The Vestal and the Fasces

Philosophy, Social Theory, and the Rule of Law

General Editors

Andrew Arato, Seyla Benhabib, Ferenc Fehér, William
Forbath, Agnes Heller, Arthur Jacobson, and Michel Rosenfeld

1. William Rehg, *Insight and Solidarity: A Study in the Discourse Ethics of Jürgen Habermas*

2. Alan Brudner, *The Unity of the Common Law: Studies in Hegelian Jurisprudence*

3. Peter Goodrich, *Oedipus Lex: Psychoanalysis, History, Law*

4. Michel Rosenfeld, *Just Interpretations: Law between Ethics and Politics*

5. Jeanne Lorraine Schroeder, *The Vestal and the Fasces: Hegel, Lacan, Property, and the Feminine*

The Vestal
and the Fasces

Hegel, Lacan, Property,
and the Feminine

Jeanne Lorraine Schroeder

UNIVERSITY OF CALIFORNIA PRESS

Berkeley / Los Angeles / London

University of California Press
Berkeley and Los Angeles, California

University of California Press
London, England

Copyright © 1998 by The Regents of the University of California

Library of Congress Cataloging-in-Publication Data

Schroeder, Jeanne Lorraine.
    The vestal and the fasces : Hegel, Lacan, property, and the
feminine / Jeanne Lorraine Schroeder.
        p.   cm. — (Philosophy, social theory, and the rule of law ; 5)
    Includes bibliographical references and index.
    ISBN 0-520-21145-6 (alk. paper)
        1. Feminist jurisprudence. 2. Property. 3. Law—Philosophy.
    4. Sex role. 5. Women—Legal status, laws, etc. (Roman law)
    I. Title. II. Series.
    K349.S37   1998
    340'.11—dc21   97-20523
                                                                    CIP

Printed in the United States of America

1 2 3 4 5 6 7 8 9

For David Gray Carlson

Contents

PROLOGUE

I. The Vestal and the Fasces   xi

II. The Feminine and Property   xv

I:
HEGEL AVEC LACAN

I. Introduction   1

A. The Death of Property   1
B. Hegel's Totality   7
C. The Hole in the Whole   8

II. The Hegelian Story of Property   15

A. The Internalist Approach of *The Philosophy of Right*   15
B. The Artificiality of the Subject   19
C. The Presupposition of Human Nature   20
D. The Impossibility of Philosophy Without
    Presuppositions; Sublation   24
E. The Tentative Presupposition   27
F. The Contradictions of Personality   31
G. Objectification and Objects   35
H. The Elements of Property   37
I. Adding the Third Term: Alienation   46
J. From Hegel to Lacan   52

III. The Lacanian Story of the Feminine   54

A. Reading Lacan   54

vii

B. The Real, the Imaginary, and the Symbolic   63
C. Adding the Third Term: The Oedipal Romance   76
D. The Phallus, Castration, and the Imaginary
    Collapse of the Symbolic into the Real   87
E. "Woman Does Not Exist"   94
F. The Woman, Property, and *Jouissance*   96

IV. An Abduction from the Seraglio   101

A. Abduction and *Jouissance*   101
B. The Radical Critique Implicit in Lacan   105

2:
THE FASCES: THE MASCULINE PHALLIC METAPHOR
FOR PROPERTY

I. Property as the *Objet Petit a*   107

II. The Axe: The Positive Version of the Masculine
     Phallic Metaphor   115

A. Waldron and the Embrace of the Masculine Phallic
    Metaphor   115
B. Some Realism about Legal Surrealism: The Positive
    Phallic Metaphor and Ostensible Ownership   130

III. The Bundle of Sticks: The Negative Version of the
      Masculine Phallic Metaphor   156

A. Chix Nix Bundle-o-Stix: A Critique of the Attempted
    Negation of Physicality   156
B. Musings on the Myth that the Uniform Commercial
    Code Disaggregated and Killed Property   185

IV. The Fasces: Axe and Bundle of Sticks   220

A. Constraints   220
B. The Denial of the Feminine   225

3:
THE VESTAL: THE FEMININE PHALLIC METAPHOR
FOR PROPERTY

I. Virgin Territory: Property as the Inviolate Feminine
    Body   229

A. Radin's Definition of Property   236
B. Pluralism, Pragmatism, and Contradiction   249

C. Market Rhetoric   253
D. Fungible Property   258

II. A Return to Hegel's Theory of Property   262

A. Radin's Misreading   262
B. Hegel and Community   271
C. The Starting Presupposition of Personality   273
D. Limitations of Positive Law   283
E. Is Hegel Useful in a Feminist Challenge
    to Masculinism?   285

III. The Implications for Feminist Property Theory   287

4:
THE WOMAN DOES NOT EXIST: THE IMPOSSIBLE
FEMININE AND THE POSSIBILITY OF FREEDOM

I. Never Jam Today: The Impossibility
    of Takings Jurisprudence   293

A. Introduction   293
B. The Permissible Limitation on Property   295
C. The Liberal Dilemma of Takings Law   296
D. Quality and Quantity   305
E. The Movement of Sublation   309
F. Takings and Freedom   317

II. The Impossibility of the Feminine and the
     Possibility of Freedom   321

A. Lacanian Freedom   321
B. I've believed . . . impossible things . . .   326
C. The Necessary Loss of Virginity   329

EPILOGUE: VESTA, THE PHALLIC WOMAN   335

INDEX   339

Prologue

I. THE VESTAL AND THE FASCES

The fasces symbolized the majesty of Roman law. It was an axe attached to a bundle of sticks. Consuls, emperors, and other high-ranking officials were escorted in public by lictors bearing the fasces as the visible representation of the enforcement powers of the state.[1] Offenders could be mercifully flogged with one of the sticks or justly executed with the blade.

The Vestals symbolized the sanctity of the Roman family.[2] These priestesses of the goddess Vesta guarded the sacred hearth of Rome,[3]

---

1. Mary Beard, *The Sexual Status of Vestal Virgins*, 70 J. Roman Stud. 12, 17 (1980); Sarah B. Pomeroy, Goddesses, Whores, Wives, and Slaves: Women in Classical Antiquity 213 (1975).

2. There were six Vestals at any given time, at least in historical times. (According to legend, in the earlier periods there were fewer Vestals.) Pomeroy, *supra* note 1, at 211; J.P.V.D. Baldson, Roman Women: Their History and Habits 235 (1962). They were chosen as little girls from the most respected families. Originally only patricians could be Vestals. Later, when it became increasingly difficult to recruit families willing to dedicate their daughters, the eligibility was expanded to other respectable, but non-noble, children. *Id.* at 236; Pomeroy, *supra,* at 213–14.

3. "The hearth with its undying flame symbolized the continuity of both family and community." Pomeroy, *supra* note 1, at 210. As is true in America today, the Romans saw a close link between private familial morality and public ethics. "The Vestal Virgins were the emblem of the State's morality and the guarantee of its economic well-being." Baldson, *supra* note 2, at 14.

ensuring the continuing warmth, intimacy, fertility, and order of the families of individual Romans.[4]

During their thirty years of service,[5] the six Vestals were required to maintain the strictest chastity. Impurity was punishable by premature burial.[6] But unlike the holy virginity of Christian nuns,[7] the Vestals' chastity was not a more perfect, spiritual form of life or a reproach to matrons. Their maidenhood was not exemplary but extraordinary—a form of ritual purity. It emphasized, through contrast, that matrimony and maternity were the norms.[8] The Vestals dedicated themselves so that others could marry.[9] They were guardians of the family. They officiated at fertility

---

4. As well as that of the state. When public calamities occurred, such as the loss of an important battle, suspicion of the Vestals' chastity was raised. Pomeroy, *supra* note 1, at 210–11; Baldson, *supra* note 2, at 239.

5. The initiate was required to be between the ages of 6 and 10. Pomeroy, *supra* note 1, at 211. *See also* Beard, *supra* note 1, at 14 n.19; Baldson, *supra* note 2, at 236.

6. Not "live burning" as asserted in a denunciation of feminist scholarship. Kenneth Lasson, *Feminism Awry: Excesses in the Pursuit of Rights and Trifles,* 42 J. Legal Educ. 1, 11 n.43 (1992).

It seems that only ten (or some say twenty) Vestals were punished in the traditional manner throughout Roman history. The corespondents were executed by being whipped to death. This may have been more efficient than being buried alive, but perhaps was more humiliating. Death by whipping was generally limited to slaves. Only a Vestal was buried. Some see this extraordinary mode of execution as uniquely related to her sacred status. She was not executed like a criminal who needed to be punished, but hidden away as a sacred vessel which had been polluted.

It has been suggested that the Vestal might have been the symbolic wife of the state or of the Pontifex Maximus. This might at first blush suggest that the unfaithful Vestal's crime might have been considered parallel to adultery. But this would ignore the fact that Roman adulteresses were not punished in such a bizarre fashion. In fact, the charges made against the unchaste Virgin were incest and high treason. Because the Vestal's purity was ritual in nature, her defilement impacted on her ability to approach the goddess on behalf of the people. This endangered the welfare of society. Baldson gives detailed descriptions of the execution ceremony. Baldson, *supra* note 2, at 240–41. *See also* Beard, *supra* note 1, at 16; Pomeroy, *supra* note 1, at 211; The New Larousse Encyclopedia of Mythology 104 (F. Giraud ed. & R. Aldington & D. Ames trans., 1968).

7. Jeanne L. Schroeder, *Feminism Historicized: Medieval Misogynist Stereotypes in Contemporary Feminist Jurisprudence,* 75 Iowa L. Rev. 1135 (1990) [hereinafter Schroeder, *Feminism Historicized*].

8. Peter Brown, The Body and Society: Men, Women, and Sexual Renunciation in Early Christianity 8–9 (1988).

9. Upon the expiration of their official term, they could leave the temple and marry. Few did so. Beard, *supra* note 1, at 14 n.21. This may have been because at the end of their official thirty-year term they would have been somewhat old (i.e., between 36 and 40 years) to begin childbearing, or because Roman superstition held that it was unlucky to marry a Vestal. Perhaps it was simple disinclination. Why would a woman who had such unique legal privileges and prestige choose to leave this life to become subject to a man?

There has been considerable debate among classicists as to whether the Vestals symbolized

rights.¹⁰ They guarded a ritual phallus which may have symbolized the ineffable goddess herself.¹¹

The Vestals' isolated world of women may have been less a convent than a seraglio without a visible sultan. The Vestals may have been symbolically married to the state. The Vestal did not dress as a maiden but wore the headdress of a Roman bride, and the *stola,* or dress, of a Roman matron. The Vestal's investiture ceremony—the *captio,* or "capture"—was reminiscent of a Roman wedding. The state's high priest, the Pontifex Maximus, roughly seized the initiate from her father in a mock abduction in memory of the legendary rape of the Sabine women by the followers of Romulus.¹² He called her *Amata,* a mysterious name that implied she was both captured matron and invincible maiden.¹³

---

a royal wife or daughter. Their virginity and some of their ritual tasks were filial in nature. Yet other functions, such as the keeping of the hearth, the baking of the sacred cake, and their prominent roles in fertility rights, were matronly. Their dress was ambiguous. They wore the stola of Roman matrons, with the veil and distinctively plaited hair of Roman brides. Beard, *supra* note 1, at 13–16.

10. Baldson, *supra* note 2, at 237–38. *See also* Beard, *supra* note 1, at 13; Pomeroy, *supra* note 1, at 211.

11. Unlike other classical deities, Vesta was rarely represented by a cult image. There were few statues of her, although her visage occasionally appeared on coins. New Larousse Encyclopedia of Mythology, *supra* note 6, at 205. Instead of the customary cult image, Vesta's temple housed a sacred fire and a phallus called the *fascinus.* Vesta was the flame itself. The phallus might relate to Vesta's function in fertility cults (in which a sacred, phallic ass played a noted role), but it might also have invoked the goddess herself because it was related to the fire stick used to start the holy fire. The goddess of the hearth was sometimes considered a personification of this fire stick which was inserted in a hollow in a piece of wood and rotated, in an obviously phallic matter, to light her flame. Vesta was also associated with the worship of such phallic masculine gods as Mars and Bacchus. In many of the myths surrounding the cult of Vesta, a penis appeared within her flame and impregnated a virgin. The first Roman king and perhaps Romulus himself were believed to have been conceived by a union between such a Vestal phallus and a Vestal Virgin. Beard, *supra* note 1, at 12, 19, and 24–25. *See also* New Larousse Encyclopedia of Mythology, *supra* note 6, at 214.

12. The symbolism of the *captio* (like everything else regarding the Vestals) is ambiguous. Scholars debate whether or not the Vestal's seizure was intended as a mock abduction representing the more ancient form of marriage by rape. It was similar to, but not identical with, a Roman wedding. In a wedding, the bridegroom seized the bride from the arms of her mother. The Vestal was snatched from her father. The cut of the Vestal's vestments was that of the traditional bridal veil, but the Vestal wore the pure white of a priest rather than the passionate flame red of the bride. By historical times, Roman marriage had become consensual and rape was no longer a legal way of entering into a marriage. Marriage by rape was, however, recognized by Germanic law well into the Middle Ages. Schroeder, *Feminism Historicized, supra* note 7, at 1165. *See also* James A. Brundage, Law, Sex, and Christian Society in Medieval Europe 129 (1987).

13. It is unclear what this title means. *Amata* might have been an archaic form of

The Vestals were guardians of the private yet lived a paradoxically public existence. Unlike other priests, they lived at the temple they served.[14] The temple of the goddess was built to look like an ancient Roman house, yet it was located in the center of the marketplace.[15] It was every Roman's right freely to enter this temple by day, although men were strictly barred from the house of the virgins at night. The Vestals attended and blessed most important government functions.[16] They were the repositories of the Sibylline books containing the prophecies of Rome's future periodically consulted by the consuls and emperors.[17] They had reserved boxes at the arenas and theaters.[18]

Most mysteriously, upon their investiture these priestesses, who were paradoxically both symbolically raped virgins and unviolated wives, were also elevated to the legal status of men.[19] The Vestals, alone of all women, were escorted by the fasces.[20]

"Beloved" (from *amare,* to love), reflecting her status as wife. On the other hand, it may have meant "unconquered" in the sense of virgin and forever unmarried. Beard, *supra* note 1, at 13–15. *See also* Baldson, *supra* note 2, at 182–84.

14. The other major priests, such as the Pontifex Maximus, had "official" residences in the forum, but actually lived in private homes like other citizens. The Vestals actually lived in a house next to the temple during their entire tenure. Baldson, *supra* note 2, at 235.

15. Properly speaking, this building was referred to as *aedes Vestae* and was not augurated as a temple in the strict sense. Beard, *supra* note 1, at 13 n.9.

16. Baldson, *supra* note 2, at 238. The sacredness of the Vestals was so great that it was thought that no one would dare invade their house. Accordingly, they served as holy repositories of state treasures.

17. They also guarded other treasures such as the Palladium, believed to have been brought by Aeneas from Troy, as well as official documents, such as the wills of the emperors and other important officials.

18. Augustus gave the Vestals the privilege of sitting in the imperial box. Other women were relegated to less prestigious seats. Pomeroy, *supra* note 1, at 214; Beard, *supra* note 1, at 13. They also had other unique privileges denied to other women, such as the right to travel through the streets of Rome in two-horse carriages (other women being confined to litters and sedan chairs). Baldson, *supra* note 2, at 238; Pomeroy, *supra* note 1, at 213. The Vestals' privileges were so great that occasionally women of the imperial family were granted the rights of honorary Vestals, rather than Vestals being granted the rights of princesses. Pomeroy, *supra* note 1, at 214; Baldson, *supra* note 2, at 116.

19. The Vestals had many attributes of Roman men. Upon her investiture, the initiate's father lost his dominion (*manus*) over her, in the same way a father loses his dominion over his daughter upon marriage. But unlike the case of a married woman, her *manus* did not vest in their symbolic spouse (the state, or the Pontifex Maximus). Rather, unlike daughters or wives, but like a *pater familias,* the Vestal held her own *manus.* She could write wills, and give testimony, like male citizens but unlike wives (at least in the earlier period; women were apparently granted similar testamentary rights later in the empire). *See* Pomeroy, *supra* note 1, at 213.

20. *Id.;* Baldson, *supra* note 2, at 238.

The seeming paradox posed by the juxtaposition of the symbolizations of the private and the public as well as its eventual explanation is suggested by true and folk etymologies of the terms the Romans used to describe them. The virgin is *virgo*. The rod bound to form the fasces is *virga*. *Vir* is man. A woman who has the virtue of a man—like a Vestal—is a *virago*. *Fasces* means "bound." *Fas* is divine law—that which binds man to god? The Vestal's ritual phallus is *fascinus*, which means not merely the male organ but also enchantment and the evil eye. It is the source of the English "fascination" and is obviously related to the *fasces*, but how? Clearly, we are fascinated with the phallus. When we are fascinated, are we spell*bound*?

From the standpoint of the political philosophy of G.W.F. Hegel and the psychoanalytic theory of Jacques Lacan, the public and the private serve complementary functions and are mutually constituting. Both the law and the virgin served as the representation of the Other, the external object by which the Roman man was able to define himself as an acting subject—a Roman citizen. The Vestal and the fasces cannot be separated because they are one and the same: *virgo* is *virga* is *vir*; Vesta is *fascinus* is *fasces* is *fas*.

II. THE FEMININE AND PROPERTY

This book is an encounter with Hegelian and Lacanian theory that shows that property—the law of the marketplace—and the Feminine are both *Phalluses* in the technical psychoanalytic sense of the lost

---

Beard notes that although in the later empire the wives of consuls or emperors were on rare occasion escorted by lictors, this was a late development. During most of Roman history, the only other exceptions to the general rule associating the fasces with high-ranking men concerned other female priests, and these instances were extremely rare. For example, Livia—one of the most powerful women in Roman history—was denied her request for the fasces in her capacity as wife of Augustus. She was, however, occasionally accompanied by lictors when officiating as chief priest of the cult of the deified Augustus. Once again, Beard argues that this masculine moment symbolized the intentionally ambiguous sexual status of Roman priestesses which enabled them to act as the point where human and divine meet. As I discuss in the last chapter of this book, this ambiguous transition between man and God is, in Hegelian philosophy, the moment of sublation, and, in Lacanian psychoanalysis, the impossible Feminine. Beard, *supra* note 1, at 17 n.46.

object of desire.[21] They serve parallel functions in the creation of subjectivity as intersubjectivity mediated by objectivity. Property, according to Hegelian philosophy, and the Feminine, according to Lacanian psychoanalysis, are fictions we write to serve as the defining external objects enabling us to constitute ourselves as acting subjects. By serving as objects of exchange between subjects, property and the Feminine simultaneously enable subjects to recognize other humans as individual subjects—they enable us to desire and be desired. This creation of subjectivity is simultaneously the creation of the realm which Lacan called the symbolic: law, language, and sexuality.

In other words, the reason the Vestal is always accompanied by the fasces is that, at one moment, the Vestal *is* the fasces—both the Feminine and the legal regime of property are *Phallic*. The binding of the *virgo* as *virga* to create the *fasces* is the writing of the *fas*—the creation of law and subjectivity. As a consequence, the actualization of human freedom requires not only the recognition of property rights but also the simultaneously impossible but necessary goal of feminine emancipation.

Lacan explained how sexuality is created by the imaginary identification of the symbolic concept of the *Phallus* with seemingly real biological analogues—the male organ and the female body. I will show how a parallel conflation occurs in jurisprudence and legal doctrine—the symbolic or legal concept of property is described through elaborate metaphors of the penis and the virgin. This is an intuition or "abduction" which comes to us so easily as to seem natural. Indeed as a psychoanalytic matter, we may not be capable of speaking about property without resorting to phallic concepts.

My theory seeks to be a thoroughgoing reconstruction of both feminist and property theory. It gives a more complex and faithful account of sexual difference than does either of the two dominant schools of legal feminism—different-voice feminism and so-called radical feminism—which I believe merely adopt traditional gender stereotypes. It also helps to explain why we, as a society, tenaciously cling to certain property-law doctrines despite their disutility, and to certain theories despite empirical evidence to the contrary.

This book is intended for lawyers as well as jurisprudes and critical the-

---

21. Lacan's terminology is intentionally confusing. I will usually distinguish the psychoanalytic concept of the *Phallus* from the anatomical analogy by capitalizing and italicizing the former. Not all of the sources I quote, however, will adopt this rule of capitalization, but I believe that the context in which these terms are used will clarify their meaning.

orists, although different sections will no doubt appeal to different segments of my audience. I believe that my theory is not merely of abstract jurisprudential interest. I have personally found that my approach has been extremely useful not only in my teaching but also in my doctrinal scholarship and in my legal practice as a commercial lawyer.[22]

Hegelian-Lacanian theory is an account not only of the structure of law but of the unconscious thinking processes which underlie our conscious legal thinking. Like a compass, it not only can help us locate our position when we know that we are lost, it can also occasionally show us that we are actually heading in a direction different from where we thought we were going. Once our position is located and our direction is reoriented, there is no immediate use for the compass and it can be safely put away temporarily while we rely on other markers to continue our journey. A reader of a travelogue can appreciate the resulting description of the author's ultimate destination even if she does not know how the author got there. She could not retrace the route and reproduce the trip—or successfully engage in a new but similar journey—without this information, however.

Similarly, I believe that Hegelian-Lacanian theory helps us not only to determine what is wrong with legal theories or doctrines that we intuit are faulty (such as, in my case, the so-called bundle of sticks theory of property) but also to reevaluate and critique theories and doctrines to which we cling because they are so intuitively attractive despite empirical evidence to the contrary (such as the commercial law doctrine of ostensible ownership). Hegelian-Lacanian theory helps us do this by revealing the unacknowledged, unconscious, but implicit assumptions, metaphors, and imagery—similar to what Thomas Kuhn would call paradigms—underlying the law. Once this initial analysis is completed, psychoanalysis, like a compass, can be temporarily put away in favor of the familiar conscious thought process of traditional legal analysis. Consequently, the lawyer reading this book, like the reader of the travelogue, may appreciate my ultimate legal analysis even if he does not know or understand the path that led me there. But he could not fully understand, reproduce, or critique my analysis, or engage in similar analysis or critique, without this information. Let me explain in greater detail.

---

22. Of course, it helps to strip the theory of its postmodern terminology and translate it into standard legalese. The general term "physical metaphor" can easily replace the more specific "phallic metaphor." Judges and clients are taken aback if one talks about penises, but they readily accept a discussion of the common error of confusing property rights with the sensuous grasp or immediate physical custody of tangible things.

I see myself as first and last a lawyer writing about law, not a philosopher. I had a successful practice as a finance lawyer in New York City for twelve years prior to entering academia and continue to consult in commercial litigation. In addition to theoretical work of the type reflected in my book, I also write highly technical commercial law doctrinal articles aimed at the practicing attorney. All of this work is intimately related to my developing jurisprudential theory. That is, I do not view myself as a Lacanian academic who happens to apply her theory to law. Rather, I am a lawyer who turned to Lacan and Hegel in order better to understand and practice law.

In my experience, law is in large part a subset of rhetoric. By this I do not mean that law is contentless cant, nor am I making the cynical layperson's gibe that lawyers are just sophists, or prostitutes, who can and will say anything for a buck. Rather, I mean that law is social, it governs relationships between and among people and, therefore, must be communicated in order to function. As such, law only exists in its expression—whether in statute, legal opinion, or argument. Law's content is, therefore, inextricably linked to its form. Consequently, I believe that understanding the symbolic order of language can greatly enhance our understanding of the symbolic order of law as well as lawyering.

It has become a banal cliché to claim that selfhood is socially constructed. Probably no expression has become so shopworn and meaningless so fast. Nevertheless, I do believe that in our postmodern economy it is increasingly true that we define our personality in terms of legal rights and responsibilities—that is, legal subjectivity. This can perhaps be most graphically seen in the civil rights, women's rights, and more recently disabled and gay rights movements where the claims of a group for social recognition and equality have been largely played out (as the common terminology suggests) in terms of claims for legal rights. This is just as true in areas of so-called private law which defines much of our relationships with people other than our immediate family—such as our employers, co-workers, students, landlords, shopkeepers, to name a few—where legal rights increasingly replace status. Indeed, even our family relationships have an important legal component as well as emotive and cultural ones. At least in our society, law and personality are, therefore, intimately, if not inextricably, interconnected. This suggests both that the study of personality (i.e., psychoanalysis) should enrich our understanding of law and that the study of law should enrich our understanding of personality.

Specifically, as a practicing lawyer I had long been troubled by the inadequacies of the law of intangible property, most specifically the law governing security interests in investment securities. I was particularly troubled by the continued use of what seemed to me inappropriate and unsuccessful analogies to physical relations with tangible property. And yet I could simultaneously neither account for the use of such analogies nor imagine any other way of thinking about intangibles. Indeed, the very term "intangibles" indicates how hard it is to think of intangibility except in terms of tangibility. It is this precise problem (which is reflected in chapter 2, section II.B on ostensible-ownership theory, and in much of my technical commercial-law scholarship) which led me to seek a way to analyze the structure of property law, specifically, and of legal thinking, generally.

In addition, when I graduated law school in 1978, it was quite uncommon for women to practice finance law. I found that although I was very skilled in understanding conventional legal analysis, I also had a talent for formulating novel modes of analysis, lines of arguments, and structures for transactions. I was conceited enough to attribute this in part to my own creativity, but I began to think that something more was going on. As a feminist I was, not surprisingly, intensely interested in the role of women lawyers and how this was affected by actual or illusory gender and sexual differences. I believed that I was perceiving a marked empirical difference in the type of imagery and metaphors which I and the few other women lawyers I knew tended to find, at least initially, to be appropriate to describe the legal world, on the one hand, and those initiated by my male colleagues, on the other. This is not to suggest that male and female lawyers could not or did not understand each other after discussion. Indeed, our success as lawyers shows the contrary. But I observed that male and female lawyers would often join discussion from different starting places. This led me to suspect that the problem of legal imagery and metaphors with which I had been struggling might also be related to sexuality. This seemed consistent with my other underlying assumptions that law is rhetorical in nature and that personality is in large part legal subjectivity. That women and men tend to speak differently as an empirical matter is a phenomenon widely recognized among linguists, although there is substantial disagreement as to the essential nature of these differences, let alone their cause. Nevertheless, I believed that the differences I perceived in masculine and feminine legal rhetoric did not follow traditional sexual stereotypes such as the cliché, embraced by different-voice feminists, that women think more in terms of relationship and men more in terms of individual rights. Not only did I believe that traditional finance law (i.e., as practiced by men) was intensely and expressly concerned with building and maintaining relationships of the type celebrated by different-voice feminism, but I observed that I, and a large percentage of women lawyers whom I eventually met in practice, were intensely individualistic, competitive, and self-involved.

After several years, my interest in feminism led me to explore Lacanian theory. At around the same time, my interest in property led me to read Hegel. Eventually, I began developing my theory of the legal nature of sexuality and the erotics of property. Law is a practice as well as a theory, however. As the cliché goes, the proof of the pudding is in the eating. Consequently, I set about the task of applying my analysis to a large number of property issues. As I have stated, many of these applications appear in the book. Others I have incorporated in my practice as an expert in the law of investment securities. I have recently begun a new long-term project of applying my analysis to Law and Economics theory. If the reader finds my analysis of specific legal questions covered in this book to be insightful, then this is strong evidence (but, of course, not definitive proof) of the validity of my approach.

As should be obvious from this Prologue, I use a lot of wordplay, including true and folk etymologies and classical allusions. This is relatively unusual in jurisprudential writings and I fear might be initially off-putting to some lawyers. At worst I might be accused, as Hegel often is, of confusing puns with analysis, of finding too much significance in purely accidental and inconsequential similarities between words and images. This argument misses the point that in Hegelian and Lacanian theory subjectivity, law, and language are considered to be mutually constituting. The structure of language, therefore, reflects the unconscious structure of law and personality. As a result, the similarities identified in wordplay as well as in humor are not always accidental; they can be serendipitous, suggesting unexpected connections between ideas as well as words. If nothing else, I hope they are occasionally amusing, leavening what might otherwise be a tediously dry narrative.

I proceed as follows: in chapter 1, I present the parallels between Hegelian and Lacanian theory at a high degree of theoretical abstraction. In chapter 2, I explore the dominance of the masculine phallic metaphor for property in American law. The masculine metaphor recalls the imagery of the fasces. In its affirmative mode the archetype of property is expressly or implicitly visualized as the grasping of a physical thing in one's hand like an axe. In its negative mode, it reinstates the metaphor through simple negation and the image of the bundle of sticks. The former privileges the masculine property element of possession and the latter the masculine element of alienation through exchange. Using the work of a number of prominent legal scholars, I will first show not only how this metaphor is developed in jurisprudence but also how it is played out in contemporary commercial law doctrine. I then return to a theoretical analysis and argue that all of the variations on the masculine metaphor are failed attempts to achieve immediate relations through disparagement of the Feminine in her role as the mediatrix of subjectivity.

In chapter 3, I examine an alternate jurisprudential theory of property recently offered by Margaret Jane Radin. I show how Radin implicitly adopts a feminine phallic metaphor in which property is visualized in terms of the female body. Indeed, to Radin the archetype of "personal property" is not just metaphorically but, in many cases, literally the female body as the object of desire. At first blush, Radin might be seen as adding the feminine property element of enjoyment missing from masculinist theory, thereby completing a single harmonious and complete property theory. This is wrong. As Lacan showed, the masculine and feminine positions are not opposites or complements which can together form a satisfying whole. Each is itself a failed attempt at wholeness. Correspondingly, Radin's feminine theory cannot be added as a corrective of the failed masculine theory of property, because it is itself a failed attempt at a simple comprehensive account of property. It is true that in order to further the development of (feminine) personhood, Radin seeks to protect the object of desire from violation in the masculine regime of exchange by privileging the feminine property element of enjoyment or *jouissance*. But by doing so she imagines the feminine object of desire as a virgin—the Vestal. She silently enjoys her own feminine integrity but never engages in the market intercourse which is necessary for subjectivity. Like the masculinist theorists I discuss in chapter 2, she denies the Feminine her role as mediatrix of subjectivity. As Radin's theory is based in large part on a common misreading of Hegel, I use the opportunity of critiquing Radin to further develop my reading. I argue that my reading of Hegel and Lacan demonstrates that the actualization of human freedom does require us to continue the task attempted by Radin—the recognition of the feminine rights of property and the creation of an impossible feminine subjectivity.

In chapter 4, I use my theory to analyze the Takings Clause of the U.S. Constitution. I argue that although the Takings Clause accurately reflects that a private property regime is necessary for the actualization of freedom, an understanding of Hegel's concepts of quality and quantity shows it is not possible for the Takings Clause to serve its traditional function as the bulwark protecting private freedom from government oppression. I conclude by arguing that this impossibility of Hegelian property reflects the impossibility of the Lacanian Feminine which, ironically, is the condition precedent of freedom. ~~The~~ Woman does not exist. She is that which cannot be constrained by the *Phallic* order of the symbolic. Exiled from symbolic order of law into the real, the Feminine changes the impossible into the forbidden, and therefore not merely possible but ethically necessary. The impossible Feminine is the potentiality of a freedom which has not yet been actualized.

1

Hegel avec Lacan

J.-A. Miller: . . . In short, are we to understand—Lacan against Hegel?
Lacan: What you have just said is very good, it's exactly the opposite of what Green just said to me—he came up to me, shook my paw, at least morally, and said, the death of structuralism, you are the son of Hegel. I don't agree. I think that in saying Lacan against Hegel, you are much closer to the truth, though of course it is not at all a philosophical debate.

Dr. Green: The sons kill the fathers![1]

I. INTRODUCTION

A. The Death of Property

Twentieth-century jurisprudence discovered that property, like God, was dead. Wesley Newcomb Hohfeld revealed that the unity, tangibility, and objectivity that were property's very essence were illusions—property was a mere phantom. Property was not a single identifiable thing but an aggregate of parts, an arbitrary collection of legal rights. Property was a "bundle of sticks"—a *fasces*.[2] Hohfeld predicted that once property is recognized as a mere collection of other rights, it loses its distinctive quality and its essence. It therefore does not, or at

---

1. Jacques Lacan, The Four Fundamental Concepts of Psycho-Analysis 215 (Jacques-Alain Miller ed. & Alan Sheridan trans., 1981) [hereinafter Lacan, Four Fundamental Concepts].
2. *See infra* chap. 2, sec. I.

I

least should not, exist as a meaningful legal category.[3] Moreover, he continued, the traditional distinction between *in personam* rights—with respect to persons—and *in rem* rights—with respect to things—is irrational. According to Hohfeld, only tangible objects can qualify as things, but not all property rights involve tangible objects. Without objectivity, property can only be a wraith, a myth.[4] The rabble might still believe in the old gods of property, but the educated "specialists" now see property as vulgar superstition.[5] If the populace could only be reeducated, then property would cease to be worshiped. This ghastly apparition could then finally be exorcised and replaced by a logical and scientific dichotomy between rights enforceable against specific individuals and rights enforceable against the world.

3. Among the writings attacking the viability of property (either generally or in a specific context) are Thomas C. Grey, *The Disintegration of Property, in* Property 69 (J. Roland Pennock & John W. Chapman eds., 22 Nomos, 1980) [hereinafter Nomos, Property]; Charles W. Mooney, Jr., *Beyond Negotiability: A New Model for Transfer and Pledge of Interests in Securities Controlled by Intermediaries,* 12 Cardozo L. Rev. 305 (1990); James Steven Rogers, *Negotiability, Property, Identity,* 12 Cardozo L. Rev. 471 (1990); Joseph K. Sax, *Some Thoughts on the Decline of Private Property,* 58 Wash. L. Rev. 481 (1983); Joseph William Singer, *The Reliance Interest in Property,* 40 Stan. L. Rev. 611 (1988); Kenneth J. Vandevelde, *The New Property of the Nineteenth Century: The Development of the Modern Concept of Property,* 29 Buff. L. Rev. 325 (1980).

4. See, for example, Jennifer Nedelsky's characterization of the commonly held American view of property in her excellent account of the significance of property to the Framers of the U.S. Constitution:

How can "the tradition" be characterized by both coherence and endurance and by an apparently unlimited mutability in the purported core of the structure? The paradox itself suggests the answers: it is the myth of property—its rhetorical power combined with the illusory nature of the image of property—that has been crucial to our system. And it is this mythic quality that current changes [i.e., disaggregation] in the concept may threaten.

Jennifer Nedelsky, Private Property and the Limits of American Constitutionalism: The Madisonian Framework and Its Legacy 224 (1990).

5. According to Thomas Grey, "specialists" such as lawyers and economists already recognize the disintegrating nature of property, although lay people naively cling to a unitary, objective, physicalist ideal. As lay people eventually accept the specialist view, property will lose its traditional inspirational role. Grey, *supra* note 3, at 69, 76–79.

Other members of the legal priesthood who identify the death of "traditional" property seek to employ a technique successfully used by the early Church—harnessing the spiritual power of the discredited religion by accepting pagan ritual but changing the object of worship. That is, in order to win over the devotees of the old dead gods, the new God usurps the titles of His defeated predecessors so that He might be worshiped in a familiar form. Thus, certain self-styled progressives do not want the memory of discredited property to wither away entirely. Rather, they wish to preserve the powerful inspirational rhetoric of property but redirect it away from its traditional conservative and reactionary roles. *See infra* text accompanying chap. 4, notes 21–22.

But if a unitary and tangible conception of property is an illusion, like Banquo's ghost, it continues to haunt property's murderers. Those scholars who expressly claim to adopt an analysis of property as a disaggregated bundle of sticks implicitly reinstate a unitary view of property which places primacy on physical possession of tangible objects. As Sir James Frazer illustrates, the murder of the mythic hero—whether it be Osiris, Tammuz, Adonis, Jesus, or Superman—is only a precursor to his resurrection.[6] The separate sticks of property are always tightly rebundled into the fasces.

And so I argue that property is alive and well. Most people in our society continue to hold a strong intuitive belief that property significantly differs from other legal rights. Let us not forget that since the "fall" of Communism in Eastern Europe and the recent official encouragement of private markets in China, the international belief that private property is necessary for economic development—and, at least in the West, for political freedom—is probably stronger now than it has been in a century. Yet many legal academics who study the situation persist in arguing either that property is dying or that the concept is incoherent, a mere mythic presence, a contentless rhetorical trope or cynical political tool.[7] I fear that these theorists risk sounding very foolish—saying that because they cannot understand the phenomenon, it does not exist and the rest of the world is delusional or suffering from false consciousness.[8] It is time-honored practice that when we do not understand something, we beat it with a stick. This has been property's sufferance of late.

In contradistinction, in this book I argue that Hegel's analysis explains how property is not only coherent as a concept but logically necessary for the creation of subjectivity and the eventual actualization of human freedom. Moreover, I demonstrate that property as an economic and legal practice is healthy and functioning. In other words, it is mod-

---

6. *See* Sir James George Frazer, The Golden Bough: A Study in Magic and Religion 283–397 (Theodore H. Gaster ed., abr. ed. 1951).

7. Nedelsky, *supra* note 4, at 8–9, 223–25, 239, 243, 247, 254.

8. Alan Brudner makes a similar point:

So far from reflecting on the nature of property in light of 1989, many . . . have attempted to reveal a conceptual dynamic in private property that moves in a direction diametrically opposed to the momentum revealed in history. At a time when publicly-owned enterprises and resources are being massively transformed into private property; at a time when socialist law is being overthrown in favour of the legal categories of private law, our theorists disclose the inherent instability, indeed the conceptual impossibility, of private property.

Alan Brudner, *Editor's Introduction,* 6 Canadian J.L. & Jurisprudence 183, 183 (1993).

ern property jurisprudence and doctrine, and not property itself, that is incoherent.

This phenomenon can be explained through Lacanian psychoanalysis. Modern property theory is in the grip of what I will call a phallic metaphor. Just as we conflate the *Phallic* concept of the psychic object of desire with the male organ and the female body to create the positions of sexuality, we use metaphors of the male organ and the female body to describe the *Phallic* concept of property as the legal object of desire. These seductive metaphors, and not property, are incoherent.

The phallic notion of property is exacerbated by—or more precisely, is reflected in—the inherent ambiguity of the word "property" in contemporary English. The word "property" is now colloquially used to refer to the thing owned, in addition to the legal rights of ownership.[9] Moreover, the owned thing is typically conceptualized as a physical thing—such as a car or a wedding ring—and the right of property is typically conceptualized as physically holding that thing. Our very terminology for non-physical things—"intangible" or "noncorporeal" property—reflects the presumption that tangibility and corporeality are the norm.

Modern theorists fall into phallic conflation by describing property as both thing and right not in terms of just any physicalist imagery but in terms of phallic imagery. Specifically, property is metaphorically identified with seeing, holding, and wielding the male organ or controlling, protecting, and entering the female body. Loss of property is correspondingly imagined as mutilation or violation. The imagery of the bundle of sticks is itself a possessory and tangible metaphor. A stick is something that one can, and stereotypically does, see and hold in one's hand. And so, while most contemporary legal commentators dutifully intone the insight—typically attributed to Hohfeld[10]—that property is neither a thing nor the rights of an individual over a thing but rather a legal relationship between legal subjects, few of them successfully or consistently resist the temptation of identifying property with the owned object.

Moreover, the bundle-of-sticks analysis does not solve the metaphysical problems supposedly inherent in the unitary, possessory, tangible concept of property. It merely postpones, and thereby replicates,

9. This conflation of the legal right of a person with respect to a thing and the thing with respect to which the legal right is asserted may only go back to the seventeenth century. Prior to that time, one usually spoke of having a property in a thing. *See* Charles Donahue, Jr., *The Future of the Concept of Property Predicted from Its Past, in* Nomos, Property, *supra* note 3, at 28.

10. *See, e.g.,* Vandevelde, *supra* note 3, at 359–61.

the unitary theory and its problems.[11] If property is merely a bundle of arbitrary sticks, this bundle consists of separate little sticks, each a separate unity with its own metaphysical problems. These, of course, are addressed by supposing that each "stick" is itself a separate bundle of smaller little sticks, *ad infinitum*. This is the classic bad infinity of "turtles all the way down."[12]

Consequently, the "bundle of sticks" metaphor marks a key psycho-

---

11. Penner makes a similar point about the inaptness of the "bundle of sticks" approach as an alternative to traditional property. "It should strike us as a bit surprising that the best we can do to explain the nature of property is to treat it as a bundle of lesser units. Contract and tort would seem to be as amenable to the same disintegrative approach." J.E. Penner, *The "Bundle of Rights" Picture of Property*, 43 UCLA L. Rev. 711, 739 (1996).

12. I refer to the famous unending terrapin tower which is fast becoming a cliché of infinite regress and spurious infinity. *See, e.g.,* James Boyle, *Introduction* to *A Symposium of Critical Legal Studies*, 34 Am. U. L. Rev. 929, 929 (1985); Anthony D'Amato, *Can Legislatures Constrain Judicial Interpretation of Statutes?* 75 Va. L. Rev. 561, 571 (1989); Steven Winter, *Bull Durham and the Uses of Theory*, 42 Stan. L. Rev. 639, 646 (1990). There are many versions of this story. My favorite involves the seeker of wisdom who travels to the far ends of the earth to consult a holy man about the meaning of life. "The world," the sage said, "lies on four columns which are supported by four enormous elephants." "On what, O Wise One, do the elephants stand?" asked the student. "The elephants," the sage replied, "stand on the back of the great cosmic turtle." The conversation continued: "But, Master, on what does the cosmic turtle stand?" "The cosmic turtle stands on the back of an even greater turtle." "Yes, Teacher, but on what does the greater turtle stand?" "On the back of a yet greater turtle." "But Sir, on what does that turtle stand?" "On the back of an even greater turtle." "And on what . . . " "Listen, Buster, it's turtles all the way down!"

Roger Cramton traces the anecdote back to William James (with rocks—the more amusing turtles having been added by later rewriters who knew a little about Hindu mythology). Roger C. Cramton, *Demystifying Legal Scholarship*, 75 Geo. L.J. 1, 1–2 (1986); William James, The Will to Believe and Other Essays in Popular Philosophy 104 (1897). Despite this, the story continues to have a life of its own, appearing in two general forms. In one, the anecdote poses as the cosmological myth of some exotic people. *See, e.g.,* Charles Krauthammer, *Beware the Study of Turtles*, Time, June 28, 1993, at 76 (told by a "swami" to a "sultan"); Mark C. Taylor, *Current Interest in O.B. Hardison's "Disappearing Through the Skylight,"* L.A. Times, Nov. 4, 1990, Book Review, at 12 (with elephants as well as turtles, a popular version of an Indian creation myth); Carol Shifflett, *Clay's the Villain*, Wash. Post, Nov. 9, 1985, at F1 (related by an "Oriental sage" to a "Western traveler"); Dennis L. Breo, *In the Beginning . . . Armed with the Tevatron and, They Hope, the Supercollider, Fermilab's Nobel Prize—Winning Director and His Scientists Are Seeking to Discover How the Whole Universe Came to Be*, Chi. Trib., Nov. 6, 1988, Magazine, at 10 (classical Greek mythology, with Atlas standing on a turtle); Joan Williams, *Critical Legal Studies: The Death of Transcendence and the Rise of the New Langdells*, 62 N.Y.U. L. Rev. 429, 455 (1987) (Indian story about questions asked by Englishman); Mark Tushnet, *Following the Rules Laid Down: A Critique of Interpretivism and Neutral Principles*, 96 Harv. L. Rev. 781, 792 (1983) (Indian cosmology related by a wise man to a traveler).

The other version is a variation of the James anecdote. Sometimes the story involves a scientist giving a lecture on astronomical theory only to be countered by the superstitions of an audience member. *See* Judge Alvin B. Rubin, *Honest Judges Offer More Than Disclosure*

analytic moment in recent property theory. Progressives plotted the murder of property. In order to make sure it stayed dead, they disaggregated property, in the same way that the evil god Set dismembered the corpse of the murdered god Osiris.[13] But, like Osiris's dismemberment, property's disaggregation has not prevented its resurrection. Rather, it enabled the resurrected god to fill the entire universe.[14] Thanks to the "bundle of sticks" imagery, property threatens to permeate all legal relations. That is, Hohfeld was right that a disaggregated reconceptualization of property makes it indistinguishable from other legal rights. He was wrong in thinking that this proved that property was illusory. It is equally consistent with

---

Forms, Manhattan Lawyer, June 6, 1989 (Stephen Hawking); Simon Barnes, *Beetles & Turtles,* The Times (London), Jan. 11, 1992 (Bertrand Russell); *Rest Assured,* Christian Sci. Monitor, Sept. 15, 1981 (William James). It is alternately presented as an old joke or an actual encounter involving a famous scientist. *See, e.g.,* Robert Wright, *Did the Universe Just Happen? Edward Fredkin's Theory Is Just Not of Physics but of Metaphysics; It Leads to Speculation About the Supreme Being and the Purpose of Life,* Atlantic, Apr. 1988; Kenny Hegland, *Legal Theory: Goodbye to 2525,* 85 Nw. U. L. Rev. 127 (1990); Jerry J. Phillips, *Opinion and Defamation: The Camel in the Tent,* 57 Tenn. L. Rev. 647 (1990). In all but one of these examples, the ignorant amateur cosmologist is misogynistically described as an old woman (sometimes in tennis shoes). The exception is Professor Hegland, who merely refers to an anonymous heckler.

I have no idea whether the anecdote actually originated with James. It is such a good story that I suspect that it has been around in one version or another for an infinitely long time.

13. According to Egyptian mythology, Set murdered his twin brother, the corn god Osiris. First, Set tried hiding the corpse. Isis, Osiris's widow and sister, found the body and conceived the child-god Horus from her dead husband. Set, determined not to be defeated twice, again killed Osiris and tore him into fourteen parts which he strewed throughout Egypt. The New Larousse Encyclopedia of Mythology 18–19 (F. Giraud ed. & R. Aldington & D. Ames trans., 1968); *see also* Joseph Campbell, The Mythic Image 27 (1974).

14. The grieving Isis once again set out in search of her husband's body. She built a temple to him wherever she found a piece of his body. Paradoxically, the myths say both that she buried each body part where she found it and that she brought all the pieces together, reconstituted the body, invented embalming, made Osiris into the first mummy, and then raised him from the dead. Although variants of the myth give different explanations for this apparent paradox—for example, Isis only buried facsimiles of the body parts, the body parts miraculously multiplied, and so on—they agree on the point that the dismemberment and multiple burials of Osiris enabled Isis to spread his divine presence and worship throughout Egypt. The resurrected Osiris now reigns as the god of death and resurrection. The New Larousse Encyclopedia of Mythology, *supra* note 13, at 18–19.

Particularly interestingly for the purposes of this book, the only part of Osiris's body that Isis could not find was his phallus—apparently a fish or a crab ate it—so the divine phallus remains forever lost in the world. *Id.;* Frazer, *supra* note 6, at 424–25. Lacan uses the metaphor of Osiris's lost phallus to describe his concept of the Phallus as the lost object. Jacques Lacan, *The direction of the treatment and the principles of its power* [hereinafter Lacan, *The direction of the treatment*], in Jacques Lacan, Écrits: a Selection 226, 265 (Alan Sheridan trans., 1977) (1966) [hereinafter Lacan, Écrits].

the conclusion that not only is property real but all legal rights must be reinterpreted in terms of property. In Hegelian terms, property as pure nothing is the same thing as property as all-encompassing being. Disaggregation as ceasing-to-be is also a coming-to-be. If, however, we intuit that not all legal rights can be analyzed in terms of property, we must return to property and identify its essence which distinguishes it from other relations.

B. Hegel's Totality

I suggest a parallel between Hegel and Lacan which should surprise neither Hegelians nor Lacanians. Hegel was a totalizing philosopher. He argued that the same structures and dynamics pervade all forms of human experience. In *The Philosophy of Right*,[15] Hegel described the dialectic through which a person becomes a legal, social, and political subject. A Hegelian would expect that the formation of a person as a psychoanalytical subject would follow the same dialectic. Hegelian philosophy purports to be a circular (or perhaps spiraling) system. Hegel did not merely show that his conception of subjectivity logically and necessarily developed from the application of his dialectical system. He also suggested that if one started instead with his conception of subjectivity, one would necessarily develop a dialectical system. This was Hegel's project in *The Phenomenology of Spirit*.[16]

Lacan often acknowledged Hegel's influence on his rewriting of Freud. But he frequently tried to distinguish himself from his intellectual forebear, as illustrated by the quotation at the head of this chapter. I believe, however, that Lacan's "science of desire"[17] derived as much from the Hegelian insight that "the desire of man is the desire of the other" as it did from the Freudian theory of the unconscious.[18] Unlike the person hypothesized by classical liberal philosophy, unlike the masculine stereotype

---

15. G.W.F. Hegel, Elements of the Philosophy of Right (Allen W. Wood ed. & H.B. Nisbet trans., 1991) [hereinafter Hegel, The Philosophy of Right].

16. G.W.F. Hegel, The Phenomenology of Spirit (A.V. Miller trans., 1975) [hereinafter Hegel, The Phenomenology].

17. *See* Jacques Lacan, The Seminar of Jacques Lacan, Book VII, The Ethics of Psychoanalysis 1959–1960 (Jacques-Alain Miller ed. & Dennis Porter trans., 1992) (1988) [hereinafter Lacan, Seminar VII].

18. *See* Edward S. Casey & J. Melvin Woody, *Hegel, Heidegger, Lacan: The Dialectic of Desire, in* Interpreting Lacan 75 (Joseph Smith & William Kerrigan eds., 6 Psychiatry and the Humanities, 1983) [hereinafter Interpreting Lacan] for an elegant introduction to the influence of Hegel on Lacan.

of pop psychology and different-voice feminism, the Hegelian and Lacanian subjects are not preexisting, self-standing, autonomous individuals seeking to maximize their utility by owning and controlling things and
people. Both Hegel and Lacan recognized that subjectivity is a human
creation—a hard-won achievement but an incomplete and imperfect
one. The subject is not autonomous but is driven by an erotic desire to
be recognized by another human being—to be desired by another person. Subjectivity can only be intersubjectivity, and this intersubjectivity
must be mediated by objectivity.

The influence of Hegel's theory of desire, as developed in *The Phenomenology of Spirit* in particular, on Lacan's early work is widely recognized.[19] I am making a slightly different point. I am arguing that Hegel
continued to exert an indirect and, perhaps, unconscious influence on Lacan throughout his life which is reflected in his late theory of feminine
sexuality. I wish to show the similarity between Lacan's account of the
origin of law, language, and sexuality and Hegel's account of the origin
of law, property, and contract in *The Philosophy of Right*.

The interrelationship between Hegel and Lacan goes deeper than mere
similarity. If Hegel was right that the totality of his dialectic is a logical
necessity, and if I am right that the application of Hegel's dialectic results
in Lacanian theory of the psychoanalytic subject, then one should be able
to go back and reread Hegel and find the Lacanian subject already waiting there. If Lacan is a true son of Hegel, this can only be because Hegel's
Minerva was already great with her Freudian child.

C. The Hole in the Whole

*Lacan's real is always traumatic it is a hole in discourse; Lacan
said "trou-matique" [literally "hole-matic"]; in English one*

See also Elizabeth Grosz, *Jacques Lacan: A Feminist Introduction* 64–65 (1990); Bice
Benevenuto & Roger Kennedy, The Works of Jacques Lacan: An Introduction 130 (1986);
Stuart Schneiderman, Jacques Lacan: The Death of an Intellectual Hero 22, 99 (1983); Jean-
Luc Nancy & Phillipe Lacoue-LaBarthe, The Title of the Letter: A Reading of Lacan 30,
121–27 (F. Raffoul & D. Pettigrew trans., 1992).

19. *See, e.g.,* Anthony Wilden, *Lacan and the Discourse of the Other, in* Jacques Lacan,
Speech and Language in Psychoanalysis 159, 163, 284–93, 306 (trans. with notes and com-
mentary by A. Wilden, 1968) [hereinafter Lacan, Speech and Language]; Casey & Woody,
supra note 18, at 75; Wilfried Ver Eecke, *Hegel as Lacan's Source for Necessity in Psychoanalytic
Theory, in* Interpreting Lacan, *supra* note 18, at 113; and Nancy & Lacoue-LaBarthe, *supra*
note 18, at 121–27.

*could perhaps say "no whole without a hole"? I would be
inclined to translate Lacan's "pas-tout"—one of his categories—
by (w)hole.*[20]

One might now be tempted to argue that my comparison
of Hegelian and Lacanian subjectivity is inept because Hegel was the theorist of the "whole" and Lacan was the theorist of the "hole."[21]

Hegel was, of course, a totalizing philosopher. To the casual reader this
might suggest that, even if he argued that no individual moment of subjectivity could adequately encompass human consciousness, we have the
potential to be part of an adequate whole—that is, the totality of *Geist* (of
which subjectivity is but one moment).[22] The creation which we call the
human subject is, according to this analysis, simultaneously true as a moment of the whole and yet false and inadequate because it is merely part
of the whole.

In contrast, one might be tempted to argue that Lacan rejected Hegel's
totality.[23] Like Hegel, Lacan thought that subjectivity, or even human consciousness, standing alone, is inadequate to the task of explaining personhood because it is only one moment of the psyche. But unlike Hegel,

---

Lacan's work went through different periods. Slavoj Žižek, For They Know Not What
They Do: Enjoyment as a Political Factor 148 (1991) [hereinafter Žižek, For They Know
Not What They Do]. Nevertheless, his theory remained deeply Hegelian.

20. Jacques-Alain Miller, *Microscopia: An Introduction to the Reading of Television, in*
Jacques Lacan, Television: A Challenge to the Psychoanalytic Establishment at xi, xxiii (Joan
Copjec ed. & Denis Hollier et al. trans., 1990) (1974) [hereinafter Lacan, Television].

21. Wilden makes this distinction in his otherwise excellent discussion of Hegel's
influence on Lacan.

Lacan is speaking at both the psychological and the political level, for he is attempting
to show the impossibility of the final reconciliation of [Hegel's] Phenomenology,
whether it is viewed at the individual or at the societal level.

Wilden, *supra* note 19, at 307.

22. But the individual who fully recognizes this [i.e., his own historicity and tempo-
rality] and understands that history is a human creation, is no longer a mere creature of
history. . . . By fully understanding his own historicity, Hegel claims to transcend it, not
by ascending to a realm of Platonic Ideas, nor by escaping into a timeless mystic unity,
but precisely by insisting that man's freedom makes him radically temporal and historical; and yet to understand this history is to transcend it in a knowledge that is absolute
because it grasps the truth of all the antecedent forms of consciousness and culture, and
knows itself to be the product of those forms. It thereby comprehends the whole of history within itself.

Casey & Woody, *supra* note 18, at 87.

23. *Id.* at 97–99.

Lacan did not think that there was an adequate whole in which the in-adequate subject could participate. Lacan thought there was an unfillable hole—an unresolvable lack—at the center of the human psyche. There is no totalizing unity with *Geist*. This argument distinguishes Hegel and Lacan. For example, according to Edward S. Casey and J. Melvin Woody,

> Hegelian phenomenology and Lacanian psychoanalysis part company here. For Lacan would forswear such a claim to absolute knowledge, empha-sizing that the analyst must abjure any comparable assertion of omni-science. And this is surely not because of any modesty on Lacan's part, but because of his conviction that there is no final insight or definitive version of truth to be had.[24]

Consequently, one might try to maintain that Hegel was ultimately profoundly optimistic while Lacan remained profoundly pessimistic. The inadequacy of the Lacanian subject remains inadequate; the creation re-mains mere fiction.[25] Thus,

> the subjection of man to culture foredooms him to what Hegel called 'the unhappy consciousness,' the consciousness of self as a dual-natured, merely contradictory being. Lacan reinforces Freud's grim conclusion that the contradiction is insuperable, that history can promise no final recon-ciliation, no splendid synthesis, not even an arena for the attainment of authenticity: cuttings and splittings, human lives in tatters, are all that re-main in this darkened vision.[26]

That is, a Lacanian might concede that the proof of a theory of the sub-ject is the role it plays in the complete totalizing whole of *Geist*. But, in-sofar as there is always a hole in the middle of any potential whole, he cannot make a claim for the essential truth of his theory *by definition*.

Unfortunately, this analysis presents a misleading dichotomy between Hegel and Lacan. It misstates Lacan's conception of the split subject as well as Hegel's conception of his totality.

When Lacan asserted that the subject is "split," he was making pre-cisely Hegel's point that the subject is not the self-sufficient, atomistic in-dividual of liberalism. Rather, subjectivity is created in part from exter-nal forces. Whether or not the human infant has an innate capacity for

---

24. *Id.* at 89.
25. Nancy and Lacoue-Labarthe give an excellent example of this analysis of Lacan's de-pendence on, and difference from, Hegel. Nancy & Lacoue-Labarthe, *supra* note 18, at 121–25.
26. Casey & Woody, *supra* note 18, at III (quoting Lacan).

speech and desire, this capacity can only be actualized through the relationships with other persons and by submission to an existing symbolic order of law, language, exchange, and sexuality. Lacan emphasizes that one implication of this process is that, at one moment, that which is most ourselves—our subjectivity—is externally imposed upon and therefore alienated from ourselves. This sense that part of ourselves is not ourselves but is somehow cut off from ourselves is one aspect of what Lacan called "castration."

As we shall see, this parallels Hegel's understanding that the abstract person can only actualize his capacity by submitting to other persons and a regime of law, exchange, and property. These institutions are created by mankind generally but are imposed on each man individually. Our legal subjectivity is, therefore, both internal and external to ourselves. Consequently, even though the Hegelian concept of totality relates to the whole, the Hegelian system is radically incomplete at the level of the individual subject, in the same way as Lacan's is. If a Hegelian were to stay with the Lacanian at her level of analysis—that is, of the subject—he would also present a similar picture of an incomplete, split, and radically negative subject. On this analysis, Hegel's theory seems optimistic only in the abstract sense that one might find intellectual satisfaction in the thought that *Geist* is working through the world. The theory, however, presents a fundamentally negative image of the individual as a moment separated from Spirit.

Moreover, Hegel's totalizing unity is a dynamic process based not only on the incomplete negative subject but on sublation—which I shall merely introduce here but discuss in detail later. In sublation, contradictions are not merely negated. They are also preserved. And yet there is always implicitly an unsublated trace, a vanishing mediator, an unaccountable fourth, which implicitly remains after the triadic operation of the dialectic.[27] The resulting whole of sublation is, therefore, simultane-

27. Michel Rosenfeld lucidly discusses the necessary interrelationship between Hegel's *Science of Logic, The Phenomenology,* and *The Philosophy of Right* in Michel Rosenfeld, *Hegel and the Dialectics of Contract,* 10 Cardozo L. Rev. 1199 (1989) [hereinafter Rosenfeld, *The Dialectics of Contract*].

As Rosenfeld says:

The Philosophy of Right traces the dialectical journey that leads from the perspective of the abstract person to that of the modern state. . . . Thus, we are led back to the struggle for recognition and to the celebrated dialectic between lord and bondsman which Hegel addresses in the Phenomenology.

Id. at 1220.

ously contradictory. Slavoj Žižek, probably the most forceful proponent of the Hegelian influence on Lacan, insists that negativity lies at the heart of Hegel's totality:

> The picture of the Hegelian system as a closed whole which assigns its proper place to every partial moment is therefore deeply misleading. Every partial moment is, so to speak, "truncated from within", it cannot ever fully become "itself", it cannot ever reach "its own place", it is marked with an inherent impediment, and it is this impediment which "sets in motion" the dialectical development. The "One" of Hegel's "monism" is thus not the One of an Identity encompassing all differences, but rather a paradoxical "One" of radical negativity which forever blocks the fulfillment of any positive identity. The Hegelian "cunning of Reason" is to be conceived precisely against the background of this impossible accordance of the object with its Notion; we do not destroy an object by mangling it from outside but, quite on the contrary, by allowing it freely to evolve its potential and thus to arrive at its Truth: . . . [28]

To Žižek, the difference between Kant and Hegel is not, as is usually thought, that Kant identified a hole at the center of our understanding and concluded that we were incapable of grasping the thing-in-itself directly while Hegel developed a new form of logic which enabled him to get to the thing-in-itself. Rather, Hegel used the same reasoning as Kant but came to a startlingly different conclusion: the hole is part of the thing-in-itself, the totality requires an intrinsic emptiness.[29]

In this analysis, Hegel's system is like Lacan's—closure does not imply fullness. The hole that lies at the center of the Hegelian totality is reflected in the emptiness at the heart of the Lacanian split subject. If one finds the Lacanian subject depressing, then one should find the Hegelian subject equally dreary. On the other hand, if the Hegelian dialectic of subjectivity reflects the possibility of the actualization of human freedom, then one should find Lacan similarly optimistic. I shall argue that it is precisely the negativity at the heart of the split Lacanian subject that opens up the possibility of radical freedom. This radical negativity is the impossible Feminine—Vesta, the hidden goddess.

The Hegelian dialectic is easily misconstrued as a crushing teleologi-

28. Žižek, For They Know Not What They Do, *supra* note 19, at 68–69.
29. Slavoj Žižek, The Indivisible Remainder: An Essay on Schelling and Related Matters 110 (1996) [hereinafter Žižek, The Indivisible Remainder]. Hegel makes this point forcefully in his *Lesser Logic:*

> Further deficiencies in the treatment of the Antinomies I have pointed out, as occasion offered, in my [*Greater Logic*]. Here it will be sufficient to say that the Antinomies are

cal necessity that inexorably leads humanity forward toward union with *Geist*. In the political context, the result is seen as union of the individual citizen with the state. Hegel's metaphor for the totality of the state, "the march of God in the world,"[30] can suggest foreboding pictures of goose-stepping storm troopers to a late-twentieth-century reader. Hegel's notorious formulation of the necessity that logic be objectified in the world—"what is rational is actual; and what is actual is rational"[31]—can sound like a depressing combination of grim determinism and a Panglossian defense of the status quo. These are serious misconceptions.

The progression of the dialectic is logically, but not empirically, necessary. The logic of intellect—*Geist*—works its way through the world, but not necessarily in any specific, preordained way. Any number of events, including, most importantly, the free acts of human subjectivity, can affect the course. The lack of inevitability is, paradoxically, logically necessitated. If, as Hegel argues, the progression of *Geist* is the actualization of human freedom, then, even at its highest development in the state, there must remain a moment of pure, free, and arbitrary subjectivity. I will argue that this moment of radical freedom which must be created and preserved is the Feminine.

The necessity of the dialectic is retrospective rather than prospective—

---

not confined to the four special objects taken from Cosmology: they appear in all objects of every kind, in all conceptions, notions, and Ideas. . . .

. . . But . . . Kant . . . never got beyond the negative result that the thing-in-itself is unknowable, and never penetrated to the discovery of what the antinomies really and positively mean. That true and positive meaning of the antinomies is this: that every actual thing involves a coexistence of opposed elements. Consequently to know, or, in other words, to comprehend an object is equivalent to being conscious of it as a concrete unity of opposed determinations.

G.W.F. Hegel, Hegel's Logic 78 (William Wallace trans., 1975) [hereinafter Hegel, The Lesser Logic].

30. Hegel, The Philosophy of Right, *supra* note 15, at 279. This unfortunate connotation is partly a matter of translation. Nisbet chose to translate the word "*Gang*" as "march." Although one meaning of "*Gang*" is "walk" or "march," it is not equivalent to these English words. For example, Walter A. Kaufman insisted that the translator should interpret the phrase as the "way of God." Shlomo Avineri, Hegel's Theory of the Modern State 176–77 (1984) (citing Walter A. Kaufman, Hegel's Political Philosophy 279 (1971)). Avineri himself argues that the meaning of the statement is not to justify any specific or existing governmental system, but "that the very existence of the state is part of a divine strategy, not a merely human arbitrary artefact." *Id*. at 177.

31. Avineri provides an excellent explanation of the meaning of this phrase based on Hegel's concepts of "rationality" and "actuality." *Id*. at 126–27 (noting that Hegel distinguished actuality from "all that exists").

it looks backward rather than forward. The retroactivity of the dialectic is reflected in Hegel's famous metaphor in his preface to *The Philosophy of Right:*

> When philosophy paints its grey in grey, a shape of life has grown old and cannot be rejuvenated, but only recognized, by the grey in grey of philosophy; the owl of Minerva begins its flight only with the onset of dusk.[32]

Only at the end of the day can we retrospectively examine events. No external "natural" standard exists by which one can judge the truth of Hegelian totality. In Hegelian philosophy, truth claims rest on the explanatory power of the resulting whole.[33]

One might agree or disagree as to the similarities and consistencies between Hegel's philosophical system and Lacan's psychoanalytical theory taken as wholes. My principal point, however, is the similarity between two aspects of their theories which at first blush might seem widely diverse—Hegel's theory of the role of property and Lacan's theory of the role of the Feminine as Phallic Mother. Both theories explain the role which the exchange of the object of desire plays in the constitution of subjectivity as intersubjectivity mediated by objectivity.

This seemingly narrow point, however, leads us inevitably back to the broader one. Both men believed that their respective theories of the creation of subjectivity were inextricably linked to the rest of their theories. One cannot understand or accept this one aspect of their theory, except in the context of the complete theoretical system of which it is an essential part. Consequently, similarities between the Hegelian and Lacanian accounts of the creation of subjectivity are some evidence for the propo-

---

32. Hegel, The Philosophy of Right, *supra* note 15, at 23. A few sentences earlier, Hegel wrote that "on the subject of issuing instructions on how the world ought to be: philosophy always comes too late to perform this function." *Id.* Žižek explains, "It is essential to grasp . . . this kind of relationship of contingency to necessity, where necessity derives from the retroactive effect of contingency—where necessity is always a 'backwards-necessity' (which is why Minerva's owl flies only at dusk). . . ." Žižek, For They Know Not What They Do, *supra* note 19, at 130. Hegel's statement also implies that Hegel thought he was writing at the end of a particular era of history. "This new world, which Hegel heralded . . . , is already reaching its maturity and is somehow, slowly but surely, on its way out." Avineri, *supra* note 30, at 129.

33. For example, Hegel accepted the concept of the absolutely free will as a moment in the individual, but unlike liberalism, he not merely claimed to posit it but attempted to prove it. "The deduction *that* the will is free and of *what* the will and freedom are . . . is possible only within the context of the whole [of philosophy]." Hegel, The Philosophy of Right, *supra* note 15, at 36–37.

sition that there is a broader, necessary consistency between their respective theoretical systems.

And so I now turn to explications, first, of Hegel's theory of property and, second, of Lacan's theory of the *Phallus*.

II. THE HEGELIAN STORY OF PROPERTY

A. The Internalist Approach of *The Philosophy of Right*

Hegel introduced his theory of property in the first part of *The Philosophy of Right,* in which he discusses the development of the legal subject, abstract right, and law.[34] These will, in turn, lead logically, although not necessarily historically or biographically, to the development of the family, civil society, the state, and the individual.

Hegel's initial account of property, like his account of abstract right, civil society, and the state generally, purports to be an internal one:

> To consider a thing rationally means not to bring reason to bear on the object from outside in order to work on it, for the object is itself rational for itself.[35]

That is, Hegel explores the rationality of property within the rhetoric of property.

This is opposed to an external or utilitarian analysis which purports to examine the purposes property-law concepts are supposed to serve. One example of an external analysis would be a Law and Economics or utilitarian approach which asks whether property law is "efficient" and how

---

34. That is, law in the sense of *Recht,* or "abstract right." Positive law (*Gesetz*) will not be written until the logically subsequent stage of social development which Hegel calls "Civil Society."

35. Hegel, The Philosophy of Right, *supra* note 15, at 60. According to Alan Brudner,

> [a] faithful account of property law invokes no principle of unity that treats as dissimulating rhetoric the discourse by which the law of property presents itself. The unity it discloses is intuited and corroborated rather than concealed by that discourse.

Alan Brudner, The Unity of the Common Law: Essays in Hegelian Jurisprudence 21 (1995) [hereinafter Brudner, Unity of the Common Law]. In this section I cite extensively Brudner's excellent account of Hegel's dialectic of property. Although I greatly admire Brudner's work, I differ with him in that I believe he finds more positive content and temporality in Hegel than I think can be warranted.

property law can be used for "wealth maximization."[36] "Pragmatists" on the left similarly take an instrumentalist approach by attempting to use property concepts and rhetoric to support any number of external social goals.[37] Another example of the externalist, instrumentalist approach can be seen in certain schools of analysis of the term "property" as used in the Takings Clause of the U.S. Constitution, which I discuss in the last chapter of this book. This approach asks, "What concept of property best serves the purpose of protecting the individual from the power of the state?"[38] The purpose of this analysis is not to examine the concept of property within the "private" law of property. Rather, it is to create a definition of the word "property" that can serve as a useful tool for the presupposed "public" law purpose of analyzing the respective rights and powers of the state and its citizens.[39]

Instrumentalist or conceptualist views tend to see property as a creature of positive law. Any normative content in property law must, accordingly, be externally provided. Neo-Hegelian Alan Brudner comments that these instrumentalist approaches might tell us something about the goals the scholars want property to serve, but are not likely to tell us very much about property per se.[40] Starting one's analysis from a presupposed arbitrary external purpose will almost inevitably lead to disappointment when it is found that property rules refuse to cooperate with the goals

36. *See, e.g.*, Richard Posner, Economic Analysis of Law (4th ed. 1992). I am aware that some practitioners of Law and Economics try to distinguish their concept of wealth maximization from utilitarianism. Nevertheless, I find the two movements close enough to lump them together for my limited purposes.

37. *See, e.g.*, Singer, *supra* note 3, in which Singer tries to use property concepts to establish a basis for judicial recognition of a legal right of workers to acquire a plant scheduled to be closed.

38. This notion of property, of course, lay behind Charles Reich's advocacy of the recharacterization of certain entitlements against the state as the "new" property. "The institution called property guards the troubled boundary between the individual and the state." Charles Reich, *The New Property,* 73 Yale L.J. 733 (1964).

39. *See, e.g.*, Frank Michelman, *Property, Utility and Fairness: Comments on the Ethical Foundation of "Just Compensation,"* 80 Harv. L. Rev. 1165 (1967); Margaret Jane Radin, *Property and Personhood,* 34 Stan. L. Rev. 957 (1982) [hereinafter Radin, *Property and Personhood*]; Margaret Jane Radin, *The Liberal Conception of Property: Cross Currents in the Jurisprudence of Takings,* 88 Colum. L. Rev. 667 (1977).

40. Thus, no matter how numerous the instances of agreement between law and the instrumentalist's goal, identifying them will reveal nothing intrinsic about law and everything about the interests of the onlooker who is absorbed by a curious, surface feature of the object.

Brudner, Unity of the Common Law, *supra* note 35, at 23.

imposed upon them.[41] For example, I will show in the last chapter of this book that it is logically impossible for property to fulfill the constitutional function assigned to it as standing as the barrier between the individual and the state. Consequently, Brudner argues that instrumentalist analyses are virtually destined to result in conclusions that property concepts are "incoherent,"[42] contradictory, or merely rhetorical,[43] or otherwise requiring reform or deserving abandonment. This approach also frequently leads to nominalism. Property itself is seen as having no essence but merely as a title for a legal conclusion—a bundle of sticks.

The libertarian branch of liberalism tries to justify the positive law of property by reference to a natural-law–labor theory of property. Like other classical liberal theories, this approach presupposes the priority of the autonomous individual. As articulated by John Locke, an individual acquires a legitimate property interest in an external object when he commingles his own labor with it.[44] This is, once again, an instrumentalist and externalist theory—property serves as the boundary of the public/private distinction.[45] Contemporary libertarian Robert Nozick argues that the only way truly to understand the political realm (which includes an analysis of the legitimacy of the state's right to interfere with what Nozick identifies as the individual's right to property) is by reference to some other "nonpolitical" realm.[46] Nozick starts with a concept of the autonomous individual who is prior to the state. He locates property rights not in positive law but in natural law—the individual is *entitled* to any and all property which he acquires directly or indirectly through legitimate appropriation. The state can be justified, therefore, only insofar as it recognizes the individual's prior *entitlement* to property. Nozick's approach presumes,

41. If understanding law means disclosing its own significance rather than imposing a foreign one, then an instrumentalist approach will succeed only if legal rules embody a conscious goal-oriented intention, . . . for only then are the rules veritably *for* the goal: their instrumentality is their true significance.

Id. at 22.

42. Such critiques are usually, but not exclusively, associated with Critical Legal Studies. *See, e.g.,* Duncan Kennedy & Frank Michelman, *Are Property and Contract Efficient?* 8 Hofstra L. Rev. 711 (1980); Sax, *supra* note 3; Singer, *supra* note 3.

43. For example, Posner states that "the true grounds of legal decision are concealed rather than illuminated by the characteristic rhetoric of opinion." Posner, *supra* note 36, at 21.

44. John Locke, Two Treatises of Government (Peter Laslett ed., 2d ed. 1967) (3d ed. 1698, corrected by Locke).

45. Nedelsky, *supra* note 4, at 8.

46. "The only way to fully understand the whole political realm is to explain it in terms of the nonpolitical." Robert Nozick, Anarchy, State, and Utopia 6 (1974). The alternatives

rather than explains, property. Hegelians would argue that Nozick's externalist approach might at most tell us something about his conception of nonpolitical life but is unlikely to provide much insight into the nature of the polity or property.

Another problem frequently identified in the libertarian version of the labor theory of value is its uneasy relationship between natural and positive law. Traditionally, liberalism has identified authenticity with nature and the individual in opposition with artificiality, the social contract, and the state.[47] On the one hand, the proponents of the labor theory justify the legitimacy of property on the grounds of natural law — it is the inherent right of the individual. On the other hand, they realize that for legitimate, labor-based property rights to exist, there must be a state to enforce the rights. Otherwise, property devolves into mere physical possession by the strongest individual — an illegitimate regime. Libertarians argue that individuals enter into the social contract precisely to protect property rights. Moreover, probably all modern American lawyers agree with the familiar cliché, associated with Hohfeld,[48] that property, like all legal categories, is a relationship between and among legal subjects. No atomistic individual could, then, have property rights which preexist the relationships of society. Consequently, the labor theory of property implicitly presupposes the state, and property is always already a creature of positive law — a paradox which causes insuperable problems for classic "takings" jurisprudence under the U.S. Constitution.

The internalist analysis, in contradistinction, claims to be an attempt to examine property law's own understanding of property law. This means it tries to determine whether there is any internal unity and logic to property both as an abstract matter and as concretely applied.[49]

which Nozick identifies and rejects are to view it as emerging from the nonpolitical but irreducible to it, or to view it as completely autonomous. Neither of these alternatives accurately describes the way Hegelians conceive of their internalist method.

47. See, e.g., Nedelsky, supra note 4, at 91. In this book, I am not attempting to give a comprehensive account of either classical or modern liberal political theory. In particular, many contemporary scholars working in the liberal tradition recognize an essentially social aspect of human nature in addition to an atomistic aspect. I am self-consciously using extremely simplified epitomes of liberalism purely as a foil for my discussion of Hegelian theory.

48. Hohfeld, of course, was not the discoverer of this truism, but he explicated it so well that it has become inextricably linked to his name. I discuss Hohfeldian property theory at length in chap. 2, sec. III.A.

49. See, e.g., Brudner, Unity of the Common Law, supra note 35, at 21–25.

B. The Artificiality of the Subject

The Philosophy of Right is the *Bildungsroman*[50] of personality. It is the story of the self-actualization of the abstract person into the complex individual located in the modern state. The initial stage in this philosophical biography is the person's achievement of subjectivity by being recognized as a legal subject by a person she recognizes as a legal subject. To Hegel, subjectivity is intersubjectivity mediated by objectivity. Property serves as this initial mediator. Although this struggle for recognition is described as a matter of necessity, this should not suggest that we experience this process as one of cold logic.[51] Because the freedom which is the essence of personality can only be actualized through recognition by another whom we in turn recognize, we are driven by an insatiable desire for the other. To Hegel, the search for love rules man's universe.[52] As Michel Rosenfeld has put it:

> The struggle for recognition is part of the dialectic of self-consciousness. Self-consciousness for Hegel is desire. . . .
>
> Indeed, once it is understood that the aim of desire is the preservation of self-consciousness, then it seems logical to conclude, as Hegel does, that self-consciousness can only achieve satisfaction in another self-consciousness. If desire seeks to maintain identity, then self-consciousness must seek an object which provides it with recognition. And the only ob-

---

50. Arthur J. Jacobson, *Hegel's Legal Plenum, in* Hegel and Legal Theory 115 (Drucilla Cornell, Michel Rosenfeld & David Gray Carlson eds., 1991).

51. Of course, to say that it is logically necessary for the free abstract person to actualize its freedom in concrete existence sounds as if the abstract person is not free at all but bound by necessity. This misunderstands the retroactive nature of Hegel's logic. He is considering the concept of the abstract free person retroactively from the position of a concrete individual situated in society. He is asking, "How did we get here from there?" And he is concluding not that it had to happen this way but that it must have happened this way.

To use a lurid but vivid example I have used elsewhere, from my standpoint sitting here at my computer in the summer of 1996, it is logically necessary for my parents to have had sexual intercourse sometime around September 1953. But what could have been more free and contingent from my parents' point of view back then?

This is not to suggest that there is no necessity in Hegel. As I shall explain at length in this essay, according to Hegel's dialectic logic abstractness, or pure potentiality, is at another moment identical to concreteness or actuality. At another moment, however, potentiality and actuality are totally separate. And the argument that a result is logically required does not result in any prediction as to the actual empirical result.

52. The mutual recognition which constitutes subjectivity must be one of love not only in the sense of mutual admiration but also in the Lacanian sense of seeing in another more than she is. Attempted recognition in hate results in the failed lord-bondsman dialectic where the lord might force grudging obeisance from his bondsman, but this recognition does not "count" because the lord cannot recognize the bondsman as an equal person.

ject which can provide recognition to a self-consciousness is another self-consciousness.[53]

Hegel's analysis of property and subjectivity is, therefore, desperately erotic to the point of hysteria. We desire the objects of property not for their own sake but derivatively as means to our true desire—the desire of and for other persons.

C. The Presupposition of Human Nature

Perhaps the biggest problem we Americans have in understanding Hegel is that we tend to view political philosophy through the lens of our liberal philosophical tradition. Most schools of classical liberalism follow natural-law or intuitionist philosophies. They start from a presupposition of the state of nature or an intuition of the good and then posit a linear, logical, and developmental progression from this originary point. Human nature in its hypothesized natural state is conceived as "authentic" and normatively superior to "artificial" states. Deviations from this authenticity must be explained and justified. Specifically, if the free individual is posited as existing in the state of nature or is intuited as the authentic mode of being, the community and the state pose problems *by definition*. One of the most familiar ways to solve this problem is by theorizing that free individuals consent to live under the state through a real or hypothetical social contract. In other words, in liberal theory temporal order of development of the artificial state from the natural autonomous individual has essential normative significance for what constitutes a good or just community.

Hegelianism claims to differ from liberalism in that it does not presuppose the existence of the subject in the sense of the autonomous individual.[54] This may, at first blush, seem inconsistent with the fact that Hegel, like Kant, used the abstract concept of free will as the starting place for his philosophy of right. Moreover, as indicated by its title, the recognition of formal rights plays a critical role in *The Philosophy*

---

53. Rosenfeld, *Dialectics of Contract, supra* note 27, at 1220–21.

54. In contrast to the libertarian, Hegel argues that individual selfhood is established as an end not prior to or outside of community but rather as an organic requirement of community. . . . In contrast to the communitarian, Hegel argues that community is authentically an end only insofar as it recognizes the rebellion of the self against its primacy. . . .

Brudner, Unity of the Common Law, *supra* note 35, at 17.

of Right, as it does in liberal political philosophy. This might suggest to a casual reader that Hegel held that human beings begin historically or empirically as autonomous individuals endowed with natural rights in the liberal sense of these terms. This would be a serious misreading.

The Hegelian critique is that liberal theory risks degenerating into a truism. Liberalism starts by presupposing that the essential human person is a pre-social, autonomous, self-acting individual.[55] This initial assumption or intuition identifies the social as a problem that needs to be solved *by definition.* It follows that once social life has been identified as a problem, the legitimacy of the state also becomes problematical. A libertarian, for example, may very well be entitled to claim that he has proved that his conception of the minimal state is the only form of government which can be legitimated as consistent with *his* notion of human nature.[56] The problem is, Hegel believes that liberals never adequately discuss how they originally decided on the notion of human nature which would serve as the bulwark of their political theory. Human nature is implicitly, or explicitly, declared to be self-evident, a matter of intuition, or otherwise in no need of explanation.

From a Hegelian viewpoint, a philosopher presupposing autonomous individualism is equivalent to a magician sneaking the rabbit into the hat. Hegel, of course, observed the same individualistic behavior in late-eighteenth- and early-nineteenth-century Western societies, as did liberal

55. As that great liberal tract, the Declaration of Independence, states: "We hold these truths *to be self-evident,* that all men are created equal, that they are endowed by their Creator with certain unalienable Rights . . . " (emphasis added).

56. Needless to say, libertarianism is not the only form of contemporary liberalism. There are, for example, egalitarianism, utilitarianism, and contractarianism. Michel Rosenfeld, Affirmative Action and Justice: A Philosophical and Constitutional Inquiry (1991) [hereinafter Rosenfeld, Affirmative Action]. Each of these derives slightly different conceptions of the just state from slightly different formulations of the individual.

Nozick's approach can be contrasted, for example, with that of John Rawls. Rawls also presumes the classical liberal view of the autonomous individual. But Rawls expressly tells the reader that he is doing so for reasons of intuition rather than logic. He in effect invites the reader to follow his argument so that we can decide whether the result of his intuition is intuitively attractive to us.

Perhaps I am being too hard on Nozick for not taking this initial step. Nozick is addressing liberals familiar with the liberal tradition. It may be that he is justified in assuming that his readers are well aware of the initial intuitive step which they all must take and is not wasting precious pages in repeating this. Indeed, his express recognition of the influence of Rawls on his thought might be shorthand for this—a sort of incorporation by reference. Indeed, *Anarchy, State, and Utopia* can be read as a rejoinder to Rawls's *Theory of Justice.* Nozick can then concentrate on his purpose of convincing other liberals why his libertarian conception of the state is more consistent with the liberal conception of the person than other possible liberal theories such as utilitarianism or egalitarianism.

philosophers and politicians of the time. But he did not argue that this meant that the essentially individualistic nature of humanity is self-evident, let alone pre-given. Indeed, it is questionable if essential individualism is ever empirically observable, whether humanity is studied sociologically (within our present culture), anthropologically (cross-culturally), historically (within the development of our culture), biographically (with reference to the history of our own personal lives), or psychoanalytically (with reference to the theory of the development of psychic subjectivity). Sociologically, individuality is observed in daily intercourse, but so are altruism, love, and communitarianism. Anthropologically, as far as we know, human beings have always lived in familial, tribal, or other social groups and have never lived as the solitary nomads of the primal liberal myth. As a historical matter, the concept of the liberal individual is a recent development of Western thought. Even if it has roots in classical philosophy and Christian theology, the individual as we know it today was only fully described in the so-called Enlightenment. Biographically, we are not born autonomous but as helpless infants totally dependent on others for all of our needs. Consequently the private is as problematical as the public. Liberalism identifies the individual and seeks to explain society. Hegel argues that the individual and society are equally in need of explanation.

The Hegelian approach is not antiliberal but *extra*liberal. The fact that individualism is not assumed to be pre-given in no way implies that it is illusory or unimportant. Hegel's eventual conclusion that individualism is artificial in no way implies that it is unreal or inessential. Hegel rejects the liberal identification of the authentic as the natural, in opposition to the inauthentic as the artificial. Rather, as etymology indicates, that which is artificial is made by art.[57] As a human creation, autonomy is an achievement, a great accomplishment to be treasured, nurtured, and aggressively defended. Individuality is a moment in the essential nature of the human

57. It is said that upon being shown the newly built St. Paul's Cathedral, King William III exclaimed, "How awful! How pompous! How artificial!" and knighted Christopher Wren. My colleague Paul Shupack reports that he first heard this delightful but probably apocryphal anecdote from John Rawls in a philosophy course delivered at Harvard College in the early sixties. I have not been able to find the original source. I have since read or heard many variations of this anecdote attributing the quotation variously to King William III or Queen Anne. I lean toward the former. St. Paul's was "completed" in the sense that the last stones were laid in 1710 during Anne's reign. However, it had been considered sufficiently complete that it had been dedicated and services had begun to be held in it by 1696, during William's. In any event the specific details of the story cannot be true because Wren was knighted before the cathedral was built.

creator and may be logically prior to other moments of humanness, but it is not necessarily either our initial natural state or our final self-creation.

In other words, Hegelians would argue that it is they who truly cherish the concept of the individual, while liberals take individuality and individuals for granted. In addition, unlike liberal philosophers, Hegel does not, and cannot, resort initially to consent theory to justify contract or property, let alone the state. He does not argue, as did Locke, that we enter into the social contract to protect our property to which we are naturally entitled by investing our labor into it.[58] Nor did he argue, as did Hobbes, that property was a creation of the social contract.[59]

As clarified by Seyla Benhabib, social-contract theory presupposes the existence of autonomous individuals capable of entering into, performing, and enforcing contracts.[60] To be the classical liberal individual and to be a person capable of entering into contractual relationships are one and the same thing. One could say the same thing about the liberal concept of property—property, as a legal category, requires not merely one individual who can serve as an owner but other individuals against which the owner asserts her property rights. If the concept of the individual is problematic, then so are property, consent, and contract. The problem is, of course, that the autonomous individual can only express her freedom—the ability to own property and enter into contract—in social relationships. The task of Hegelian political philosophy and jurisprudence is precisely to explain how the individual, property, and the ability to contract came into being.[61]

To put this another way, the liberal person in the "state of nature" is by its very definition pre-social and abstracted from all social intercourse. We

58. Michel Rosenfeld, *Contract and Justice: The Relation Between Classical Contract Law and Social Contract Theory,* 70 Iowa L. Rev. 769, 788 (1985).

59. *Id.* at 791.

60. The act of contract cannot generate the conditions of its own validity but presupposes background norms and rules the compliance with which confers validity on the contractual transaction. Hegel derives these background norms and rules from the rights of personality and property.

Seyla Benhabib, *Obligation, Contract and Exchange: On the Significance of Hegel's Abstract Right, in* The State & Civil Society: Studies in Hegel's Political Philosophy 159, 162 (Z. Pelczynski ed., 1984) [hereinafter The State & Civil Society].

61. Unlike [liberal contractarian philosophers] Hegel does not take as his starting point the condition of an isolated self motivated to recognize the right of others through the fear of death (Hobbes) or through an intuitive and presocial knowledge of the natural law (Locke). Nor does Hegel understand "persons" to be Kantian moral agents endowed with the noumenal ability to act in accordance with the categorical imperative. He proceeds from the condition of a society of individuals who have recognized one another's

must explain, therefore, how these abstractions come to become social. It begs the question to argue that an act of social intercourse—contract— is the origin of the institution of social intercourse—society and property. One would be arguing that liberal society was created by autonomous individuals who contracted to form liberal society which created the individuals who created liberal society, and so on. Once again, the towering turtles raise their unending heads. To put this another way, liberals presume that the abstract autonomous person is already a subject, in the sense of a being who is capable of bearing legal rights. Hegel argues that the abstract person is too empty a concept to sustain this burden precisely because all legal rights are social relationships. Property serves a function in the creation of sociality by giving the person sufficient content to bear the weight of subjectivity.[62] Or, more accurately, property and legal subjectivity will be mutually constituting.

D. The Impossibility of Philosophy Without Presuppositions; Sublation

In the introduction to the first chapter of his *Greater Logic*,[63] Hegel discusses his goal of creating a philosophy without pre-

---

entitlement to be persons in order to describe the concrete forms of interaction compatible with this norm.

Benhabib, *supra* note 60, at 160. *See also id.* at 170.

62. Alan Brudner presents still another way of looking at this problem. He argues that insofar as property is the act of the abstract free will to objectify itself, it is by definition a unilateral act by which the will recognizes itself as its own end. Basing property on consent of another denies this and denies the will's appetite for infinite appropriation. As Brudner states, "A complete property must therefore embody a reconciliation between the right to exclusive possession and the right to freedom of acquisition." Brudner, Unity of the Common Law, *supra* note 35, at 56. The resolution of this problem will be exchange and the concomitant right of alienation of property. But we cannot derive this from a preexistent ability of the person to consent because, as we have seen, the starting point of the individual will (as imagined by liberalism) is pre-social. Brudner also says:

Among the many difficulties with this solution [i.e., presupposing the ability to consent, rather than logically deriving and creating the ability to consent] one in particular concerns us most. No person could rationally, that is, consistently with his claim to be an end, consent to a unilateral and exclusive appropriation by another; for this would be to acquiesce in his permanent exclusion from the thing and hence in a permanent disparity between his self-conception and reality.

Id. at 55.

63. G.W.F. Hegel, Hegel's Science of Logic (A.V. Miller trans., 1969) [hereinafter Hegel, The Greater Logic].

suppositions. To put it simply, he concludes that it is impossible to *begin* a logical analysis without intentionally, if tentatively, adopting presuppositions.[64] One needs an initial working hypothesis or abduction. I have just explained that Hegel criticized other philosophers for basing their theories on unexamined presuppositions. Does this mean that Hegel himself is open to the same criticism despite his denials?

Hegel would argue "No." The problem with most philosophers is not that they *start* from presuppositions, which is inevitable. It is that they never *return* to critique their initial presuppositions. Presuppositions should only be accepted tentatively as working hypotheses to be developed and tested. Hegel argued that his totalizing philosophy and dialectic logic of *Aufhebung* (frequently translated into the dreadful English word "sublation") always turns back on itself. This enables one not only to develop the logical consequences of a hypothesis but also to return to and analyze the starting point—to test the hypothesis.

> The essential requirement for the science of logic is not so much that the beginning be a pure immediacy, but rather that the whole of the science be within itself a circle in which the first is also the last and the last is also the first.[65]

Sublation is a process by which internal contradictions of earlier concepts are resolved, but not in the sense of suppressing difference. The German word *aufheben* means paradoxically to preserve as well as negate.

> *"To sublate"* [i.e., *"aufheben"*] has a twofold meaning in [German]: on the one hand it means to preserve, to maintain, and equally it also means to cause to cease, to put an end to. Even "to preserve" includes a negative element, namely, that something is removed from its immediacy and so from an existence which is open to external influences, in order to preserve it. Thus what is sublated is at the same time preserved; it has only lost its immediacy but it is not by that account annihilated.[66]

In trying to understand the dialectic, many Americans are hampered by having been taught a crude caricature of sublation as a simplistic trinity of thesis, antithesis, and synthesis. That is, a thesis is presented, an in-

---

64. And yet we must make a beginning: and a beginning, as primary and underived, makes an assumption, or rather is an assumption. It seems as if it were impossible to make a beginning at all.
Hegel, The Lesser Logic, *supra* note 29, at 3.
65. Hegel, The Greater Logic, *supra* note 63, at 71.
66. *Id.* at 107.

ternal contradiction or antithesis in the original thesis is identified, and the two are resolved in a harmonizing synthesis, which destroys all previous contradictions. This serves as a new thesis, starting the logical process over. This formula is designed more as a means to discredit Karl Marx (who expropriated Hegel's method) than to understand philosophy. Indeed, this is how I was introduced to it in high school.

The problem with this description is that it suggests that sublation destroys all difference and deviation by converting them into an oppressive compromise.[67] Rather, as the German term implies, sublation preserves, as well as negates, the prior concept. Sublation is not merely tertiary—it is quadratic.

Thesis and antithesis exist in contradiction. Through sublation these contradictions are simultaneously resolved into synthesis so that at one moment thesis and antithesis are revealed as identical. Yet there always remains an unmediated moment, a hard kernel of unsublated contradiction, a phantom fourth, the trace or *différance* of deconstruction, that resists mediation.[68] That is, in sublation we have not only the thesis and antithesis and the moment of identity of synthesis, but also simultaneously the moment of difference which resists sublation.

In sublation the difference identified in the earlier stage is always preserved because it is always a necessary moment in the development of the later. To gussy it up with more fashionable terminology, the earlier concept is at one moment always already the subsequent concept, but simultaneously the very existence of the latter concept requires that the earlier concept is not yet the later concept.

Sublation (i.e., synthesis) can never destroy the differentiation between self and other (thesis and antithesis) precisely because sublation is the recognition that at one moment self and other are truly the same while at another moment they are truly different. Moreover, the moment of identity is itself different from the self-identity of self and other. In other words, in the differentiation of self and other, identity is a possibility. It is through sublation that the possibility of identity is actualized. But at

67. Even as brilliant a philosopher as Charles Sanders Peirce criticized Hegel for subsuming "secondness" (awareness of distinctions) into "thirdness" (interrelations). *See* John E. Smith, *Community and Reality, in* Perspectives on Peirce: Critical Essays on Charles Sanders Peirce 92, 96, 103 (R. Bernstein ed., 1965) [hereinafter Perspectives on Peirce]. Other scholars, however, recognize a cross affinity between Peircean secondness and thirdness and Hegelian sublation. *See, e.g.,* Paul Weiss, *Charles S. Peirce, Philosopher, in* Perspectives on Peirce, *supra* at 120, 133–34.

68. *See* Žižek, For They Know Not What They Do, *supra* note 19, at 179.

the same time, self and other must remain differentiated in order for actualization to remain possible. Hence Hegel's famous slogan of "the identity of identity and non-identity."[69]

This is a necessary result of the circularity of the dialectic. Although worded in terms of the proactive resolution of what initially appeared to be contradictions into an implicit and inevitable whole, sublation is simultaneously the retroactive breakdown of what initially appeared as a harmonious whole into unresolved inherent contradiction.[70]

E. The Tentative Presupposition

I. HEGEL V. LIBERALISM As a theoretical matter, Hegel's logic should eventually result in the same totalizing whole regardless of where one chooses to start. As a practical matter, however, one has to start somewhere.[71] For practical reasons, some starting points are more productive than others. Hegel's chosen starting place for the Logic is *pure being*.[72] The starting place chosen for *The Philosophy of Right* is the most abstract concept of selfhood which he calls *"absolutely free will"*—that which is an end in itself, and is not the means to some other entity's end.[73] The fact that he logically derives the notions of property and abstract right from the notion of the absolutely free will before he derives the notion of the family does not mean that he thinks ancient human beings actually developed commercial and contractual relationships before they adopted the affective relationships of family.[74] He is not taking the liberal position that the free individual is prior to society. Indeed, the autonomous individual of liberalism was only recognized relatively late as a historical matter.

It is true that in his analysis as a logical starting place, Hegel did start

69. Hegel, The Greater Logic, *supra* note 63, at 74.

70. Slavoj Žižek, Tarrying with the Negative: Kant, Hegel, and the Critique of Ideology 122–23 (1994) [hereinafter Žižek, Tarrying with the Negative].

71. Philosophy forms a circle. It has a beginning, an immediate factor (for it must somehow make a start), something which is unproved which is not a result. But the *terminus a quo* of philosophy is simply relative, since it must appear in another terminus as a *terminus ad quem*. Philosophy is a sequence which does not hang in the air; it is not something which begins from nothing at all; on the contrary it circles back into itself.

Hegel, The Philosophy of Right, *supra* note 15, at 225.

72. Hegel, The Greater Logic, *supra* note 63, at 82.

73. Hegel, The Philosophy of Right, *supra* note 15, at 37.

74. Consequently, Richard Posner's attempt to explain sexual behavior and family relationships in terms of economic decision making by autonomous individuals would have been anathema to Hegel. Richard Posner, Sex and Reason (1992).

with a creature bearing a strong family resemblance to liberalism's abstract individual. This may be, in part, because Hegel needed to address liberalism directly and immediately, as the foremost political philosophy of the time. But Hegel's dialectic is too generous ever to try to prove that his philosophical predecessors were simply wrong. Hegel agreed with Kant that there are reasons to begin one's consideration of a concept with its simplest, most universal, primitive, immediate, and minimal—and therefore least adequate—manifestation. If one wishes to study mankind generally—to make a universal statement as to human nature—there are advantages to abstracting down to the lowest common denominator.[75] Hegel then builds upward to show how the more adequate, complex, and fully developed concept is already logically inherent in the more primitive.

Consequently, Hegel might be said to have started with liberalism and accepted that it contains a true if inadequate moment. His point was to show that liberalism's theory of the person was only partial. Accordingly, it logically and necessarily already includes its negation which will lead to the development of a more adequate concept of the person. If liberals start, and end, with the abstract, autonomous individual, Hegel starts with the autonomous individual, continues through a more complex notion of the subject, and ends with the rich concept of the individual in a state. As I have said, liberalism assumes that the abstract person is already a subject, whereas Hegel argues that the abstract person cannot yet perform this role. As Alan Brudner writes:

> Our account of property law thus takes as its starting-point personality, conceived initially in the quite insular, decontextualized, and disembodied manner just described. It begins with this abstract self not because it aligns itself with a particular ideology for which this self is an unexamined prejudice, but because any quest for an unconditioned end as the foundation of right must begin with the abstraction from everything given or conditioned and hence with the most vacuous of concepts. Any richer or more affirmative conception of the self must prove itself worthy of rights from this starting-point, that is, through the immanent negation of abstract personality

75. It seems, rather, that Hegel's aim is to start from what we might call the minimum characterization of a person; this minimum characterization is as someone capable of distinguishing what is him from what is not or, in Hegel's terms, capable of externalizing his will. This minimal, and thus abstract, personality allows two crucial distinctions to be made, between myself and other persons and between myself and what I can have an effect upon.

Alan Ryan, *Hegel on Work, Ownership, and Citizenship, in* The State & Civil Society, *supra* note 60, at 178, 185.

as the sole unconditioned reality. So, while our account of property law begins with decontextualized personality, it does not remain there.[76]

Or, to put it another way, liberal theory's presupposition that the individual is prior to society gives individuality preeminent, exclusive normative import. The normative import in Hegelian philosophy is different. Since the autonomous individual is a true moment of personhood, the state must always preserve and respect individualistic abstract rights. However, insofar as there are also other true moments of personhood, the state can and must take other values into account as well.

2. THE ABSTRACT PERSON AND THE KANTIAN CONSTRUCT As a nineteenth-century German, Hegel could not have done otherwise than to start his political analysis from the version of liberalism developed by Immanuel Kant,[77] rather than those more familiar to American lawyers developed by John Locke, Thomas Hobbes, Jean-Jacques Rousseau, and Jeremy Bentham. Nevertheless, Hegel is relevant to American jurisprudence in that all of these theories share the notion of authentic human nature as containing elements of autonomy, self-standing individualism, and a natural right to negative liberty. Kant is an excellent starting point for the critique of liberalism precisely because he takes this shared notion of the autonomous individual in the state of nature to its logical extreme.

To oversimplify, Hegel agreed with Kant that the most basic, simple, and abstract (and, of course, least adequate) notion of what it could be to be a person is the notion of self-consciousness as free will.[78] The bare minimum essence of personality which distinguishes some*one* from some*thing* is "consciousness of oneself as simple, contentless self-relatedness that is undetermined by inclination and unrestricted by anything given."[79]

Hegel explained the minimal concept of the abstract person as follows:

> The *universality* of this will which is free for itself is formal universality, *i.e.* the will's self-conscious (but otherwise contentless) and *simple*

76. Alan Brudner, *The Unity of Property Law,* 4 Canadian J.L. & Jurisprudence 3, 14–15 (1991) [hereinafter Brudner, *Unity of Property Law*].

77. Hegel's imperative of abstract personality—"[b]e a person and respect others as persons"—is "consciously modeled on Kant's categorical imperative." Avineri, *supra* note 30, at 37.

78. Hegel, The Philosophy of Right, *supra* note 15, at 67–68.

79. Peter Benson, *Abstract Right and the Possibility of a Nondistributive Conception of Contract: Hegel and Contemporary Contract Theory,* 10 Cardozo L. Rev. 1077, 1165 (1989).

reference to itself in its individuality. . . . [T]o this extent the subject is a *person*.

. . . .

Personality contains in general the capacity for right and constitutes the concept and the (itself abstract) bases of abstract hence *formal* right. The commandment of right is therefore: *be a person and respect others as persons.*[80]

So, even though Hegel starts with free will, he is not *presuming* that free will is a necessary aspect of human nature. That can only be demonstrated retroactively through the internal logic and consistency of the entire totalizing philosophy. That is, the primitive concept of the abstract person is abstracted from the more developed concept of the individual living in the state.

To be free is to be the means to one's own ends, rather than the means to the ends of another.[81] The Kantian construct is a totally negative notion of personhood. To be free means not to act under compulsion. In order truly to have free will, the person can have no needs, desires, relations, or other pathological characteristics.[82] As a consequence, pure freedom is totally arbitrary—if the person acted for a reason, it would be bound by that reason, and not be free.[83] The person at the start is, therefore, a pure negativity. The free person can only be defined in terms of what it is not. "For the same reason [*Grund*] of its abstractness, the necessity of this right is limited to the negative—*not to violate* personality and what ensues from personality."[84]

To say that essence of personality is pure negativity may initially seem depressing because in this society we tend to identify the negative as the opposite of the affirmative and, therefore, as that which is bad. But, as I shall emphasize throughout this book, the Hegelian concept of negativity can be seen as not just hopeful but as the very basis of human freedom. The negative and the affirmative require each other. Pure negativity is not nothing, but pure potentiality. It is the very possibility, and therefore ability, to grow, create, and love. And so, as we shall explore in the next section, the abstract negative person as free will contains an internal contradiction which sets the engine of the dialectic in motion.

80. Hegel, The Philosophy of Right, *supra* note 15, at 67–69.
81. *Id.* at 67.
82. *Id.* at 67–70.
83. *Id.* at 48–49.
84. *Id.* at 69–70.

F. The Contradictions of Personality

The problem with conceptualization of the self as absolutely free will is that it is empty, abstract, arbitrary, and negative[85]—it is, by definition, totally stripped of all distinguishing characteristics. It is also, by definition, subjective (in the sense of solipsistic and impoverished) even as it claims to be universal. But real people are not abstract. They have content and concrete existence, experience themselves positively, and interrelate with other people. Since subjectivity is the ability to interrelate with others through legal rights, the empty abstract person cannot be a subject, as liberalism claims.

According to the reasoning of the dialectic, to be potential, abstract concepts must be manifested or actualized in concrete form. This is one of the meanings of Hegel's (wrongly) notorious assertion that "what is rational is actual, and what is actual is rational."[86] If one starts with the person as abstract free will, then, in order for the concept of freedom to have "meaning"—that is, determinate being—it is logically necessary that the abstract person become a specific, concrete individual with positive existence.

For something to be possible it must be actualized—the failure of something eventually to become actualized means, in retrospect, that it had not been, in fact, possible. Something only retroactively becomes potential once it has already been fulfilled. This is why the abstract person as free will is driven to actualize its potential freedom as concrete freedom.[87] But the dialectic works the opposite way as well. The logically later concept cannot exist except for the logical necessity of the continuance of the earlier, and the earlier cannot exist except for the logical necessity of the possibility of the later. The later concept is actuality, but the earlier concept is the possibility which allows it to come into being.

This concept of potentiality may initially seem opposed to our intuitions. We have a strong sense that many things that could happen, in fact, won't. Or, to put it another way, we feel that the fact that things turned out one way does not mean that things could not have been different. Isn't this why we are so moved by Marlon Brando's claim in *On the Waterfront*[88] that he "could'a been a contender"?

---

85. *Id.* at 27.

86. Hegel, The Philosophy of Right, *supra* note 15, at 20.

87. That is, freedom is negative and, therefore, mere possibility. Right is the actualization of freedom. *Id.* at 35.

88. On the Waterfront (Columbia 1954). By my use of this example, I am not implying

I would argue that a more thoughtful reading of this line of dialogue shows that our intuitions are actually in accordance with the Hegelian view. When Brando asserts that he could have been a contender, he is not really making a claim about his abstract potentiality sometime in the past. Rather, he is making a claim about his actuality in the present. He is asserting a difference between the authentic internal essence of his selfhood and the illusory external accidents of his circumstances. Hidden deep below a shabby facade of failure lies a true noble self—the contender—only temporarily and unfairly obscured. His argument is based on a misuse of the Hegelian dialectic of potentiality and actuality. He says, in effect, "If you agree that I had the potential of being a contender in the past, then you must conclude that I am in actuality a contender today despite all appearances to the contrary because potentiality must always ripen into actuality." He is a frog asserting that he is now a prince because he once was one.

Brando's argument is facetious precisely because he tries to apply the dialectic prospectively. He wants us to believe in predestination. His statement strikes us as tragic, or more accurately, pathetic, because we intuitively understand that the dialectic can only be applied retroactively. He is deceiving himself not only about his present nobility but about his past promise. Only now that the owl of Minerva has flown can we look back and recognize from the fact that he is so obviously not in actuality a contender today that he never really had the possibility of being one. It is now painfully obvious that he never had the guts. He is a frog today, because he was only a polliwog yesterday.[89]

And so the negative concept of abstract personality as free will contains contradiction and must go under. The self-consciousness as free will

---

that Hegel formulated a theory of necessity at the level of the empirical individual. He is not a Pangloss who believes that, because right and freedom must be actualized in the world, then everything in the world is in fact right.

> When understanding turns this "ought" against trivial external and transitory objects, against social regulations or conditions, which very likely possess a great relative importance for a certain time and special circles, it may often be right. In such a case the intelligent observer may meet much that fails to satisfy the general requirements of right; for who is not acute enough to see a great deal in his own surroundings which is really far from being as it ought to be? But such acuteness is mistaken in the conceit that, when it examines these objects and pronounces what they ought to be, it is dealing with questions of philosophic science. The object of philosophy is the Idea: and the Idea is not so impotent as merely to have a right or an obligation to exist without actually existing. The object of philosophy is an actuality of which those objects, social regulations and conditions, are only the superficial outside.

Hegel, The Lesser Logic, *supra* note 29, at 10.

89. This understanding of possibility can also be seen in the common folktales known

on the one hand has positive existence, but on the other hand has no positive attributes and is pure negativity.[90] As such, even though the free will is on the one hand an individual, on the other hand it is indistinguishable from all other individuals and, therefore, is not individual.[91] Moreover, to be truly free the person must be beyond desire; yet, as Hegel explained in *The Phenomenology of Spirit,* self-consciousness as negativity is nothing but desire.[92] Self-consciousness claims to be free, but since it is totally negative, its freedom can only be potential. It is, therefore, driven to actualize its freedom in order retroactively to prove its claim.

In order to resolve these contradictions, the will needs to give itself content by embodying or expressing itself somehow.[93] In order to obtain the subjectivity that will eventually enable the person to develop into a full individual and actualize his freedom, the abstract person needs to objectify himself. As we shall see, although the will must be objectified to obtain positive freedom, immediate, binary object relationships will be inadequate to this task. According to Hegelian philosophy, subjectivity is a triune relationship—intersubjectivity mediated through objectivity. One can achieve subjectivity if and only if one is recognized as a subject

---

as Cinderella stories. The familiar characterization of these as rags-to-riches stories—in which a poor girl is passively rescued by a good marriage—is a vulgar masculinist misunderstanding. In these stories, the heroine always starts as a girl of high estate—usually a princess or at least, as in the best-known version, that of Perrault, the heiress of a wealthy bourgeois. She is only temporarily plunged into a state of debasement and bodily filth upon the death of her mother (and, frequently, the attempted incest by her father). Aided by the supernatural intercession of her dead mother, Cinderella actively seeks out an ideal mate who can recognize her true self and thereby enable her to actualize her possibility revealed at the beginning of the story. That is, Cinderella is a true Hegelian-Lacanian subject. *See, e.g.,* Marina Warner, From the Beast to the Blond: On Fairy Tales and Their Tellers (1994).

90. Hegel, The Philosophy of Right, *supra* note 15, at 46–49; Brudner, Unity of the Common Law, *supra* note 35, at 21, 36.

91. Hegel, The Philosophy of Right, *supra* note 15, at 41–42, 54–55; Brudner, Unity of the Common Law, *supra* note 35, at 26–28, 229–30.

92. Hegel, The Phenomenology, *supra* note 16, §167.

93. The activity of the will consists in cancelling [*aufzuheben*] the contradiction between subjectivity and objectivity and in translating its ends from their subjective determination into an objective one, while at the same time remaining *with itself* in this objectivity.

Hegel, The Philosophy of Right, *supra* note 15, at 57.

The person must give himself an external *sphere of freedom* in order to have being as Idea. The person is the infinite will, the will which has being in and for itself, in this first and as yet wholly abstract determination. Consequently this sphere distinct from the will which may constitute the sphere of its freedom, is likewise determined as *immediately different* and *separable* from it.

Id. at 73.

by another person, whom one recognizes as a subject. Human beings are driven by an erotic desire for mutual recognition.[94] Property is "a moment in man's struggle for recognition."[95] Abstract personality cannot be recognized by others because it has no positive individuating characteristics. Only through the possession and enjoyment of objects can the abstract person become individualized and thereby recognizable as a subject. Through the exchange of objects with another person one person can recognize another person as an acting subject deserving of rights. And through recognition by that other person, the first person can recognize herself as a subject capable of bearing rights. Consequently, in Hegel, subjectivity can only be achieved in what Lacan called the "symbolic"—the social order of law and language.

One of the steps in the will's development is property. Property is a means by which the abstract person objectifies itself. The self as abstract will claims to be essential reality, but the existence of external things, that is, objects, and our dependence on external reality contradict this.[96] The self, therefore, needs to appropriate external objects—it must own property.[97] The self becomes particularized and concrete, rather than abstract, through ownership.[98] Potentiality becomes actuality.

94. *See* Rosenfeld, *Dialectics of Contract, supra* note 27, at 1220–21.

95. Avineri, *supra* note 30, at 89.

96. It is therefore a self stripped of all corporeal, mental, and affective characteristics. It has no concrete needs, values, or goals, no qualities of physical or moral character, no attributes of social or economic status, nor any citizenship. It is simply and abstractedly a person. This conception of the essential reality as a self shorn of individuating features is paradoxically determined by an individualistic premise. Specifically, it is determined by the assumption that the individual's isolated or pre-social condition is its natural one, or that the atomistic individual has a fixed and stable reality. Since the determinate individual has the significance of the atomistic one exclusive of others, the self can arrive at a normative foundation only by abstracting from determinateness per se, for the latter is equated with the merely contingent and relative, with that true only for this individual or for that. *No value that I seek as an isolated individual can objectively bind others to respect it, for such a value enjoys no privileged position with respect to their own. If I am necessarily isolated from others (if there is no natural community), then all values have this significance.*

Brudner, *Unity of Property Law, supra* note 76, at 19 (emphasis added).

97. "Because this reduction of things to an end is regarded as objective and absolute, it is said to be constitutive of a property." Brudner, Unity of the Common Law, *supra* note 35, at 42.

We can understand property, then, as the objectively realized claim of the person to be the end of things. . . . The universal and objective significance of property is that it embodies the end-status of personality.

Id. at 43.

98. First, property is here private property, because it is the embodiment of the self of

G. Objectification and Objects

Before we turn to how property leads to intersubjectivity and contract, let us examine a little more closely what Hegel meant by objectivity and ownership. This is useful because the English translation of Hegel uses such words as "things," "objects," and "possession," which have an unfortunate tendency to suggest the very phallic metaphor for property—the physical holding and seeing of tangible things—that I am criticizing. Upon careful reading, however, it becomes clear that Hegel did not hold such unsophisticated concepts.

First, I wish to remind the reader of the ambiguity of the English word "property." On the one hand, as Hohfeld so eloquently explained, in a technical legal sense the term "property" refers to a legal interrelationship between at least two subjects.[99] On the other hand, we also use the word "property" to refer to the object which is the subject of the property relationship. That is, property is both the term for the system of possession, enjoyment, and exchange and the name of the thing possessed, enjoyed, and exchanged within this system. In this book, I use both meanings of the word "property." When I refer to "property" as a type of *Phallus,* and compare it to the Feminine, I am primarily referring to "property" as the object of desire. When I refer to the legal regime called property, the psychoanalytic parallel is the linguistic system of ownership and exchange called sexuality.

Second, although the word "object" in colloquial English often refers to physical things, in philosophical and psychoanalytical discourse the term "object" refers to anything that is not a subject, that is, that which is not itself capable of having will.[100] Hegel's definition of "object" is logically necessitated by his starting definition of the subject as free will. The subject is initially the will in the sense of being one's own end in oneself, rather than the means to the ends of another. External things which themselves

---

the atomistic individual, external and indifferent to others. At this stage the presumed end of things is the singular self, the self of the discrete individual, a self that therefore excludes the self of other individuals. The realization of this self as an absolute end is private property.

Id.

99. *See* Wesley Newcomb Hohfeld, Fundamental Legal Conceptions as Applied in Legal Reasoning 65 (W. Cook ed., 1919) [hereinafter Hohfeld, Fundamental Legal Conceptions].

100. What is immediately different from the free spirit is, for the latter and in itself, the external in general—a *thing* [*Sache*], something unfree, impersonal and without rights.

Hegel, The Philosophy of Right, *supra* note 15, at 73.

have will (i.e., other human beings) cannot rightfully be objects of property. This is because appropriation is the infusion of the will of a subject into an object.[101] External things which do not have their own ends but are merely the means to the ends of another can properly serve as objects. Objects lack the subject's capacity of self-transcendence, are not ends in themselves, and, therefore, offer no moral resistance to their appropriation.[102] They can only be means to the ends of a will, and therefore appropriation of property by a will is legitimate.[103]

In other words, an object is defined as that which is not a subject. This means that if one starts with a definition of the subject as abstract person, then a strict subject-object distinction is a simple definitional truism at this stage (but only at this stage) in the dialectic.

All external characteristics are, then, "objects." Although tangible things can be objects, it is not their tangibility which establishes their objectivity. Rather, it is negation by the subject that does it. Potential "objects" of property cannot be limited to actual physical things such as land and cattle, or even intangibles such as debts and intellectual property. Since the concept of the object is defined in terms of what is not (i.e., the subject), anything that "can be conceived as immediately different from free personality"[104] can be a "thing," including desk, apartment, bank account, and stock portfolio, as well as my talents and ideas:

> Intellectual . . . accomplishments, sciences, arts, even religious observances (such as sermons, masses, prayers, and blessings at consecrations), inventions, and the like, become objects . . . of contract; in the way they

101. Slavery is wrong precisely because it is a system by which human beings are treated as the means to another's ends. Animals do not have "will" as that term is used in the Hegelian system. They are, therefore, proper objects of property. Hegel, The Philosophy of Right, *supra* note 15, at 86–88.

Our bodies are a special type of property, as I discuss briefly in chapter 3. Our responsibilities to the state also preclude an unqualified right of alienation through suicide. *Id.* at 102.

102. [T]he person stands opposed to a world of particular things, some forming its own natural endowment, others lying outside it. A "thing" is a being that is not a person, or that lacks the capacity for self-transcendence. Lacking this capacity, the thing is not an unconditioned end and so offers no moral resistance (has no right) against its use and destruction by other beings.

Brudner, Unity of the Common Law, *supra* note 35, at 42.

103. Being a thing is essentially external, its notion is not contradicted if it is given a purpose from the outside. In other words, what is essentially external *can* be used *merely* as a means: its end can be given to it by something that is other than it.

Benson, *supra* note 79, at 1164.

104. *Id.*

are bought and sold, etc., they are treated as equivalent to acknowledged *things*.[105]

Consequently, Brudner argues (correctly in my opinion) that the view expressed in much modern jurisprudence that the dematerialization of property is a recent invention inconsistent with, and subversive of, classic property theory is simply wrong.[106] It is wrong on a jurisprudential basis, given the work of Hegel and others, not to mention the long history of nontangible forms of property recognized by the common law, such as incorporeal hereditaments.[107] Indeed, as I shall discuss in chapter 2, section II.B, classical liberal jurisprudence as reflected in Blackstone's *Commentaries* and classical liberal political theory as reflected in the writings of Madison and the other Federalists both expressly adopt a definition of the objects of property which is fundamentally the same as Hegel's. They also include whatever is necessary for concrete personality: body, beliefs, opinions, talents, and so on. Property includes all that is proper to man.

H. The Elements of Property

Hegel identifies three essential elements of property: possession, enjoyment, and alienation. For an interest to be "property," it must contain all three elements. These elements should not, however, be confused with any specific empirical manifestation of the elements, but should be understood as extremely abstract logical and symbolic concepts. Moreover, it does not follow from the proposition that the concept of property necessarily contains three elements that all legal interests either contain complete manifestations of all three elements or lack all three com-

---

105. Hegel, The Philosophy of Right, *supra* note 15, at 74.

Anything, capacity or activity "external" to the person, can become an object of property. Externality does not mean simply that the thing is physically distinct from the person. Objects like books, works of art and mechanical inventions are external to the person, not in virtue of being physically distinct from him, but in virtue of being objectifications (*Entaeusserungen*), i.e. concrete embodiments of human skills, talents and abilities.

Benhabib, *supra* note 60, at 163.

106. Brudner, Unity of the Common Law, *supra* note 35, at 42 n.46. Brudner, in particular, takes Radin to task for misunderstanding what Hegel means by the external nature of things.

107. *Id.* "All the same, Hegel stretched the notion of property in other contexts in much the same way that theorists of the 'new property' do." Ryan, *supra* note 75, at 179.

pletely. Some manifestations of property will be more complete and "adequate" actualizations of the abstract possibility of the concept than others. According to Alan Brudner:

> Because these conditions will be the necessary and jointly sufficient ones of an objectively valid mastery of things, they will stand to each other not as isolated "sticks" in a "bundle," but as co-essential elements of a totality. That is to say, they will form what are commonly called the "incidents" of ownership—the particular rights that are involved in the notion of property. . . . Property in the full sense will be the interconnected totality of all its partial realizations. It will be possible to distinguish, therefore, between an imperfect and a fully realized property, and therefore between superior and inferior and superior (or relative and absolute) titles to things; and it will be possible to parcel out for finite periods some of the constituent elements of property while keeping intact its atemporal notion, thereby making possible the ideas of a remainder and a reversion.[108]

1. POSSESSION The most rudimentary or logically "first" element of property is possession[109]—the intersubjectively recognizable identification of a characteristic (object) to a specific person (subject). Possession is the most primitive element of property as an empirical matter in that one can have a right of possession of an object without any right of enjoyment or alienation, as in a simple bailment,[110] but in order to enjoy or alienate an object one must first have some rudimentary right to possess it. To have possession of something is to have "external power over" it so that the will is embodied in it.[111] Possession is "man's physical and anthropological capacity to appropriate externality for human purposes."[112]

By referring to possession, Hegel did not mean physical, sensuous holding. Even though the German word "*Besitz*" as well as its English cognate carry unfortunate physicalist connotations, both words are more accurately defined as "occupancy" or "ownership."[113] Indeed, the English word might be even less physicalist than the German used by Hegel.

---

108. Brudner, Unity of the Common Law, *supra* note 35, at 45.

109. Hegel, The Philosophy of Right, *supra* note 15, at 76–88; Brudner, *Unity of Property Law, supra* note 76, at 23.

110. A familiar example is a hatcheck at a restaurant. While you are dining, the restaurant has the right of physical possession of your checked coat until you request it back, but the maître d' may not wear it or try to sell it to other diners.

111. Hegel, The Philosophy of Right, *supra* note 15, at 76.

112. Benhabib, *supra* note 60, at 171.

113. 12 The Oxford English Dictionary 171 (1989).

"*Besitz*" is derived from the same root as "*Sitz*" (sitting or seat) and implies occupancy in the sense of the place one physically sits or camps. German mythographer Erich Neumann suggests that the concept of possession as sitting derives from the nomadic nature of ancient German tribes who only temporarily possessed any specific piece of land by camping.[114] The English word "possession," on the other hand, derives from a root meaning "power" and is etymologically related to such concepts as possibility and potency.[115] In this light, possession relates not to physicality per se but to the power of the subject with respect to objects and other subjects. Consequently, in chapter 2, section II.B.3, I suggest that if I were granted the privilege of drafting the terminology of property from scratch, I might prefer the term "objectification" to convey the Hegelian concept of possession.

Hegel's definition of possession follows from his realization that the "objects" of property are not necessarily, or even archetypically, tangible.

> Given the qualitative differences between natural objects, there are infinitely varied senses in which one can take control and possession of them, and doing so is subject to equally varied kinds of limitation and contingency.[116]

Nor, by "rudimentary," did he imply that the concept of property originated historically in the physical possession of tangibles, and expanded to include other interests by analogy and metaphor. Property originates in the internal necessity of the will.

---

114. Neumann, who has a Jungian perspective on mythology, goes further and suggests that "*Besitz*" also invokes the images of the mother goddesses worshiped by the Germans and displayed in their camps. "*Sitz*" was not just the generic term for "seat," it also referred specifically to the king's throne which in turn was identified with the mother's lap. German gods—and German kings—were depicted seated in the lap of the great mother goddess, in the same way as the ancient Egyptians depicted Horus seated in Isis's lap and Catholics depict Jesus seated in Mary's lap. This identification is specifically reflected in religious terminology. "Isis," the name of the great ancient Egyptian goddess, means "throne." Erich Neumann, The Great Mother: The Analysis of the Archetype 98–99 (Ralph Manheim trans., 1963). Even today, one of the Blessed Virgin's traditional titles is "Seat of Wisdom."

Neumann's point is that we confuse the source of power in property. The king thinks that his seat is a throne because he is a king, whereas he is only king because he sits on the throne. Similarly, men speak of possessing women in intercourse, but the man who thinks he possesses the woman is, in fact, possessed by his desire.

In other words, from the Jungian perspective, in possession, the object controls the subject, not the other way around. This is consistent with Hegel's analysis. The subject does not preexist the legal concept of property—it is constituted through property. We do not possess things because we are subjects, we are subjects because we possess things which make us recognizable to others.

115. Joseph T. Shipley, The Origins of English Words: A Discursive Dictionary of Indo-European Roots 326, 579 (1988).

116. Hegel, The Philosophy of Right, *supra* note 15, at 82.

Physical custody is, therefore, merely one possible way for possession to be actualized. This follows from the recognition that the class of objects cannot be limited to tangible things. Indeed, because physical custody is the most determinate[117] form of possession, it is the most inadequate—a brute fact easily defeated by a brute.[118] For possession to serve its function, it must be intelligible by others.

> The essence of possession is thus *intelligible* possession. . . . As an aspect of intelligible possession, a person's connection with the object is conceived independently of physical contingencies. Therefore, something is one's own only if one's will should be recognized as present in the object, regardless of whether at any particular moment one has *physical* possession of it.[119]

Consequently, Hegel identified at least two other, and more complete, ways of taking "possession" of an object: forming it and marking it.[120] Forming the object is superior to physical holding because

> [t]o give form to something is the mode of taking possession most in keeping with the Idea, inasmuch as it combines the subjective and the objective.[121]

Moreover,

---

117. Ever since "critical" legal scholars announced that the law was "indeterminate," there has been a tendency to associate determinacy with "good" and indeterminacy with "bad." Indeed, the slogan "law is indeterminate" is intended as a critique. In Hegel, determinacy is a descriptive, not a normative, term. Some things are more determinate, but this means that they are more contingent and less universal. Other things are more universal, but they are then less determinate.

118. From the point of view of the senses, *physical seizure* is the most complete mode of taking possession, because I am immediately present in this possession and my will is thus also discernible in it. But, this mode in general is merely subjective, temporary, and extremely limited in scope, as well as by the qualitative nature of the objects.

Hegel, The Philosophy of Right, *supra* note 15, at 84.

119. Benson, *supra* note 79, at 1180. Similarly, Brudner states:

> [P]ossession is a "property"—a right to possession—one that binds others whether or not the occupier is subsequently present. A distinction thus arises between sensuous and juridical possession, the latter dependent on the former but striving to transcend its limitations.

Brudner, Unity of the Common Law, *supra* note 35, at 140.

120. Hegel, The Philosophy of Right, *supra* note 15, at 85–86. *See also* Brudner, *Unity of Property Law, supra* note 76, at 143.

121. Hegel, The Philosophy of Right, *supra* note 15, at 85–86.

[t]aking possession by designation is the most complete mode of all, for the effect of the *sign* is more or less implicit . . . in the other ways of taking possession, too. If I seize a thing or give form to it, the ultimate significance is likewise a sign, a sign given to others in order to exclude them and to show that I have placed my will in the thing. For the concept of the sign is that the thing does not count as what it is but as what it is meant to signify.[122]

If marking is the most complete form of possession, it is, consequently, the most indeterminate.[123] That is, there is a considerable role to be played by positive law (whether by statute, custom, or whatever) in specifying which modes of marking will be considered legally cognizable in any specific society. Unlike Locke,[124] Hegel did not present possession of specific property by specific individuals as being normatively justified, but only as a logically required starting point for the abstract person.

What does it mean, then, to recognize that an object is possessed by (assigned to) a subject? At first blush, possession seems individualistic, but it implicitly requires the existence of others. Property, like all legal claims, is relational in the sense that it is a set of rights and obligations between and among legal subjects.[125] Consequently, property cannot be a natural right or attribute of an autonomous individual in the state of nature, as Locke insists. Possession is not merely the objective relationship of assignment of object to a subject, therefore. Although my property interest in an apple might include the right to possess it, in

---

122. *Id.* at 88.

123. *Id.*

124. Locke argued that, although in the state of nature the object world belongs in common to all men, an individual is entitled to such property with which he has intermixed his labor, with certain limitations. Locke, *supra* note 44.

It is a common misperception that Hegel, like Locke, justified property on the basis of first appropriation. *See, e.g.,* Steven R. Munzer, A Theory of Property 69–70 (1990). I believe that this is a misreading of the following sentence:

That a thing [*Sache*] belongs to the person who *happens to be the first* to take possession of it is an immediately self-evident and superfluous determination, because a second party cannot take possession of what is already the property of someone else.

Hegel, The Philosophy of Right, *supra* note 15, at 81. In context, I believe that this sentence is merely a descriptive definition of possession—the right and power of a first-in-time claimant to exclude later-in-time claimants—not a normative judgment of the justice of any individual's claim to possession of any specific object. Hegel does not seek to justify any property claim of any individual specifically, but to justify a property regime as abstract right, generally, on the grounds that it furthered the creation of subjectivity and the actualization of freedom.

125. Hohfeld, Fundamental Legal Conceptions, *supra* note 99, at 65–115.

the sense of holding it in my hand, and the right to enjoy it, in the sense of eating it, my legal right cannot be reduced to the brute fact of my holding and eating it. A monkey can hold and eat an apple, but it cannot *own* it. Possession as a legal right, as opposed to a brute fact, is the intersubjective relationship whereby a specific object is assigned to an identifiable subject *as opposed to another subject*. In other words, possession of an object by one person can only be understood in terms of the exclusion of others from the same object.[126] But more important, the person takes possession of property so that he can become recognizable by other persons.

Consequently, "possession" is the intersubjective recognition that a specific object is identified to a specific subject in the sense that the subject has some legal entitlement and ability to exclude others from the object.[127] I say "some ability" because as an empirical matter this might include different combinations of Hohfeldian rights, privileges, powers, and immunities. The highest manifestation of this may be free and clear "ownership" by an individual of those personal goods which are exempt property in bankruptcy—such as a wedding ring or glass eye. That is, the owner has the right, power, and privilege to exclude almost everyone else from these objects and the immunity from having her property interests taken or violated by others. Most possessory rights are much more constrained. Even "fee simple absolute" ownership of real property is not absolutely perfect possession.[128]

The Hegelian notion of possession, therefore, contains a contradiction in that it is solipsistic but can only be understood in terms of other persons. To possess something is to exclude others, thus possession seems to separate us. But insofar as the will was totally free of contingency, it was *already* separate. Possession, therefore, reflects rather than causes separation. At the same time, possession is dependent on other persons. The element of possession—the intersubjectively recognizable identification of an object to a subject—therefore presupposes the existence of another

126. "[T]aking possession confers the title of property only if the individual is situated in a context of social relations that legitimatize this act." Benhabib, *supra* note 60, at 172.

127. Elsewhere, I have argued extensively that intersubjective recognition is a necessary and essential element of possession on the grounds that it furthers both the classical liberal value of autonomy and the Hegelian teleological purpose of the actualization of freedom. Jeanne L. Schroeder, *Some Realism About Legal Surrealism,* 37 Wm. & Mary L. Rev. 455, 509–516 (1996).

128. *See, e.g.,* Stewart E. Sterk, *Neighbors in American Land Law,* 87 Colum. L. Rev. 55 (1987), for a discussion of the limits on fee simple ownership.

subject who can recognize this identification. This means that possession is separate but contains the promise of relationship.

2. ENJOYMENT   The next element of property is use—or what I prefer to call the "enjoyment"—of property. Standing alone, possession cannot achieve the person's goal of recognition because mere identification of an object to a person looks the same to an outside observer as identification of the object with the person. Passive owner is confused with owned object. In enjoyment, the person actively relates to the object. By using the object, the will actualizes the fact that the object is a means to the person's ends.

> [T]he thing, as negative in itself, exists only and *serves* it.—*Use* is the realization of my need through the alteration, destruction, or consumption of the thing, whose selfless nature is thereby revealed and which thus fulfills its destiny.[129]

What constitutes "use" or enjoyment will depend on the actual object.[130] Just as possession should not be equated with physical custody, enjoyment cannot be limited to sensuous consumption. The nature of the right of enjoyment varies with the type of object involved. A tomato can be eaten, but one can also admire its beautiful color or fragrance or even use it as a weapon by throwing it at some politician. Although during the term of a lease, the lessee has the right to sensuous exploitation of the leased object, the lessor also retains a right of enjoyment in the form of economic exploitation (i.e., the right to rent). Enjoyment is often conflated with possession in the sense of physical custody, because one frequently, or even usually, needs to be in immediate physical contact with, or at least close proximity to, a tangible object in order to enjoy it. But even in the case of tangible goods, the rights of possession and enjoyment are distinguishable. As reflected in the cliché that you can't have your cake and eat it too, it is often the case that enjoyment destroys the object of

129. *Id.* at 89.

130. Hegel distinguished between partial or temporary use of a thing and ownership in a way that might imply that temporary interests can never be property or that there can never be more than one interest in the same piece of property. *Id.* at 90.

One should always keep in mind Hegel's concept of the object as anything external that the various partial temporal property interests in the "same" piece of real estate (i.e., a life estate, a fee subject to a condition subsequent, a remainder, etc.) can in Hegelian terms be reanalyzed as several complete ownership interests in different objects. For example, he describes a pledge as the granting by the debtor of possession, use, and right to alienate the *value* of the collateral. Any excess value belongs to the debtor. *Id.* at 112.

desire and, therefore, also destroys the other two property elements. Consumption is the ultimate form of enjoyment.

Enjoyment is the most solipsistic element of property, in that the subject turns inward to the object and away from other subjects. Enjoyment, standing alone, is, therefore, also inadequate. The danger of enjoyment is dependence on the object.[131] Rather than being the means to her own ends (the definition of freedom), the person risks becoming subjected to the ends of the object. Because the enjoyer only has positive existence through enjoyment of her object, she is an addict who is a slave to, and lives only for, the object. This is inconsistent with the free nature of the person and with the function of property to actualize that freedom. So long as the person remains fascinated—spellbound—by the enjoyment of the object, she cannot turn to others.

Enjoyment also fails because solitary enjoyment implicitly presupposes the existence of others who must be excluded so that the object can be enjoyed,[132] and who must observe if property is to fulfill its purpose. But without mutual recognition the enjoyer remains virgin and sterile, while the observer is reduced to perverse voyeurism. Moreover, to say that enjoyment presupposes exclusion is only another way to say that possession is the most primitive element of property. That is, although it is possible to have the naked right of possession (exclusion) without also having a right to enjoyment, it is hard to imagine having any right to enjoyment without first having some minimal right of possession.

Enjoyment is intersubjective not just because the mutual enjoyment of the same object by two different subjects can be inconsistent, but because one's enjoyment of one's own object can hinder or even preclude the ability of another to enjoy his own object. To give an easy example, even rabid libertarians would probably agree that society can legitimately limit the rights of car owners to enjoy their cars by driving them on the sidewalk because that would interfere with the rights of pedestrians to enjoy their bodily integrity. Another example is environmental nuisances. A factory owner's enjoyment of his object by exploiting its productive capacity and incidentally polluting the underlying aquifers can interfere with

---

131. Brudner, *Unity of Property Law, supra* note 76, at 31.

132. In possession and use, first of all, the person verifies its primacy in a self-contradictory way, for it finds itself dependent on things for the confirmation of its mastery of them. Hence the very act that cancels the independence of the object also reinstates it.

Id.

a neighbor's ability to enjoy her water.[133] Exactly what these limitations are (i.e., what degree of interference we will tolerate as a legal matter)[134] must be determined by practical reasoning (i.e., positive law).

The first two elements of possession and enjoyment also reduce property to a brute fact, mere contingency, rather than a right, in the sense of something essential to humanity.[135] These contradictions cannot remain. In order to actualize her freedom, the person needs to rid herself of the enslaving object.[136] This requires the third element of property—alienation.

3. THE TRIUNE NATURE OF PROPERTY Before we continue further, it might be helpful to stop again briefly to examine where we have been. At this point, the Hegelian conceptualization of property appears to be binary, containing only two terms—the owning will and the owned object. But, as we have seen, this apparently binary relationship contains contradictions. These contradictions will be resolved through the addition of a third term—the other which recognizes the self's property interests and in relationship to which the self can assert its objectification through property. Through sublation, property is always already becoming a relationship between subjects, and subjectivity can only be intersubjectivity.

In my discussions of possession and enjoyment, I have shown that intersubjectivity is implicit and potential, but latent. It is only in alienation through exchange that it becomes express and actualized.

One should also note that even at this point before the recognition of the third term, the purpose of property and the three Hegelian elements of property are already implicitly and inherently intersubjective. The Hegelian analysis contradicts modern assertions that the Hohfeldian conception of property as relational between persons is a recent development inconsistent with the classic view that property is a relationship between

133. I apply my property analysis to environmental nuisances in Jeanne L. Schroeder, Three's a Crowd: Calabresi and Malamed's Repression of the Feminine (1997) (unpublished manuscript, on file with author).

134. Of course, legal restrictions are not the only limitations society places on enjoyment. Other restrictions are imposed by religious belief, customs, and etiquette. That is, rudeness is legal but intolerable.

135. [W]e have not yet bridged the gulf between fact and right. Possession and use are sensuous acts that claim to ground a conceptual or unconditioned right to exclude. Yet the supposedly unconditioned right is thus far self-contradictorily conditioned by physical possession and use.

Brudner, *The Unity of Property Law, supra* note 76, at 31–32.

136. *Id.* at 34.

a person and a thing.[137] It also contradicts the misinterpretation according to which Hegel reaffirms the liberal position that property is prior to community.[138] Rather, Hegel shows that the liberal position is contradictory. If community presupposes property, property also necessarily presupposes community.

This Hegelian conclusion as to the triune nature of property parallels the common-law concept of personal property. In contemporary property law there must be a subject asserting the property rights (possession, enjoyment, and alienation). There must be an object in which the property rights are asserted via appropriation by the subject. And there must be at least one third person against which the property rights are asserted.

I. Adding the Third Term: Alienation

Accordingly, a person can have existence in relation to another only when each side has recognizable determinate existence through its being embodied as an owner of a thing. The relation between persons must be mediated through external things and must consequently be a relation between persons qua owners of things. For there to be such a relation, it must be possible for me to acquire or alienate something, not merely as an external thing, but as property—as what already embodies the will of another. My acquiring or alienating a thing would then occur through my relation to the other's will. This brings us to the third

---

137. The division of right into the right of *persons and things* . . . and the rights of *actions,* . . . like the many other divisions of this kind, aims primarily to impose an external order upon the mass of disorganized material between us. The chief characteristic of this division is the confused way in which it jumbles together rights which presuppose substantial relations, such as family and state, with those which refer only to abstract personality. . . . To enlarge upon the lop-sidedness and conceptual poverty of this division into the *right of persons* and the *right of things,* which is fundamental to Roman law . . . , would take us too far. Here, it is clear at least that *personality* alone confers a right to *things,* and consequently that personal right is in essence a *right of things—* "thing" . . . being understood in its general sense as everything external to my freedom, including even my body and my life.

Hegel, The Philosophy of Right, *supra* note 15, at 70–71.

Of course, Hohfeld himself did not purport to be inventing a new way of looking at law. Rather he created a taxonomy to describe classic legal concepts in an elegant, consistent, and therefore more readily usable, vocabulary. He made more readily apparent certain aspects of property which had not traditionally been recognized—a not inconsiderable achievement. Hohfeld, Fundamental Legal Conceptions, *supra* note 99. Unfortunately, as I discuss in chap. 2, sec. III.A, his specific attempt to analyze and reconceptualize property per se was woefully inadequate.

138. Radin, *Property and Personhood, supra* note 39, at 972.

phase of property, namely contract, which according to Hegel, completes its deduction.[139]

I. ABANDONMENT AND GIFT   Hegel described alienation as the third fundamental element of property.[140] Possessory rights tell you whom you can exclude from the object of desire. Enjoyment rights tell you what you may do with and to your object of desire. Alienability rights tell you how to rid yourself of the object you once desired.

We have seen how the person cannot remain in lonely enjoyment but must extricate herself from the trap of objectivity. To understand alienation, we must return to the logic of property as the objectification of the will: the free will is simultaneously totally universal and totally solipsistic, and, therefore, seeks to resolve its contradictions by making itself into something recognizable by others. Alienation enables the will to reassert its mastery over an object through indifference.

> It is possible for me to *alienate* my property, for it is mine only in so far as I embody my will in it. Thus, I may abandon . . . as ownerless anything belonging to me or make it over to the will of someone else as his possession—but only in so far as the thing . . . is *external* in nature.[141]

Abandonment is one way of demonstrating the nothingness of the object. But mere abandonment cannot be enough because in property the will is attempting to objectify itself. If the subject merely abandons the object, he destroys his objective confirmation.[142] The only way out of this dilemma is to achieve objective confirmation through the recognition of the act by an equal acting subject—both subjectivity and objectivity must become intersubjectivity.

And so simple abandonment of the object is a self-defeating retreat back into abstraction and away from recognizability.[143] The person must, therefore, find a way of untangling herself from the object, while simul-

139. Benson, *supra* note 79, at 1183.
140. *Id.*
141. Hegel, The Philosophy of Right, *supra* note 15, at 95. "By getting rid of the thing, I show conclusively that it belongs to me rather than I to it." Brudner, *Unity of Property Law, supra* note 76, at 34.

As I shall discuss in chapter 3, the logic of property will recognize that the continued possession of certain objects (such as the body) is necessary for the development of personality (i.e., recognizability) and should not be subject to the regime of exchange.

142. "If I abandon it . . . however, I lack objective confirmation for my claim of right to dispose of it according to my will." Brudner, *Unity of Property Law, supra* note 76, at 34.
143. *Id.*

taneously maintaining sufficient connection to the object to remain recognizable and enabling her to enter into a relationship of mutual recognition by another person.

Gift is more adequate than abandonment because it more explicitly recognizes the third term. Although superior to abandonment, gift is, surprisingly, also inadequate to this function. Although we tend to think of gift as benevolent, the dialectic of gift is similar to the malevolent lord/bondsman dialectic. True, in a gift the donee can recognize the donor as a person with identifying characteristics who is indifferent to the object given and is, therefore, free. The problem is that the donee's recognition doesn't count. This is because, in gift, the donor treats the donee as the means to the donor's end of achieving freedom.[144] The donee does not herself exercise subjectivity in receiving the gift—she is literally the object of the donor's affection. The donor cannot requite the donee's love precisely because he has selfishly demanded love from her rather than helping her become lovable. The donee is a bondswoman who can never satisfy her lord's desire for recognition.[145] How often have we seen this failed dialectic played out in actual "love" affairs?

Since the donor does not achieve his goal of being recognized by another subject, he also fails in achieving the subjectivity he desires. Instead of achieving the self-other relationship of mutual recognition, the donor remains in a subject-object relationship. Moreover, after the gift is made

144. *Id.*

145. Although we tend to think of gifts as benevolent, from a Hegelian property analysis they are parallel to the malevolent relationship described in Hegel's famous lord-bondsman dialectic. The lord, seeking recognition, enslaves a bondsman who is forced to bow down in obeisance. This does not have the desired result, however, because the lord has reduced the bondsman to a degraded state. By enslaving the bondsman, the lord has refused to recognize the bondsman as an equal human being whose judgment counts. Or, to put it the other way, the lord can only maintain his status as a lord by refusing to recognize the bondsman as a human being. The recognition by the bondsman is unsatisfying precisely because the lord craves admiration from someone better than himself, yet the lord cannot allow himself to admit that the bondsman is even his equal. Hegel, The Phenomenology, *supra* note 16, at 114–21.

Similarly, admiration which is bought—as in the case of gift—is suspect. We despise those who take bribes. Consequently, there is something unsatisfying in the recognition of thanks precisely because we do not really admire another person when he is thanking. It is a servile act. By demanding love, rather than giving it, the donor, like the lord, reduces the donee, like the bondsman, to an inferior position. The donee whose love is demanded is perceived as pathetic and clinging, and not lovable. This is why the seducer's desire turns to loathing the moment his paramour asks "When will I see you again?"

This is not to imply, of course, that gifts never have benevolent social functions. It merely implies that the relationship of gift does not further the specific function assigned to property, namely the creation of legal subjectivity.

(as in abandonment), the giver is once again left without an identifying object in his possession. He squandered his object in a failed attempt at recognition and is once again left unrecognizable.

2. EXCHANGE The only way of making a person lovable is to love her—recognize her as a subject worthy of recognition. As Lacan explained, love must precede lovability.[146] To love is, precisely, to see in someone more than she is. This results in the alchemy in which the beloved is able to give back to the lover that which she doesn't have.[147] It is only at the moment when she, whom I now recognize as a subject, in turn recognizes me as a subject, that I truly know myself as "I."[148] She is my mirror, and I am hers. In exchange—contract[149]—one person does not give an object to the other; two persons exchange objects.[150] Not only is the first party thereby recognized as a free subject by the counterparty, but since the counterparty is also alienating an object, the counterparty is simultaneously recognized as a free subject by the first party. Because in contract the two parties are briefly united in a common will—the agreement to engage in the exchange—they share ends.[151] Neither is reduced to the subhuman objective level of a mere means to the ends of the other. This is the moment of mutual recognition between subjects which can only be achieved through the mediating object in the relationship known as property, contract, and abstract law.[152]

> A person, in distinguishing himself from himself, relates himself to *another person,* and indeed it is only as owners of property that the two per-

146. "Not so long ago, a little girl said to me sweetly that it was about time somebody began to look after her so that she might seem lovable to herself." Lacan, Four Fundamental Concepts, *supra* note 1, at 257.

147. Miran Božovič, *The Bonds of Love: Lacan and Spinoza,* 23 New Formations 69 (1994).

148. "To love is, essentially, to wish to be loved." Lacan, Four Fundamental Concepts, *supra* note 1, at 253.

149. For simplicity, I am using the term "contract" to describe its more complete manifestation in exchange. Hegel, however, was careful to recognize that even gift has a contract aspect. "A contract is *formal* insofar as the two acts of consent whereby the common will comes into being—the negative moment of the alienation of a thing . . . and the positive moment of its acceptance—are performed separately by two separate persons: this is a *contract of gift.*" Hegel, The Philosophy of Right, *supra* note 15, at 106.

150. This is as much the case in service contracts as in sales contracts. The services performed are as much an object (in the sense of being separable from the concept of personhood) as the money paid.

151. *Id.* at 102–03.

152. *Id.* at 104.

sons really exist for each other. Their identity *in themselves* acquires existence . . . through the transference of the property of the one to the other
by common will and with due respect for the rights of both—that is, by
contract.[153]

Law is essential to this dialectic because it is only by being accorded
rights that a person obtains the dignity of a subject who is capable of bearing rights. Law, contract, and the legal subject who is capable of contract
are mutually self-constituting. The abstract person creates rights not so
he can immediately claim them for himself, but in order to accord them
to the other in order to bestow on her the dignity of subjectivity so that
she may in turn recognize him and return the gift of subjectivity.

Contract recognizes a moment in which two persons are united,
bound together in a common will at the same time that they recognize
each other as separate individuals having specific rights and duties. The
parties to contract are simultaneously the same and different, actualizing
the identity of identity and difference.

> But as the existence of the *will*, its existence for another can only be *for the
> will* of another person. This relation . . . of will to will is the true distinc-
> tive ground in which freedom has its *existence*. This mediation whereby I
> no longer own property merely by means of a thing and my subjective will,
> but also by means of another will, and hence within the context of a com-
> mon will, constitutes the sphere of *contract*.[154]

And so we see, property simultaneously leads to the creation of both
the contract[155] and the contracting person; they are mutually constituting. The object of property in this stage of development is the external
object of desire exchanged between subjects. This exchange does more
than merely enable persons to recognize each other as acting subjects.
Rather, this mutual recognition is precisely what makes us into subjects
with the capacity of acting and contracting.

For this reason, alienation—the exchange value of property—is essential to the idea of property as a moment in the formation of personality precisely because it subordinates the object to intersubjective rela-

153. *Id*. at 70.
154. *Id*. at 102.

155. [Contract] is the process in which the following contradiction is represented and
mediated: I *am* and *remain* an owner of property, having being for myself and excluding the will of another, only in so far as, in identifying my will with that of another, I
cease to be the owner of property.

Id. at 104.

tionship. Property is not about things, it is about people. True, in property people desire, possess, and enjoy objects, but only derivatively as a means of achieving their true desire—the desire of the other.

In most traditional liberalism, the authentic human being is the autonomous individual supposedly encountered in a hypothesized state of nature. This liberal tenet means that negative freedom is all that the state and other individuals can offer. To Hegel, however, this categorical imperative is merely the bare minimum that human beings owe each other, and fails to describe the more complex interrelations of which individuals are capable within families and communities.

> If someone is interested only in his formal right, this may be pure stubbornness, such as is often encountered in emotionally limited people. . . .
> [F]or uncultured people insist most strongly on their rights, whereas those of nobler mind seek to discover what other aspects there are to the matter . . . in question. Thus abstract right is initially a mere possibility. . . . [156]

I have been describing the Hegelian dialectic in terms of desire and love, but the relationship achieved at the level of abstract right is only the cold impersonality of the marketplace. But Hegel's precise point is that although the market seems cold and abstract it is, in fact, fundamentally but potentially erotic. As its name suggests, *abstract* right is the most abstract, and therefore the least adequate, form of human relationships.[157] Consequently, it is only the first logical step in, and not the culmination of, the process of the development of the personality and the actualization of freedom. This is why the last two-thirds of *The Philosophy of Right* concern how abstract right is sublated into the more adequate relationship of morality, which in turn is sublated into ethical life, thereby enabling the development of a complex individuality within a complex society. This means that, in contrast to utilitarian liberalism, Hegelianism refuses to analyze all human relations in terms of economic man interacting in the marketplace.[158] This also means that, in contrast to libertarian liberalism, property rights, although necessary, cannot be absolute. Property rights will necessarily be limited not only by prop-

---

156. *Id.* at 69.

157. Brudner describes the interpretation of all human relationships in terms of contract as "the distorted image peculiar to persons who define their worth independently of all connection to others." Brudner, *Unity of Property Law, supra* note 76, at 37.

158. *See also* Avineri, *supra* note 30, at 139. Indeed, to describe more complex relationships, such as marriage, in terms of contract is not just impossible, it is "disgraceful." Hegel, The Philosophy of Right, *supra* note 15, at 105.

erty's own internal limitations but by the higher requirements of morality and ethics.

J. From Hegel to Lacan

I now explore how the Feminine serves a function in the psychoanalytic-linguistic theory of Lacan parallel to the function of property in Hegel's theory of subject formation. At first blush, Hegel and Lacan seem to adopt different starting places for their analyses. As we have seen, Hegel tried to derive a philosophy without presuppositions, even as he realized that one must tentatively adopt a working presupposition in order to start the logical process. He chose to start with the Kantian construct—the most universal, and thereby abstract, conception of the individual—in order to derive the development of the complex, concrete experience of actual human beings. Hegel's description of the development of the subject and the society purports to be logical, not literally temporal in the psychological or historical sense. The logical necessity of the theory is retroactive, not prospective.

Lacan explored the development of the psychoanalytic subject. One might initially assume that his starting place and ending place are given as a biographical and empirical matter—we all start out as babies and we end up as adults.[159] This makes the theory sound like a temporal, biographical account based on the observation that babies are speechless but learn to speak as children.[160] The autonomous individual of liberalism would have no place in Lacan's theory, if for no other reason than that if he did exist, he would have no need of a psychiatrist's couch.[161] On fur-

---

159. Of course, this is only "given" in the vaguest sense. Isn't the whole problem of psychology and ethical philosophy that there can be great disagreement as to how a baby "starts" (i.e., how much of our personality and language capabilities are hardwired in our genes, and how much is software programmed into us later) and where we end up (i.e., are human beings inherently selfish, altruistic, individualistic, communitarian, good, bad, all or none of the above?)?

160. The human subject is created from a general law that comes to it from outside itself and through the speech of other people, though this speech in its turn must relate to the general law.

Juliet Mitchell, *Introduction I* to Jacques Lacan and the école freudienne, Feminine Sexuality 1, 5 (Juliet Mitchell & Jacqueline Rose eds. & Jacqueline Rose trans., 1985) [hereinafter Lacan, Feminine Sexuality].

161. The Hegelian subject much more nearly recognizes the people encountered in therapy than does the autonomous self-interested individual of liberal political theory. Lacan's formulation that "the desire of man is the desire of the other" was specifically intended as

ther reflection, however, it becomes apparent that Lacan's theory, like Hegel's, is not inductively derived from the observation of children and does not necessarily purport to be an accurate description of human biography. Rather, as Lacan insists, his theory is a fiction—a story retroactively written through abduction and dialectic logic to explain a Hegelian conception of the person.

To Lacan, the subject is the subject of language.[162] In other words, subjectivity is intersubjectivity mediated through objectivity—just as it is in Hegelian philosophy. Human beings are driven by an erotic desire for mutual recognition; one can achieve subjectivity if and only if one is desired as a subject by another person whom one recognizes and desires as a subject.[163] In order to become a speaking subject, the infant, like the Hegelian abstract person, must become recognizable and recognized by another speaking subject. Through the symbolic exchange of the *Phallus* as object of desire with another person—that is, language and the law as prohibition—the person can desire the other person as a speaking and desiring subject. And through recognition by that other person, the first person can recognize himself as a speaking subject capable of desire.

This subject's position with respect to possession, enjoyment, and exchange of the *Phallus* is sexuality. Sexuality is not, therefore, a biological function, although it is patterned by biology.[164] Consequently, the moment a person attains sexuality is simultaneously the moment of creation both of subjectivity as intersubjectivity and of law as prohibition. In Hegel,

---

a description of hysteria. Lacan, Écrits, *supra* note 14, at 264. But this is because Lacan believes that hysteria is not an aberration but the fundamental human condition. Žižek, The Indivisible Remainder, *supra* note 29, at 167.

162. "I have long established in the structure of the subject, defined as the subject that speaks . . . " Jacques Lacan, *Introduction to the Names-of-the-Father Seminar* [hereinafter Lacan, *Names-of-the-Father Seminar*], *in* Lacan, Television, *supra* note 20, at 81, 82. "For Lacan the subject is constituted through language. . . . The subject is the subject of speech (Lacan's '*parle-être*'), and subject to that order." Jacqueline Rose, *Introduction II* to Feminine Sexuality, *supra* note 160, at 27, 31; *see also* Mitchell, *supra* note 160, at 5.

163. "If I have said that the unconscious is the discourse of the Other (with a capital O), it is in order to indicate the beyond in which the recognition of desire is bound up with the desire for recognition." Jacques Lacan, *The agency of the letter in the unconscious or reason since Freud* [hereinafter Lacan, *The agency of the letter*], *in* Lacan, Écrits, *supra* note 14, at 146, 172.

164. "[A]ny difficulties experienced by the individual in assuming his or her own sex, bear no direct relation to the biological facts of what is called intersexuality." The école freudienne, *The phallic phase and the subjective import of the castration complex* [hereinafter the école freudienne, *The Phallic Phase*], *in* Lacan, Feminine Sexuality, *supra* note 160, at 99, 107. In the words of Mitchell, "the actual body of the child on its own is irrelevant to the castration process." Mitchell, *supra* note 160, at 17. "It is only . . . through deferred action that previous experiences such as the sight of the female genitals becomes significant." *Id.* at 16.

property, subjectivity, and law were mutually constituting. In Lacan, sexuality, subjectivity, and law are mutually constituting. Property in Hegelian philosophy, therefore, serves a function parallel to that of the *Phallus* in Lacanian psychoanalysis.

Like Hegel's, Lacan's reasoning is dialectic, retroactive, and abductive, not empirical, progressive, or inductive.[165] He does not argue, as Freud sometimes seems to have done, that our adult sexuality is the culmination of an *empirical* process starting with our literal desire to have sexual union with our mothers and to kill our fathers. Rather, the logic of subjectivity and consciousness requires intersubjective recognition achieved through a regime of possession, enjoyment, and exchange of an object of desire. It is only when we retroactively try to understand this purely psychoanalytic process that we identify or conflate the stages with actual empirical stages we have lived through. Psychoanalysis is not an account of what the child is actually experiencing. It is, rather, the story told by the adult looking back at his own childhood. That is, we are not the way we are because we desired our mother, but our memory of our desire for our mother only retroactively takes on importance because of who we are today.

III. THE LACANIAN STORY OF THE FEMININE

A. Reading Lacan

The gender types described by Lacan are at least superficially consistent with contemporary gender stereotypes—many of which are highly misogynist. I would hope that feminists and feminist fellow travelers do not dismiss his theories out of hand because of this. I find his account not merely provocative but evocative. In particular, I find that his typology of the Feminine and Masculine functions much more accurately fits my experience of myself and others than does the pop psychology of cultural feminists. Lacan does reveal a tragic, misogynist world. But to condemn him for doing so is to kill the messenger because of the message.[166] A theory of misogyny is not necessarily a misogynist theory.

---

165. Žižek, Tarrying with the Negative, *supra* note 70, at 37, 58, 66, 200–01, 208, 211, 219; Slavoj Žižek, Looking Awry: An Introduction to Jacques Lacan Through Popular Culture 13, 17, 69–71, 78 (1992) [hereinafter Žižek, Looking Awry].

166. As Mitchell states, Lacan's "task is not to produce justice but to explain this [i.e., existing sexual differences]." Mitchell, *supra* note 160, at 8.

More important, Lacan is, probably unintentionally, subversive of the gender status quo. I will show throughout this book that Lacan's very propositions undermine his conclusions from within. The Masculine is supposed to be the position of subjectivity, and the Feminine that of objectivity. The Feminine symbolizes lack—she does not exist. But it is only this radical negativity of the Feminine which can represent the negative that is at the heart of the split Lacanian subject. It is only this negativity which opens up a space in human existence for desire, creation, and freedom. It is the denial of the Feminine in what Lacan called "castration" which transforms the impossible into the merely forbidden.

Paradoxically, then, it is this impossibility of the Lacanian Feminine which creates the possibility of Hegelian freedom. Consequently, Lacanian theory shows that the self-actualization of human freedom requires not only property rights but feminine emancipation. This latter requires the impossible task of going beyond the limits of castration and creating an affirmative speaking feminine subjectivity. This is the concept of Hegelian freedom as "the ought"—that which, according to sublative logic, is the always already and the not yet. But it is never the now.

But we run before our horse to market.

I. THE PATRIARCHAL FAMILY In reading Lacanian theory one needs to keep several things in mind. First and foremost, Lacan's theory does not "explain" patriarchy in a scientific or causative sense. Rather, it presupposes patriarchal family structures.[167] Lacan's method was abduction—the logic of imagination.[168]

Abduction is the logical process by which we try to imagine possible

---

167. It is significant that this myth does not in fact explain patriarchy, for it already presupposes it. For the father to have control of all the women, for the sons to be dominated by him, patriarchy must already exist.

Grosz, *supra* note 18, at 69.

As Lacan noted:

Judging from experience [the function of woman as the symbolic object of exchange among men] can only happen within an androcentric and patriarchal framework, even when the structure is secondarily caught up in matrilineal ancestries.

Jacques Lacan, The Seminar of Jacques Lacan, Book II, The Ego in Freud's Theory and in the Technique of Psychoanalysis 1954–1955, at 272 (J.-A. Miller ed. & S. Tomaselli trans., 1988) [hereinafter Lacan, Seminar II].

168. *See generally* Jeanne L. Schroeder, *Abduction from the Seraglio: Feminist Methodologies and the Logic of Imagination*, 70 Tex. L. Rev. 179 (1991) [hereinafter Schroeder, *Abduction from the Seraglio*].

explanations of initially surprising phenomena. As Julia Kristeva explains, she accepts Lacan's theory of castration as a working hypothesis because of its great explanatory power. She compares it to the "Big Bang" theory of the birth of the universe, which cannot be directly observed. Nevertheless, if we were to treat the story of the *Phallus* or the story of the Big Bang as though it were true, then so many initially surprising things we observe about human behavior, in the one case, or astrophysics, in the other, would no longer be surprising but would be a matter of course.[169] It is a retroactive attempt at explaining the past, as opposed to a prospective prediction of the future. Consequently, Charles Sanders Peirce argued that abduction was better termed "retroduction."[170]

In other words, Lacan did not merely observe infants acquiring language and deduce that conventional gender roles would inevitably develop. Rather, he observed the existence of the patriarchal family and tried to imagine a satisfying story which might make its existence seem understandable. This means that Lacan purports neither to show how patriarchy originally came into being as a historical matter nor to argue that patriarchy is inevitable. At most, it suggests the structures through which Western patriarchy, once in place, reproduces itself.[171]

On the one hand, the theory holds out to feminists at least a theoretical possibility of change—a rewriting of gender roles. On the other hand, Lacan's retroactive account of patriarchy as a self-reproducing system takes seriously the crushing "reality" of the fiction of gender roles as lived. We cannot not merely wish away unhappiness and oppression.

2. THE ARTIFICIALITY OF SEXUALITY Lacan can be seen as retelling Hegel after Freud, or perhaps more accurately, as rewriting Freud through Hegel.[172] Lacan's greatest contribution to Freudian psychoana-

---

169. Julia Kristeva, The Kristeva Reader 197–98 (Toril Moi ed. & Alice Jardine et al. trans., 1986).

170. Schroeder, *Abduction from the Seraglio, supra* note 168, at 115 n.15.

171. That is, the theory simultaneously recognizes that the status quo is not natural while recognizing that we do not develop into persons in a vacuum but within a specific society. As a consequence, anatomical difference does not cause sexual difference in a psychoanalytical sense, but sexual difference is retroactively overlaid onto anatomical difference "according to a pre-existing hierarchy of values." Rose, *supra* note 162, at 42.

172. Lacan's insistence that he was "returning" to Freud should not be confused with an uncritical acceptance of Freud's theories. Lacan was perfectly aware that the theories of the historical Freud were not totally systematized but contained contradictory strands and a lingering naturalism. But this is to be expected in the works of any innovator. Lacan thought that much of contemporary Freudian psychoanalysis, particularly American object-relations theory, was unsuccessful because it had, so to speak, taken the wrong fork in Freud's theory. Lacan, therefore, argued that it was necessary to return to Freud in the sense of reopening his work to recover what had been lost. *Id.* at 28.

lytic theory may be that he moved it away from the anatomical and natural.[173] Freud himself wavered between naturalistic and fictional accounts of the psyche.[174] In his theory of "penis envy," Freud at times came close to saying that the penis is so impressive that the mere sight of it arouses an actual desire in little girls to want one of their own; the primal sighting (or non-sighting) of the little girl's lack of a penis causes the little boy to fear physical castration. The psychological experience of loss is a retroactive reinterpretation of these primal events. The traditional Freudian theory of the oedipus complex risks becoming an assertion concerning biological lust which is supposedly experienced by children as an empirical, biological matter.

In contradiction:

> Sexuality . . . [on Lacan's rewriting of Freud] is not, in spite of popular conceptions, governed by nature, instincts or biology but by signification and meaning.[175]

This signification is given by the man looking back at the child he once was.[176] Penis envy and castration anxiety are retroactive, imaginary reinterpretations of earlier psychoanalytic experiences of loss, rather than the other way around.[177]

---

173. "Lacan's central insight has been to correct the biological readings of Freud's account of gender differentiation through the castration complex." Drucilla Cornell, *The Doubly-Prized World: Myth Allegory and the Feminine*, 75 Corn. L. Rev. 644, 660 (1990) [hereinafter Cornell, *Doubly-Prized World*].

174. *See, e.g.*, Grosz's account of Freud's account of the subject, sometimes taking what she refers to as a realist approach, while at other times taking a narcissistic approach. Grosz, *supra* note 18, at 24–31.

Wilden notes that although Freud "stated quite adamantly the discontinuity between psychic and other realities (biological reality . . .), . . . he had nevertheless indicated his own carelessness about maintaining the distinction in his writing." Wilden, *supra* note 19, at 199.

175. Grosz, *supra* note 18, at 13. Note that in this passage, Grosz is emphasizing the non-anatomical aspect of Freud which Lacan developed further. In context, Grosz's point is that Freud wavered between the symbolic interpretation of sexuality and an anatomical, naturalist interpretation.

176. "The legibility of sex in the interpretation of the unconscious mechanisms is always retroactive." Lacan, Four Fundamental Concepts, *supra* note 1, at 176. Freud was preoccupied with the actual *historical* event experienced by the child that would create subjectivity. "But for Lacan, this is not some mythical moment of our past, it is the present order in which every individual subject takes up his or her place." Rose, *supra* note 162, at 36.

177. My disagreement with Judith Butler's reading of Lacan is so profound that a point-by-point refutation is beyond the scope of this book. Basically, I believe that her misreading springs largely from a failure to appreciate the retroactive nature of the dialectic. Thus, she thinks it is a criticism of Lacan's theory of the mirror stage that the infant is described as becoming aware of its body through the sight of its organs, which she believes Lacan

3. SEXUALITY AS LANGUAGE When Lacan speaks about "men" and "women," he is not speaking about empirically anatomical male and female human beings.[178] He is, rather, referring to the "Masculine" and the "Feminine" as psychoanalytical, or linguistic, positions which human beings must take up to become speaking creatures. These positions are only generally associated with the biological sexes.[179] That is:

> For Lacan, men and women are only ever in language ("Men and women are signifiers bound to the common usage of language" . . .). All speaking beings must line themselves up on one side or the other of this division, but anyone can cross over and inscribe themselves on the opposite side from that to which they are anatomically destined.[180]

To say that Lacan sought to destroy any lingering biological determinism in Freud's theories while explaining how gender difference becomes mapped upon biological sexual difference[181] is not to imply that biological sexual difference does not exist or is not important. Lacan's

---

considered to be typified by the male genitals, when the signification of the *Phallus* and its identification with the penis only takes place in the later oedipal stage. Judith Butler, Bodies That Matter: On the Discursive Limits of "Sex" 78–79, 86 (1993) [hereinafter Butler, Bodies That Matter]. This is not, however, a contradiction if one realizes that the signification of the organs in the mirror stage is not the empirical experience of the infant. Rather it is signification given by the adult looking at children and reconstructing his experience. Butler also seems peculiarly insensitive to how Lacan's theories developed over time, comparing his very early work on the mirror stage which dated from the 1930s, which arguably reflect traces of classic Freudian biologism, with his late writings on sexuality in the 1970s.

I do agree with Butler, however, that the Lacanian system, with its dichotomy of male and female sexuated positions, has not to date developed a satisfying account of homosexuality. But then, in my opinion, neither does Butler.

178. Lacan teaches us that there are not such "things" as men and women in any theoretically pure sense. As split subjects we are all defined as both Masculine and Feminine, because there can be no pure referent outside of the system of gender representation that designates our sex.

Cornell, *Doubly-Prized World, supra* note 173, at 672.

179. This account of sexual desire led Lacan, as it led Freud, to his adamant rejection of any theory of the difference between the sexes in terms of pre-given male or female entities which complete and satisfy each other. Sexual difference can only be the consequence of a division; without this division it would cease to exist. But it must exist because no human being can become a subject outside the division into sexes. One must take up a position as either a man or a woman. Such a position is by no means identical with one's biological sexual characteristics, nor is it a position of which one can be very confident—as the psychoanalytical experience demonstrates.

Mitchell, *supra* note 160, at 6.

180. Rose, *supra* note 162, at 49.

181. Grosz, *supra* note 18, at 13; Cornell, *Doubly-Prized World, supra* note 173, at 660.

point is that our experience of sexuality as speaking, conscious subjects can never be simply reduced to our biological sex for the same reason that property cannot be reduced to our sensuous relationship with physical things. Sexuality is artificial, and therefore authentic to man the artist. The sexual status quo is neither natural nor inevitable in the sense that anatomy is destiny. Nevertheless, Lacan hypothesizes a mechanism by which a sexual status quo—once in place—maintains its position.

Male superiority is neither biologically nor psychoanalytically true. Rather it is a fantasy. Yet it is a fantasy in which we live.[182] If gender is a lie, it is a lie that we *believe*. We must adopt a sex in order to become adult subjects. As we shall see, the theory holds that identification of these psychological categories with biological analogues is practically inevitable in our society, even if it is erroneous. Anatomy is, therefore, hardly irrelevant.

> [A]natomy is what figures in the account: for me "anatomy is not destiny," but that does not mean that anatomy does not "figure" . . . , but it only figures (*it is a sham*).[183]

That is, the fictional sex we "choose" and live tends to be correlated, more or less strongly, with our anatomical sex. Lacan captures this by using terms for his psychoanalytical concepts, like *Phallus* and castration, which suggest this conflation. Consequently, a Lacanian would deny the fashionable sex/gender distinction (which identifies the former with anatomical difference and the latter with social difference) precisely because it presupposes that we can tell the difference and achieve an immediate experience of the "real" of anatomy as distinct from our imaginary and symbolic interpretations.[184]

Neither does my reading of Lacanian theory require a denial of the physical and anatomical concept of the brain, in favor of a psychic explanation of the mind. Nor is his linguistic theory necessarily incompatible

---

182. For example, as Ellie Ragland-Sullivan explains, "[i]n this signifying nexus, males defend against imaginary castration anxiety by linking identity, discourse, and sexual apparatus to a fantasy of superiority *qua* difference." Ellie Ragland-Sullivan, *The Sexual Masquerade: A Lacanian Theory of Sexual Difference, in* Lacan and the Subject of Language 49, 59 (E. Ragland-Sullivan & M. Bracher eds., 1991).

183. Rose, *supra* note 162, at 44 (quoting M. Safoan, *la sexualité féminine dans la doctrinne freudienne* 131 (1976). Ragland-Sullivan criticizes Rose for stressing the role of anatomy in the development of sexual identity.

184. *See* Mitchell, *supra* note 160, at 2. Curiously, this is one of the few points of agreement between Lacanian theory and MacKinnon's so-called feminism unmodified. Jeanne L. Schroeder, *The Taming of the Shrew: The Liberal Attempt to Mainstream Radical Feminism,* 5 Yale J.L. & Feminism 123, 138–39 n.42 (1992) [hereinafter Schroeder, *The Taming of the Shrew*].

with theories that emphasize the physical capacity of the human brain for language.[185] Lacan's idea is held by many philosophers of science.[186] Human consciousness cannot experience the physical in an unmediated way. Human beings, as speaking subjects, do not have a direct unmediated relationship to our biological sexuality. We always filter our experience of the physical through the orders of the real, the imaginary, and the symbolic. The moment we are aware that we are experiencing a sensation, the second we are aware of ourselves as differentiated from an object or sensation, our mind has mediated the experience of the brain.[187] The moment we think about our sexual experiences (let alone fantasize or speak about them), we have already interpreted them.[188]

4. THE ANATOMY OF TRUTH Lacan's truth about lies is a story told through metaphors of male anatomical experience. But this leaves open the question whether other different "true" stories—perhaps feminine stories—could be told to explain other aspects of ourselves.

This possibility, of course, is more than just a little problematical. As we shall discuss, Lacan posits that the subject is psychologically positioned as masculine. What then could it possibly mean to tell a feminine story if we always speak in a masculine voice?[189] It would not be an answer merely

185. Nevertheless, some Lacanians insist on such an incompatibility. For example, Ragland-Sullivan states: "There are . . . no innate Chomskian tendencies or capacities for language." Ellie Ragland, Essays on the Pleasures of Death 193 (1995).

186. Including Peirce and Karl Popper. See Schroeder, Abduction from the Seraglio, supra note 168.

187. Charles Sanders Peirce developed a particularly clear illustration of the mediated nature of consciousness:

Imagine me to wake and in a slumberous condition to have a vague, unobjectified, still less unsubjectified, sense of redness, or of salt taste, or of an ache, or of grief or joy, or of a prolonged musical note. That would be, as nearly as possible, a purely monadic state of feeling.

Charles Sanders Peirce, Collected Papers, vol. 1, Principles of Philosophy 149 (E. Hartshorne & Paul Weiss eds., 1931) [hereinafter Peirce, Collected Papers]. But as soon as one becomes conscious that one is tasting something, there is no longer one thing, the pure essence of the taste. There are two, the taste and the taster. You no longer have an unmediated experience of the quality of taste, but a mediated or interpretive experience. You can speculate that a few seconds before, you might have had an immediate, purely physical, experience, but you can never know this directly.

188. Cornell, Doubly-Prized World, supra note 173, at 672. It is "never a question of arguing that anatomy or biology is irrelevant, it is a question of assigning their place. [Lacan] gave them a place—it was outside the field of psychoanalytic enquiry." Mitchell, supra note 160, at 20.

189. Lacan's assertion, however, is also a way of insisting that women cannot tell of the experience of Woman, because it is exactly this universal experience which is beyond rep-

to attempt to tell the story of development through female anatomical metaphor.[190] Mere negation or reversal is always a reinstatement, not a rejection, of hierarchy. In negation, the categories of the original hierarchy are accepted, and thereby strengthened and essentialized; one merely argues about the relative valorization of the categories. Lacan's point of the essential antinomy of sexuality remains.[191] If the Feminine is the position of lack (radical negativity), then any attempt to identify positive content replicates the deluded masculine fantasy that we can tame and dominate the Feminine by defining her.

For example, as I shall discuss, Lacan's psychoanalytical term of art *Phallus* is the lost object of desire and the signifier of subjectivity. It does not designate the male organ. The identification of the *Phallus* with the male

---

resentations. Lacanianism, in other words, seems to undermine all attempts on the part of feminists or anti-feminists to tell us what Woman is. She is the beyond. At the same time, Woman, or the Feminine, is "there" in her absence, as the lack that marks the ultimate object of desire in all subjects. To say that She is unknowable is not, then, to argue that Her lack is not felt. Indeed, Woman as lack is constitutive of genderized subjectivity. Even so, Woman does not exist as a "reality," present to the subject, but as a loss.

Cornell, *Doubly-Prized World, supra* note 173, at 661.

190. Luce Irigaray, whose Lacanian-influenced writings are filled with female imagery, at first blush seems to be making this mistake. Cornell argues that this literal-minded analysis misses Irigaray's point:

Because of her refiguring of sexual difference, Irigaray has been falsely accused of once again understanding anatomy as destiny. But this accusation only makes sense if Irigaray is understood as *describing* the female body and then drawing conclusions about what women *are* from this description. Instead, the second aspect of her deconstruction should be understood to undermine the identification of gender with her "sex," now in the name of feminine desire. Sexual difference, in other words, reaches into the definition of desire itself. Irigaray, in effect, challenges Lacan's own writing of the split subject as a masculine version of desire. Perhaps women desire differently. Who's to *know*?

Drucilla Cornell, Beyond Accommodation: Ethical Feminism, Deconstruction, and the Law 16 (1991) [hereinafter Cornell, Beyond Accommodation].

Grosz is also extremely compelling in her discussion of Irigaray's attempt to explore the feminine and female imagery without falling into the trap of reinstating Lacan's binary sexual system, which is by definition *Phallic. See* Grosz, *supra* note 18, at 170–83. *See also* Judith Butler, Gender Trouble: Feminism and the Subversion of Gender 9 (1990) [hereinafter Butler, Gender Trouble].

191. Žižek explains the seeming contradiction whereby Lacan insisted both that the sexual positions are arbitrary and that his system of sexuality is universal. What is necessary (universal) in Lacan's system is the fundamental antinomy or noncomplementarity of sexuality where one "sex" is defined as the universal (the symbolic order) and the other as the exception to the order. But this antinomy can be played out in any number of ways. Consequently, in Lacan, the usual situation whereby there is one universal theory which has many particular manifestations is reversed. In Lacan there is one particular idea (sexual antinomy) which has many "universals" (sexual hierarchies) in different societies. Žižek, The

organ and the female body is, like all identification, imaginary. Lacan intentionally uses this misleading term in order to reflect conflations retroactively made by the subject upon taking on sexual identity and subjectivity.

Several feminists such as Grosz, Cornell, and Irigaray have, however, challenged Lacan's claims to a neutral terminology. Is he in fact engaging in a conflation of the psychic and the anatomical even as he denies it?[192] That is, by using terminology which invokes the anatomical male organ to describe the object of desire, Lacan might be making the error of describing the psyche through phallic (as opposed to *Phallic*) metaphor. Lacan's very terminology may not merely reflect but actually predetermine the conclusions of his analysis. Lacan's claims of nonessentialism might degenerate into the essentialization of the Feminine as silence. Sexuality is not biological, but biological men and women usually take up the fantasy positions of psychic men and women: but if *all* is fantasy, then the fantasy we live is the only reality. Theoretically we might be able to live another fantasy—but not in the current world. Our current fantasy is the only reality we can know. Nevertheless, I believe Lacan's misogynist paradox, whereby sexuality is not inevitable but always already predetermined, precisely describes the structure of society and the impossible task facing feminism. Lacan's terminology is *not* neutral. But this is because society is not.

Indivisible Remainder, *supra* note 29, at 217. Lacan's *Phallic* language reflects how the sexual antinomy is universalized in contemporary Western society.

See also Jeanne L. Schroeder, *Feminism Historicized: Medieval Misogynist Stereotypes in Contemporary Feminist Jurisprudence* 74 Iowa L. Rev. 1135 (1990) [hereinafter Schroeder, *Feminism Historicized*]; *and* Schroeder, *Abduction from the Seraglio, supra* note 168.

192. Even though Lacan claims the *Phallus* is not the penis, Elizabeth Grosz writes:

The phallus and penis can only be aligned if there are those who lack it. It is assumed on the basis of division and dichotomy, represented by the lack attributed to women. . . . In spite of Lacan's claims, the phallus is not a "neutral" term functioning equally for both sexes, positioning them both in the symbolic order. As the word suggests, it is a term privileging masculinity, or rather, the penis. The valorization of the penis and the relegation of female sexual organs to the castrated category are effects of a socio-political system that also enables the phallus as the "signifier or signifiers," giving the child access to a (sexual) identity and speaking position within culture.

Grosz, *supra* note 18, at 122.

Similarly, Cornell states:

Despite this facially gender-neutral account [i.e., of the development of language through the child's relationship with the mother], however, Lacan goes further and appropriates signification in general to the masculine. Although Lacanians maintain the difference between the penis and the phallus—the phallus represents lack for both sexes—

But this seeming predestination is the inevitable effect of a retroactive dialectic. Lacan's theory of sexuation posits its necessity only in the sense that, standing here today as adults in this society, this is the process which *must have happened*. It is not necessary in the sense that, from the standpoint of any empirical infant, this is the process that *must* happen in all societies in all times. Theoretically the child could undergo different forms of sexuation in different types of societies. In addition, as we shall see, the Lacanian alchemy allows us to transform the impossible into the merely forbidden. As I shall discuss, to the Lacanian and the Hegelian, the existence of prohibition contains within it not merely the possibility but the ethical imperative of its transgression. It is precisely by denying feminine subjectivity that Lacan requires it. Consequently, implicit in the Lacanian-Hegelian notion of necessity is the possibility of reform. But we will never know whether it is really possible until we actualize it.

B. The Real, the Imaginary, and the Symbolic

According to Lacan, we exist in the three orders of the symbolic, the imaginary, and the real.[193]

[I]n the relation of the imaginary and the real, and in the constitution of the world such as results from it, everything depends on the position of the subject. And the position of the subject—you should know, I've been repeating it for long enough—is essentially characterized by its place in the symbolic world, in other words in the world of speech.[194]

In one of Lacan's last seminars, he uses the metaphor of a "Borromean Knot" to describe the relationship between these orders. This "knot" consists of three rings that are not interlinked but are held together through overlapping.[195] The metaphor points out that although each ring and each realm is distinct and does not interpenetrate any other, the whole of the knot and the psyche depends on the interrelationship between the three;

---

it remains the case that, because the penis is visible and can represent the lack, the penis can stand in for the would-be-neutral phallus. The phallus as the transcendental signifier, then, cannot be totally separated from its representation as the penis.

Cornell, *Doubly-Prized World, supra* note 173, at 661.

193. *See generally* Grosz, *supra* note 18.

194. Jacques Lacan, The Seminar of Jacques Lacan, Book I, Freud's Papers on Technique 80 (J.-A. Miller ed. & J. Forrester trans., 1988) [hereinafter Lacan, Seminar I].

195. Lacan, *Names-of-the-Father Seminar, supra* note 162, at 88. Lacan provided a visual representation of the "Borromean Knot":

remove one, and the whole system collapses. The metaphor of the inter-locking rings is also designed to counteract the tendency to hierarchize the three regimes—placing the symbolic realm above the imaginary, and the imaginary above the real. Another advantage of the metaphor of rings is that it offers an alternative to the common internal-external metaphors for human experience. A point within a ring can be described either as external to the ring or as internal to it. Because the three rings overlap, the metaphor illustrates how (as I shall discuss later) the object cause of desire, which Lacan calls the *objet petit a,* can exist in more than one or-der simultaneously.

The symbolic is the order of law and language.[196] Since the Lacanian subject is the speaking subject, subjectivity is primarily in the symbolic—law, language, symbolization, and signification. In other words, the sub-ject is not only the subject *of* language, it is also subject *to* language.[197] The imaginary, as its name indicates, concerns the order of nonverbal imagery.[198] It includes simple identification and differentiation of the

Schneiderman, *supra* note 18, at 33. For brief descriptions of the metaphor of the "Borromean Knot," *see id. and* Žižek, Looking Awry, *supra* note 165, at 5, 143.

According to Rose:

> Lacan termed the order of language the symbolic, that of the ego and its identifications, the imaginary (the stress, therefore, is quite deliberately on symbol and image, the idea of something which "stands in"). The real was then his term for the moment of impos-sibility onto which both are grafted, the point of that moment's endless return.

Rose, *supra* note 162, at 31.

196. *Id.* at 80. Because Lacan's subject is the subject of language, his psychoanalytic the-ory is also a linguistic theory consisting in large part of a rewriting of Ferdinand de Saus-sure. *See* Lacan, *The agency of the letter, supra* note 163, at 146.

197. "For Lacan the subject is constituted through language. . . . The subject is the sub-ject *of* speech (Lacan's "parle-être"), and subject *to* that order." Rose, *supra* note 162, at 31. *See also* Mitchell, *supra* note 160, at 1, 5.

198. The Freudian ego, for example, is imaginary in that it is one's image of oneself. The imaginary is the least worked-out of the Lacanian orders. Like all great thinkers, Lacan refined his theories constantly throughout his life. In his early work, Lacan concentrated

type of which animals are capable. Lacan's concept of the real is subtle and paradoxical. The real is our sense of the limit to the symbolic and the imaginary—that which cannot be captured in language or images. It is the world of impossibility, limitations, and necessity.[199] The real is pure immediacy. It is the uterine unity that collapses all distinctions not only of people but of time and space. It is that which we feel we lose the moment we mediate our experience through imagery or language. To speak of or visualize the real is to lose touch with reality. Yet our sanity literally requires that we treat the real as though it were reality.[200] We necessarily insist on a piece of the real in our symbolic and imaginary experience.[201]

For some purposes it is useful, although admittedly simplistic, to say the real stands in for the physical or "object" world preexisting outside of human consciousness and language—that is, nature. Standing for the biological or natural, the real includes the realm of the infant before it

----

on the distinction between the symbolic and the imaginary. In his late work, however, Lacan had changed his concentration to the distinction between the symbolic and the real, with the real taking over some of the function which had originally been ascribed to the imaginary. Compare, for example, Lacan, Seminar I, *supra* note 194, with Lacan's twentieth seminar, *Encore* (portions of which have been translated as Jacques Lacan, *God and the Jouissance of the Woman, in* Lacan, Feminine Sexuality, *supra* note 160, at 127 [hereinafter Lacan, *God and Jouissance*]; *and* Jacques Lacan, *A Love Letter (Une lettre d'âmour), in* Lacan, Feminine Sexuality, *supra* note 160, at 149 [hereinafter Lacan, *Love Letter*]. "With the development of Lacanian teaching in the sixties and seventies, what he calls 'the Real' approaches more and more what he called, in the fifties, the Imaginary." Slavoj Žižek, The Sublime Object of Ideology 162 (1989) [hereinafter Žižek, Sublime Object]. Consequently, it is not absolutely clear what functions were left to the imaginary in late Lacan. Because my theories are based largely on the late Lacanian theories of feminine sexuality and on the works of Slavoj Žižek, this book reflects this change of emphasis to the real.

199. The Real cannot be experienced as such: it is capable of representation or conceptualization only through the reconstructive or inferential work of the imaginary and symbolic orders. Lacan himself refers to the Real as "the lack of a 'lack.'"

Grosz, *supra* note 18, at 34.
Grosz explains:

The child, in other words, is born into the order of the Real. The Real is the order preceding the ego and the organization of the drives. It is an anatomical, "natural" order (nature in the sense of resistance rather than positive substance), a pure plenitude or fullness. . . . The Real is not however the same as reality; reality is lived as and known through imaginary and symbolic representations.

Id.
200. Indeed, in Lacanian theory, psychosis consists in large part of a subject's inability to maintain the barrier between the real and reality. *See, e.g.,* Žižek, Looking Awry, *supra* note 165, at 20.
201. *Id.* at 17, 33.

develops consciousness. Psychoanalytically, it also means all other forms of limitation of which we do not have direct experience, including the gods and death.[202] It is the hard kernel that "exists when all . . . imaginary and symbolic factors are annihilated."[203]

Before I give the plot of Lacan's *Bildungsroman* of sexuality, let me once again emphasize that the story I am about to tell is a retroactive re-creation of the development of the psyche. We will speak as though the infant actually, empirically passes through three orders of consciousness even though these orders are, in fact, mutually constituting. Lacan retroactively imagines the infant passing successively through these orders, but as he passes into the next order he never leaves the previous order.

This reflects the Hegelian dialectic in which each stage in the development of the subject is sublated into the next stage. All difference is not destroyed in sublation. An unsublated trace always remains. The "earlier" orders of psychic development, the real and the imaginary, do not totally disappear into the order of the symbolic to form consciousness.

Indeed, the two seemingly "earlier" orders do not, in fact, preexist the symbolic—the three are mutually constituting. Although we experience the real as that which preexists and binds the symbolic, in fact, the real, the imaginary, and the symbolic are mutually constituting. It is the ordering of the symbolic which walls off an outside called the real which retroactively serves as the impossible limit to the symbolic. The impossibility of a closed system has been familiar at least since Gödel proved that no mathematical system can be complete. Rather its closure always depends on assumptions imposed on the system from the outside.[204] The real is logically required by the concept of the symbolic by

---

202. "The gods belong to the field of the real." Lacan, Four Fundamental Concepts, *supra* note 1, at 45.

> The gods and the dead are real because the only encounter we have with the real is based on the canceling of our perceptual conscious, or our sense of being alive: the real is real whether we experience it or not and regardless of how we experience it. The real is most real when we are not there; and when we are there, the real does not adapt itself or accommodate itself to our being there. The concept of the real implies the annihilation of the subject.

Schneiderman, *supra* note 18, at 76.

203. Renata Salacel, *Editorial: Lacan and Love,* 26 New Formations at v (1994). "The real may be represented by the accident, the noise, the small element of reality, which is evidence that we are not dreaming." Lacan, Four Fundamental Concepts, *supra* note 1, at 60.

204. *See generally* Roger Penrose, Shadows of the Mind: A Search for the Missing Science of Consciousness (1994); Douglas R. Hofstadter, Gödel, Escher, Bach: An Eternal Golden Braid (1979).

the same reasoning.[205] We retroactively abduct the existence of the real from the traces or stains it seems to have left in the symbolic. As in Hegelian sublation, the creation of the symbolic reveals the necessary precondition of the real and the imaginary. That is, consciousness is a Borromean Knot of the three orders. The knot cannot exist unless there are at least three rings to overlap.

Lacan called the process of entering the symbolic (i.e., becoming a human subject who is capable of speech) "castration." It is the understanding that we only exist as subjects within law and language, yet law and language are external to, and imposed on, our subjectivity. It is reflected in our sense of being separated from a mythical, imaginary sense of unity with the Other (associated, of course, with the uterine union with the Mother). Castration is the loss of the mythical object of desire which is called the *"Phallus"*—the symbol of subjectivity.[206] This separation is the creation of law which is always the law of prohibition: Thou shall not merge back into unconscious union with the world. In the imaginary, this union is the utopian mother-child dyad. Consequently, in modern West-

205. Miller, *supra* note 20, at xxiv.

206. The école freudienne, *The phallic phase, supra* note 164, at 116–17; Jacques Lacan, *The direction of the treatment, supra* note 14, at 226, 265.

On the one hand, this is different from the naturalistic side of Freud which sometimes seems to argue that sexuality is literally created when the boy sees the female genitals and then for the first time understands and fears the possibility that he could lose his own, or the girl's seeing the male genitals and immediately understanding that she is maimed. On the other hand, it is also different from those object relationists who argue that "castration" is merely the culmination of numerous small natural losses, such as the loss of the breast at weaning.

Castration is not any natural (real) loss as object-relations psychologists have wrongly concluded. It is, rather, the moment our sense of loss acquires sexual signification. That is, the real of castration is an event: the Big Bang of the symbolic. In the words of Mitchell:

> There is a fundamental distinction between recognizing that the castration complex may refer back to other separations and technically seeing these separations as castrations. . . . Freud's [i.e., Lacan's interpretation of the non-naturalistic side of Freud] account is retroactive: fearing phallic castration the child may "recollect" previous losses, castration gives them relevance. . . . For Freud, history and the psychoanalytic experience is always a reconstruction, a retrospective account.

Mitchell, *supra* note 160, at 18–19. In Lacan's words:

> The fear of castration is like a thread that perforates all the stages of development. It orientates the relations that are anterior to its actual appearance—weaning, toilet training, etc. It crystallizes each of these moments in a dialectic that has as its centre a bad encounter. If the stages are consistent, it is in accordance with their possible registration in terms of bad encounters.

> The central bad encounter is at the level of the sexual.

Lacan, Four Fundamental Concepts, *supra* note 1, at 64.

ern society this law of prohibition takes the form of the incest taboo.[207] That is, the command, "Thou shalt not merge with the real" becomes "Thou shalt not identify with the Feminine" and, finally, "Thou shalt not sleep with your mother." Paradoxically, it is law's prohibition and its maiming of subjectivity in castration which create not only the possibility of but also the conditions for human growth, love, and freedom.[208] "[L]ove is a mirage that fills over the void of the impossibility" of the relationship between the two sexes.[209]

I. THE OPENING CHAPTERS OF THE PSYCHE'S BILDUNGSROMAN   Just as Hegel "started" his analysis of property with an account of the abstract will, so Lacan "started" with the infant. When viewed retroactively, the infant seems to exist wholly in the order of the real. In the real, the infant has no consciousness. Its relation to the world is immediate; it experiences itself as one with the object world, including its "Mother." Most specifically, it has no awareness of the separation of itself and the rest of the world. As Hegel stated, the infant has being-in-itself, mere implicit being.[210] At this point the infant experiences itself and its Mother as one.

Or more precisely, it has no sense of itself as a self, and no sense of its mother as a person.[211] It is, therefore, misleading to say that the infant

---

207. In Lacanian usage, the "incest taboo" does not refer to the literal prohibition of biological incest but to the law of exclusion:

> Thus, the incest taboo is not so much a biological "no" as it is a strong cultural injunction to boys to identify away from the maternal and the feminine, to substitute the name of a lineage to the desire of a mother. . . .

Ragland-Sullivan, *supra* note 182, at 50–51.

208. "Law and desire, stemming from the fact that both are born together, joined and necessitated by each other in the law of incest . . . " Lacan, *Names-of-the-Father Seminar, supra* note 162, at 89.

209. Salacel, *supra* note 203, at v.

210. Hegel, The Lesser Logic, *supra* note 29, at 181. At least one commentator has previously pointed out the similarity between Lacan's concept of the real and Hegel's concept of "being in itself." John Muller, *Negation in "The Purloined Letter": Hegel, Poe, and Lacan, in* The Purloined Poe: Lacan, Derrida, and Psychoanalytic Reading 343 (John P. Muller & William J. Richardson eds., 1988).

211. Which is why I am using the impersonal pronoun "it" to describe the selfhood of the infant in the first two stages.

> The child forms a syncretic unity with the mother and cannot distinguish between itself and its environment. It has no awareness of its own corporeal boundaries. It is *ubiquitous*, with no separation between itself and "objects", for it forms a "primal unity" with its objects. It cannot recognize the absence of the mother (or breast).

Grosz, *supra* note 18, at 34.

"experiences" union with the Mother because as soon as it starts becoming aware of experience, it begins to be aware of itself as distinct from the Mother. Awareness is not experience but the interpretation of experience. It is entering the mirror stage that will bring it into Lacan's next order of existence, the imaginary.

The imaginary is the order of the image and, therefore, of identity and difference.[212] It is the order of meaning, of captivation and ensnarement.[213] Based on mirror images, the imaginary sees difference in terms of simple negation—the sexes are imagined to complement each other perfectly as yin and yang, active and passive, autonomous and connected, individualistic and nurturing, and so on. In this mirror stage, the child starts becoming aware of itself as separate through the mediating function of sexuality.[214] This is the beginning of the subject/object distinction.[215] The infant becomes aware of the Mother as Other—as radical alterity.[216]

Note that the term "Mother" means the person initially recognized by the infant as the other, rather than his female parent. Consequently, it is sometimes written as "(M)other" by English-speaking Lacanians. In a patriarchal family structure, this person is also usually the child's mother in the usual sense, or a person socially recognized as a mother surrogate (i.e., nanny, nurse, guardian, widower, or whatever), hence the choice of terminology. The fact that the other, as second term, is identified with

---

212. Rose sees Lacan as assigning unity to the imaginary in his earlier texts, but as identifying the fantasy of sameness within language (i.e., the symbolic) in his later work. I agree that it is not clear precisely what role the imaginary plays in late Lacan.

213. Jacques Lacan, The Seminar of Jacques Lacan, Book III, The Psychoses 1955–56, at 54 (Jacques-Alain Miller ed. & Russell Grigg trans., 1993) [hereinafter Lacan, Seminar III].

214. Jacques Lacan, *The mirror stage as formative of the function of the I as revealed in psychoanalytic experience* [hereinafter Lacan, *The mirror stage*], *in* Lacan, Écrits, *supra* note 14, at 1, 2.

215. Grosz explains this as the beginning of the subject/object distinction. Grosz, *supra* note 18, at 35. Rose observes:

> For Lacan the subject is constituted through language—the mirror image represents the moment when the subject is located in an order outside itself to which it will henceforth refer. The subject is the subject *of* speech (Lacan's *"parle-être"*), and subject *to* that order. But if there is division in the image, and instability in the pronoun, there is equally loss, and difficulty in the word. Language can only operate by designating an object in its absence. Lacan takes this further, and states that symbolization turns on the object as absence.

Rose, *supra* note 160, at 31. According to Jane Gallop: "But Lacan posits that the mirror constructs the self, that the self as organized entity is actually an imitation of the cohesiveness of the mirror image." Jane Gallop, Reading Lacan 38 (1985).

216. *Grosz, supra* note 18, at 42. Grosz explains, "It is by identifying with and incorporating the image of the mother that it [the infant] gains an identity as an ego." *Id.* at 43.

(m)other in our society (and that, as we shall see, the third term will be identified with father) will determine the positions of sexuality.

Lacan's punning and metaphoric terminology is intentional. The infant *sees* its *mirror*—thereby enters the *image*-inary—in the *mirror stage*.[217] It recognizes itself by seeing itself reflected in Mother who functions as its mirror. The experience of recognition is primarily one of vision—it sees the Mother, it sees its hand and begins to recognize parts of its body.

This concept of the Feminine as alterity has been misunderstood by so-called different-voice feminist legal scholars, such as Robin West, who are strongly influenced by the works of Carol Gilligan and other object-relations psychologists. On the basis of the assertion that most empirical psychological studies of childhood have concentrated on boys, they conclude that theories that claim to explain the development of personality, generally, are, in fact, accounts of masculine personality, specifically. They presume from this that since mainstream theory asserts that personality (i.e., masculinity) originates in a recognition of difference from the Mother, then feminine personality must originate in a recognition of similarity to the mother. From this they conclude that although men (whose development is characterized by separation) may be the autonomous individuals of liberal philosophy, women (whose development is characterized by connection) are more interrelated, following an ethic of care rather than justice.[218] This vision of an affirmative Feminine which is the simple negation or mirror image of the Masculine is, as we shall see, not merely imaginary, but a masculine fantasy. Moreover, this particular conclusion is a non sequitur which springs from a fundamental confusion about the level of differentiation on which the theory relies.

The *initial* differentiation which is the starting point of Lacanian per-

217. In this stage the child becomes fascinated with actual mirror images. Grosz, *supra* note 18, at 36–37. This phenomenon is familiar to all of us who have seen infants squealing with delight at their reflected images, pictures in books, and other newly discovered "mirror images."

Lacan points out that the difference in capacity for language between human and ape first becomes apparent in this stage. Human and simian infants experience similar development up to this point. Both become fascinated with mirrors at approximately the same age. Eventually both the child and the chimp realize that the image in the mirror is itself, and not another animal on the other side. The chimp loses most of its interest. The child's fascination increases. Lacan, *The mirror stage, supra* note 214, at 1.

218. I use the term "different-voice feminism" because the psychological study which has had the greatest influence on American feminist jurisprudence is Carol Gilligan, In a Different Voice: Psychological Theory and Women's Development (1982). This school of feminism is often called "cultural" feminism. *See, e.g.,* Robin West, *Jurisprudence and Gender,* 55 U. Chi. L. Rev. 1 (1988).

sonality is the awareness that I and the Mother are not literally the same person—that is, the ability to formulate the third person pronoun (which precedes the development of the first person, let alone the second person). This cognitive step of recognizing the existence of another person as different must take place before the ability to identify, let alone evaluate, similarities to and differences from that other person. The former—mere imaginary identification of identity and nonidentity—is purely dual in nature and must be the same for both the girl and the boy in the mirror stage. That is, in the mirror stage, all children, male and female, both identify with the Mother yet recognize their difference from the Mother.

Indeed, for the different-voice feminist to posit that the girl child initially recognizes her similarity to the Mother and the boy initially recognizes his difference prior to the oedipal stage is to presuppose a natural or biological sexual difference which does not explain the psychoanalytic and social significance of sexuality.[219] The two-party mother-child dyad is an imaginary relationship. In the imaginary, one can identify "meaning," in the sense that one can identify that X is like or not like Y, but all meanings (i.e., differences and similarities) have the same valorization because there is no external standard of comparison. For example, the blue-eyed little boy would see himself as like his mother in that she has blue eyes and different from her in that she lacks a penis, and the brown-eyed girl may see herself different from her blue-eyed mother despite their similarity in genitalia. But neither specific difference nor similarity could have precedence over the other.

Signification is not imaginary but symbolic. In order for a child to learn to privilege a specific anatomic difference, he must identify a third term to serve as the basis of comparison—what Lacan will call the Father. Consequently, the creation of sexual differentiation cannot take place in the mirror stage but must wait until the oedipal stage.

In other words, although both different-voice feminists and Lacanians agree that femininity is identification with the Mother and masculinity is identification away from the Mother, their respective interpretations of

219. Most different-voice feminists, including Carol Gilligan, present their theory as a psychological or social construction account of empirically observable gender differences. West is one of the very few who recognize that the theory implicitly requires a presumed natural, biological sexual difference. Unfortunately, her "connectedness thesis" uses bodily metaphor to explain supposedly psychic differences. She argues that women are more socially connected and interrelated than men, because women are physically connected to other human beings through childbearing, nursing, being penetrated during sexual intercourse, and through menstruation (which presumably reflects the ability to bear children). West, *supra* note 218, at 14.

this phenomenon are wildly disparate. Different-voice feminists believe that children identify with or away from their mother on the basis of their pre-given (i.e., natural) sexuality and that this difference causes gender characteristics. In contradistinction, Lacanians believe that sexuality is itself the *decision* to identify with or away from the mother. This decision can only be made when the child enters into the symbolic. Accordingly, one's sexuality is not necessarily correlated with one's biology.

Consequently, although the mirror stage is the child's first awareness of self, at this point it can only experience itself as that which it is not.[220] It is not the "Other"—Lacan's term for radical alterity, which is identified with the role of the Mother, the unconscious, and the symbolic order.

The infant is not yet a subject, and to say the same thing, it does not yet recognize the Mother as another subject. She is just Other. Infant and other are merely negatives, oppositions. It is not an individual, it is not-Mother.[221] It can now conceive of mother in the third person as "she" (or, perhaps at this stage, "it") but cannot yet think of itself as "I," let alone recognize "you."

The infant during the mirror stage, existing only in the real and the imaginary, resembles the Hegelian abstract personality—pure negativity.[222] The mirror stage is consequently both a stage of great gain—the experience of self—and incalculable loss and violence. Since the child has no memory of alterity prior to the mirror stage, in the imaginary the in-

---

220. Only at this moment [i.e., the mirror stage] does [the child] become capable of distinguishing itself from the "outside" world, and thus of locating itself *in* the world. Only when the child recognizes or understands the concept of absence does it see that it is not "one" complete in itself, merged with the world as a whole and the (m)other.

Grosz, *supra* note 18, at 35.

For Lacan the subject is constituted through language—the mirror image represents the moment when the subject is located in an order outside itself to which it will henceforth refer.

Mitchell, *supra* note 160, at 31.

221. In the mirror stage the child develops an imaginary body-image.

This is the domain in which the self is dominated by images of the other and seeks its identity in a reflected relation with alterity. Imaginary relations are thus two-person relations, where the self sees itself reflected in the other. This dual, imaginary relation—usually identified with the pre-oedipal mother-child relation—although structurally necessary, is an ultimately stifling and unproductive relation. The dual relationship between mother and child is a dyad trapping both participants within a mutually defining structure. Each strives to have the other, and ultimately, to *be* the other in a vertiginous spiral from one term or identity to the other.

Grosz, *supra* note 18, at 46–47.

222. The mirror stage both affirms and denies the subject's separateness from the other. If we look more directly at the privileged stage for acting out of the drama of the mir-

fant retroactively imagines that it had once been one with Mother before the mirror stage (as opposed to having been merely unaware of alterity). Consequently, as we shall see, when the child enters the symbolic, he will identify his subjectivity (castration) as loss or denial of the Feminine.

In other words, the relation between the infant and the object world, like the relationship between the will and the object of property in possession and enjoyment, is ostensibly dual. Because the relationship between the infant and the Mother is not yet mediated by a third term, the infant can only imagine union as absorption and destruction of separate personhood.[223] This binary system is unstable and looks forward toward, and presupposes, its own overthrow. The self in the imaginary is contradictory in the same way as property before exchange—the infant is now both separate from and dependent on the defining Other. This can only be resolved by the addition of a third term. Or, more accurately (as we are looking backward over our shoulders), the third term is not added but is revealed as being always already there. The very act of recognizing the third term is simultaneously the creation of the imaginary binary mother-child opposition in the mirror stage and the real mother-child union prior to the mirror stage, as necessary preconditions to the tertiary symbolic relationship of adult sexuality.

2. LONGING IN THE THREE ORDERS   Before discussing the third term, it is helpful to consider the categories of longing which correspond to the orders of the real, the imaginary, and the symbolic: "need," "demand," and "desire," respectively.[224] In the first stage, the infant experiences the real longing of need.[225] Needs are particular by definition. If one can be satisfied by a substitute, then one didn't *need* the missing ob-

---

ror stage—that is, at the mother-child relation, in which the mother takes on the position of the specular image and the child that of incipient ego, the mirror stage is an effect of the discord between the *gestalt* of the mother, a total unified, "completed" image, and the subjective, spatially dislocated, positionless, timeless, perspectiveless, immersing turmoil the child experiences.

Grosz, *supra* note 18, at 42.

223. *Id.* at 50–51.

224. Need, demand, and desire are expressions or effects of the orders of human existence Lacan defines as the Real, the imaginary, and the symbolic. . . . The child's "development" from need to demand and desire is congruous with its movement out of the Real and into the imaginary and symbolic.

Id. at 59.

225. *Id.* at 59–60.

ject, one only wanted it. For example, if one is dying of thirst, only drink will do. Need is always full in the sense that it is either fulfilled or not. That is, either you need something or you don't.

We have seen that, in the mirror stage, the realization that the Mother is Other—radical alterity—is the start of the infant's realization of self. As a result, it not only has needs.[226] It also recognizes that it lacks[227]—it demands of the (M)other.

> Demand takes the form of the statement, "I want . . . " or the command "Give me . . . ". In Lacan's understanding, the demand is always transitive for it is always directed to an other (usually the mother). By being articulated in language, a language always derived and learned from the (m)other, demand is always tied to otherness.[228]

Demand is not yet conscious language. It is the call to the Other.[229] Unlike need, demand is not full. The infant can and does demand because it is aware that it wants something, and that there is someone else who has something which it does not have.[230] "Ask yourselves what the call represents in the field of speech. Well, it's the possibility of refusal."[231] As a result, unlike need, demand is general. "From this point on, the particularity of his need can only be abolished in demand, a demand which can never be satisfied, since it is always the demand for something else."[232] That is, even if the Mother gives us everything we ask for, we are never satisfied because we really want her love and our demand is for an irrefutable proof

---

226. *Id.* at 60.

227. *Id.* at 35.

228. *Id.* at 61.

229. Lacan, Seminar I, *supra* note 194, at 84.

230. Let us, therefore, start with lack, inscribed at the roots of the structure in so far as the subject is constituted in a dependency on the speech of the Other. From this point on, the particularity of his need can only be abolished in demand, a demand which can never be satisfied, since it is always the demand for something else. This is also why the particularity of need has to resurface in the desire which develops on the edge of demand.

The école freudienne, *The phallic phase, supra* note 164, at 116. The anonymous authorship of this article is a good example of Lacan's insufferable egotism.

François George mocks the Lacanians who swallow the gross injustice that no one has the phallus except Lacan: an injustice manifested, for example, in the outrageous fact that, in the Lacanian journal *Scilicet,* all articles were published anonymously except Lacan's, which bore his signature.

Gallop, *supra* note 215, at 42–43.

231. Lacan, Seminar I, *supra* note 194, at 87.

232. The école freudienne, *The phallic phase, supra* note 164, at 112.

of the love. This, of course, is the inherent anxiety of deductive reasoning. No amount of positive evidence provided by the mother can ever verify the hypothesis that "Mommy loves baby" while every instance in which a demand is not instantly satisfied threatens to falsify it.

The infant desperately wants and demands to reexperience union with the lost Mother. This is a terrible, violent, and frightening demand.[233] If it and the Mother become one again, then they will no longer be two. One must disappear.[234] The new infantile self is terrified that it is the infant who will disappear. After all it is the Mother who is all-powerful, who has been the source of fulfillment of its needs, and who is now the object of its demands. But if it is the Mother who disappears, then the infant will no longer have a mirror. If the infant has no mirror in which to see itself, will the infant disappear?[235] In the binary Mother-child relationship, the infant is like the abstract person in enjoyment—totally dependent on the object as other: a Mother-addict.

When the third term is added, the child enters the symbolic and becomes a subject, who, like a Hegelian subject, desires. Desire is what is left when need is separated from demand. "[T]he particularity of need . . . resurface[s] in the desire which develops on the edge of demand."[236] Desire is sexual in that it is the creation of the linguistic categories of sexuality, but it is a conflation to identify it with anatomical sexual urge. Lacan is talking about the desperate Hegelian drive for recognition. "[D]esire is intrinsically inter-subjective. Consciousness desires the desire of another to constitute it as self-consciousness. . . . [D]esire is thus a movement, an energy that is always transpersonal, directed to others."[237] For the subject, desire is the symbolic experiential counterpart of need and demand

---

233. Grosz, *supra* note 18, at 61.

234. At first, before language, desire exists solely in the single plane of the imaginary relation of the specular stage, projected, alienated in the other. The tension it provokes is then deprived of an outcome. That is to say that it has no other outcome—Hegel teaches us this—than the destruction of the other.

The subject's desire can only be confirmed in this relation through a competition, through an absolute rivalry with the other, in view of the object towards which it is directed. And each time we get close, in a given subject, to this primitive alienation, the most radical aggression arises—the desire for the disappearance of the other in so far as he supports the subject's desire.

Lacan, Seminar I, *supra* note 194, at 170. *See also* Grosz, *supra* note 18, at 62.

235. Grosz, *supra* note 18, at 50–51.

236. The école freudienne, *The phallic phase, supra* note 164, at 116. Grosz, *supra* note 18, at 66.

237. Grosz, *supra* note 18, at 65.

in the real and imaginary. Like demand, and unlike need, desire is always incomplete.

> Desire is a fundamental lack, a hole in being that can satisfied only by one "thing"—another('s) desire. Each self-conscious subject desires the desire of the other as its object. *Its* desire is to be desired by the other, its counterpart.[238]

Thus

> any satisfaction that might subsequently be attained will always contain this loss within it. Lacan refers to this dimension as "desire". The baby's need can be met, its demand responded to, but its desire only exists because of the initial failure of satisfaction. Desire persists as an effect of a primordial absence and it therefore indicates that, in this area, there is something fundamentally impossible about satisfaction itself. It is this process that, to Lacan, lies behind Freud's statement that "We must reckon with the possibility that something in the nature of the sexual instinct itself is unfavorable to the realization of complete satisfaction."[239]

Just as the Hegelian abstract person desired recognition from another subject, the child now desires that the Mother desire him. As the Hegelian person sought to possess objects so that he could be recognized by other subjects, the Lacanian seeks to identify and possess whatever object it is that the Mother desires.

C. Adding the Third Term: The Oedipal Romance

1. ENTER THE FATHER   It is in his search for the Mother that the child encounters Father. Once again, this is not the actual male parent but a symbolic father.

> To Freud [i.e., as reinterpreted by Lacan], if psychoanalysis is phallocentric, it is because the human social order that it perceives refracted through the individual human subject is patro-centric. To date, the father stands in the position of the third term that *must* break the asocial dyadic unit of mother and child.[240]

Consequently, Lacan often calls him the Name-of-the-Father.[241] Nevertheless, empirically the role is usually filled by the male parent in the pa-

---

238. *Id.* at 64.
239. Mitchell, *supra* note 160, at 6 (citations omitted).
240. *Id.* at 23.
241. Benevenuto & Kennedy, *supra* note 18, at 133; *see also Translator's Note* to Lacan, *Four Fundamental Concepts, supra* note 1.

triarchal family. The sexuated positions are not the result of the actual bi-ography of a specific child located in an empirical family, but the signification given by society to the roles played by family members. That is, even if one's primary caretaker is one's biological male parent, the child will understand that our society considers him to be taking on the role of mothering.[242] The symbolic Father is the lawgiver, who, as the Mother's lover, must possess the object of desire. With the recognition of the Fa-ther, the child recognizes that the world is not divided into the duality of infant-M(O)ther. The Father is the child's rival. The law imposed in the Name-of-the-Father is prohibition—the incest taboo. The child may not

---

Both Freud and Lacan believed the symbolic Father who imposes the law is the dead Father in whose name the child writes the law. The child not only wants to murder the Fa-ther as hated rival for access to the M(O)ther, in his mind he has already done so. Out of guilt for this psychic murder, the child denies it by writing and then submitting to the Law of the Father, namely, thou shalt not have access to the Mother and thou shalt not murder the Father. The child pretends the Father wrote the Law of the Father but, in fact, the child wrote the Law of the Father in the Name of the Father. Consequently, in Lacanian theory, the symbolic function of the Father is often called the Name-of-the-Father. *See* Grosz, *supra* note 18, at 67–69.

The child's strategy is to say "I cannot have murdered the Father because I am law-abid-ing and the law says I may not murder the Father," but this strategy is not effective. Indeed, it is the failure of this strategy that makes the law effective through the child's unforgivable guilt for having broken the law.

The child's strategy shows that Lacan's conception of dialectical necessity, like Hegel's, is retroactive. Only by prohibiting the murder of the father and incest with the mother do these unspeakable, impossible acts become speakable and possible. The child "murdered the Father" before the child wrote the Law of the Father. The child broke no law and cannot be guilty. The child creates his own guilt by retroactively writing and applying a law that is al-ways already broken. "We are able to speak only under the aegis of the paternal metaphor—of the dead (murdered) father who returns as his Name." Žižek, For They Know Not What They Do, *supra* note 19, at 105. "In a way, Freud was already aware of it when, in Totem and Taboo, he wrote that, following the primordial patricide, the dead father 'returns stronger than when he was alive'. . . ." *Id.* at 134. It is ironic, but it is only by submitting to the law that we become subjects who could have a relationship with the Mother and Father. We were not even capable of the transgression which we retroactively believe we were guilty of. *See* Jeanne L. Schroeder & David Gray Carlson, *The Subject Is Nothing,* 5 Law & Critique 94 (1993) (reviewing Žižek, For They Know Not What They Do, *supra* note 19).

242. "It seems that the father does not have to be present (i.e., there does not have to be a *real* father) for the acquisition of this vague name-of-the-father." Benevenuto & Kennedy, *supra* note 18, at 133.

See Translator's Note to Lacan, Four Fundamental Concepts, *supra* note 1, at 281–82.

This hypothesis is, interestingly, recognized by certain different-voice feminists who em-phasize the activities which they correctly insist on calling "mothering" even when the ac-tual caretaker is the father or even a nanny. *See, e.g.,* Martha Albertson Fineman, The Neutered Mother, the Sexual Family, and Other Twentieth Century Tragedies (1995). For a Lacanian critique of Fineman, see M.M. Slaughter, *Fantasies: Single Mothers and Welfare Reform,* 95 Colum. L. Rev. 2156 (1995).

regain union with the Mother and may not murder the Father (i.e., the child must identify away from the Feminine and toward the Masculine). This separation from the Mother is experienced as the psychoanalytic concept of "castration" or permanent loss of the Phallic Mother. As recompense for the loss of the (M)Other, the child is promised access to other women and entrance into the society of Fathers through exchange.[243] In order to form the *fasces* of property and to write the *fas* of law, the *virgo* must become *virga*—bound and carried by men.

Once a third term is introduced, the Mother is no longer merely the child's mirror, its negation. Nor is the Father. This allows the child to start to experience himself as an individual rather than merely not-Mother.[244] The infant realizes that he is not the Mother's entire life. He has a rival; she desires the Father. The child imagines that he was once whole, in union with the Mother. Now that they are separated, by necessity, they must both be incomplete. The Mother's incompleteness or castration is confirmed when the child observes that his mother desires his father (or other persons filling the Father's role).[245] He now realizes that Mother is not the all-powerful, self-sufficient, totally Other. If she were, she wouldn't desire.

---

243. Lacan, Seminar I, *supra* note 194, at 262. This promise is never kept because it is impossible to keep. Because the Father does not have the *Phallus,* he can never keep his promise to exchange it. Consequently, nothing is ever really exchanged, there are no sexual relationships, and the subject is nothing. Schroeder & Carlson, *supra* note 241, at 100–01.

244. The imaginary is the order of demand and appropriation: exchange is not possible between two individuals for whom there is no third term. In order for the dyadic structure to give way to the plurality constituting the symbolic order, the narcissistic couple must be submitted to symbolic regulation. Within the confines of the nuclear family, this order is initiated by a third family member—the father . . . .

Grosz, *supra* note 18, at 68.

The separation of the child from its mother "is the action upon which all subjectivity is based, the moment in which the human individual is born. It is also a necessary condition for the existence of language . . . . This is also the moment in which culture is born." Catherine Clément, The Lives and Legends of Jacques Lacan 87 (A. Goldhammer trans., 1983).

245. These [i.e., clinical] facts go to show that the relation of the subject to the phallus is set up regardless of the anatomical difference between the sexes, which is what makes its interpretation particularly intractable in the case of the woman and in relationship to her, specifically on the four following counts:

. . . .

(3) as to why, correlatively, the meaning of castration only acquires its full (clinically manifest) weight as regards symptom formation when it is discovered as castration of the mother; . . .

Jacques Lacan, *The meaning of the phallus* [hereinafter Lacan, *The meaning of the phallus*], *in* Lacan, Feminine Sexuality, *supra* note 160, at 74, 76.

If she desires Father, Father must be greater than she, he must have whatever object she desires. The psychological term for this object of desire is the *"Phallus."*[246] The *Phallus* is one of the Names-of-the-Father;[247] that is, it is the universal signifier of subjectivity. The incest taboo creates the symbolic by prohibiting the child from reuniting with the Phallic Mother. Law as prohibition is, therefore, the denial of the Feminine.

The irony, of course, is that the child turns to the Father solely out of desire for the Mother. The imaginary trinity of the relationship of wholeness is not Child-Mother-Father but Child-Mother-*Phallus*.[248] In the symbolic, the Father is recognized solely in order to hold the *Phallus* for the other two. But "sexual difference is constructed at a price."[249] The price the Father demands for holding the *Phallus* is castration—the permanent loss of the Mother. This has to be the case; if it is the Father who is holding the *Phallus*/Mother, obviously the child cannot also hold it/her. The turn to the Father is, therefore, a *père-version*.[250] Consequently, adult sexuality is, in fact, quadratic. The imaginary trinity is replaced with the symbolic trinity of Child-Mother-Father which is haunted by the ghostly *Phallus* that resists sublation in the symbolic and is exiled into the real.

In order to learn what the *Phallus* is, the child wants to learn what the Name-of-the-Father is in order determine what it has that the (M)other

---

Grosz, *supra* note 18, at 68. "Both sexes must accept the mother's castration; each must give her up to develop an exogamous libidinal relation and a symbolic and speaking position independent of her." *Id.* at 71.

246. The duality of the relation between mother and child must be broken . . . . In Lacan's account, the phallus stands for that moment of rupture. It refers mother and child to the dimension of the symbolic which is figured by the father's place. The mother is taken to desire the phallus not because she contains it (Klein), but precisely because he does not. The phallus therefore belongs somewhere else . . . . Castration means first of all this—that the child's desire for the mother does not refer *to* her but *beyond* her, to an object, the phallus, which status is first imaginary (the object presumed to satisfy her desire) and then symbolic (recognition that desire cannot be satisfied).

Mitchell, *supra* note 160, at 35.

247. Another Name-of-the-father, another term for the Phallus, is, as we will see, The Woman (i.e. the feminine) . . . . Woman [*la Femme*] is "one of the Names-of-the-Father": the figure of Woman, its fascinating presence, simultaneously embodies and conceals a certain fundamental impossibility (that of sexual relationship). Woman and Father are two ways for the subject to "give way as to its desire" by transforming its constitutive deadlock into an external agency of prohibition or into an inaccessible Ideal.

Žižek, For They Know Not What They Do, *supra* note 19, at 276 n.51.

248. Lacan, Seminar III, *supra* note 213, at 319.

249. Rose, *supra* note 162, at 28.

250. Ragland, *supra* note 185, at 12–13.

lacks yet desires.[251] Unfortunately, the Name-of-the-Father, the (M)other, and the *Phallus* are linguistic concepts which cannot literally be seen. All the child can actually do is look at biological fathers and see how they differ anatomically from biological mothers. In a vain attempt to capture the real *Phallus*, in the imaginary the subject identifies the (real) *Phallus* with something that only *seems* real—that is, a physical object. He conflates the penis with the *Phallus*.[252] Being a subject—a person who has the *Phallus* and is therefore desired as a subject by another—is confused with the empirical status of being a biologically male human being—a person who has a penis who inspires anatomical lust in biologically female human beings like his mother.[253]

And yet, as we shall see, paradoxically, men do not escape castration. Lacan insisted on the "universality of the process of castration as the unique path of access to desire and sexual normativisation. . . . "[254] Castration anxiety and penis envy are merely the masculine and feminine response to the universal initiation right of subjectivity.

2. CASTRATION As I discuss in more detail later, the *Phallus* thus becomes the signifier of subjectivity. But the subject did not exist until it recognized the *Phallus* as signifier. That is, the *Phallus* is a signifier with-

---

251. The signifiers that seem to answer the question "what do I want/what does mother want" give a pseudo- or semi-answer. She wants something that is referred to the father's name. Not his penis, *per se,* but whatever fulfillment he is supposed to provide for her unconscious desire.

Ragland-Sullivan, *supra* note 182, at 56.

252. Sexual difference is based on the significance that this experience of "sighting" comes to have in the symbolic. To have the penis is identified with being potent, able to satisfy the mother's desire. This fantasy identification explains why, for Lacan, the symbolic is never fully separated from the masculine imaginary, in which the masculine subject invests in the illusion that he can regain what he lost, the power to forever call her back.

Cornell, Beyond Accommodation, *supra* note 190, at 38.

The penis is removed from its merely anatomical and functional role within ("natural") need . . . to the role of object . . . in a circuit of demand addressed to the (m)other. It is then capable of taking on the symbolic role of signifier at the level of desire, an object of unconscious fantasy.

Grosz, *supra* note 18, at 116.

253. The price of the subject's access to the world of desire is that the real organ must be marked at the imaginary level with this bar, so that its symbol can take up its place as the signifier of this very point where the signifier is lacking. And when Freud gives the boy's narcissistic attachment to his penis as his motive for renouncing the mother, he is indicating how the imaginary function lends itself to such symbolization.

The école freudienne, *The phallic phase, supra* note 164, at 117.

254. *Id.* at 118.

out a signified. The subject is nothing, a zero, which exists only because it is signified. Signification—that is, the symbolic order of language— brings the fiction of subjectivity into being by the trick of making zero count as one.[255] Subjectivity is created when the subject claims to have the *Phallus* as the signifier of subjectivity.

The child retroactively insists that the Name-of-the-Father imposes law as prohibition against the child.[256] Castration is the "Big Bang" of subjectivity—the originary moment when our primeval unity exploded to create the expanding universe of our split subjectivity. Because we nostalgically long for this lost sense of wholeness which we locate in the real, we want to reverse this process and collapse the three orders of the psyche. We retroactively try to recapture the real by collapsing the symbolic back into it. We do this by conflating symbolic and real concepts, by imaginary identification of physical (i.e., seemingly real) objects with the lost objects of desire. As a result, the law of prohibition (thou shalt not merge with the real but enter the symbolic, thou shalt deny the Feminine and identify with the Masculine) is reimagined as the incest taboo (thou shalt neither sleep with thy mother nor murder thy father, lest thou be castrated). The Mother is the Father's object of desire, the child may not have her. We insist that it is the Father who castrates the child by forever separating him from his *Phallus*.[257]

But this is not the case. Like the eunuch priests of the great mother goddess Cybele, we castrate ourselves in a failed attempt to identify with and worship the Feminine. But without the *Phallus*, we can never join with her. The symbolic (i.e., law as prohibition, language, and sexuality) is necessary for desire to be created and to function. Desire is that which by definition cannot be filled.[258] The law, which separates the subject from

---

255. Žižek, For They Know Not What They Do, *supra* note 19, at 50.

256. "The father regulates the child's demands and its access to the mother by prohibiting (sexual) access to her." Grosz, *supra* note 18, at 68. "Indeed, the figure of the male *qua* male might be called the cultural lie which maintains that sexual identity can be personified by making difference itself a position." Ragland-Sullivan, *supra* note 182, at 50–51.

Lévi-Strauss' symbolic function depends on the law of incest, while Lacan's notion of the Symbolic Order depends on the law of the father.

Benevenuto & Kennedy, *supra* note 18, at 102.

257. He construes the father's (or mother's) prohibitions as castration threats, and these eventually lead him to renounce his desire of the mother because of his fear of the organ's loss, i.e. because of the father's authority and power as "possessor" of the phallus.

Grosz, *supra* note 18, at 68.

258. Lacan, *The meaning of the phallus, supra* note 245, at 71, 81–83; Grosz, *supra* note 18, at 64–67.

its object of desire, makes desire possible. Language itself is the barrier which separates us from the imaginary and the real.[259] And so we see, just as with Hegel, the moment of the creation of law is the moment of creation of the subject: subjectivity and law are mutually constituted.

3. POSSESSION, EXCHANGE, AND SEXUALITY   The first element of the masculine position of subjectivity is the same as Hegel's first element of property—possession. The first masculine response to the universal condition of castration is simple denial. The Masculine lies and claims not to be castrated, to still *have* the *Phallus*. The "proof" of this is that he has a penis. In the masculine imaginary, therefore, only anatomically male persons are recognized as being full persons. This masculine strategy is obviously untenable. Deep in one's heart, everyone feels one is castrated. Consequently, the Masculine adopts a second fallback position.

The other element of the masculine position is the third Hegelian element of alienation through exchange. From the masculine position, the origin of law and of subjectivity as intersubjectivity is created by an attempted exchange of the object of desire.

---

259. Žižek explains the development of subjectivity from the mirror to the oedipal stage as follows:

> Before the reign of Law, Mother (the "primordial Other") appears as the "phantom of the Omnipotence"; the subject depends totally on its "whim," on its arbitrary (self) will, for the satisfaction of its needs; in these conditions of total dependence on the Other, the subject's desire is reduced to the demand for the Other's love—to the endeavor to comply with the Other's demand and thus gain its love. The subject identifies its desire with the desire of the Other-Mother, assuming a position of complete alienation: it finds itself totally submitted to the Other-without-place, non-subjected to any kind of law, which, according to its momentary whim, can satisfy or not satisfy the subject's demand.
>
> The advent of symbolic Law breaks this closed circle of alienation: the subject experiences how the Other-Mother itself obeys a certain Law (the paternal Word); the omnipotence and self will of the Other are thereby "checked", subordinated to an "absolute condition". . . . [T]he Other is no longer a figure of full omnipotence: what the subject obeys is no longer the Other's will but a Law which regulates its relationship to the Other—the Law imposed by the Other is simultaneously the Law which the Other itself must obey.
>
> The "Other's whim"—the fantasy-image of an omnipotent Other upon the self-will of which our satisfaction depends—is therefore but *a way to avoid the lack in the Other:* the Other *could have* procured the object of full satisfaction; the fact that it did *not* do so depends simply upon its inscrutable self-will.

Žižek, For they Know Not What They Do, *supra* note 19, at 265–66.

Lacan's insight that prohibition itself creates the possibility of and desire for transgression originated with St. Paul. Lacan, Seminar VII, *supra* note 17, at 83.

Since the Child imagines that he once had the *Phallus* (i.e., wholeness, union with the Mother) prior to the mirror stage, he must retroactively explain its loss, but in a way that can deny his loss. He tells himself that the Father threatened to take away the *Phallus* which the male child conflates with his penis. The Father and son reached an agreement that if the son submitted to castration (the Law-of-the-Father), the Name-of-the-Father will recompense him by allowing him to adopt the Father's name and marry another woman.[260] The son would then be recognized as a speaking subject, a member of the symbolic community, and thereby regain his wholeness. As in Hegel, the son sees himself and the Father as being mutually constituted as subjects through the exchange of the object of desire.[261] Each recognizes the other as a subject objectified through objects of desire, yet not dependent on any specific object of desire. Through this symbolic exchange of the Phallic Woman, the community of subjects is created, just as the actual exchange of property constitutes abstract right, the first stage in the eventual development of the community of the state.[262]

Of course, a typical initial reaction to this theory is that this story seems less satisfactory for girls than for boys.

260. The renunciation is only temporary; he gives up the mother in exchange for the promise (a "pact" between father and son) of deferred satisfaction with a woman of his own.

Grosz, *supra* note 18, at 68.

At bottom, the woman is introduced into the symbolic pact of marriage as the object of exchange between—I wouldn't say "men," although it is men who effectively are supports for it—between lineages, fundamentally androcentric lineages. To understand the various elementary structures is to understand how these objects of exchanges, the women, circulate between these lineages. . . . The fact that the woman is thus bound up in an order of exchange in which she is object is really what accounts for the fundamentally conflictual character, I wouldn't say without remedy, of her position—the symbolic order literally subdues her, transcends her.

Lacan, Seminar I, *supra* note 194, at 262.

261. "Thus, at the moment when sexual exchange, governed by the law of supply and demand, is initiated, the woman comes to figure as the object of *jouissance*." The école freudienne, *The phallic phase, supra* note 164, at 121.

262. This pact, in other words, founds patriarchy anew for each generation, guaranteeing the son a position as heir to the father's position in so far as he takes on the father's attributes.

Grosz, *supra* note 18, at 68.

The parallels between Lacan's concept of the role of the symbolic exchange of Woman in the formation of the subject and language and Lévi-Strauss's structuralist anthropological theory of the role of the exchange of actual women in the origin of culture is obvious and has been frequently noted. *See, e.g.,* Butler, Gender Trouble, *supra* note 190, at 36–43; Grosz, *supra* note 18, at 126.

For her, the oedipus complex involves no rewards, no authority, no compensation for her abandonment of the mother; rather, it entails her acceptance of her subordination. It involves the "discovery" that what the boy has been threatened with—castration—has already taken place in the girl. He believes that she and the mother are castrated. In her "recognition" of her narcissistic inadequacy, the girl abandons the mother as a love-object, and focuses her libidinal drives on the father now recognized as "properly" phallic. The girl has quickly learned that she does not have the phallus, nor the power it signifies. She comes to accept, not without resistance, her socially designated role as subordinate to the possessor of the phallus, and through her acceptance, she comes to occupy the passive, dependent position expected of women in patriarchy.[263]

Didn't Lacan admit that there is "something insurmountable, something unacceptable in the fact [that woman is] placed as an object [of exchange] in a symbolic order to which, at the same time, she is subjected just as much as the man"?[264]

Because of the conflation of gender and sex, the female child, insofar as she takes on the position of "woman," tends to identify with her mother, as the castrated self. She can never fully join the community of castrating Fathers because she, and they, conflate her lack of the penis with the inability to have the *Phallus*.[265] She, therefore, can only aspire to be the *Phallus*,[266] to be the object of desire for men. As a woman she is forever barred

---

Of course, for feminists, one of the most significant aspects of these theories is that the community is conceived as a community *of men* that necessarily excludes women. As Butler says (specifically referring to Lévi-Strauss but in a context which compares his theory of the incest taboo with Freud's):

> The relation of reciprocity established between men, however, is the condition of a relation of radical nonreciprocity between men and women and a relation, as it were, of nonrelation between women.

Butler, Gender Trouble, *supra* note 190, at 41.

263. Grosz, *supra* note 18, at 69.

264. Lacan, Seminar II, *supra* note 167, at 304–05.

265. The *différences* between genitals become expressed in terms of the presence or absence of a single (male) term. The Real, where the vagina, clitoris, or vulva have the same ontological status and functional utility as the penis and testicles, must be displaced and recoded if women's bodies are to be categorized as *necessarily* incomplete. The narcissistic imaginary order mediates between the Real, in which there is no lack, and the symbolic, where women represent *for men* a lack men have disavowed.

Grosz, *supra* note 18, at 117.

266. The mother . . . is positioned in relation to a signifier, the phallus, which places her in the position of *being* rather than *having* (the phallus, the object of the other's desire).

Grosz, *supra* note 18, at 71.

from the intersubjective regime which creates subjectivity because she is the object of that regime.

As a result, women experience *Peniseid* (penis envy) not in the literal sense of wanting an actual penis but in the sense of a depressive nostalgic longing for an imaginary lost state of wholeness[267] — of a subjectivity and community she is denied insofar as she is positioned as a "woman." The desire to *have* the *Phallus* is forever thwarted because the symbolic order names the *Phallus* as that which is possessed and exchanged only between those positioned as "men." Insofar as she is recognized as a "woman," she is a person without a *Phallus* — she is castrated. Castration is, therefore, denial of an affirmative femininity.

But in fact, the girl's situation only seems less satisfactory than the boy's at first blush. Lacan's description of the woman as object of exchange comes from one of his earliest seminars, and, even then, he recognized that men as well as women were subjected. As his ideas developed, it became clear that the apparent exchange between those who are positioned as "men" cannot be truly satisfactory, because it is not real. It is a lie. Indeed, the Masculine failed strategy for dealing with castration is, in fact, the simultaneous adoption of two mutually inconsistent strategies. First, the Masculine merely denied castration, he claimed that he still does have the *Phallus*. Second, when he was forced to recognize that he has lost the Phallic Mother, he claimed that he narrowly escaped castration in the sense of the involuntary taking of the *Phallus* by his retroactive consent in exchange for a promise for a replacement in the future. "For whereas in the earlier texts the emphasis was on the circulation of the phallus in the process of sexual exchange, in these texts it is effectively stated that if it is the phallus that circulates then there is no exchange (or relation)."[268] Desire can never be satisfied. The son exchanges something he does not have (access to the Phallic Mother, identity with the Feminine) for something that does not exist (the *Phallus,* access to the Feminine) in order to achieve something with no content (subjectivity).[269]

267. *See* Gallop, *supra* note 215, at 148; Jacques Lacan, *The signification of the phallus* [hereinafter Lacan, *The signification of the phallus*], *in* Lacan, Écrits, *supra* note 14, at 281, 289.
268. Rose, *supra* note 162, at 48.

269. Lacan rejects all usual attempts to account for the prohibition of incest: from utilitarianism to Lévi-Strauss, they all promise something in exchange for this radical renunciation; they all present it as a "reasonable" decision which provides a greater amount of long-term pleasure, a multitude of women, and so on — in [short], they all refer to some Good as its ground, contrary to Lacan for whom the prohibition of incest is unconditional, since it is radically unaccountable. In it, I give *something in exchange for nothing* — or (and therein consists its fundamental paradox) in so far as the incestuous

Castration is universal. Those who are positioned as men dread the loss of their subjectivity through the loss of its signifier, the *Phallus,* precisely because it is always already lost—it is exiled into the real. Men are trying to deny the horrible truth. Men experience castration fear not in the literal sense of fearing genital mutilation but in the sense of a morbid dread of confronting the "fact" of their symbolic castration. In other words, men are every bit as castrated as women are, but the masculine strategy is different from the feminine strategy. Men identify with the Name-of-the-Father who bears the *Phallus.* They try to assert their paternal wholeness by projecting their lack onto Woman as the symbol of lack. They do this by the imaginary identification of the *Phallus,* which everyone lacks, with the one organ that men have but women lack. In this sense, Woman is the symptom of man.[270]

Although this formulation makes it sound as if femininity is subordinated to masculinity, one can read it to mean the opposite. Women are in the arguably more successful psychic position in that they are not self-deluded in quite the way that men (always unsuccessfully) try to be. It is not Woman who is a mutilated man, as men claim. Rather, men are failed women—*vir* is incomplete *virgo.*[271]

The real is, therefore, not the threat of castration,[272] it is the fact of a castration which has always already occurred. There is a hole, a lie, and a

---

object is in itself impossible, I give *nothing in exchange for something* (the "permitted" non-incestuous object).

Žižek, For They Know Not What They Do, *supra* note 19, at 230–31.

270. One should not confuse this with a simple misogynist view of the feminine as dependent on, inferior to, or somehow less authentic than the masculine. In Lacan's theory, "symptom" does not have the layperson's meaning. Žižek explains:

If, however, we conceive the symptom as it was articulated in Lacan's last writings and seminars . . . namely, as a particular signifying formation which confers on the subject its very ontological consistency, enabling it to structure its basic, constitutive relationship toward jouissance, then the entire relationship between the symptom and the subject is reversed: If the symptom is dissolved, the subject loses ground under his feet, he disintegrates. In this sense, "Woman is a symptom of man" means that *Man himself exists only through woman qua his symptom:* all his ontological consistency hangs on, is suspended from, is "externalized" in his symptom. In other words, man literally ex-sists: his entire being lies "out there," in woman. Woman, on the other hand, does *not* exist, she *insists,* which is why she does not come to be only through man. Something in her escapes the relation to Man, the reference to the phallic enjoyment; and, as is well known, Lacan endeavored to capture this excess by the notion of a *"non-all" feminine jouissance.*

Žižek, Tarrying with the Negative, *supra* note 70, at 188 (footnote omitted).

271. Ragland-Sullivan, *supra* note 182, at 62.

272. As Butler contends. Butler, Bodies That Matter, *supra* note 177, at 104–05.

fiction at the heart of subjectivity.[273] The subject is nothing.[274] There are no sexual relations, only failed attempts because all human relations must be mediated and mediation is impossible.[275] This leads to love—the impossible relation of seeing in someone more than she is and in giving back more than one has in order to fill in the hole of subjectivity. Love is seeing the lost kernel of the real in the other.[276]

As is so often the case, this truth is reflected in classical mythology. The personification of the perfect sexual relationship—marriage—is the god Hymen. The god also personifies the female organ which prevents sexual union and bears his name to this day. As a result, any attempt to actualize Hymen necessarily destroys Hymen. As Lacanian theory insists, the promise of sexual union is only established by its very impossibility.

This perhaps explains the morbid fascination of many traditional societies with the physical virginity of women. Although we seek immediate relations, there is always a ghostly third mediating sexuality. In the imaginary, this third is identified with the seducer whose presence is abducted from the scar of defloration. Men dream that if they can just keep the virgin intact, perhaps union can be achieved.

D. The Phallus, Castration, and the Imaginary Collapse of the Symbolic into the Real

Let me explain in greater detail how the sexual roles described in the previous section become mapped onto anatomical sexuality. According to Lacan, in the imaginary we conflate the symbolic concept of the *Phallus* with seemingly real—but actually physical—analogues. Why? Let us stop briefly and reconsider the location of the *Phallus*. Sex-

---

273. Gallop suggests:

If we understand the nostalgia resulting from the discovery of the mother's castration [as a homesickness], then the discovery that the mother does not have the phallus means that the subject can never return to the womb. Somehow the fact that the mother is not phallic means that the mother as mother is lost forever, that the mother as womb, homeland, source, and grounding for the subject is irretrievably past. The subject is hence in a foreign land, alienated.

Gallop, *supra* note 215, at 148.

274. Schroeder & Carlson, *supra* note 241, at 101; Žižek, For They Know Not What They Do, *supra* note 19, at 50.

275. Grosz, *supra* note 18, at 136; Ragland-Sullivan, *supra* note 182, at 67.

276. Consequently,

For Lacan, love is an entanglement, a knot, of imaginary gratifications and symbolic desires. It is always structured with reference to the phallus, which, in a sense, is the

uality is created by law—the symbolic. The *Phallus* would, therefore, seem to be a symbolic object. But in the symbolic, we are castrated from the *Phallus*. Since the *Phallus* is the signifier of subjectivity, it is that which cannot itself be signified. In other words, we cannot achieve the *Phallus* in the symbolic—it is defined as that which cannot be captured in language. This means that the *Phallus* must be in the order of the real. Although sexuality is created in the symbolic, sexual relationship is impossible in the symbolic.

Like differentiation, the achievement of subjectivity is a moment of pain and loss, as well as gain. According to both Hegel and Lacan, in order to be a speaking subject we must experience ourselves as individuated subjects separate from other individuals and the world. All relations are mediated through the symbolic exchange of the object of desire. Subjectivity is intersubjectivity mediated through objectivity. Consequently, when we experience ourselves as speaking beings, we lose our sense of being one with the world which we imagine we must have had as infants. This sense of loss is *castration*.

And yet we long for immediate relations and union with the Other. In order to achieve this, we want to destroy mediation and reduce the symbolic back to the real. By doing so we engage in the fantasy that if we can acquire the "real" object that we imagine is the cause of our desire, then we will achieve our desire. So we imagine that the real *Phallus,* created by the symbolic, is actually a real object. This doomed operation is the "masculine metaphor of property" which is the subject of the second chapter of this book. The imaginary, being the realm of mirror images, meaning, and negation, is a fantasy of perfect sexual fit. It is the fantasy that we can find an object which will plug the hole left by castration.

This operation is doomed for two reasons which I shall discuss in greater detail later. First, the real cannot be reduced to reality. The acquisition of any real object can never satisfy our desire. Second, and more important, if one were actually to achieve immediate relationships, one

---

third term coming between lovers. The subject demands a wholeness, unity, and completion which it imagines the other can bestow on it. The symbolic, on the other hand, requires a subject irrevocably split, divided by language, governed by the phallus and the other. Love relations aspire to a union or unity that is strictly impossible. The two can never become *One*. The desire for the One is, for Lacan, the desire of the Other, the Other beyond the other. . . . In other words, the Other always intervenes between the subject and the other. There is no direct, unmediated relation between the sexes.

Grosz, *supra* note 18, at 137.

would necessarily lose subjectivity, freedom, and sanity. Castration—the creation of the real and the loss of the *Phallus*—is the erection of the wall that binds and delineates the symbolic. If we regained the *Phallus* and entered the real, both the real and the symbolic would cease to exist by definition. Those who fail to maintain these walls are psychotics. Consequently, in order to preserve our subjectivity, we impose upon ourselves an injunction not to merge with the Other, despite our desire to do so. This is the *incest taboo*—law as prohibition. We tell ourselves that the law has been imposed upon us by the Father, but in fact we can only impose it on ourselves.

As we have seen, we retroactively identify the symbolic *Phallus* with something we imagine to be real that one of the anatomical sexes physically has and that the other physically is. Two possible positions that an individual can take with respect to the *Phallus* are that of *having* the *Phallus* and that of *being* the *Phallus*.[277] This is reflected in European languages that divide all predicate forms into having and being.[278] It is a (psychoanalytically) unexplained historical fact that in masculinist societies, such as our own, the Masculine is the dominant sex and the Feminine the subordinate. We identify the seemingly "superior" position of subjectivity—having and exchanging the *Phallus*—with the Masculine, and the "inferior" position of objectivity—being and enjoying the *Phallus*—with the Feminine. The penis (what males have) and the female body (what females are) are identified in the imaginary as the real correlates to the *Phallus*.[279] The symbolic—that is, legal and linguistic—concepts of sexuality are imagined as anatomy. Paradoxically, the *Phallus* is the signifier of both male subjectivity and the Feminine.

It is easy to see how the *Phallus* in the role of what women are becomes identified with the female body. But the mere fact that we need to erect a part of the male anatomy to stand in for the *Phallus* in the role of what men have does not in and of itself explain why the penis is chosen as the privileged organ. Why not the beard, or the deep voice? The penis is chosen not because of its impressiveness but because of its fragility. The *Phallus* is not merely the object of desire, it is the *lost* object of desire. Its stand-in, therefore, must be something which suggests the possibility of loss.

277. *Id.*
278. *Id.*
279. *Id.* at 133. This is totally arbitrary; in a different hypothetical society the position of having the *Phallus* could be identified with some part of women's anatomy; in that case, the Lacan equivalent in this hypothetical society would not use the term "phallus" for this concept.

The penis can play this role not only because of its failure to appear on women but also because of its disappearance on men. The penis stands in for the *Phallus* because of its unpredictable failure to stand up.

Lacan's theory of castration subtly echoes St. Augustine's theory of sexuality, which has so greatly influenced traditional Christian teaching.[280] St. Augustine, like Lacan, insisted that human beings are irreparably split. Adam's sin sundered the prelapsarian harmony between man and God, man and woman, and soul and body.[281] God literally inscribed Adam's Fall into the male body as a constant reminder of Original Sin.[282] Before the Fall, the penis was a limb subject to the conscious control of the soul like an arm and a leg.[283] As soon as Adam and Eve ate of the Forbidden Fruit, they "knew that they were naked."[284] St. Augustine interpreted this as meaning that Adam had the first involuntary erection.[285] The loss of control of the penis is, therefore, the holy symbol of the debased and split nature of man in the state of sin — in Augustine's words, man's desire "is divided against itself."[286] Although this can be seen in the embarrassing masculinity of inopportune tumescence, it is even more forcefully shown by the humiliating failure of impotence.[287] What was once limb is now limp.

Consequently, the penis can stand for the lost *Phallus* because it is already partly gone. It is what men think of simultaneously as being most themselves yet not themselves. It seems to have a mind of its own. How can men have the *Phallus* when they do not even control the penis?

The facts that the *Phallus* is the symbol of the Feminine and that the *Phallus* is exiled into the *real* means that the Phallic Mother (i.e., the ideal

---

280. I discuss Augustinian theory and show how it is reflected in Catharine MacKinnon's supposedly radical theory of sexuality in Schroeder, *The Taming of the Shrew, supra* note 184.

281. Peter Brown, The Body and Society: Men, Women, and Sexual Renunciation in Early Christianity 405, 407, 418 (1988); *see also* Augustine, The City of God 413–14, 416–17, 457, 471 (Marcus Dods trans., 1950).

282. Augustine called sexuality the *poena reciproca*. The human body serves as a "tiny mirror, in which men and women could catch a glimpse of themselves." Brown, *supra* note 281, at 418.

283. Augustine, *supra* note 281, at 470–72.

284. *Genesis* 3:7.

285. Augustine, *supra* note 281, at 422, 440, 465; Brown, *supra* note 281, at 416.

286. Augustine, *supra* note 281, at 465; Brown, *supra* note 281, at 417.

287. [S]ometimes this lust importunes them in spite of themselves, and sometimes fails them when they desire to feel it, so that though lust rages in the mind, it stirs not in the body. Thus strangely enough, this emotion not only fails to obey the legitimate desire to beget offspring, but also refuses to serve lascivious lust. . . .

Augustine, *supra* note 281, at 465.

of the Feminine) does not exist.[288] She is beyond the discourse and interpretation of the symbolic realm of language and beyond the imagery of the imaginary. She is at least partly in the real in this technical sense — that which serves as the limit and the impossible. We are speaking subjects, however, who only exist in discourse.

As I have already emphasized, the fact that Lacanian theory helps us understand that our psyches contain delusional aspects does not imply that we can simply choose not to believe our delusions. We experience ourselves as our lies and live our lies. Our lies are our truth. We cannot leave the lies of the symbolic without giving up the language which is created in the symbolic. We cannot reverse repression without becoming babbling infants.

> Many feminisms envision woman's freedom as lying just around the corner. Freedoms will readily be won, for example, by our changing language lest language—itself the mask of patriarchy—appropriate woman's voice. . . . But such one-dimensional terms do little to address the larger questions attached to women's and men's issues. In Lacan's clinical work, he came to understand that any dismantling of ego, language, or desire placed the analysand at the risk of death. The "self" may only be imagined, but individuals live from such "necessary fictions."[289]

That is, repression is not a mental disease. We need language and repression to function and speak.[290] Repression is not the suppression of desire, it is the creation of desire. Lacan believes he is telling truth about lies, because lies are the only truth we are capable of.[291]

Moreover, as we have seen, the community of subjects is constituted

288. As I shall discuss shortly, this does not suggest that anatomical female human beings are less real than males, but that the Feminine per se is beyond the grasp of the symbolic order of language and consciousness. It defines the Feminine as beyond discourse. Jacques Lacan, *God and Jouissance, supra* note 198, at 144; *see also* Rose, *supra* note 162, at 50.

289. Ragland-Sullivan, *supra* note 182, at 54.

290. Consequently, although Lacanians encourage analysands to engage in the free-association of metonymy in sessions as a means of accessing the unconscious, derepression in daily life cannot be a goal.

> The patient must say "whatever comes into his mind." This violates the most basic conventions of any culture. Just think what any group of human beings would be like if everyone went around free-associating out loud. All civility would go by the boards.

Clément, *supra* note 244, at 62.

291. If the penis is identified with the phallus, not only on the level of fantasy, but also as reinforced by a cultural system of patriarchal pregiven conventions, then Woman, who lacks the penis, is "seen" as lacking the affirmative qualities associated with the phallus.

through the symbolic exchange of the *Phallus* between Father and son. Unfortunately for those of us who are positioned as women, the *Phallic* object of desire, which is identified with the Feminine, is conflated not only with the phallic male organ but with actual women. For this linguistic system to work, those who position themselves as men (who tend to be those who are also biologically male) must objectify women. The feminist cliché that men treat women as sex objects takes on new meaning in Lacan. The theory gives essential significance to empirically familiar phenomena. Many men identify themselves with, and through, social groups which are characterized primarily through their exclusion of women—fraternities, private "business clubs," the priesthood, and until very recently the military, academia, and government. We continue to try to lead our lives this way even though it doesn't and can't work. In order to experience themselves as subjects, men need to seek to experience women as objects. To deny castration, men project their own lack onto the Feminine. Man requires Woman as his symptom. Feminine aggressiveness is destructive of masculinity because it gives the lie to the femininity of lack. If man recognizes feminine positivity, then he also confronts his own negativity and castration which his sexual position requires him to deny.

Lacan particularly notes that the institution of patriarchal marriage requires the exchange of women as objects. Giving women property rights, therefore, threatens the very structure of our society. This is because Lacan, as a good Hegelian, agrees that allowing a woman to own and exchange property with subjects must lead to the recognition of her as a subject. If she becomes a subject, she can no longer serve her function as object.[292] And so a Lacanian feminist would agree with the rhetoric of the American religious right—feminine emancipation is a threat to traditional family values.

I have argued elsewhere that both American cultural and radical feminist jurisprudes are implicitly and imminently conservative in that they

---

But from within her own feminine "identification" she is also the one who cannot bring the desired other back. As a result, women suffer a severe sense of inadequacy—not, now, because they do not have a penis, but because they cannot make up for their primary narcissistic wound.

Drucilla Cornell, The Philosophy of the Limit 173 (1992) [hereinafter Cornell, Philosophy of the Limit].

292. In other words, it is when the woman begins to emancipate herself, when she has the right to property as such, when she becomes an individual in society, that the significance of marriage begins to be abraded.

accept and reinstate, rather than effectively critique, the masculinist status quo. This is because they accept the traditional American stereotype of masculinity and femininity, although they disagree as to what women's response to these stereotypes should be (i.e., different-voice feminists celebrate the feminine stereotype, while radical feminists denigrate it and encourage women to adopt behavior more similar to the masculine stereotype).[293] That is, both schools accept the characterization (associated with Carol Gilligan)[294] that men tend to be more separate, individualistic, concerned with right and justice. This liberal ideal is treated as an empirically accurate description of men. Women, who in this view are the negative of men, are declared to be (either essentially or as a result of social conditioning) more relational and communitarian, concerned with needs and care.[295] This, of course, is the imaginary view of sexuality in which the sexes are mirror images and, therefore, perfect complements. Different-voice feminism's insistence that girls never separate from their mothers in the way that boys do, that women are fundamentally and essentially connected to other human beings and its simplistic view of spontaneous, immediate relationship of self and other,[296] reflects the masculine strategy of denying castration and imagining that one still has union with the

---

Lacan, Seminar II, *supra* note 167, at 263.

293. *See* Schroeder, *Feminism Historicized, supra* note 191; *and* Schroeder, *Abduction from the Seraglio, supra* note 168.

294. *See, e.g.,* Gilligan, *supra* note 218.

295. *See, e.g.,* West, *supra* note 218. Cornell has criticized cultural feminists such as West as confusing sociology (how people act in social groups) and psychology. Cornell, Beyond Accommodation, *supra* note 190, at 50–51.

Grosz criticizes Nancy Chodorow's work on mothering, a mainstay of different-voice feminist jurisprudential thought, as using psychoanalysis to provide a sociological explanation. That is, she concentrates on "behavioral patterns, tendencies, and regularities of social life." Grosz, *supra* note 18, at 21. Chodorow does not, in Grosz's view, question the distinctions between masculine and feminine, the psyche and reality, consciousness and unconsciousness. Consequently, Chodorow "leaves the structures of patriarchal, and particularly phallocentric, oppression intact and unexplained," *id.* at 22, and is imminently conservative. Lacan also suggests that Chodorow is also implicitly, if unintentionally, misogynist. She adopts the traditional approach of blaming women for our problems. Chodorow says, in effect, that if someone has a mental illness, the mother should be blamed for not living up to Chodorow's ideal of being a good mother. I have made similar arguments about the implicit and inherent conservatism of cultural feminisms elsewhere. *See* Schroeder, *Feminism Historicized, supra* note 191; *and* Schroeder, *Abduction from the Seraglio, supra* note 168.

296. This view of different-voice feminism is most starkly expressed by Robin West in *Jurisprudence and Gender, supra* note 218. For example, West asserts,

More generally, women do not struggle toward connection with others, against what turn out to be unsurmountable obstacles. Intimacy is not something which women fight

Feminine. The true Feminine, in contradistinction, is the acceptance of castration and the resulting need for mediation in relationship. Consequently, different-voice feminism, like all attempts to give positive content to the radical negativity of the Feminine, is merely another masculine fantasy.

As we shall see in chapter 2, where I explore masculine phallic metaphors for property, the simple, immediate, one-to-one relationship privileged by cultural feminism as being characteristically feminine reflects the psychoanalytically masculine strategy of denying castration. In contradistinction, the feminine position is the acceptance of castration as the impossibility of binary relationship and the insistence on the necessity of mediation.

Many read Lacan as saying that women *should* take on the traditional masculine fantasy roles—such as the mother-whore dichotomy—so that masculinity can be maintained.[297] The man known as Jacques Lacan may or may not have actually drawn the misogynist normative conclusion that women should submit to masculine fantasies of femininity in order to support the norm of masculine subjectivity. Nevertheless, his theories, intentionally or not, actually subvert the gender hierarchy.[298] It is the Masculine which is the key to community. The masculine subject is not individualistic, because the subject is an intersubjective linguistic concept totally dependent on the exchange of *Phalluses* with other men.

E. "Woman Does Not Exist"

The assertion that "Woman does not exist" is perhaps the most notorious and most misunderstood catchphrase associated with Lacan.[299] We can now explore what this means in greater detail.

---

to become capable of. We just do it. It is ridiculously easy. It is also, I suspect, qualitatively beyond the pole of male effort.

West goes further than most other different-voice feminists such as Gilligan in that West tries to make the uncastrated nature of the feminine "real" by positing that women's connection to others is not merely psychological but physical. "[W]omen are actually or potentially materially connected to other human life. Men aren't." *Id.* at 14.

297. *See, e.g.,* Teresa Brennan, History After Lacan 9–10 (1993); Somer Brodribb, Nothing Mat(t)ers: A Feminist Critique of Postmodernism 3, 97 (1992).

298. "The Lacanian account turns [the cultural feminist] story on its head." Cornell, *Doubly-Prized World, supra* note 173, at 664.

299. Clément points out that this quotation is frequently used by the ill-informed as evidence of Lacan's "deep-seated misogyny." "He doesn't like women. He said they don't

During the mirror stage, the infant experienced the tragedy of separation from the Mother/(m)other and demanded that she come back. Now
he sees himself as a separate subject and desires the Mother. The Mother
is the object of his desire. Mother is his *Phallus*.[300]

The problem, of course, is that the subject can never again reunite with
the Mother because of the incest taboo. Or, more accurately, it is castration from the *Phallus* pursuant to the law as prohibition which creates
subjectivity. If the subject regained the *Phallus,* it would cease to be a subject. He can never again have the Phallic Mother. The Phallic Mother as
the Feminine represents the dream of an unmediated relationship with
the other. This utopian relationship exists in the real.

> If we understand the nostalgia resulting from the discovery of the mother's
> castration in this way, then the discovery that the mother does not have
> the phallus means that the subject can never return to the womb. Some-
> how the fact that the mother is not phallic means that the mother as mother
> is lost forever, that the mother as womb, homeland, source, and ground-
> ing for the subject is irretrievably past. The subject is hence in a foreign
> land, alienated.[301]

"Woman, as a result, is identified by her lack of the phallus. She is difference *from* the phallus"[302] even as she also "is" the *Phallus*—but the *Phallus* which is always desired and never obtained. The Feminine is therefore
projected as "lack."[303] She does not exist as "not-all" in the sense of "not
all subjects are phallic."[304]

Consequently, the quotation about Woman ascribed to Lacan can be
misleading. Indeed, it is a misquotation. The more accurate translation
is "~~The~~ Woman does not exist":

---

exist." This interpretation is "nonsense of monumental proportions." Clément, *supra* note
244, at 51.

300. "The man has the illusion of having the phallus, in the sense of the potency to
keep her. The woman 'is' for him as the phallus, as his projected desire." Cornell, Beyond
Accommodation, *supra* note 190, at 38.

301. Gallop, *supra* note 215, at 148.

302. Cornell, Beyond Accommodation, *supra* note 190, at 38.

303. Once projected into language, however, the primary identification with the mother
is projected only as lack. The phallic Mother and what she represents cannot be expressed
in language . . . . Thus, Kristeva insists that the Feminine, when "identified" as the phallic Mother, embodies the dream of an undistorted relation to the Other which lies at
the foundation of social life, but which cannot be adequately represented.

Cornell, *Doubly-Prized World, supra* note 173, at 660–61.

304. Grosz, *supra* note 18, at 138.

[T]he woman can only be written with *The* crossed through. There is no such thing as *The* woman, where the definite article stands for the universal. There is no such thing as *The* woman since of her essence—having already risked the term, why think twice about it?—of her essence, is not all.[305]

As negative to the man, woman becomes a total object of fantasy (or an object of total fantasy) elevated into the place of the Other and made to stand for its truth. Since the place of the Other is also the place of God, this is the ultimate form of mystification.[306]

As we shall explore, this insistence that the Feminine has no positive content increases, rather than destroys, her presence. She is the potential moment of negativity as radical freedom which is the heart of subjectivity.

F. The Woman, Property, and *Jouissance*

The Phallic Mother, like property, constitutes the subject through signification. My analogy is still, however, incomplete. I have shown that our masculine subject lies to himself in saying that he *possesses* the Phallic Mother. He seeks self-recognition through the fiction that he engages in the *alienation and exchange* of the Phallic Mother with other male subjects through submission to the incest taboo and initiation into the symbolic. But, Hegel argued, there are three necessary elements of a full property necessary for the formation of a subject. It is not enough to possess and alienate the desired object of property. One must also have the ability to *enjoy* the object. Our split masculine subject cannot achieve his desire and *enjoy* the Feminine. If he did so, he would no longer be the masculine subject. We have seen that, by definition, language is the bar to enjoyment which makes desire possible.[307] But that does not mean that enjoyment cannot occur. Not everyone is always positioned as masculine speaking subjects totally trapped in the symbolic. Consequently, we must now approach subjectivity from the feminine position of being and enjoying the *Phallus*.

It is fairly simple to see how the Lacanian idea of having and exchanging

305. Lacan, *God and Jouissance, supra* note 198, at 144.
306. Rose, *supra* note 162, at 50.

307. Law is the agency of prohibition which regulates the distribution of enjoyment on the basis of a common, shared renunciation (the "symbolic castration"), whereas superego marks a point at which *permitted* enjoyment, freedom-to-enjoy, is revered into *obligation* to enjoy—which, one must add, is the most effective way to block access to enjoyment.

Žižek, For They Know Not What They Do, *supra* note 19, at 237.

the *Phallus* (which is conflated with having a penis) recalls the elements of possession and alienation of property. Lacan's concept of feminine *jouissance* is more complex. But it captures Hegel's critique of the solipsistic, addicted side of enjoyment which requires the additional element of alienation or castration.

The French word *"jouissance,"* which can be literally translated as "enjoyment," includes both the legal concept of quiet enjoyment of property and sexual orgasm.[308] In *jouissance* the subject takes on the feminine position of being the object of desire and submerges into the real. Being and enjoying the *Phallus* become one and the same. This is like the Hegelian subject who becomes so identified with the object of enjoyment that she cannot reach out to others. Nevertheless, even as Hegel showed that enjoyment standing alone is inadequate, he insisted that it is indispensable to the logic of subjectivity.

The order of the real is that which is beyond, and therefore limits, the symbolic realm of language and law. Consequently, by submerging with the real, the subject loses her subjectivity in the sense of losing her place in the symbolic. She cannot speak to others and achieve the intersubjective recognition which is the condition of subjectivity while standing in the feminine position of *jouissance.* This is because the moment she tries to describe her experience of *jouissance,* she is no longer in an unmediated relationship with the real. To speak is to interpret experience in the symbolic. To picture it is to interpret it in the imaginary. In order to attain subjectivity, therefore, she must reject her enjoyment and submit herself to the symbolic.[309] This is why the speaking subject is not merely the subject *of* the symbolic, he is always also subject *to* the symbolic.

---

308. There is no precise English cognate for the French word *"jouissance"* used by Lacan. Literally, it refers to enjoyment or joyfulness generally. It includes the legal right of "enjoyment" of property, but is also a slang term for sexual orgasm specifically. Benevenuto & Kennedy, *supra* note 18, at 179. Lacan's term is not perfectly translatable because it is defined as that which is beyond the masculine, symbolic order of language.

If, as Lacan taught, unconscious drives do not always wish one's good, feminist theories that have equated *jouissance* with pleasure and the erotic pleasure of sexual freedom to gender liberation, have missed the meaning of Lacan's rethinking of the links between repetition, the death *beyond* the pleasure principle, and *jouissance.*

Ragland-Sullivan, *supra* note 182, at 70.

Jouissance is not the same as what Lacan calls "pleasure" (*plaisir*). Pleasure, for Lacan, is bound to desire as a defence against jouissance, and is a prohibition against going beyond a certain limit of jouissance. Jouissance, like death, represents *something whose limits cannot be overcome.*

Benevenuto & Kennedy, *supra* note 18, at 179.

309. Grosz, *supra* note 18, at 139.

This parallels Hegel's argument that to obtain subjectivity the person cannot lose herself in enjoyment but must become indifferent to the objects of desire and turn to others. This causes a paradox. If one abandons the object of desire in order to escape the trap of enjoyment, one loses the recognizability which is the purpose of property. Castration creates the potential for desire while simultaneously making desire impossible to satisfy.

But this in turn makes *jouissance,* like Hegelian enjoyment, necessary to subjectivity, even though it is inadequate. Subjectivity is only created by the incest taboo which walls off the real from the symbolic. But one cannot forbid what is impossible. *Jouissance*—the momentary achievement of the Feminine as merger with the real—is the transgression of the incest taboo which proves that what was once impossible is now merely forbidden.

Because the symbolic is linguistic, women, in a curious way, can never "speak" in a feminine voice. Anatomically female persons must always in a way take on the masculine position in order to speak.[310] That is, language is *Phallic* in that the *Phallus* is the universal signifier of the speaking subject. In order to be heard, one must take the position of the one who has the *Phallus.* To have the *Phallus* is to be symbolically masculine. People who are positioned as women must somehow take on the position of, or mime, the Masculine to act as a speaking subject. The Feminine is silenced because she is the object of the symbolic exchange between subjects. To form the *fas/fasces* the *virgo/virga* is not merely bound, she is gagged. The Feminine is defined as that which is not *Phallic.* The Feminine is that which cannot be captured in language (enjoyed in the symbolic order of consciousness). In the words of Drucilla Cornell:

> Although both genders are cut off from the repressed Mother, and, theoretically, have access to the position of the other, only men, to the degree they become traditional, heterosexual men, are fundamentally "connected" to one another in the order of the symbolic. Without this connection, there would be no ground for masculine identity.[311]

---

310. In one sense, in so far as [the girl] speaks and says "I", she too must take up a place as a subject of the symbolic; yet, in another, in so far as she is positioned as castrated, passive, an object of desire for men rather than a subject who desires, her position within the symbolic must be marginal or tenuous; when she speaks as an "I" it is never clear that she speaks (of or as) herself. She speaks in a mode of masquerade, in imitation of the masculine, phallic subject. Her "I", then, ambiguously signifies her position as a (pale reflection of the) masculine subject; or it refers to a "you" the (linguistic) counterpart of the masculine "I".

Grosz, *supra* note 18, at 71–72.

311. Cornell, *Doubly-Prized World, supra* note 173, at 664. This passage, slightly edited, also appears in Cornell, Beyond Accommodation, *supra* note 190, at 52.

Women, insofar as they are identified with the Feminine, are isolated from community.[312] It is only by taking on the masculine role of subjectivity that they have access to community. In Cornell's words, "to enter into the masculine world, women must take up the masculine position."[313]

But slippage always occurs.[314] The gag temporarily falls from the virgin's mouth. In this slippage we glimpse the real. Access to the real cannot come directly through words but through that which is beyond words, what Lacan calls the *jouissance* or *enjoyment* of and by the Feminine. But we only glimpse her; the Feminine remains "Eurydice twice lost."[315]

Consequently, Lacan posits that woman experiences an *enjoyment* which is beyond the *Phallic*. Those who are positioned as men, of course, also experience *enjoyment* in the sense of the nonverbal access to the unconscious, but the *enjoyment* of women is posited as something different, something more.[316]

> There is woman only as excluded by the nature of things which is the nature of words, and it has to be said that if there is one thing they themselves are complaining about enough at the moment, it is well and truly that—only they don't know what they are saying, which is all the difference between them and me.
>
> It none the less remains that if she is excluded by the nature of things, it is precisely that in being not all, she has, in relation to what the phallic function designates of *jouissance,* a supplementary *jouissance.*[317]

In other words, *jouissance* as access to the real is that which is beyond speech, and therefore not symbolic and not *Phallic*. It is consequently associated with women. Men, who define their sexuality as not women, need

---

312. Cornell, *Doubly-Prized World, supra* note 173, at 664; Cornell, Beyond Accommodation, *supra* note 190, at 53–54.

313. Cornell, Philosophy of the Limit, *supra* note 291, at 175.

314. "[T]he sliding of the signified under the signifier, which is always active in discourse (its action, let us note, is unconscious), is the function of the dream." Lacan, *The agency of the letter, supra* note 163, at 160. And yet "the efficacy of the unconscious does not cease in the waking state." *Id*. at 163.

315. Lacan, Four Fundamental Concepts, *supra* note 1, at 25. Lacan's metaphor also beautifully captures the retroactive nature of Hegelian and Lacanian dialectics. Hegel and Lacan, like Orpheus, are glancing backward. But according to Lacan, the Feminine, like Eurydice, escapes our understanding. The second she is glimpsed, we enter the symbolic and she is lost.

316. "[M]asculine *jouissance* differs from feminine *jouissance,* except perhaps, in the case of male mystics . . . . " Ragland-Sullivan, *supra* note 182, at 63.

317. Lacan, *God and Jouissance, supra* note 198, at 144.

The woman belongs on the side of the Other in this second sense, for in so far as *jouissance* is defined as phallic so she might be said to be somewhere else. The woman is implicated, of necessity, in phallic sexuality, but at the same time it is "elsewhere" that she

to reject *enjoyment*.[318] Being non-*Phallic,* the experience of *enjoyment* is by definition beyond discourse. Even to think it, let alone speak it, is to enter the Phallic world of the symbolic and lose *jouissance*.[319] But without *enjoyment* of the Feminine, how can we be complete?

Is this theory misogynist?[320] On the one hand, Lacan might argue that it "accords women the possibility of refusing a pleasure and desire that is not theirs."[321] On the other hand, he not does permit them to claim "one that is there."[322] This leads Elizabeth Grosz to ask:

> If phallic *jouissance* is "the *jouissance* of the idiot," what is a *jouissance* beyond the phallus? Women can't know and won't say. It is not clear from Lacan's discussion whether it is because this *jouissance* is in itself unknowable; or simply that women can't know it.[323]

Should we see *jouissance* as an empowering, ecstatic possibility through

---

upholds the question of her own *jouissance,* that is, the question of her status as desiring subject. Lacan designates this *jouissance* supplementary so as to avoid any notion of complement, of woman as a complement to man's phallic nature (which is precisely the fantasy). But it is also a recognition of the "something more", the "more than *jouissance*" which Lacan locates in the Freudian concept of repetition—what escapes or is left over from the phallic function, and exceeds it. Woman is, therefore, placed *beyond* (beyond the phallus). That "beyond" refers at once to her most total mystification as absolute Other (and hence nothing other than other), and to a *question,* the question of her own *jouissance,* of her greater or lesser access to the residue of the dialectic to which she is constantly subjected. The problem is that once the notion of "woman" has been so relentlessly exposed as a fantasy, then any such question becomes an almost impossible one to pose.

Rose, *supra* note 162, at 51 (citations omitted).

318. In relation to the man, woman comes to stand for both difference and loss: "On the one hand, the woman becomes, or is produced, precisely as what he is not, that is sexual difference, and on the other, as what he has to renounce that is, *jouissance*". . . .

Id. at 49.

319. Grosz, *supra* note 18, at 139.

320. Julia Kristeva, at least in her earlier writings, seemed to suggest that woman, through *jouissance* and the experience of actual pregnancy and mothering, might be able to have access to the Phallic Mother. *See, e.g.,* Kristeva, *supra* note 169, at 204; Drucilla Cornell & Adam Thurschwell, *Feminism, Negativity, Intersubjectivity,* 5 Praxis Int'l 484, 488 (1986). Kristeva apparently abandoned this concept in her later writings. *See* Cornell, Beyond Accommodation, *supra* note 190, at 7, 41–50. See also Grosz's critique of Kristeva as Lacan's "dutiful daughter." Grosz, *supra* note 18, at 150–73. Cornell has posited the feminine as a messianic ideal of the "not yet," as opposed to the Lacanian concept of the castrated never again. Cornell, *Doubly—Prized World, supra* note 173.

321. Grosz, *supra* note 18, at 139. Cornell sometimes comes close to taking this position. "Her *jouissance* overflows any attempt to confine her or to designate her desire." Cornell, Beyond Accommodation, *supra* note 190, at 17.

322. Grosz, *supra* note 18, at 139.

323. *Id.*

which women can glimpse the psychological goal of union with the Feminine, or a rationalization for the traditional infantile, idiotic, and silent role of women?

It is both. Lacanianism is a misogynist theory only in the sense that it is an account of misogyny. As such, it opens up the possibility of moving beyond misogyny. The Feminine is the silent Phallic Mother who is always already lost in castration. But she is also the freedom of not being bound by the law of castration which has not yet been achieved.

IV. AN ABDUCTION FROM THE SERAGLIO

A. Abduction and *Jouissance*

I have referred to the phallic metaphor of property as an "abduction" in the sense of the logic of imagination[324] as developed by pragmaticist philosopher Charles Sanders Peirce. He considered abduction to be a form of logic equal to induction and deduction. It is an absolutely essential element of science and philosophy because it is the only form of logic capable of generating new ideas.[325]

The process of abduction is as follows: I observe a surprising thing. I do not like to stay surprised. Consequently, I try to make up a story which, if it were true, would make the surprising thing no longer surprising but a matter of course.[326]

An abduction is not proof.[327] Its causality is retroactive. It is only the way

324. Schroeder, *Abduction from the Seraglio, supra* note 168. The term has other more common sexual and violent meanings. Other terms for abduction in the sense of the logic of imagination are "retroduction" and "hypothesis."

325. *Id.* at 180.

326. *Id.* at 179–81. To give a silly example, if I were to see a magician make his assistant float through the air, I might initially be surprised because in my experience women aren't so buoyant. Consequently, I start spinning explanatory stories: for example, it's all done with mirrors. This story, if it were true, would make the surprising thing no longer surprising because I believe from my previous experience that it is ordinary course that one can use mirrors to make things appear to be where they are not (e.g., in midair). This abduction might become my working hypothesis which I deem worthy of further exploration. If I had the opportunity to go up on stage, I could test my abduction inductively by trying to touch the airborne assistant in order to determine if she were physically located where she appeared to be. If I could touch the assistant, I would abandon the hypothesis that I was looking at a mirror image and try to abduct a new hypothesis to test.

327. There are differences of opinion on this, of course. One way one can avoid testing one's abductions is by developing a meta-abductive theory which explains why one's abductions are true. For example, if one theorized that our thought process is governed by a God seeking to reveal Himself to us, one might also theorize that God reveals Himself

we generate hypotheses. If I decide an abduction is worthy of serious consideration, I will tentatively accept it as my working hypothesis as to the
state of the world, to be tested through other means such as the familiar
logical processes of induction and deduction accepted by traditional American science, or by the circular and retroactive dynamic of the dialectic, accepted by Hegelians and Lacanians. Generally, we consider an abduction
to be worthy of further testing when it seems "natural" and "reasonable" to
us, in the colloquial sense of those words.[328] That is, through abduction we
try to take the surprise out of surprising things. We, therefore, try to abduct
explanations consistent with the ordinary course of our life experiences.

As I shall explain in chapter 2, the traditional abduction of property
law reflects the experience of the Masculine. In chapter 3, I shall show
how Margaret Radin has tried to abduct an alternate property law which
reflects the experience of the Feminine. Both traditional jurisprudence and
Radin's theories are replete with phallic metaphors. The former adopts
the phallic metaphor of property as the male organ, and the latter, the phallic metaphor of property as the female body. The former emphasizes possession and exchange, and the latter, enjoyment.

The point of my analysis is not to suggest that phallic metaphors are
psychoanalytically inevitable in all cultures and under all circumstances.
The goal of psychoanalysis is not the recognition of inexorable fate but
the furthering of human freedom through the increase of knowledge. Nor
am I arguing in the alternative that the phallic metaphors are delusional
instruments of oppression. Indeed, Lacan's linguistic theory holds that

---

through our instinctive thoughts—our abductions about God. We would then believe that
our abductions are always (or usually, leaving room for demonic interference) true and in
no need of further confirmation. Leibniz's theory whereby our mind, as God's creation, has
a natural ability to understand the world, as God's creation, is, perhaps, a more palatable
semireligious meta-abductive theory.

But not all meta-abductive theories are religious. It can be argued that Peirce himself
occasionally fell back onto a meta-abductive theory of the similarity between the structures
of our mind and scientific truth about the object world to explain why our (collectively, if
not individually) abductions can be expected to be correct a statistically significant percentage
of the time. *Id.* at 183–85.

328. To return to my example, I would probably reject the following initial abductions
because they do not sound "natural" or "plausible" to me, given my past experiences (in
fact, they sound downright ridiculous, more surprising than the surprising thing they are
supposed to be explaining): "the magician has magic powers," "the assistant is an angel,"
or even "I am locked in an insane asylum and am experiencing hallucinations." I would only
start seriously considering such explanations of the surprising thing after testing and elim-
inating all other hypotheses which initially sounded more reasonable.

metaphors and metonymy are always necessary elements of all language and, therefore, law.

I am merely suggesting reasons why these particular metaphors for property—the male organ and the female body—might seem so "natural" and reassuring. Lacan explains how we tend to conflate the psychological concept of the Phallus/the Feminine (the object of desire) with the physical organ of the penis and the female body, to equate the *Phallic* with the phallic. In parallel, we might have a psychological tendency to conflate the parallel legal *Phallic* concept of property (as the object of desire) with the phallic metaphors of holding and seeing or entering, enjoying and protecting. The psychological conflation can serve positive functions, such as the development of gender identity and the creation of language. But it can also cause tragedy in the form of mental illness, the oppression and rage of women, and the despair of men. Similarly, I am suggesting that the parallel jurisprudential conflation might also serve positive functions, as well as risk not merely confusing, but unjust, legal results. This does not necessarily mean that we should abandon such metaphors, but does mean that we should be aware that we use them, so that we can consider whether it is the best alternative.

Lacan offers one explanation for the use of masculinist phallic metaphors in the law. Another explanation might initially seem simpler. Until very recently, all lawyers were men. In this simplistic view, the empirical fact that some of us are now biological women should add a feminine "different" voice to the law.

The power of Lacanian theory to me lies in its insight that things are not so simple. It suggests that insofar as I am writing this and communicating with you, I am also speaking in the masculine voice. Even different-voice feminists speak in a masculine rather than a "different" voice. They adopt a stereotype of femininity which is merely the negative of the archetype of masculinity. It essentializes what they believe is the empirical experience of women who are psychically positioned as the defining other of man. Consequently, the purported "Feminine" of the different-voice feminist is in fact a mirror image reflecting back the Masculine. Different-voice feminism's account of sexuality is, therefore, imaginary in the technical Lacanian sense. Its image of femininity is the masculine fantasy that woman has an affirmative content that can fill the hole carved in man by castration, enabling the sexes to achieve immediate relation.

Does this mean that legal abductions can only replicate the Masculine? I have stated that Lacanian psychoanalysis does not explain the inevitability of patriarchy or the use of phallic metaphors to describe *Phallic* concepts such as property. However, in our society it is mandatory that we adopt a sexual identity with respect to having or being the *Phallus* to even be able to speak. Doesn't this show that, while patriarchy may not be natural or inevitable, it has a rapacious reproductive potency?

The very terminology of abduction makes it initially appear to be masculine. As I have explained elsewhere,[329] the more common meaning of the English word "abduction" is not the logic of imagination, but kidnapping for sexual purposes. To be blunt, it means rape. Abduction was one of the ancient forms of marriage[330]—indeed, the form memorialized in the Vestal's initiation rite of *captio* (capture).

At first blush, this might suggest either the symbolic exchange of the Feminine posited by Lacan as the origin of the subject and law, or the actual abduction or exchange of women posited by Claude Lévi-Strauss as the origin of culture. But at second look, the image is more ambiguous. The thinker does not rape his ideas, he is raped by them; he is ravished by his imagination, taken by a new thought. The imagery reflects the masculine vision of female sexual experience—silent, passive, and orgasmic. And so, at one moment, the theory of abduction is the masculine myth of the feminine joy of rape.

But it is more. The imagery of imagination as abduction is *precisely* the Lacanian concept of the Feminine's access to the real through *jouissance*. Lacan said that the masculine subject is stuck in the symbolic order of language. The terminology of abduction reflects the concept that in order to give birth to new ideas and to experience *jouissance*, "he" must take on the position of the Feminine. That is, if we need to take up the position of the Masculine to speak, we must take up the position of the Feminine to enjoy.

This is the fundamental anxiety of masculinity which Freud called castration fear. To achieve subjectivity, the Masculine must identify lack with the Feminine, and then turn away from her. And yet, in fact, all human beings experience *jouissance,* the experience of the Feminine. Consequently, according to Žižek, the real problem with the real (and with ~~the~~ Woman who doesn't exist) is not that it (she) is unattainable, but that it (she) cannot be avoided.[331] We must all face our castration.

---

329. Schroeder, *Abduction from the Seraglio, supra* note 168, at 115–17.

330. In classical Roman times, marriage was contractual, but the concept of marriage through abduction continued into the Middle Ages. Schroeder, *Feminism Historicized, supra* note 191, at 1165.

331. Žižek, The Indivisible Remainder, *supra* note 29, at 93.

B. The Radical Critique Implicit in Lacan

We have seen how Hegel solved the paradox of subjectivity in jurisprudence through the concept of exchange. Similarly, in Lacan, the psychoanalytic subject tries to cure the paradox of desire and castration—the need to simultaneously be, have, enjoy, and lose the *Phallus*—through an attempted regime of exchange. As I have just said, the law which castrates and thereby constitutes the psychoanalytic subject is the law of prohibition: thou shalt respect the borders of the symbolic order by renouncing the real and the Feminine in the form of *jouissance;* thou shalt no longer be the *Phallus* or enjoy it.

This attempt at resolution is, of course, impossible. The Feminine cannot be exchanged because she is lost in the real and cannot be described in the symbolic. Men invent imaginary fantasy images of Femininity to take her place.[332] Of course, this makes her even harder to grasp. As the Hegelian dialectic of property showed, by treating the subject of love as the object of desire (in the regime of possession and exchange), men cannot achieve the goal of affirmative subjectivity as intersubjectivity. Since their own femininity is prohibited, women often hopelessly attempt to live this fantasy image. They proudly proclaim that they are speaking in a feminine "different voice," when they are, in fact, merely reciting a script written for them in the Masculine.[333]

The Lacanian story is one of emptiness and desire. It denies the sexual status quo by showing that masculine superiority is a sham, a pathetic lie. It reverses our sexual stereotypes—accepted as much by radical and cultural feminists as by traditionalists—that men are more independent and autonomous and women more relational and communitarian. It is only in our masculine aspect that we can be members of the symbolic community. The radicalism of Lacan resides in the fact that it is not a mere reversal in the sense of a mirror image which would merely reflect back upon the status quo. Rather, it is a subtle warping and revalorization of the status quo. The Lacanian community of castrating Fathers is not that of warmth and fulfillment imagined by cultural feminists. It is based on repression, castration, and law.[334] It is not, therefore, surprising that men often engage in aggressive attempts at individuality in order to achieve a separation from community which they cannot

332. *See* Lacan, *Love Letter, supra* note 198, at 50.
333. *See* Schroeder, *Abduction from the Seraglio, supra* note 168, at 120–51.
334. Cornell, *Doubly-Prized World, supra* note 173, 664; Cornell, Beyond Accommodation, *supra* note 190, at 53–54.

achieve.[335] Similarly, as Julia Kristeva argues, many women engage in desperate clinging and seemingly relational behavior in a desperate attempt to have relations and achieve the closeness of community which is always denied them.[336]

If this were all that Lacan had to say, however, his theory would merely be a depressing condemnation of society. It is depressing precisely because it simultaneously reveals our life as a fiction, but as one which we are incapable of rewriting. There is, however, another optimistic, affirmative, and creative way of reading Lacan.

Through castration we have exiled the Feminine—immediate relationship and *jouissance*—to the real. As we have seen, the real is the realm of the impossible, of the limit. This constitutes the Feminine as radical negativity. We Americans with our "positive attitude" assume that the negative is bad, that to identify the Feminine with the negative is to denigrate her. Indeed, it is precisely the negative hole at the center of the split masculine Lacanian subject which is often considered his most depressing discovery. This is a serious misreading.

Hegel shows that negativity is the very condition of freedom. It is the failure of constraints. It is the emptiness as the heart of subjectivity which allows us to desire and love. Consequently, although Lacan speaks of the Masculine as the subjective position, only the Feminine in her radical negativity can symbolize the free subject.

One might assume from this that since the Feminine is exiled to the real, then, by definition, freedom cannot be achieved. No. Castration as the incest taboo is an alchemy. It turns the impossible into the forbidden. It is not merely impossible for a speaking subject to enter the real, to be feminine. The Name-of-the-Father prohibits us from doing so. Prohibition, however, necessarily implies the possibility of its transgression. In denying the Feminine it, in fact, creates the Feminine as the possible—the not yet.

---

335. Cornell, *Doubly-Prized World, supra* note 173, at 664–65.
336. Kristeva, *supra* note 169, at 201.

2

The Fasces:

The Masculine Phallic Metaphor for Property

I. PROPERTY AS THE *OBJET PETIT A*

In chapter 1, I argued that the phallic metaphor haunts property discourse because it is an abduction that comes so easily to us as to seem natural. Both property, according to Hegelian philosophy, and the *Phallus,* according to Lacanian psychoanalysis, serve as the defining objects of desire that enable us to create ourselves as acting subjects through the creation of law. The parallel roles reserved for property and for the *Phallus* in the political and psychoanalytic philosophies of Hegel and Lacan are the reason these metaphors so frequently recur in discourse about property law. Just as we conflate the psychoanalytic concept of the *Phallus* with the male organ and the female body, so we use these anatomical metaphors to describe the *Phallic* relation of property.

Although sexuality is an essentially symbolic or linguistic category, it becomes mapped onto anatomical differences by a conflation which I have called the imaginary collapse of the symbolic into the real. This is a doomed attempt to deny castration, recover the Feminine, and experience the *jouissance* of immediate relationships. The imaginary collapse of the symbolic and the real that Lacan noted at the psychic level is reflected in a similar conflation at the legal level. Property, like sexuality, exists at the linguistic-legal level of the symbolic in the sense that property, subjectivity, and law are mutually constituting. Property cannot, therefore, belong in the animalistic, physical, impossible, prelegal realm which we locate in the order of the real. It does not exist primarily to satisfy our physical, limiting, *needs.* Property is *Phallic* and, as such, is an object of insatiable symbolic desire, not of satiable real need or even imaginary demand. Because desire can only be played out through intersubjectivity mediated through objectivity, desire and its objects are symbolic categories. That is, we desire the object of desire derivatively as a means of achieving our true desire—the love of other subjects.

According to Lacan, we sublimate our desires and identify the object of desire with a specific object that Lacan called the *objet petit a*.[1] Although this object a is an imaginary—in the technical sense—substitute for the symbolic object of desire, we make it function retroactively as the object cause of the desire.[2] The object little a, therefore, is the point at which the

1. The French term is short for "the object spelled with the little a" and designates that object which stands in for the "other" (lower case, i.e., the specific other as distinguished from the big Other of radical alterity which first includes the (M)Other in the mirror stage and later comprehends the entire symbolic order which, in our castration, seems other to us). The French word for "other" (*autre*) is obviously spelled with an "a." This subtlety is lost if the word is translated literally and directly into English—for the obvious reasons that both "object" and "other" are spelled with an "o."

Lacan considered the concept of the *objet petit a* his most important contribution to psychoanalysis. In this book, I am not attempting to give a full account of this rich and complex concept, but I refer to one aspect of the little a as the retroactive cause of desire. *See* Jacques Lacan, The Four Fundamental Concepts of Psycho-Analysis 17, 62, 76–77, 103–04 (Jacques-Alain Miller ed. & Alan Sheridan trans., 1981) [hereinafter Lacan, Four Fundamental Concepts]; Jacques Lacan, *God and the Jouissance of the Woman* [hereinafter Lacan, *God and Jouissance*], *in* Jacques Lacan and the école freudienne, Feminine Sexuality 137, 143 (Juliet Mitchell & Jacqueline Rose eds. & Jacqueline Rose trans., 1985) [hereinafter Lacan, Feminine Sexuality]; Jacques Lacan, *A Love Letter (Une lettre d'âmour), in* Lacan, Feminine Sexuality, *supra* at 149, 153–54; Jacques Lacan, *Seminar of 21 January 1975, in* Lacan, Feminine Sexuality, *supra* at 162, 164, 167–68; Alan Sheridan, *Translator's Note, in* Jacques Lacan, Écrits: A Selection at vii, xi (Alan Sheridan trans., 1977) (1966) [hereinafter Lacan, Écrits]; Bice Benvenuto & Roger Kennedy, The Works of Jacques Lacan: An Introduction 175–76 (1986); Elizabeth Grosz, A Feminist Introduction to Lacan 75–78 (1990).

Through the psychoanalytical process of sublimation, the *objet petit a* stands in for the Other—and thereby functions as the object cause of our desire. This object can conventionally take the form of a woman or, more fetishistically, a body part such as a breast. But an infinite number of objects can so function to put the chain of desire into motion. The imaginary object need not be sublime in the conventional sense of beautiful or nonsexual. It often takes the form of the disgusting, obscene object of morbid fascination. *See* Grosz, *supra* at 75–77, 80–81; Jacques Lacan, *Introduction to the Names-of-the-Father Seminar, in* Jacques Lacan, Television 81, 82 (Joan Copjec ed. & Denis Hollier et al. trans., 1990) (1974) [hereinafter Lacan, Television]; Lacan, Television, *supra* at 3, 21; Slavoj Žižek, For They Know Not What They Do: Enjoyment as a Political Factor 148, 231, 255 (1991) [hereinafter Žižek, For They Know Not What They Do]; Jacqueline Rose, *Introduction II* to Lacan, Feminine Sexuality, *supra* at 27, 48.

2. That is, "the subject calls for recognition on the appropriate level of authentic sym-

lyzing property. They are, in fact, two sides of the same coin. The masculine imagery of property is a fasces—simultaneously both axe and sticks.

When we adopt the positive masculine phallic metaphor, we try to reduce property to physical objects we control. This is a strategy to avoid confronting the triune mediated nature of property and subjectivity. Property is reduced to possession, conceptualized as the simple immediate binary relation of subject to object—property is the wielding of the axe. While this accurately recognizes that a property interest in a physical object may include the right sensuously to see and grasp, property cannot be reduced either to sensuous contact or to the physical thing itself which is the object of the property right. Nor does the sensuousness of the contact or the physicality of the object epitomize the property relation. This seems to be self-evident, and yet we continue to identify property with physicality—to imagine that we can collapse the symbolic into the real.

When the implicit physicalist imagery underlying this view of property is made express, it appears painfully naive. But those writers who do confront the inadequacy of the imagery of property as tangible object do not escape the lure of the masculine phallic metaphor. Despite their protests to the contrary, they cannot imagine property as anything *other* than a phallic, physical object. As a result, they feel forced to condemn not this incompetent image of property but the entire institution of objective property. They argue that property as we know it does not exist (or is in the process of disappearing) and attempt to propose a new definition. This alternate approach of legal discourse insists that property is an unmediated binary legal relationship between subjects—a relationship that does not require a mediating *res* or object. The fasces of property is unbundled into a random and contingent bundle of rights with no essential characteristics.

I have suggested that the axe and the bundle of sticks—the positive and negative manifestations of the masculine phallic metaphor—reflect the failed two strategies by which the Masculine tries to avoid confronting castration and achieve the wholeness of immediate binary relationship. The first strategy is simple denial—the subject insists that he still has "it." In law this is done by repressing the relational, mediated

---

relationship of property to a binary one (either subject-object or subject-subject). I criticize them for not seeing that, in fact, they are two necessary aspects of a single tertiary regime, and for repressing the feminine element of enjoyment, which lies at the heart of environmental disputes.

aspect of property and emphasizing the binary relation of subject to owned object in possession. Under the second strategy he pretends that he gave up the original *Phallus* in exchange for a promised future access to an object of desire. In law this is done by repressing the objective mediator of property and emphasizing the binary relation of subject to subject in exchange.

If we view property theory in terms of this urge to deny castration and achieve wholeness by collapsing the three orders, we gain insight into the tendency to picture property concepts in terms of phallic metaphor. We envision property in terms of the archetype of the penis and the female body. In the former manifestation, we imagine property as a physical object that we see, hold, and wield. In the latter manifestation, we imagine it as a physical object that we either protect from invasion or occupy and enjoy. When men speak of possessing a woman in sexual intercourse, they are not merely using a metaphor or invoking an analogy to the possession of property. The two are not merely similar; they are psychoanalytically identical.[8]

If the conflation of the *Phallic* concept of property with phallic concepts of physicality reflects our psychic constitution, its recurrence no longer seems merely surprising. It risks seeming inevitable. It may be impossible for people situated in our society to speak about property without descending to phallic imagery to describe *Phallic* concepts. Thus, on one level I mean to critique, but not to criticize, those legal writers who reinstate the phallic metaphor of property even as they purport to deny it. On another level, however, I argue that psychoanalytical theory's exposure of the identification of the symbolic and the real *as imaginary* as a doomed attempt to collapse the three orders of the psyche enables us to rethink the relation and to try to imagine other, more adequate ways of thinking about property. The attempted collapse of the three orders through the use of the phallic metaphor is doomed because it is merely a denial or repression of the *fact* of castration—consciousness consists of three orders, the subject is split, and immediate sexual relations are impossible. What is required is not the denial but the sublation or transcendence of castration.

This will not be an easy task, however. The postmodern subject hypothesized by Lacan is paradoxically constrained by its own radical freedom. If subjectivity, law-property, and language-sexuality are mutually

8. Erich Neumann, The Great Mother: The Analysis of the Archetype 98–99 (Ralph Manheim trans., 1963).

constituting, then the subject is not merely the subject *of* the symbolic order; the subject is also subject *to* the symbolic order. Because the symbolic order in which we are currently located is neither natural nor inevitable, Lacanian thought holds out the theoretical possibility of creating radically different alternate orders. But changing the symbolic order would entail simultaneously and radically changing the subject. Destroying the symbolic would destroy the subject. The question, therefore, is whether the symbolic and subjectivity can be sublated in the sense of preserved as well as negated. This is the goal of achieving the Feminine in her guise as the not yet.

In this chapter, I will examine the work of a number of legal theories and doctrines which reflect the masculine phallic metaphor for property. I will discuss the positive version of the metaphor first and then turn to the negative. In each case, I will first present an example of the use of the metaphor in legal theory, and then follow it with an example from commercial law.

Representative of those who wield the axe of positive masculine phallic jurisprudence is Jeremy Waldron. Waldron agrees that contemporary neo-Hohfeldian analysis makes the task of defining property difficult, but he argues that it can be done by applying a Wittgensteinian family-resemblance analysis starting with the archetype of ownership of physical objects. Waldron represents the revival of property theory against the twenty-year assault that property has undergone from both the Critical Legal Studies and Law and Economics movements.[9] I will show that Waldron's implicit masculine theory of property is inadequate because it reduces property to possession and conflates possession with sensuous grasp of tangible things and thereby has no account of the rights of enjoyment and alienation and can only deal with intangible property indirectly through analogy.

After examining Waldron's theory, I then turn in section II.B to what must be the most extreme version of the masculine phallic metaphor in positive law—the commercial law doctrine of "ostensible ownership" as

9. Most of the writers I discuss in this section are generally associated with the liberal or critical left. This is because I am intuitively drawn toward the progressive political position and, therefore, find left-leaning jurisprudence more interesting. The reader should not infer from this that the right is any less guilty of the phallic metaphor. I am, perhaps, more critical of what I consider insufficient arguments offered in support of positions I wish to support than of those I wish to oppose on other grounds. I am in the early stage of applying my property theory to Law and Economics. *See* Schroeder, Three's a Crowd, *supra* note 7.

explicated by Douglas Baird and Thomas Jackson. This is presented as an example of the pernicious effect of unconscious use of this metaphor—unwieldy and confusing legal doctrine. This dogma holds that property is so archetypally physical that any property interest which cannot literally be reduced to the grasp of a tangible thing (either because the interest is noncustodial or because the object of the property interest is intangible) is problematic and fraudulent as a matter of law. Such interests are to be voided unless they can be "cured" through elaborate analogies to sensuous grasp. I will show that, regardless of the historicity of the doctrine, its presumptions are absurd as an empirical matter. We cling to this doctrine for psychoanalytic reasons despite its inaccuracy and disutility. Here I return to the Hegelian property theory introduced in chapter 1 and show how it enables us to get beyond the phallic metaphor in order to address directly the issues which the ostensible ownership tries unsuccessfully to solve.

I next consider the thesis that property, if not dead, is in the process of disintegration. Thomas Grey is probably the most prominent theorist who adopts the bundle-of-sticks metaphor. He argues that if property cannot be conceived as a unitary right with respect to tangible things, then it must lose its meaning as a legal category. Because property cannot have this meaning, it does not exist. But this thesis depends on the proposition that property only has meaning if conceptualized as the sensuous grasp of physical things by a single human being. I will show that the bundle-of-sticks theory of property is inadequate because it insists on denying the existence of property despite its continued existence as a well-recognized category of law and a vigorous legal and economic practice.

Finally, I turn to the supposed doctrinal basis for Grey's allegation of the disintegration of property. By examining the writings of Karl Llewellyn, I will disprove the well-known cliché that by rejecting common-law "title" analysis, the drafters of the Uniform Commercial Code (the "U.C.C.") disaggregated property into a bundle of sticks. The U.C.C., in fact, not only incorporates traditional unitary property concepts, it adopts the positive masculine phallic metaphor with a vengeance through a radically physicalist notion of property. Indeed, the realists departed from the common law precisely because they perceived it as insufficiently physical. In other words, although it is a common assumption among lawyers that the U.C.C. imagines property as a bundle of sticks, it in fact implicitly reimagines property as an axe. Or, more accurately, it unstably alternates between the two.

II. THE AXE: THE POSITIVE VERSION
OF THE MASCULINE PHALLIC METAPHOR

[O]ne must discard the prejudice that truth must be something tangible.[10]

A. Waldron and the Embrace of the Masculine Phallic Metaphor

1. **DEFINING PROPERTY** Jeremy Waldron is one of the few contemporary theorists who have tried to defend the institution of private property from attacks by progressives within the rights tradition without adopting the predominant "right wing" rights position—libertarian absolutism.[11] In his insightful book The Right to Private Property,[12] Waldron specifically examines a modified Lockean natural-law liberal philosophy or liberty justification, as well as a Hegelian speculative philosophy or freedom justification.[13]

Unfortunately, Waldron unwittingly adopts the affirmative masculine phallic metaphor—property as axe. His definition of property reduces property to the single element of possession and envisions possession as the sensuous grasp of a tangible thing. Other rights with respect to other things are not property per se, although they might be analogized to property.

Waldron's analysis is particularly illuminating because, on the one hand, he avoids the error that many defenders of property make in assuming

10. G.W.F. Hegel, Hegel's Science of Logic 50 (A.V. Miller trans., 1969).

11. *See generally* Jeremy Paul, *Can Rights Move Left?* 88 Mich. L. Rev. 1622 (1990) (reviewing Jeremy Waldron, The Right to Private Property (1988)). I will not here address Waldron's often insightful analysis of how to reconcile the concept of an individual's rights to private property with the rights of the community to limit those rights. For present purposes I am only interested in the imagery implicit in Waldron's definition of property, or what Paul calls "the somewhat tedious, early portions of the book." *Id.* at 1640.

12. Jeremy Waldron, The Right to Private Property (1988).

13. I use the term "liberty" to refer to the negative freedoms—that is, freedom "from"—emphasized by classical liberal natural-rights theories. I use the term "freedom" to refer to concepts of affirmative freedoms—that is, freedom "to"—emphasized by Hegel, among others.

Of course, libertarianism also traces its origins to Locke. The differences between libertarian absolutism and other Lockean liberty theories of property spring primarily from the greater emphasis given by the latter to the so-called Lockean proviso: One is entitled to property with which one has intermixed one's labor so long as there is "enough, and as good left in common for others." John Locke, Two Treatises of Government bk. II 27, §27, 288 (Peter Laslett ed., 2d ed. 1967) (3d ed. 1698, corrected by Locke).

that the core concept of property is self-evident and not in need of expli-
cation.[14] Rather, he takes seriously the literature questioning the coherence of the concept of property and acknowledges that he cannot purport to justify property without first defining it:

> Many writers have argued that it is, in fact, impossible to define private
> property—that the concept itself defies definition. . . . If private property
> is indefinable, it cannot serve as a useful concept in political and economic
> thought: nor can it be a point of interesting debate in political philoso-
> phy. Instead of talking about property systems, we should focus perhaps
> on the detailed rights that particular people have to do certain things with
> certain objects, rights which vary considerably from case to case, from ob-
> ject to object, and from legal system to legal system.[15]

On the other hand, Waldron does not fall into the error committed by many
leftist critics who adopt the bundle-of-sticks imagery. As we shall see, these
critics assume that if a simple, sharp-edged analytic definition of property
is not possible, then no definition of property is possible. On this view property ceases to exist as a meaningful legal and economic institution.

> A term which cannot be given a watertight definition in analytic ju-
> risprudence may nevertheless be useful and important for social and po-
> litical theory; we must not assume in advance that the imprecision or in-
> determinacy which frustrates the legal technician is fatal to the concept in
> every context in which it is deployed.[16]

Waldron makes reference to modern and postmodern theories of fuzzy
definitions:

14. Richard Epstein, in contrast, acknowledges Thomas Grey's critique (which I shall
discuss in detail in section III.A) but largely dismisses it: "The great vice in Grey's argument is that it fosters an unwarranted intellectual skepticism, if not despair. He rejects a
term that has well-nigh universal usage in the English language because of some inevitable
tensions in its meaning, but he suggests nothing of consequence to take its place." Richard
Epstein, Takings: Private Property and the Power of Eminent Domain 21 (1985).
  Epstein thinks that Grey confuses the problem of applying a concept in various complex contexts with the vagueness of the concept itself. I agree. I distinguish Waldron from
Epstein, however, in that the former more directly recognizes his responsibility to grapple
with and articulate the concept of property, whereas Epstein assumes that its meaning is
uncontroversial. Specifically, he believes that Blackstone's definition is more than adequate
for most purposes. Those issues that seem vague should be kept in the proper perspective
as belonging at the margins of property issues. *Id.* at 22–23.
  Epstein also thinks that political considerations drive Grey's critique more than real
difficulties in definition. I believe that there is some truth to Epstein's complaint.
  15. Waldron, *supra* note 12, at 26.
  16. *Id.* at 31.

I want to consider whether any of the more interesting recent accounts of the nature and meaning of political concepts—such as Wittgenstein's idea of family resemblance, the idea of persuasive definition, the distinction between concept and conception, or the idea of "essential contestability"—casts any light on the question of the definition of private property.[17]

Waldron argues that "private property is a *concept* of which many different conceptions are possible, and that in each society the detailed incidents of ownership amount to a particular concrete *conception* of this abstract concept."[18] Waldron defines the "concept" of property as follows:

The concept of property is the concept of a system of rules governing *access to and control of material resources*. Something is to be regarded as a material resource if it is a material object capable of satisfying some human need or want. . . . Scarcity, as philosophers from Hume to Rawls have pointed out, is a presupposition of all sensible talk about property.[19]

He continues:

The concept of property does not cover all rules governing the use of material resources, only those concerned with their allocation. Otherwise the concept would include almost all general rules of behaviour. . . . As Nozick puts it, the rules of property determine for each object at any time which individuals are entitled to realize which of the constrained set of options socially available with respect to that object at that time.[20]

I concur with Waldron's conclusions as to both the need for and the possibility of defining property and distinguishing it from other legal relations. In particular, Waldron's approach toward definitions, his recognition that property is and will probably remain a flourishing legal and economic institution in spite of—or because of—its open-ended and fluid nature, and his realization that the institution of private property seems intuitively related to liberty and freedom considerations are much more successful than the analysis offered by critics such as Grey which I discuss

17. *Id.*
18. *Id.* Waldron also writes:

For one thing, private property is a concept of which there are many conceptions: legal systems recognize all sorts of constraints on the rights of owners, and the crucial question is not whether there should be constraints, but whether the particular constraints we need defeat the original aims of our right-based argument.

Id. at 5.
19. *Id.* at 31 (emphasis added).
20. *Id.* at 32.

in section III.A. Unfortunately, at the next stage Waldron's analysis devolves into precisely the unsophisticated thinking that Grey and Vandevelde associate with—and criticize as—the rigid, unworkable, traditional model of property. That is, Waldron adopts the paradigm of sensuous grasping as the norm or epitome of property against which all other forms of property must be analogized. Indeed, it is not even clear that he considers legal rights with respect to intangibles to be true property at all.

2. THE PHYSICALITY OF PROPERTY   As we have seen, Waldron first defines property as the regime for the allocation of material resources. That is, he reduces property to the single masculine element of possession—the identification of an object to a subject—and represses the elements of enjoyment and alienation. In turn, he defines the term *material resources* as those things that are possible objects of human wants and needs. In the following passage, however, he limits material objects to *physical* things, which he contrasts with *noncorporeal* things:

> I have defined property in terms of material resources, that is, resources like minerals, forests, water, land, as well as manufactured objects of all sorts. But sometimes we talk about objects of property which are not corporeal: intellectual property in ideas and inventions, reputations, stocks and shares, choses in action, even positions of employment. . . . This proliferation of different kinds of property object is one of the main reasons why jurists have despaired of giving a precise definition of ownership. I think there are good reasons for discussing property in material resources first before grappling with the complexities of incorporeal property.[21]

Note that Waldron has already taken an unacknowledged step toward the identification of property with physicality that will color the rest of his argument. He defines human wants and needs, and therefore property, in terms of purely animal satisfaction of physical limitations. This is an odd choice from a philosopher like Waldron who wishes to explore justifications of property from a Lockean and a Hegelian perspective. Neither Locke nor Hegel justifies property in terms of the satisfaction of animalistic physical needs. Rather, both justify property by reference to the most sublime and abstract notions of what makes humans truly human—liberty and freedom, respectively.

Waldron locates property in the uninterpreted, preimaginary, prelinguistic realm of the real in which humans experience "need." But, as we

---

21. *Id.* at 33.

have seen, property does not belong in the animalistic, physical realm we identify with the real, or the imagistic realm of the imaginary, in which Waldron immures it. Property is the object of human *desire*. Waldron, however, presumes that property relates to physical want—what Lacan calls "needs." He wants to find an object in the imaginary to take the place of the *objet petit a* that he can identify with some physical object to stand in for the symbolically prohibited real object of desire and function as the cause of desire. Consequently, Waldron wants to presume that property is originally a physical relationship.

This may explain why Waldron cannot—as he refreshingly admits[22]—follow Hegel's argument as to the necessary role of property in the development of human personhood. Hegelian property has nothing to do with physical requirements.[23] As I have discussed, property is the means by which the abstract person as self-consciousness attains subjectivity. This purely logical construct does not yet even have a body, let alone physical needs.

In other words, Waldron makes *precisely* the phallic metaphoric conflation that Lacan locates as the identification of gender roles—or sexuated positions—with anatomy. Waldron conflates the *Phallic* with the phallic and desire with need in an imaginary attempt to collapse the symbolic and the real.

3. WALDRON'S STATE OF NATURE Waldron defends his emphasis on corporeal objects by an appeal to something like a state of nature. Waldron argues:

> First, we should recall that the question of how material resources are to be controlled and their use allocated is one that arises in every society. . . . The question of rights in relation to *in*corporeal objects cannot be regarded

22. Waldron writes: "There are fewer difficulties with the Hegelian approach, though it has to be said that the link between private property and the ethical development of the person is rather obscure and, in any case, never established as an absolutely necessary connection." *Id.* at 4. If, however, one concludes that human nature is driven by the desire to be desired by another subject, and that subjectivity is intersubjectivity mediated by the exchange of the object of desire—as do both Hegel and Lacan—and if property is the regime of the exchange of objects, then by definition property is necessary for the development of subjectivity.

23. "The rational aspect of property is to be found not in the satisfaction of needs but in the superseding of mere subjectivity of personality." G.W.F. Hegel, Elements of The Philosophy of Right 74 (H.B. Nisbet trans. & Allen W. Wood ed., 1991) [hereinafter Hegel, The Philosophy of Right]; *see also* Merold Westphal, Hegel, Freedom, and Modernity 22 (1992).

as primal and universal in the same way. In some societies, we may speculate, the question does not arise at all either because incorporeals do not
figure in their ontology or, if they do, because human relations with them
are not conceived in terms of access and control. That is a point about
incorporeals in general. Turning to the incorporeal objects we are interested in, it is clear that questions about patents, reputations, positions of
employment, etc. are far from being universal questions that confront
every society. On the contrary, one suspects that these questions arise for
us only because other and more elementary questions (including questions about the allocation of material objects) have been settled in certain complex ways.[24]

In other words, Waldron tries to defend his analysis by hypothesizing an
anthropology of societies without incorporeals.

Of course, liberal philosophers, including Locke, have traditionally
started their analysis from a hypothetical state of nature. At first blush,
therefore, Waldron's approach might seem worthwhile for the consideration of a Lockean natural-rights justification of property. On further
reflection, however, Waldron's approach is inappropriate to an analysis
of liberal philosophy. The state of nature posited by liberals such as Locke
presupposes *pre-social* individuals. Waldron starts with a hypothesized second stage of human development in which social individuals are already
living in societies. An analysis of property as it might exist in even such a
primitive society is irrelevant to the Lockean search for a pre-social natural right of property.

More important, despite Waldron's assertions to the contrary, I believe
that it is not possible to hypothesize a society of entities identifiable as
human beings in which incorporeal property—such as status, religious objects, artistic creations, crafts, objects of beautification, and other symbolic and imaginary objects—does not play a central role. Creatures living together solely within the realm of physical needs and wants are not
human subjects but only animals living in packs. The human subject is
the speaking subject of language in the symbolic order. I can, on the other
hand, hypothesize societies of human beings where incorporeals are the
primary source of property. For example, such a society might exist on a
hypothesized tropical island with abundant fruit, vegetables, water, and
space obviating scarcity for basic human needs and wants. That is to say,
Waldron believes that tangible property is more fundamental to human
personality than incorporeal property. I argue that the opposite is true.

24. Waldron, *supra* note 12, at 34.

Waldron's approach poses even more difficulty when we move to the considerations of actual "primitive" or tribal societies. I am not an anthropologist, so I am wary of making empirical claims, but I nevertheless believe that no contemporary society exists solely in the world of physical needs without rich and complex symbolic objects of desire.[25]

In the passage quoted above, Waldron tries to suggest that those primitive societies that do have symbolic objects—such as religious objects or status—do not allocate these objects through a recognizable *property* regime. This objection fails for at least two reasons.

First, Waldron's own definition of property—a regime of access and control of scarce resources—would apply on its face equally to incorporeals and corporeals. Even if we are squeamish about speaking of religious objects and worship in terms of property, any society that recognizes a priesthood with special access and passage to the divine, that recognizes the efficacy of ritual or taboo, or that requires initiation into religious mysteries or status—such as manhood—subjects incorporeals to a regime of access and control of the objects of human wants. This is Waldron's definition of property. Indeed, in his seminal anthropological study of archaic property relations, Marcel Mauss emphasized that in so-called primitive or premarket societies property, law, family, and religion were inextricably interconnected.[26]

In contradistinction, the two philosophies on which Waldron supposedly relies—Hegelianism and Lockean liberalism—do not flinch from

25. The Tasadays are the only contemporary society I know of to approach this description. The Tasadays, a group of twenty-six people, caused a stir in 1971 when they were "discovered" in the Philippines as the only contemporary Stone Age tribe. *See, e.g.*, Further Studies on the Tasaday (D.E. Yen & John Nance eds., 1976); The Tasaday Controversy: Assessing the Evidence (Thomas N. Headland ed., 1972); Kenneth Macleish, *The Tasadays: Stone Age Cavemen of the Mindinao,* Nat'l Geographic, Aug. 1972, at 219. Arguably, the Tasadays suggest the possibility of Waldron's model of a people having little or no intangible goods. Unfortunately, since the late 1980s suspicion has spread widely in the scientific community that the Marcos regime invented the Tasadays as a crude hoax to gain control over tribal lands. Bruce Bower, *19-Year Debate over "Stone Age" Tasaday Thrives in Rain Forest,* L.A. Times, Jan. 8, 1990, at B2. See also Shannon Brownlee, *If Only Life Were So Simple,* U.S. News & World Rep., Feb. 19, 1990, at 54.

26. The things transferred were sometimes useful goods but often ritual or decorative items of spiritual significance. The purpose of the property relationship was not so much to allocate goods, as Waldron presupposes, but to establish status and relations of mutual obligation within and among families, clans, and tribes.

Moreover, what they exchange is not solely property and wealth, movable and immovable goods, and things economically useful. In particular, such exchanges are acts of politeness: banquets, rituals, military services, women, children, dances, festivals, and fairs, identifying religion with property. Hegel expressly recognized that our beliefs, religious positions, and liturgical objects are every bit as much external symbolic objects of desire as food and clothing. Similarly, as I shall discuss later, the Framers of the U.S. Constitution, who were, of course, deeply influenced by Lockean liberalism, were not shy about analyzing religion in terms of property. They sought to *justify* constitutional freedoms of speech and religion precisely on the grounds that men have a natural property right in their opinions and beliefs.

Second, if Waldron wishes to assert that primitive regimes of access to religious or other symbolic objects significantly differ from the type of access and control that we associate with property, he has the burden of articulating that difference. Waldron recognizes that his stated project of justifying property requires that he be able to define property and distinguish it from other interests, and he starts from the proposition that a philosophic project requires careful definition. If he cannot identify the difference between the regime of access to religious and status objects and other regimes, his attempted definition of property fails on his own terms.

Most important, there is a practical problem with Waldron's specific choice of the limited concept of property that serves as the starting point for his analysis. When one chooses to argue from a simple hypothetical, the ultimate issue is not whether there is any empirical society that matches the hypothetical. Rather, the question is whether the hypothetical simplifies and epitomizes fundamental aspects of our society so as to serve as a useful analytical model. Indeed, Waldron is very sensitive to the idea that property exists not merely as an abstract philosophical concept but as a fundamental legal, economic, political, and social institution in our society. Unfortunately, I believe that Waldron's hypothetical is so alien as to be misleading.

As we have seen, Waldron has reduced the concepts of material resources and human wants to what I have referred to as seemingly real needs. The problem with this should be obvious. By reducing these concepts in this fashion, he has excluded from his starting analysis of property all interests beyond those necessary for subsistence. As a result, all property interests in the symbolic economy—including incorporeals and

---

in which economic transaction is only one element, and in which the passing on of wealth is only one feature of a much more general and enduring contract.

Marcel Mauss, The Gift: The Form and Reason for Exchange in Archaic Societies 5 (W.D. Halls trans., 1990).

luxury goods defined broadly as anything above the satisfaction of animal need—have already been identified as problematic. It is possible to take the position that no institution of property can be philosophically justified beyond the subsistence level.[27] By definition, that position would always lead to the conclusion that the property regime of a relatively wealthy, nonsubsistence economy, such as contemporary American society, could never be justified. Waldron's goal, however, is not to take the radical neo-Proudhonian or Marxian position that property is theft. He wishes to justify at least a limited property regime in a modern society. His choice as a starting point, though, seems antithetical to his purpose.

4. WALDRON'S DENIAL OF INCORPOREALITY

a. Need or Desire? In his analysis of property, Waldron's rhetoric quickly falls into the *Phallic*-phallic confusion of the physicalist metaphor for property. Waldron states, for example, that "it is often illuminating to characterize the solutions [to questions concerning the allocation of incorporeals] in terms which bring out analogies with the way in which questions about property have been answered."[28] Waldron continues:

> For example, once it is clear that individuals have rights not to be defamed, it may be helpful to describe that situation by drawing a parallel between the idea of owning a material object and the idea of having exclusive rights in a thing called one's "reputation." Such talk may take on a life of its own so that it becomes difficult to discuss the law of defamation except by using this analogy with property.[29]

Let us recapitulate Waldron's reasoning. First, he argues that property is a regime relating to the access and control of the objects of human wants and needs. Insofar as this definition refers to "wants," one does not necessarily have to limit property to the allocation of physical things. The colloquial term "want" could be read expansively to include the technical psychoanalytical concept of desire. This would make the theory con-

27. The alternate interpretations of the so-called Lockean proviso are variations on this argument. The narrow libertarian reading justifies virtually all exclusive property rights this side of starvation of the poor. An expansive reading sharply limits property rights in favor of egalitarian and communitarian values. *See* John Stick, *Turning Rawls into Nozick and Back Again,* 81 Nw. U. L. Rev. 363 (1987).

28. Waldron, *supra* note 12, at 34.

29. *Id.*

sistent with the Hegelian-Lacanian concepts of objects of property as potentially being anything external to abstract personality and of property as the regime of intersubjective exchange of the object of desire.

Waldron rejects this interpretation in his second move. Although he purports merely to restate this definition, he in fact changes it by limiting the term "want" to the Lacanian concept of need for physical objects. That is, he tries to move property out of the symbolic regime of law, into the preconscious, prelinguistic realm of the real.

Waldron's third move is to argue that by analogy we can apply to incorporeal objects legal principles developed by considering corporeal objects. In his fourth and final move, Waldron comes full circle to Grey's denial of noncorporeal property. Only corporeal object relations are property relations. Waldron no longer purports to apply principles developed in connection with corporeal objects by analogy to develop the *property* law of noncorporeals. Rather, he purports to apply *property* law concepts—which by implicit definition relate only to corporeal objects— by *analogy* in order to develop a new law of noncorporeal object relations.

Waldron continues his argument by assertorially denying the noncorporeal nature of the objects of legal relations that are traditionally considered to epitomize property. It has often been noted that the most archetypical type of property—real property—is not a right to soil or other physical things but to estates in land. Real property is not real in the Lacanian sense.[30]

Waldron attempts to counter this view:

> We might accept the argument but insist that spatial regions can still be regarded as material resources. Although they differ ontologically from cars and rocks they also seem to be in quite a different category from the complexes of rights that constitute familiar incorporeals—patents, reputations, etc. It is philosophically naive to think that the fact that we have to regard regions as property objects adds anything to the case for regarding, say, choses in action in that way. The second response is more subtle. We may concede that land, as conceived in law, is too abstract to be described as a material resource. But we may still insist that the primary objects of real

30. This disturbing nontangibility of realty is reflected in the common law. Like us, our legal ancestors had difficulty imagining the transfer of property otherwise than as the physical delivery of tangible things. Consequently, they did not recognize a conveyance by deed alone but required that it be structured as closely as possible to the physical delivery of chattel. This led to the ritual known as "delivery of seisin"—an attempt to identify a real manifestation of the symbolic relationship of property. A.W.B. Simpson, A History of the Land Law (2d ed. 1986).

property are the actual material resources like arable soil and solid surfaces which are located in the regions in question. Until recently, these resources have been effectively immovable and so there has been no reason to distinguish "land as material" from "land as site." But developments like modern earth-moving and high-rise building necessitate a more complex and sophisticated packaging of rights over these resources. Thus the concept of land as site has now had to be detached from its association with immovable resources and employed on its own as an abstract idea for characterizing these more complicated packages of rights. Still, in the last analysis, the system of property in land is a set of rules *about* material resources and nothing more.[31]

These arguments evidence Waldron's deep ambivalence concerning corporeality and property. He provides these arguments to support his assertion that, first, we should start by analyzing corporeal objects because they are more basic and, second, that real property interests are corporeal. The statement just quoted, however, seems to be an unacknowledged shift in position. After saying that he will start with the property of material objects because they are most basic, he makes an implicit admission that even though the most basic property rights concern realty, and realty is not a physical object, he finds it useful to *analogize* land to physical objects. Because it is *convenient* to think of realty interests as physical objects, we will say that realty interests are physical objects without considering whether or not this is actually the case. In other words, Waldron all but admits that he starts with material objects not because they are the most basic objects of property but because they seem simpler to think about.

b. Waldron's Empirical Arguments for the Phallic Metaphor. Waldron wants to suggest that only modern technology has made the identification of realty interests with the underlying land problematic. I question both the historical and empirical accuracy of his statement.

As any first-year law student knows, the concept of realty as a specific plot of land occupied and exploited by a single owner is a relatively modern development in Anglo-American culture. Historically, real property consisted of the system of estates.[32] Estates did not consist merely in the

---

31. Waldron, *supra* note 12, at 36–37 (footnote omitted).

32. Indeed, to be precise, when the word "property" started to come into legal parlance in the seventeenth century, it may have more accurately referred only to personal property rights of private citizens in personalty. This is because the word "property" was defined as the "highest right that a man hath or can have to any thing." G.E. Aylmer, *The Meaning*

right to occupy, farm, mine, or otherwise physically exploit specific pieces of realty; they included a complex network of rights, responsibilities, and status. The estates granted to nobility, for example, were often tied to a title and were conditioned on the obligation to provide their liege with the military service (or its financial equivalent) of a specified number of men for a specified number of days. Numerous persons held different property rights with respect to a given piece of realty. Although some of these were merely temporal divisions of the right to occupy the land—such as life estates, reversions, and so on—many others were not. Not only social status but also what we would call governmental and ecclesiastical positions and functions were tied to estates. Other real property interests included, among others, *banalities*—which included the right to operate certain "utilities" in a village such as a mill, oil press, or bake oven located in a village—and *advowsons*—the right to name clerics to a specific church and income.[33] Indeed, the traditional dichotomy between real and personal property may originally have been in large part jurisdictional rather than substantive. *Real* property rights referred not to property interests relating to land per se but to those causes of action for specific relief that could be brought in the king's court.[34]

Although many of these medieval estates exist only as vestigial organs in late-twentieth-century America, other partial estates have taken their place. Let us look at a very simple example of residential real estate in New York City—*my* apartment. A corporation named Hudson Mews Apart-

---

and Definition of "Property" in Seventeenth Century England, Past & Present, Feb. 1980, at 87, 89–94. In seventeenth-century England—and technically in the contemporary United States—only the sovereign can have property in land in the sense of the highest allodial right. Consequently, legal discussion concerning the interests in land of ordinary citizens involved not property in land but only estates. In contradistinction, anyone can have a full property in personalty. Despite this, according to Aylmer, some seventeenth-century lawyers tended to refer sloppily to property in estates owned by citizens. *Id.*

33. *See* C.B. MacPherson, Property: Mainstream and Critical Positions 7 (1978).

34. As an empirical matter, however, such real causes of action may have related primarily, though not exclusively, to claims concerning rights in land.

The name "real property" itself is taken from the procedures, the real actions, through which landowners' rights were specifically enforced. The dominant status of real property law, early established, long persisted, and in Blackstone's time that body of law, viewed as the mechanism either for the resolution of land disputes, or, as it was used by the expert conveyancers, for the cooperative, consensual organization of land ownership, remained the most important and intellectually developed branch of the common law.

A.W.B. Simpson, *Introduction* to 2 William Blackstone, Commentaries on the Laws of England, at v (A.W. Brian Simpson ed., 1979) [hereinafter Blackstone's Commentaries]. That

ment Corporation owns the equity in the building and land where I live. A bank holds a mortgage on the building granted by the corporation. Various parties including Time-Warner Cable Television, Atlantic Bell, ConEdison, and the U.S. Postal Service have easements to enter and keep objects—such as coaxial cables and telephone and power lines—on the premises. The corporation owns rights of access to hook up to the water mains and pipelines that run under the street in front of the building. The use of the land and building is subject to extensive regulation by the City and State of New York. As the building is located in an unusual (for Manhattan) location behind a private courtyard, the corporation also owns a right-of-way across a narrow strip of land—owned in fee by someone else—which separates our garden from the street. I, as tenant in the entirety with my husband, own the equity in 625 common shares of the corporation, and we are lessees of a proprietary lease granted by the corporation for the apartment in which I live. A savings and loan association owns an Article 9 security interest in the shares and the lease. Although the terms of my lease are coterminous with my ownership of the shares, both my occupancy of the lease and my ownership of the shares are subject to my performance of certain obligations under the bylaws of the corporation—including paying an amount equivalent to my pro rata share of the corporation's mortgage debt and operating expenses—and under the terms of the agreement with my S and L. The corporation also has a security interest in my rights to secure my obligations and an intercreditor agreement with my S and L governing its respective property rights as a secured creditor. My right to alienate my shares and my lease is restricted by the terms of the bylaws of the cor-

---

is, real-property actions concerned the enforcement of manorial rights, not all of which would be considered tied to land by modern standards.

Duncan Kennedy criticizes Blackstone's categorization of certain rights as real property. See Duncan Kennedy, *The Structure of Blackstone's Commentaries,* 28 Buff. L. Rev. 205, 344–46 (1979). Simpson's point is that Blackstone's characterization was not an idiosyncratic choice but a reflection of the legal practice of his time.

It is tempting to suspect that the terminology "real property" comes from its original enforcement in the royal courts. Indeed, the word "realty" can also mean "royal" and "realm." Unfortunately, these two meanings of "realty" seem to derive from entirely different roots. The former, referring to property, originates from the Latin *res,* which means "thing" or "matter." The latter refers back to *rex* or "king," which in turn relates to a root meaning "to straighten or put in line." That is, it means "ruler" in both senses of the term. 13 The Oxford English Dictionary 272, 279 (2d ed. 1989); see also Eric Partridge, Origins: A Short Etymological Dictionary of Modern English 553, 561 (1966). Perhaps the development of such similar English words for these different concepts originating in different roots is a folk etymology.

poration and my security agreement with the S and L. Although shareholders occupy most of the other apartments in my building—sometimes
individually and sometimes through various forms of joint tenancy—
some shareholders sublet their apartments to unrelated tenants. The corporation has granted the shareholders and lessees limited rights to use
the common areas of the building and the garden, as well as the right-
of-way. Each tenant has the exclusive privilege to use a portion of the
basement for storage. The corporation leases the basement apartment
to our superintendent, whose lease is coterminous with his employment,
and so on.

Commenting on modern-day estates in land, Waldron ends his argument with the following non sequitur:

> Thus, the concept of land as site has now had to be detached from its as-
> sociation with immovable resources and employed on its own as an ab-
> stract idea for characterizing these more complicated packages of rights.
> Still, in the last analysis, the system of property in land is a set of rules *about*
> material resources and nothing more.[35]

Thus, Waldron would conclude that ultimately all the interests concerning my apartment building are concerned with "material resources"
in his definition of physical things. He might try to argue that my ownership interest primarily concerns my sensuous exploitation of physical
walls, floors, ceilings, fixtures, and so on. But the interests of the financial institutions, the telephone company, the cable TV company, the elec-
tric company, the postal service, the laundry company, and Sal the Super
are *not* primarily related to the physical location. Rather, they are rights
to receive income and are not, as Waldron suggests, substantially different from the rights to income from the exploitation of any other form of
noncorporeal property. Moreover, even my apartment's value to me is not
primarily based on my physical needs. The value consists of a combination of its objective exchange value—the market price—and its subjective
use value to me. The use value relates to a variety of symbolic and imaginary concerns, as well as my real needs. Examples include the apartment's
physical attractiveness, its relative quietness, its proximity to both my office
and a wide variety of restaurants and entertainment, the artsy population
of the neighborhood, and so on. Indeed, when one compares the cramped
quarters in which we New Yorkers tend to live with the housing occupied by people of comparable economic resources in other parts of the

35. Waldron, *supra* note 12, at 36–37.

country, it is obvious that we value our property *despite* its failure to meet our real physical wants.

Waldron admits that if ownership is defined in terms of wealth, then

> we will certainly have to conjure up incorporeal things to correspond to the complex legal relations that in fact define their economic position. But if we say instead that property is a matter of rules about access to and control of material resources, but not necessarily about private ownership, then we may still say that a man's wealth is constituted for the most part by his property relations. He may not be the owner of very many resources; but the shares he holds, the funds he has claims on, and the options and goodwill he has acquired, together define his position so far as access and control of material resources is concerned.[36]

Once again, Waldron distinguishes between relations concerning non-corporeals and "property"—that is, access to material (i.e., physical) resources. The only true property is what he sees and holds. His argument seems to be based on the agrarian myth that all wealth ultimately comes down to physical things—the land, gold, and so on. Everything else is merely an indirect interest in the physical. To Waldron, all our creations—art, music, medicine, technology, knowledge—ultimately relate to satisfaction of our physical, animal needs and wants. Like the infant, we remain preconscious in the domain of the real.

But even if one accepts Waldron's assertions as to the source of wealth, it does not follow from this that property relations are primarily or even archetypically relations affecting the access to and control of physical things. His very discussion indicates that access to and control of wealth—even if defined narrowly as physical things—are legal, symbolic relations, not the mere immediate sensuous contact with, and physical exploitation of, tangible things. Property, as a legal relation, is the way we as human beings move away from mere sensuous experience of the outside world to symbolic and social relations among human beings with respect to the outside world.

Indeed, as human beings, even our needs are not purely animalistic or natural. In the words of Renata Salecl:

> For Lacan the concept of need is linked to the natural or biological requirements of human beings (food, for example). But for human beings it is essential that these needs are never manifest as purely natural needs. Needs are always defined by a symbolic context: if we are hungry, for ex-

36. *Id.* at 37.

ample, we do not simply grab the first available food, but rather we think about what we shall eat and then prepare food in a special way.

When put into words, a need becomes articulated in the symbolic order. . . . Desire arises as the excess of demand over need, as something in every demand that cannot be reduced to a need.[37]

When I eat food, my *property* in the food is not the animal act of consumption and digestion but the legal recognition of my right to possess and use or alienate the food. In our society, property rights are these *indirect, mediated* relations among people through our relationship with the external world. It is meaningless to speak of property without speaking of our relation to these noncorporeal things, even if they ultimately indirectly lead to the access to and control of corporeal things. And yet, it is impossible to do so through the positive masculine phallic metaphor that Waldron unwittingly adopts.

B. Some Realism about Legal Surrealism: The Positive Phallic Metaphor and Ostensible Ownership

1. GRASPING AT STRAWS Much of commercial law doctrine—the private law of personal property—is firmly in the grasp of the masculine phallic metaphor of property as axe. The legal concept of possession is conflated with the sensuous experience of grasping a physical thing in one's fist. This metaphor is merely inept for the analysis of noncustodial property interests in tangible chattels which, at least theoretically, could be grasped. It is bizarre when applied to the property law of intangibles which is an increasingly important subject of commercial law. Rather than being simple and intuitive as its proponents claim, the metaphor of sensuous grasping can only be maintained through increasingly elaborate auxiliary metaphors and analogies. If legal realism was an attempt to make commercial law more nearly reflect actual economic practice, then the phallic metaphor is legal surrealism.

In this section, I explore the pernicious use of the physical metaphor in commercial law scholarship and doctrine with particular emphasis on the law of perfection of noncustodial security interests and security interests in intangible property. I will concentrate on the most extreme and

---

37. Renata Salecl, The Spoils of Freedom: Psychoanalysis and Feminism After the Fall of Socialism 124 (1994).

surrealistic example of the affirmative version of the physical paradigm in commercial law—the doctrine of "ostensible ownership." To the proponents of this doctrine, property should not merely be grasped, it must be wielded in the sense of being displayed for all to see. Not only does the sensuous grasp of a physical thing erect a legal presumption that the grasper is the owner, but property interests which do not, or cannot, take the form of sensuous grasping—such as when the object of the property interest is itself intangible—are deemed to be so problematic as to be presumptively fraudulent unless "cured." I will show that by enabling us to get beyond the masculine metaphor, the Hegelian theory of property offers a more satisfactory account of existing American property law and can serve as a paradigm for critiquing and revising existing law.

2. OSTENSIBLE OWNERSHIP

a. Introduction. The traditional doctrine of ostensible ownership holds that creditors assume that property "held" by another person actually belongs to that person. In other words, this doctrine posits that the archetypical form of ownership is immediate physical contact with, and custody of, a visible and tangible object. Like Waldron, proponents of this doctrine implicitly reduce property to the single masculine element of possession. I take this imagery to its logical extreme and call it "property as sensuous grasp." Property interests that cannot be so reduced—either because the interest is nonpossessory or because the object of the property interest is itself intangible—are considered "problems" that need to be explained. In other words, this doctrine holds that reasonable creditors presume that the person in physical custody of a tangible thing is ostensibly the owner free and clear of any competing claims. Consequently, in order to prevent actual or constructive fraud on creditors, all noncustodial property interests (such as hypothecations) should be "perfected."[38] "Possession," in the sense of immediate physical custody or sensuous grasp

---

38. The presumption of a right to possession from the fact of possession, moreover, largely underlies the doctrine of ostensible ownership, by which one is presumed to own the property he possesses. Numerous decisions and statutes, including the Statute of 13 Elizabeth, c. 5 (1571) and its modern progeny, the Uniform Fraudulent Conveyances Act, rest upon that doctrine and the further assumption that creditors rely upon the debtor's possession. The purchaser or creditor who allowed a false inference of ownership to arise by leaving property in the debtor's possession could expect no leniency in resulting litigation.

David Morris Phillips, *Flawed Perfection: From Possession to Filing Under Article 9—Part I,* 59 B.U. L. Rev. 1, 4 (1979).

by the secured party, is the preferred mode of perfection because it supposedly eliminates the ostensible-ownership problems with respect to the
debtor's creditors.[39] Hypothecations of most forms of personalty are governed by Article 9 of the Uniform Commercial Code (the "U.C.C."). Article 9's primary alternate mode of perfection by filing is permitted as a
substitute — a form of fictive custody — in those situations where custody
is impossible or impractical.[40] This notion is unquestioningly adopted by
a large percentage of the academy and the courts — a computer search will
produce literally dozens of articles and cases which parrot it as dogma.

The high priests of ostensible ownership are Douglas Baird and
Thomas Jackson.[41] Starting with their 1981 article, *Possession and Owner-*

---

39. The secured party could best rebut the inference of the debtor's unfettered ownership and assert her own right in the collateral by taking possession of it. The original
purpose of recording statutes was "rebuttal of [the] fraud created by possession." Article 9, quite conservatively, tracks this historical emphasis on possession and ostensible
ownership.

Id. (quoting John Hanna, *The Extension of Public Recordation,* 31 Colum. L. Rev. 617, 622
(1931) (alteration in original) (footnotes omitted).

The legal system's original method of providing this information was to give primacy
to possession. At common law, a debtor's possession of personal property assured a
prospective creditor that the debtor could give him an unencumbered interest in that
property. Possession was indeed nine points in the law.

Douglas G. Baird & Thomas H. Jackson, *Possession and Ownership: An Examination of the
Scope of Article 9,* 35 Stan. L. Rev. 175, 180 (1983) [hereinafter Baird & Jackson, *Possession and
Ownership*].

40. [The U.C.C. takes the approach] that [a] secured creditor need not take possession
of the collateral, but if he does not, he must make a public filing in a designated place
before he can shift the risk of competing claims to other property claimants.

Baird & Jackson, *Possession and Ownership, supra* note 39, at 183.

As David Morris Phillips so accurately argues in his critique of possession as a mode of
perfection, despite the availability of filing as an alternate mode of perfection, and despite
the fact that "business people have discounted the importance of possession, especially in
its role as a perfecting mechanism" as indicated by the fact that "[f]iling, instead, dominates
as the means of perfecting security interests," Article 9 still reflects the historical "preference
accorded possessory security interests over filed security interests." Phillips, *supra* note 38,
at 3. Indeed, the filing requirements have a "structural affinity to possession reflected in the
tie between the location of filing and the place of possession." *Id.* Moreover, "possession
by the debtor generally governs the time by which . . . the secured party must so file." *Id.*
Phillips applauds amendments made to Article 9 since its original adoption which he believes have moved it further away from what I have called the physical metaphor, and argues that numerous considerations "should continue to contribute to the decline of possession's importance." *Id.*

41. *See generally* Baird & Jackson, *Possession and Ownership, supra* note 39; Douglas Baird
& Thomas Jackson, Security Interests in Personal Property (2d ed. 1987) [hereinafter Baird
& Jackson, Security Interests]; Douglas Baird, *Security Interests Reconsidered,* 80 Va. L. Rev.

ship: An Examination of the Scope of Article 9,[42] and continuing up through Baird's *Security Interests Reconsidered,*[43] they have taken the doctrine of "ostensible ownership" to its logical extreme and beyond.[44] As described by Baird and Jackson:

> Since *Twyne's Case,* . . . possession has been viewed as *the best available source of information* concerning "ownership" of most types of personal property. Separation of ownership and possession has been viewed as a source of mischief toward third parties, and for that reason as fraudulent.[45]

They identify a negative pregnant in the traditional assertion that physical custody implies ownership. They infer from this that *lack* of physical custody implies *no* ownership. That is, the doctrine holds that the archetype of property is the sole element of possession reduced to the specific example of physical custody—an immediate, binary relation of subject to object. As this is the masculine strategy of denial, all attempts to complicate this simplistic account by revealing the mediated nature of noncustodial property interests must be repressed. This is why such interests are declared constructively fraudulent and voidable unless they can somehow be restated within the metaphoric imagery of the binary archetype.

Proponents try to justify this doctrine with a combination of ethical and economic grounds.[46] Both these justifications are based on the unexamined and unverifiable empirical presumption that reasonable creditors assume (absent actual notice to the contrary) that all assets in a debtor's custody are unencumbered. This presumption is supposed to be bolstered by a historical analysis which purports to show that American

---

2249 (1994). A quick LEXIS search of law reviews reveals literally dozens of articles and notes which uncritically accept the doctrine of ostensible ownership.

42. Baird & Jackson, *Possession and Ownership, supra* note 39.

43. Baird, *supra* note 41.

44. Their casebook on secured transactions (which recapitulates arguments which they had separately or together introduced in earlier articles) is probably their most complete and sustained paean to ostensible-ownership theory. Baird & Jackson, Security Interests, *supra* note 41.

45. Baird & Jackson, *Possession and Ownership, supra* note 39, at 180 (emphasis added).

46. I explore these justifications at length in Jeanne L. Schroeder, *Some Realism About Legal Surrealism,* 37 Wm. & Mary L. Rev. 455 (1996) [hereinafter Schroeder, *Legal Surrealism*]. In his critique of ostensible-ownership theory, Phillips sets forth its traditional ethical justification of preventing fraud. Phillips, *supra* note 38. That is, since, it is claimed, reasonable creditors assume that all assets in the custody of a debtor are unencumbered, any creditor who seeks to take a noncustodial property interest has an ethical duty to put other creditors on notice so that they are not defrauded. In their defense of ostensible-ownership

law has traditionally held that noncustodial property interests are presumptively voidable on the grounds of constructive fraud. Baird and Jackson do not merely argue that this historical account explains the existing positive law of perfection of security interests. Rather they believe that rationality itself insists upon the doctrine of ostensible ownership. It, therefore, should be unloosed from the confines of its traditional jurisdiction. Accordingly, not merely noncustodial security interests but all noncustodial property interests should be subjected to a perfection regime.[47] That is, although they purport to justify ostensible-ownership doctrine in part by historical precedent, they conclude by arguing that we should adopt and expand the doctrine despite historical precedent to the contrary.

Opponents of ostensible-ownership theory have argued for years—persuasively in my opinion—that there is strong empirical evidence that, whether or not its basic underlying assumptions were ever justified, they are now obsolete.[48] In our modern economy, property interests commonly, or even typically, are not accompanied by physical custody of tangible objects, and the persons in custody of the objects of property are commonly not the owners. An excellent example of this, which I shall discuss later in this section, is one of the most important categories of personal property in the modern economy—investment securities (i.e., stocks and bonds). The vast majority of publicly traded securities are no

---

theory, Baird and Jackson recognize the traditional ethical argument but seek to justify the rule in terms of efficiency. Baird & Jackson, *Possession and Ownership, supra* note 39. That is, it is supposedly cheaper for a noncustodial claimant to put all other creditors on notice of her property interest than it is for creditors generally to incur the costs of investigating title.

47. "That we tolerate the ostensible ownership problems created by these transactions is largely an accident of history." *Id.* at 177–78. To Baird and Jackson, the traditional protections of leases, bailments, and other interests are economically irrational aberrations to a general ostensible-ownership doctrine. Indeed, they repeatedly emphasize that if we are to take the "ostensible ownership problem seriously" we should impose filing or other notoriety requirements on other forms of noncustodial interests such as bailments.

48. Many writers, including myself, question the empirical presuppositions underlying this argument. *See* Schroeder, *Legal Surrealism, supra* note 46. Probably the most trenchant critic is Charles Mooney. Similarly, Phillips states that

[c]riticism of the doctrine of ostensible ownership finds its strongest behavioral support in the actions of parties who extend secured or unsecured credit subsequent to the secured transaction. Even with respect to creditors, one can poke holes in this criticism but its case seems incontrovertible—business people look to written, not possessory evidence of ownership. And this view leads generally to recognizing filing, but not possession, as a means of notice.

Phillips, *supra* note 38, at 35.

longer evidenced by physical certificates held by the owners but are held indirectly through tiers of intermediaries in the form of electronic book-keeping entries. Consequently, the marketplace is fully aware that physical custody standing by itself has no evidentiary value.[49] In other words, creditors do not have to undertake expensive investigation to learn that encumbrances exist. They can assume, based on empirical data concerning debtors on the whole, that they do.[50]

49. The high cost and relative ineffectiveness of possession as a means of allowing efficient use of the debtor's resources and providing certainty explain why filing dominates as the perfecting mechanism. The ineffectiveness of possession as a constructive notice is the foremost reason why the law *should* recognize and encourage possession's demise. These factors are related. Any attempt to make perfection through possession more effective in providing the secured party with certainty conflicts with the debtor's use of collateral. And efforts to make perfection through possession more effective in allowing collateral to be put to its most efficient use inevitably increase the risk that third parties might mistakenly rely upon the debtor's ostensible ownership and extend credit or purchase assets unaware of the secured party's interest.

Phillips, *supra* note 38, at 8.

50. At least one critic also challenges Baird and Jackson's historic account. Charles Mooney argues that our legal and economic system has never had a general concern about the separation of ownership and possession per se. There has, however, been a concern for limiting opportunities for fraud. This fraud concern is separable from the ostensible-ownership concern that possession of personal property begets misleading appearances of ownership upon which creditors and purchasers may rely. Charles Mooney, Jr., *The Mystery and Myth of "Ostensible Ownership" and Article 9 Filing: A Critique of Proposals to Extend Filing Requirements to Lease*, 29 Ala. L. Rev. 683 (1988). According to Mooney, the landmark cases on which Baird and Jackson rely invalidated the property interests of certain parties because the facts in those situations seemed particularly amenable to being used fraudulently. *Id.* at 730.

I do not wish to restate Mooney's insightful analysis, but a brief discussion of one of the cases may give a flavor to the traditional case law. In Clow v. Woods, 5 Serg. & Rawle 275 (Pa. 1819), the debtor, Hancock, purported to hypothecate all of his property to two individuals, Woods and Sharp, *the day before* a court awarded a judgment against Hancock in favor of a certain Poe. Poe did not learn of this hypothecation until exactly a year later when he hired a sheriff to enforce his judgment against the recalcitrant Hancock. Woods and Sharp sued the sheriff for taking "their" property.

We do not know much about the parties, but the skimpy facts reported in the case are suspicious. The judgment of Poe against Hancock was for the accounting of a defunct partnership between the two men. Although the court described this as an "amicable suit," it is my experience that even friendly breakups of partnerships, like uncontested divorces, often result in bitterness. This is especially the case when there is a disagreement about the division of property. For example, in the last five years my former law firm merged with another firm, split, and then split again. Two of the splinters were incorporated into other larger firms and the third has since dissolved. Several other partners and associates left or were forced out during these troubled times. Since I had resigned and withdrawn my capital a few years before in order to teach, I was able to sit and watch with morbid fascination the pitiful and disgusting sight of former friends descending into mutual recriminations and, eventually, years of litigation.

My main argument against Baird and Jackson's theory is not, however, based on empirical claims or historical interpretation.[51] Rather, my complaint is that they attempt not only to analyze current law but also to make policy recommendations for future law on the basis of unprovable assertions of accidental and contingent empirical facts rather than a consideration of the logical functions of property.

b. Custody as Evidence of Ownership. Baird and Jackson assert:

Possession of personal property is the *best* evidence of its ownership. The law of secured transactions has ordered itself around this principle for nearly four hundred years. . . . The drafters of the [Uniform Commercial] Code did not go far enough either in abolishing metaphysical and unobservable

---

Woods and Sharp were not ordinary secured lenders of Hancock. Rather, they had signed instruments as accommodation parties for Hancock. The hypothecation was to secure Hancock's reimbursement obligation in the event the accommodation parties were ever called under their suretyship obligation. People do not act as sureties without a reason. Apparently Woods and Sharp were never called to pay under the instruments. At the time the sheriff tried to execute upon the property one year and one day after the hypothecation, the "collateral" was still being used by Hancock. Were Woods and Sharp close friends or intimate business associates of Hancock whom Hancock preferred over his former associate, Poe? Rather than being a legitimate transaction which can be characterized as an abstract constructive fraud against hypothesized future creditors, this case reeks of being an actual fraud—a sham transaction entered into for the sole purpose of defrauding Poe.

In this view, the traditional doctrine of ostensible ownership did not generally void property arrangements which separated ownership and possession as fraudulent. It merely established a rebuttable presumption of fraud—in the case of certain hypothecations and a few other forms of the noncustodial transfers. Mooney, *supra* at 729. Moreover, most instances of separation of ownership and possession have traditionally been found to be "unproblematic." Disputes among different claimants to various forms of property are usually resolved by application of a combination of "derivation" (i.e., first in time, first in right) and "negotiability" (i.e., bona fide purchaser) principles without reference to pejorative and conclusory allegations of implied fraud.

51. Although I believe that the underlying presumptions are highly unlikely to be true. As Phillips argues, Baird and Jackson must be wrong in asserting that physical custody is the *best* evidence of ownership. Custody can *never* convey unambiguous information as to ownership *precisely* because people do not take custody of goods solely or even primarily as a form of communication but for a wide variety of practical purposes. Perhaps the only instance of possession as a communicative act is the pledge. But even then, often the secured party takes custody of the collateral not merely to put the world on notice of its security interest but also as a way of policing the debtor. The significance of custody is, consequently, *always* ambiguous. "Only an abstract means of perfecting security interests avoids both the uncertainty as well as other inefficiency costs associated with perfection through possession." Phillips, *supra* note 38, at 34. That is, if avoiding ambiguity is the goal, one should require a formal act which no one would take for any reason other than for the purpose of conveying information. Consequently, even though, historically, filing was developed as a "form of constructive possession," *id.,* in fact, it better serves the functions of perfection and should

distinctions based on concepts such as "title" or in adopting the more concrete concept of possession as their benchmark.[52]

This is one of the clearest statements of property as sensuous grasping of
physical things in contemporary legal scholarship. Those legal relationships which are not physically observable are slandered as mere "metaphysics." Their phrase echoes Karl Llewellyn's embrace of the physical
metaphor in the Official Comment to U.C.C. § 2-101, which states that
under the law of sales

> [t]he legal consequences are stated as following directly from the contract
> and action taken under it without resorting to the idea of when property
> or title passed or was to pass as being the determining factor. The purpose
> is to avoid making practical issues between practical men turn upon the
> location of an intangible something the passing of which no man can prove
> by evidence and to substitute for such abstractions proof of words and ac-
> tions of a tangible character.

As Llewellyn insisted, practical men need tangible things. Baird and Jackson seem never to use the word "title" without their intended pejorative,
"metaphysical." Presumably, by "metaphysical" they intend connotations such as unreal, fictional, imperceptible, invisible, intangible, in-
audible, too abstract, excessively subtle, "airy-fairy," supernatural, ambiguous, uncertain, and so on. Certainly it is not serious enough (or, dare
I say, too feminine?) for real men who are only happy when grasping their
tangible things. But, in context, Baird and Jackson use the term to mean
the legal (symbolic) as opposed to that which physically exists (which we
locate in the real).[53] In other words, they have inadvertently limited the
word "metaphysical" to a simpleminded, folk-etymological meaning—
that which is other than the physical—and imply that only the physical is
actual. This precisely reflects our psychoanalytic urge to achieve the impossible goal of unmediated relationships through the imaginary collapse
of the symbolic into the real, as though property could be reduced to our
animalistic, natural, physical relations with the material world.

Note, however, that Llewellyn's concern expressed in the Official

---

supplant custody as the preferred norm. "[F]iling, with its attendant specifics of what, where
and how, generally avoids the recurrent pitfalls that characterize perfection through possession and produce uncertainty." *Id.*

52. Baird & Jackson, *Possession and Ownership, supra* note 39, at 212 (emphasis added).

53. Other "metaphysical notions" they identify include "'leases,' 'bailments,' and 'security interest.'" *Id.* at 190.

Comment is not the misleading nature of non*custodial* interests but of non*objective* ones—that is, property interests which "no man can prove by evidence." Unfortunately, as I shall discuss in greater detail in section III.B of this chapter, his physicalist imagery already presupposes that "objective" means "physical" and that "intangible" means "subjective." This is exactly Baird and Jackson's error.

Like all proponents of the physical metaphor for property, Baird and Jackson do at some level recognize its impracticability, if not impossibility. And they offer one of the usual "solutions": denial through the adoption of the physical metaphor and attribution of the pejorative "metaphysical" to alternates. That is, certain forms of nonphysical possession are implicitly analogized as being equivalent to physical custody.

For example, they do not defend the filing regime on its own intrinsic utility. Rather, its utility is defended by metaphor—filing is *just like* sensuous contact:

> Both public recording files and possession share one central feature: Information about competing property interests is concrete and trustworthy. It is trustworthy because the information is conveyed by events—making a filing or taking possession—that themselves determine legal systems.[54]

This is despite the fact that Baird and Jackson also recognize that filing has distinct advantages over custody in that it allows the debtor to continue to use the collateral, thereby making it more likely that the secured party will eventually be paid.

> A secured creditor need not take possession of the collateral, but if he does not, he must make a public filing in a designated place. . . . [A] filing system places fewer restrictions on the use of collateral *yet* it still provides information that allows a creditor to avoid the uncertainty caused by the possibility of debtor misbehavior.[55]

At one moment Baird and Jackson do recognize that the requirement of perfection must relate to some requirement that property interests be objectively manifest as a condition of general enforceability, but do not understand its full implications:[56]

---

54. Baird & Jackson, *Possession and Ownership, supra* note 39, at 184.
55. *Id.* at 183.
56. Of course, they try to justify this on efficiency grounds based on unverifiable empirical presumptions as to creditor behavior and the relative costs of alternate legal regimes. In contradistinction, I wish to avoid relying on that which we cannot prove. Therefore, I try to derive this requirement from jurisprudential theory of the ethical function of property.

> The doctrine of ostensible ownership assumes that such contractual divisions [i.e., of property rights] are irrelevant insofar as third party rights are concerned. What matters is that third parties be able to observe the division easily and accurately.[57]

Unfortunately, after this correct starting place, their argument gets lost. Based on historical, but unverified, empirical assumptions, they first assume that physical custody is clear and informative and can serve as an effective way of objectively evidencing a property interest. From this they draw the non sequitur that noncustodial property interests are so problematic that they must be voided unless they can be cured by analogy to custodial interests. This means that Baird and Jackson do not fully recognize that the question of objectification arises in all property claims. Because they conflate objectivity with physicality, they believe that the need for objectification (what they call the ostensible-ownership problem) is *created* not by the claim to property but by the separation of such claims and physicality. Consequently, the test of an enforceable property interest depends not on whether it is sufficiently objectified but on whether it is sufficiently physicalized:

> A party who wishes to acquire or retain a nonpossessory interest in property that is effective against others must, as a general matter, make it possible for others to discover that interest.[58]

Therefore, filing is judged by whether or not it can serve as a substitute for physical custody and thus become a form of fictive possession.[59]

A similar conflation of objectification with physicality can be seen in Stephen Munzer's otherwise insightful property analysis. Munzer makes the quite remarkable statement that the only way that "embodied entities such as human persons can have property in nonmaterial things . . .

---

57. Baird & Jackson, *Possession and Ownership, supra* note 39, at 190.

58. *Id.* at 179.

59. *Id.* Elsewhere, they note in passing that possession may not be so unambiguous or even possible, but they minimize this by assertorially denying the materiality of this problem:

> Cases might also arise in which there is ambiguity about which of two parties is in possession of property. . . . First, although the question of whether a party is in possession of property might be difficult in some cases, at least when goods are involved the inquiry will be quite straightforward. . . . Second, many problem cases do not have to be resolved on a case by case basis. . . . As we have seen, the doctrine of ostensible ownership provides potential claimants with a method for obtaining this knowledge. If a debtor is in possession of property, and there is no filing, potential claimants can be confident they will prevail over earlier claimants.

Id. at 193–94.

[is] through some physical manifestation."[60] "It is, therefore, essential to property as it can exist for human beings that it involve, at some point, material objects. Without a physical manifestation people cannot have rights in nonmaterial things."[61] He thinks that this is demonstrated by the fact that copyright and patent applications require a writing, drawing, or model.[62] But in context, it becomes clear that his real concern is intersubjective communication. He refers to recent legislation as instituting "legal conventions that allow for more transitory physical manifestations."[63] He gives as an example a California statute that recognizes property rights in "any original work of authorship that is not fixed in any tangible medium of expression."[64] Music performed but not transcribed, or a mime performance seen but not filmed, is, to Munzer, a "fleeting" physical manifestation of property.[65] Presumably, on this analysis, electronic records of property interests (such as uncertificated securities) and conveyances (such as wire transfers) are also "physical" manifestations.

Even if one buys (which I do not) their assertion that physical custody of goods is unproblematical in most cases, Baird and Jackson are presupposing an economy in which most (or at least the archetypical forms of) property interests involve tangibles. This means that the law of perfection of security interests in intangibles is developed by analogy to the presumed "norm" of tangibles. If the law of tangibles is based on the presence or absence of physical custody, the law of intangibles is developed by reference to the presence or absence of something that, by definition, cannot exist.[66] This requires the development of ever more elaborate fictions and metaphors. This is precisely the same inverted logic which Waldron used to support the positive masculine phallic metaphor in property jurisprudence.

60. Stephen R. Munzer, A Theory of Property 72 (1990).

61. *Id.* at 73.

62. *Id.*

63. *Id.* at 78.

64. Cal. Civ. Code §980(a)(1) (Deering Supp. 1989) (amended 1982), *cited in* Munzer, *supra* note 60, at 78.

65. Munzer, *supra* note 60, at 78.

66. The common law, of course, dealt with this in two ways. First, it generally made it difficult to convey property interests in intangibles. The assignment of choses in action was prohibited (although the numerous exceptions which grew up around this general proposition perhaps made it a rule more honored in the breach). 1 Grant Gilmore, Security Interests in Personal Property 196–249 (1965). Second, it "reified" certain intangible and noncustodial interests into pieces of paper called negotiable instruments, negotiable documents, and securities certificates so that we could fictively convey possession of the underlying property by handing over physical possession of the paper.

c. Benedict v. Ratner. It is significant that Baird and Jackson include the infamous case of *Benedict v. Ratner*[67] in the chapter of their casebook which covers the history of the ostensible-ownership principle.[68] In this pre-U.C.C. case, the United States Supreme Court invalidated an assignment of accounts receivable—what we would today call a non-notification security interest in accounts.[69] Specifically, the court voided a purported assignment by a corporation of all of its existing and future accounts receivable when the assignee not only lacked the right to collect the accounts but the assignor had no obligation to account to the assignee for the collected accounts. The assignee did not notify the account debtors that he was now the owner of the accounts, collect, ask for an accounting, or attempt to assert any rights whatsoever with respect to the accounts until after the corporate-assignor's bankruptcy. That is, the assignor retained the right to collect, settle, or otherwise deal in the accounts without either paying the proceeds over to the assignee or substituting new accounts. The Supreme Court found that this transaction was a fraud on the corporate-assignor's debtor *as a matter of law* (i.e., it is objectively fraudulent even if the corporate-assignor acted with subjective good faith as a matter of fact)[70] because the assignor retained, and the assignee did not obtain, "dominion" over the accounts.

Baird and Jackson's inclusion of this case as an example (or, at least, a close relative) of ostensible-ownership theory follows from their custodial/

---

67. 268 U.S. 353 (1925).

68. Baird & Jackson, Security Interests, *supra* note 41, at 51–58. Baird and Jackson do not state expressly that ostensible-ownership principles literally apply to security interests in accounts. Their placement of the discussion, however, suggests that they see a strong family resemblance.

Other authors have more expressly linked the rule of *Benedict v. Ratner* with ostensible-ownership principles. For example, "The *Twyne* rule (and perhaps the *Benedict* rule) also may reflect the early common-law dissatisfaction with the notion that possession and ownership can be separated." John Dolan, *The U.C.C.'s Consignment Rule Needs an Exception for Consumers,* 44 Ohio St. L.J. 21, 34 n.84 (1993). Dunham similarly sees a close relation between the rule of *Benedict* and ostensible-ownership doctrine:

> Perhaps the United States' most noteworthy extension of Twyne's case was articulated by the Supreme Court in *Benedict v. Ratner*. . . . Reservation and dominion over the accounts by the debtor was inconsistent with the assertion that title had been given to [the assignee]. The debtor's grant of unrestricted domain over the goods which rendered ownership more than ostensible troubled the court.

Darrell W. Dunham, *Postpetition Transfers in Bankruptcy,* 39 U. Miami L. Rev. 1, 41–42 (1984).

69. U.C.C. §§ 1-201(37) and 9-104. The term "security interest" includes virtually all assignments of accounts, including outright sales, in addition to assignments for security.

70. Although the court did not find that there was evidence of an actual intent to defraud the assignor's creditors in this case, the facts are, obviously, suspicious. Not only was

noncustodial distinction: if noncustodial interests are defined as problematical, then property interests in accounts which are, by definition, intangible must always raise the concerns which underlie ostensible-ownership theory.[71]

Baird and Jackson take the position that, when one is analyzing the validity of the *secured party's* property interest, then the logic of ostensible-ownership doctrine demands that we ask not only whether the debtor retains physical custody but also whether the *secured party* ever obtained physical custody. That is, under the classic version of the ostensible-ownership theory, the debtor's creditors supposedly would be fooled into thinking that the debtor owned his property free and clear of liens if they looked at the debtor and saw the debtor in possession of the collateral. In the rewritten theory, creditors would also be fooled into thinking that a rival creditor did not have a lien on the debtor's property if they looked at the creditor and did not see it in possession. This seems to follow directly from the underlying presumption that property *is* possession and possession *is* physical custody.

This, of course, is the logical extension of the phallic metaphor. If a secured party is claiming a property interest, it is not enough to show that the debtor has been castrated from her phallic property. Rather, the secured party must show that he now wields the *Phallus*. For this analysis, it is irrelevant whether the reason why the secured party lacks physical custody is that the debtor retains physical custody (as in classic ostensible-ownership analysis) or that the nature of the collateral makes physical custody an impossibility (as in the case of assignments of accounts and other intangibles). This approach may be implicit in the rule announced in *Benedict v. Ratner*. Justice Brandeis might be read as analo-

---

the assignee the father of the assignor's president, the assignment was made four months and three days prior to the assignor's bankruptcy at a time when the voidable preference period was four months.

71. Mooney criticizes this approach because the Supreme Court expressly denied that it was applying ostensible-ownership law precisely on the grounds that it is impossible to take physical custody of an intangible. Mooney, *supra* note 50, at 733–34. "But it is not true that the rule stated above and invoked by the receiver is either based upon or delimited by the doctrine of ostensible ownership." 268 U.S. at 362–63.

Here I will defend Baird and Jackson as accurately reflecting the logic of the case. Mooney does not recognize that Baird and Jackson's (and, implicitly, the Supreme Court's) analysis extends the reasoning underlying ostensible-ownership doctrine beyond its common-law boundaries to its logical extreme. The common law of ostensible ownership concentrated on the fact that the *debtor* retained physical custody of the collateral. But Baird and Jackson are correct in realizing that this was a red herring.

gizing ownership of accounts to the sensuous grasp of goods and fixating on the lack of physical custody, or its analogue, in the secured party. In this reading the term "dominion" stands in for physical custody of intangibles.

Perhaps tellingly, the assignee in this case was the father of the assignor's president. Does his paternal status of the assignee explain, in part, why the Supreme Court was so concerned with the assignee's lack of dominion? For the father to function as a father he needs to appear to be holding the *Phallus*. But in *Benedict v. Ratner*, the father is castrated and it is the son who wields phallic property.

Modern lawyers love to sneer at this case as a relic of a financially unsophisticated era. The drafters of the U.C.C. claimed that they rejected the rule of *Benedict v. Ratner* with respect to accounts.[72] By this they meant that they did not adopt the Supreme Court's specific solution to the secured party's lack. That is, they did not insist that the secured party take dominion and control over an assigned account. Instead, as I shall discuss below, Article 9 permits secured parties to perfect their interest through filing. Consequently, Article 9 makes it much easier for lenders to offer what is known as "nonnotification" accounts receivable financing.[73]

In contradistinction, I agree with Baird and Jackson's intuition that *Benedict v. Ratner* remains relevant because it identifies a recurring problem of commercial law, albeit in a partial and imperfect manner. Although the drafters sought to assure a different *outcome* from that of *Benedict v. Ratner*, they implicitly embraced both its obvious general conceptual errors as well as its hidden insight. This can be seen in Article 9's rules for the perfection of security interests.

---

72. Official Comment 1 to U.C.C. § 9-205 states that this section "repeals the rule of *Benedict v. Ratner*." It continues:

> The principal effect of the Benedict rule has been, not to discourage or eliminate security transactions in inventory and accounts receivable—on the contrary such transactions have vastly increased in volume—but rather to force financing arrangements in this field toward a self-liquidating basis. Furthermore, several lower court cases drew implications from Justice Brandeis' opinion in Benedict v. Ratner which required lenders operating in this field to observe a number of needless and costly formalities: for example it was thought necessary for the debtor to make daily remittances to the lender of all collections received, even though the amount remitted is immediately returned to the debtor in order to keep the loan at an agreed level.

73. U.C.C. § 9-205 provides that

> [a] security interest is not invalid or fraudulent against creditors by reason of liberty in the debtor . . . to collect or compromise accounts . . . or to use, commingle or dispose of proceeds or by reason of the failure of the secured party to require the debtor to account for proceeds or replace collateral.

3. OBJECTIFICATION: HEGELIAN POSSESSION AS AN ALTER-
NATIVE TO THE PARADIGM OF THE PHALLIC METAPHOR   The
ostensible-ownership doctrine is supposed to explain the historical development of the positive law of security interests. Extremists, such as
Baird and Jackson, argue that if one accepts the doctrine, then consistency
and utilitarian considerations demand that we extend the concept of "perfection" beyond security interests to all noncustodial property interests.
They cannot explain, however, why our supposedly efficient capitalist system has not yet done so. One is not required to "perfect" one's nonpossessory property interest in goods leased, coats left at the hatcheck in
restaurants, clothes left with the dry cleaner, and so on. In the theory of
Baird and Jackson, this remains an unexplained aberration. In this section, I suggest that a Hegelian analysis offers a much more convincing
account of current law which avoids such embarrassments. To that end,
it is helpful to review briefly the structure of Article 9 before moving on
to my analysis.

a. Attachment and Perfection.   Article 9 security interests can only be created by contract.[74] They are not merely contract interests, however, but
property interests in specific identifiable collateral. This means, among
other things, in the event of the debtor's bankruptcy, a secured party does
not share in the estate pro rata with general creditors but is entitled to
distribution out of earmarked assets. Consequently, Article 9 makes a distinction between what it calls "attachment" and "perfection" of security
interests which reflects their contractual and property aspects, respectively.

Roughly speaking, when we say a security interest has attached, we
mean that it has become enforceable against the debtor who created the
security interest as well as against a discrete class of third parties: donees
and knowledgeable buyers out of the ordinary course of business.[75] Perfection means that the attached security interest is also enforceable against
a much larger class of third parties, most significantly, subsequent lien cred-

---

74. Article 9 "applies to security interests created by contract." U.C.C. § 9-102(2). One
of the elements of attachment (i.e., creation) of a security interest is that there is an agreement. U.C.C. § 9-203(1)(a).

75. The four elements of attachment are located in U.C.C. § 9-203: (i) The security interest must be established by agreement between the debtor and the secured party, U.C.C.
§ 9-203(1)(a) (i.e., because security interests, unlike judgment liens, are voluntary conveyances, they fall within the defined term "purchase"); (ii) the security agreement must be
evidenced by one of three formalities in the nature of a statute of frauds (Official Comments
3 and 5); (iii) the debtor must have rights in the collateral, U.C.C. § 9-203(1)(b) (i.e., there
must be some object in which the debtor can assert a property interest, a special case of the

itors, the debtor's bankruptcy trustee, most subsequent secured parties, and certain others.[76] Consequently, one can have unperfected but attached security interests in many categories of collateral,[77] but there is no such thing as a perfected but unattached security interest.

Why is this so? One answer is suggested by the Hegelian theory of the function of property.

b. The Logic of Property

(1) Classical Liberalism and Autonomy.

Elsewhere I have shown that the existing positive law of property under the U.C.C. can be explained in terms of the classical liberal policy of furthering autonomy.[78] This analysis is powerful and appealing in that it probably reflects the underlying liberal jurisprudential theories actually (implicitly or explicitly) held by the drafters. It is limited, however, in that it depends on a liberal presupposition of human nature as atomistic individuality with a natural right of negative liberty as personal autonomy (and, to a lesser extent, a natural right to property). These presuppositions are, perhaps, not so universally shared in our society as they once were. As a sublation of liberalism, Hegelian property theory can preserve

---

derivation rule); and (iv) the secured party must have given value, U.C.C. § 9-203(1)(b) (i.e., in order to form the contract, consideration must be given by the secured party).

My categorical statements are roughly true. Unperfected security interests are enforceable (i.e., have priority) against a few third parties such as donees and buyers of goods out of the ordinary course of business.

76. As usual, the U.C.C. never states this general principle in so many words. Rather it adopts the transactional approach and describes (Article 9, Part 3) the priority of unperfected security interests vis-à-vis other parties (U.C.C. § 9-301), the priority of conflicting security interests (U.C.C. § 9-312), and priorities against other parties (U.C.C. §§ 9-306 and 9-310).

77. It is often thought that it is impossible to have an attached but unperfected security interest in investment securities in those states which still have the pre-1994 version of Article 8. This is an overstatement. Pre-1994 U.C.C. § 8-321(2) does provide that attached Article 8 security interests are always initially automatically perfected. This only means that it is impossible to create an attached yet unperfected security interest *ab initio*. Under pre-1994 Article 8, perfection can lapse, resulting in an unperfected yet attached security interest. *See* Jeanne L. Schroeder & David Grey Carlson, *Security Interests in Investment Securities*, 12 Cardozo L. Rev. 557 (1990) [hereinafter Schroeder & Carlson, *Security Interests in Investment Securities*].

The 1994 Revisions to Articles 8 and 9 remove this anomaly.

78. I do this in Jeanne L. Schroeder, *Death and Transfiguration: The Myth That the U.C.C. "Killed" Property*, 69 Temple L. Rev. 1281 (1997).

the liberal values of individuality, autonomy, and negative liberty as one true moment in the actualization of freedom while negating and superseding its false claims to universality.

As I discussed in chapter 1, Hegelian possession is the identification of a specific object as being "owned" by a specific legal subject with the right and power to exclude others from the object. Because the logic of property is to make the owner recognizable by others, the claim to ownership which is possession cannot be totally "subjective" in the sense of private to the so-called owner. It must be somehow public and "objective" in the sense that it is intersubjectively recognizable by the relevant legal community.

Unfortunately, the U.C.C., and much contemporary legal scholarship, conflates the English term "possession" with its more narrow meaning of physical custody, preferably in the form of sensuous grasp. Consequently, the Supreme Court's terminology in *Benedict v. Ratner*—dominion (from *dominus,* lord)[79]—may in fact be more appropriate since it does not carry the unfortunate modern physicalist connotation of "possession."

In our legal system, both the debtor and the secured party to a security interest are deemed to have property rights in the collateral, although neither has the most full and adequate manifestation of property known as unfettered ownership. In a hypothecation, the debtor has possession in the sense of the right to have physical custody of a tangible object, or is otherwise recognized as the owner of an intangible object. She has the right to enjoy the object in the sense of using it or collecting it. Article 9 gives her the power to alienate her equity interest and sometimes the secured party's interest in the collateral (despite contractual restrictions to the contrary).[80] These rights are all immediate, but they are also contingent in that their continued existence is subject to the condition that she satisfy the secured obligation. The secured party's rights of possession (through "repossession"),[81] enjoyment (through collection or strict foreclosure),[82] and alienation (through foreclosure sale)[83] are inchoate because they are all contingent upon a future default by the debtor which may never occur. Consequently, the secured party's rights remain contractual in nature unless they are somehow immediately objectified. An unperfected security interest is objective only to a very small class of people: the

79. 4 The Oxford English Dictionary 949 (1989).
80. U.C.C. § 9-311.
81. U.C.C. § 9-503.
82. U.C.C. §§ 9-502, 505(2).
83. U.C.C. §§ 9-504, 505.

debtor and parties with actual notice. Consequently, attached but un-perfected security interests are enforceable against certain knowledgeable buyers[84] and against the debtors' donees, who do not act as independent legal subjects but inherit the status of their donor.[85] The logic of prop-erty is recognition by others. In order to be a property right enforceable against a third party, it is necessary that it become objective in the sense of recognizable by that third party. It is the necessity for objectification which explains the requirement known as perfection. This is another way of saying that possession is the most primitive element of property, re-quired for the other two.

(2) Hegelianism and Pragmatism.

While the Hegelian dialectic is a powerful tool for analyzing the structures of society, it cannot answer specific questions of legal policy or daily life.[86] This is why pragmatism is a necessary correlate of Hegelian idealism. The actual form of possession for any given property claim in any given soci-ety falls outside logic and within the province of positive law. In this in-terpretation, perfection of a security interest through *filing* of a financing statement would be a form of Hegelian possession through marking rec-ognized by the positive law of the U.C.C. That is, filing is not a second-best substitution for possession as exemplified in the norm of sensuous grasping; through positive law, filing itself becomes a form of possession.

The Hegelian concept of possession can be used both to explain and to

---

84. U.C.C. § 9-301(1) provides that unperfected security interests are subordinate to, among others, buyers of farm products, buyers out of the ordinary course of business of other goods, and certain assignees of accounts and assignments to the extent they give value and do not have knowledge of the security interest. By negative pregnant, such purchasers *with* knowledge take subject to the security interest under the general derivation principle of U.C.C. § 9-201.

85. Donees take subject to an unperfected security interest granted by their donor-debtor under the general derivation principle of U.C.C. § 9-201. As discussed in chapter 1, in Hegelian theory, a donee is not asserting her subjectivity (i.e., acting as an end to her own means). Rather, she passively serves as the means to the ends of the donor. Hegel, The Phi-losophy of Right, *supra* note 23, at 102, 106–07, 111. *See also* Alan Brudner, *The Unity of Prop-erty Law,* 4 Canadian J.L & Jurisprudence 3, 34 (1991).

86. As Richard Hyland has written in the context of discussing *The Philosophy of Right:*

Hegel described what he believed to be the ever-recurring *forms* of self-reflection, at an individual and societal level. He did not dream of dictating to us either their *substantive* content or the resolution of conflicts between the individual and society. Hegel's the-ory leaves us free to resolve these issues for ourselves.

Richard Hyland, *Hegel: A User's Manual,* 10 Cardozo L. Rev. 1735, 1741 (1989).

critique some areas of property law which seem anomalous when considered within ostensible-ownership doctrine. Probably the most obvious of such apparent anomalies, as raised by Baird and Jackson, is the lack of any perfection requirement for leases and certain other arrangements where a noncustodial party has enforceable property rights. From a Hegelian viewpoint, the continued existence of this apparent anomaly can be explained if the lessor's noncustodial interest is otherwise objectively manifest in the sense of being observable, or at least discoverable, by a third-party creditor of the custodial lessee from evidence other than the self-serving subjective statements of the custodial party.[87] This turns out to be the case.

If a creditor wishes to take a security interest on equipment or other goods in the custody of a debtor, it can investigate the equipment's provenance or chain of title.[88] That is, it can demand from the debtor some evidence of the origin of the equipment—such as a bill of sale or other receipt. The creditor can then question the source of the equipment about the nature of the transaction by which the debtor obtained custody. In this way, the creditor has some ability to ascertain the existence of an adverse interest that is not totally dependent on the subjective statements of the debtor.[89] The same reasoning could in part explain the traditional solicitude for purchase money financers—at least when the financer is also

---

87. Baird and Jackson assert that there is no objective way for a creditor to learn of a leasehold or other bailment. In the case of leases, "third parties have no easy way of discovering these divisions." Baird & Jackson, *Possession and Ownership, supra* note 39, at 178. In the case of purchase money security interests, "the financer of the inventory had no independent means of learning about the contractual arrangements between [the bailor and the bailee/debtor]." *Id.* at 200.

88. Mooney, *supra* note 50, at 748–51.

89. In the teacher's manual to their casebook (which I assume, from its style, consists mainly of their lecture notes), Baird and Jackson flippantly dismiss this approach:

But what if you want to buy a personal computer sitting in my office. How do you know it's mine—that is, how do you know if you pay for it, some company won't swoop down later and take it away, saying the computer belonged to it, and that I had no right to sell it? You might ask for the bill of sale. But I'm a careless guy, and I might not have it any more. What else? You look to see that I have it in my office. Anything else? No.

Douglas G. Baird & Thomas H. Jackson, Teacher's Manual, Security Interests in Personal Property 9 (2d ed. 1987).

They do not consider, as Mooney implicitly does, that even in the absence of a bill of sale, the potential buyer could ask the computer holder for the name of his seller and then ask the seller about the nature of the transaction. Of course, if the computer holder cannot produce this evidence, the potential buyer can still protect itself by lowering the price it will offer, or put a portion of the purchase price in escrow for whatever time the buyer deems sufficient to smoke out any competing claimant.

In other words, Baird and Jackson's comment does not go to the validity of Mooney's point that provenance *can* be and often is investigated. Indeed, I practiced as a corporate

the seller of the collateral.[90] It cannot, however, justify the nonperfection of other forms of noncustodial security interests. That is, an investigation of the past chain of title of an object will not reveal the existence of a non–purchase money hypothecation.

I am not arguing that Hegelian property analysis shows that perfection of leases by filing is neither *necessary* nor a good idea. It merely argues that any given society may decide that different forms of objectification might be appropriate for different property interests for historic or pragmatic reasons. In my example, one might decide on abstract logical grounds that the unperfected interests of lessors are theoretically objective (i.e., possessory) and, therefore, property. Nevertheless, society could also pragmatically decide that investigation of provenance is too difficult, too time-consuming, and too subject to fraud by dishonest debtors who can forge fake receipts or collude with dishonest suppliers, to be considered sufficiently objective to justify enforcement of all leases against all competing interests. In other words, leases which can be discovered through investigation of provenance might be minimally objective and "possessory" in a Hegelian sense, but they are not necessarily the most adequate or full form of possessory interests.

Moreover, if lease financing is a significant rival for secured financing

---

lawyer for many years before teaching, and such investigation was a standard part of the "due diligence" undertaken in large corporate mergers and acquisitions, and various forms of "holdbacks" and escrows are customarily used to protect buyers against undiscovered potential risks such as rival claimants. Fine arts is another industry in which elaborate systems for investigating and evidencing provenance have developed.

The valid issue they do implicitly raise, however, is the pragmatic one of whether this is the better way of protecting the competing interests of buyers, sellers, and third-party claimants. Lower prices and escrows will only be imposed by the buyer if the seller is "a careless guy" who does not keep his bills of sale. But economic theory would indicate that if "careless" sellers will receive a lower purchase price (or have part of the purchase price escrowed), there will be a strong incentive to be "careful" and keep records of provenance. Nevertheless, there might be cheaper and/or less burdensome ways of achieving this purpose.

90. Because the adequacy of a form of objectification is a pragmatic rather than a logical one, it should not be surprising that one will occasionally find certain "logical" inconsistencies in application. For example, the reason given for not requiring filing in the case of leases (the possibility of investigating provenance) would seem to apply equally to justify not requiring filing for purchase money security interests ("pmsi's") retained by sellers. In fact, although we relax the filing requirements in the case of such pmsi's (e.g., U.C.C. § 9-301(2) provides that a pmsi will prevail over a judgment lien if perfected by filing within ten days of the debtor's obtaining possession of the collateral), in most cases we do require such filing.

in some industries, it might also make pragmatic sense to require the same form of objectification for all property interests. We might, therefore, pragmatically decide that with respect to some industries, or some types of collateral, creditors should have to engage in only one form of search to discover all potentially rival interests. Why make creditors search both the secured financing records and investigate provenance if it would not impose significant hardships on lessors to record their interests on a certificate of title?

For example, we have decided to require perfection formalities for all property interests—ownership, leasehold, and security interests, custodial as well as noncustodial—in aircraft and airplane engines and equipment which are frequently financed by sale-leasebacks and secured credit.[91] Similarly, although the U.C.C. does not require that leases in automobiles be perfected as a condition of enforceability against creditors, both the interests in lessors (as owners) and secured parties (as lienholders) must be noted on the certificate of title on automobiles under state certificate-of-title statutes.[92] Contrarily, in other industries we may decide that the expense imposed on the noncustodial party would not justify the investigative cost savings to third parties.

Of course, these pragmatic decisions depend on precisely the type of difficult-to-verify empirical questions which I have been seeking to avoid. But this is an inevitable characteristic of all pragmatic decisions. All we can do is develop a logical structure to help frame the type of pragmatic questions we need to ask, and develop a theory of political legitimacy for the process by which the pragmatic decision will be reached. Traditionally, in our political system, such decisions are considered to be within the competency of the legislature. My criticism of Baird and Jackson, then, is not so much that they raise a hypothesis which requires empirical investigation but that they assume the very empirical data on which a demonstration of their hypothesis depends.

---

91. In the case of aircraft and equipment, Congress has, by making recordation the exclusive mode of possession, implicitly determined that the mere fact of custody is too ambiguous to serve as objectification. Federal law makes recordation a condition of enforceability of all property interests in aircraft and equipment, including ownership and leaseholds, in addition to security interests. 49 U.S.C. § 44107 (1997 Supp.). *See* Jeanne L. Schroeder & David Gray Carlson, *Airplanes in Bankruptcy,* 3 J. Bankr. L. & Prac. 203, 217, 254–59 (1994) (discussing the predecessor statute) [hereinafter Schroeder & Carlson, *Airplanes in Bankruptcy*]. The Supreme Court has interpreted these provisions as meaning that physical custody can*not* serve as a perfecting formality for aircraft. Philco Aviation, Inc. v. Shacket, 462 U.S. 406 (1982).

92. See, e.g., Uniform Certificate of Title and Anti-Theft Act.

(3) Perfection, Filing, and Control.

An example of a pragmatic recognition that different forms of objectification may be more or less adequate is the priority regime for security interests in investment securities contained in the 1994 revisions to Articles 8 and 9 of the U.C.C. As revised, Articles 8 and 9 permit a variety of liberalized perfection alternatives for security interests in investment securities. In perhaps the most radical change from traditional law, the revisions provide for automatic perfection of security interests granted by broker-dealers and other securities intermediaries. Filing will be permitted in the case of other types of debtors. Both of these are examples of a minimum form of Hegelian possession through positive law—intersubjectively recognizable identification of object to subject.

In the case of automatic perfection, objectification consists of the general knowledge of the lending industry that securities held by broker-dealers are customarily subject to multiple competing noncustodial property claims. Based on their investigation of the actual practices of lenders in the securities industry, the drafters of the 1994 revisions to Articles 8 and 9 rejected the assumptions of the ostensible-ownership theory in light of a new ostensible-nonownership analysis: in the absence of actual notice to the contrary, reasonable creditors assume that *all* investment property held by securities professionals is encumbered. But note, the intersubjective knowledge which is "objectively" known by the lenders goes only to the existence of competing interests, generally, rather than of any specific property interests of any identified party. Consequently, revised Articles 8 and 9 only make these interests generally, but not specifically, enforceable. By this I mean all secured parties who rely only on automatic perfection and do not take one of the other objectifying acts permitted by the statute have priority over general creditors but share pro rata among themselves.[93]

Perhaps more interestingly, the revisions further provide that secured parties who take "control" of investment securities have priority over security interests perfected by alternate means (such as automatic perfection).[94] "Control" is a newly coined term of art defined as a variety of devices which give the secured party power to dispose of the property

---

93. U.C.C. § 9-115(5)(e).

94. U.C.C. § 9-115(5)(a). A "controlling" secured party who is not the debtor's securities intermediary will, however, be subordinate to the securities intermediary, who is always deemed to have "control."

without the further cooperation of the debtor. As we have seen, although physical custody can be a form of Hegelian possession, it is not the archetype of possession. Similarly, although actual physical custody of a securities certificate can be an element of control, it is not the archetypical form of control. Indeed, when a certificate is registered in the name of a specific person, mere physical custody does not even constitute control unless it is accompanied by all appropriate indorsements.

It is also significant that the forms of "control" defined by the revisions are all intersubjectively recognizable. For example, one form of investment property governed by the revisions is a new property interest known as a security entitlement.[95] For my limited purposes it suffices to say that this is what an investor has when she owns her securities indirectly through her broker or other securities intermediary. This is now the most common form of securities holding in this country. If "control" by a secured party is thought of only as the power to dispose of the collateral without the further act of the debtor,[96] then, theoretically, a debtor could give a secured party control by signing an irrevocable power of attorney to give instructions to the broker or other securities intermediary.[97] But such an arrangement could be kept entirely private between the debtor and the secured party until such time as the secured party chose to exercise its power. Consequently, such private arrangements do not fall within the defined term "control" for the purposes of the revisions. In order for a secured party to obtain "control" over a security entitlement, the securities intermediary with whom the security entitlement is maintained must agree to obey such instructions.[98] That is, there must be at least one third party who knows of the arrangement and can answer questions from other third parties.[99]

. The drafters, in effect, made a pragmatic judgment that security in-

---

95. Security Entitlement means the rights and property interest of an entitlement holder with respect to a financial asset specified in Part 5 [of Article 9].

U.C.C. § 8-102(17). Put simply, in in the vast majority of cases, when a customer holds her investment assets in an account at a securities intermediary, she will be deemed not to be the direct holder of such assets but a holder of this new sui generis property right.

96. Obtaining "control" means that the purchaser has taken whatever steps are necessary, given the manner in which the securities are held, to place itself in a position where it can have the securities sold, without further action by the owner.

U.C.C. § 8-106 cmt. 1.

97. U.C.C. § 8-106; Jeanne L. Schroeder, *Is Article 8 Finally Ready This Time? The Radical Reform of Secured Lending on Wall Street,* 1994 Colum. Bus. L. Rev. 291, 393–95 [hereinafter Schroeder, *Is Article 8 Finally Ready?*].

98. Revised U.C.C. § 8-106(c).

99. The system is not perfect. Under the revisions, the securities intermediary has no statutory duty to respond to the inquiries of others, although it does have to obey the in-

terests perfected by "control" are more public and unambiguous than those perfected by automatic perfection and, therefore, should be given priority. Similarly, although public filing is given the status of perfection by positive law, it does not as adequately serve the possessory function of excluding others as does "control"; consequently, secured parties who perfect by filing are subordinate to perfection by "control." In other words, although security interests in investment securities may be minimally objectified through notoriety or filing, "control" prevails because it is a more adequate form of objectification.

(4) *Benedict v. Ratner* Redux.

A Hegelian analysis might also offer an aphysicalist reinterpretation, and partial rehabilitation, of some aspects of the apparently physicalist legal doctrines such as ostensible ownership and the *Benedict v. Ratner* rule. The doctrine of ostensible ownership is both archaic and based on insupportable empirical presumptions. Nevertheless, just "as the toad, ugly and venomous, wears yet a precious jewel in its head,"[100] this incoherent doctrine hides a valuable germ of Hegelian property analysis buried deep within it. Such an analysis would ask: What does it mean to say that a hypothecation or assignment has created a property interest in the underlying collateral in favor of the secured party/assignee? Under contemporary commercial law theory, substance is supposed to control over form.[101] Because property rights always implicate third parties (such as creditors), courts are not supposed to look solely to the parties' self-serving characterization of their legal relationship. Consequently, we need to identify the minimum substantive requirements of property. This is another way of saying that property interests need to be at least minimally objective.

The principle that substance prevails over form usually arises when it is clear that the parties intended to create a property interest, but there is

---

structions from its customers. This is a purely pragmatic decision to protect financial intermediaries from being forced to act like a county clerk and be subject to liabilities to third parties. Nevertheless, when securities are held indirectly in the form of security entitlements, creditors are at least on notice of the securities intermediary, and can make inquiry of the securities intermediary. If a securities intermediary refuses to respond to such a third-party inquiries, and the debtor refuses to instruct the securities intermediary to respond, the potential creditor should be suspicious.

100. William Shakespeare, As You Like It, act 2, sc. 1.

101. Article 9 "applies . . . to any transaction (regardless of its form) . . . . " U.C.C. § 9-102(1). *See also* U.C.C. §§ 2-401(1), 9-202.

a dispute as to how the interest is to be characterized. The classic example is the security interest disguised as a lease.[102] But it is another example of the form/substance dichotomy which raises the concerns underlying ostensible-ownership analysis. Certain transactions which are structured in the form of present conveyances of property may, in substance, be mere options to acquire, or other forms of executory contracts to purchase property in the future. That is, when two parties to a contract self-servingly characterize the transaction as "hypothecation" or an "assignment" or another form of property interest, it does not necessarily make it so. It could just be a promise to prefer a creditor, to assign an asset, or to grant a call option on the asset exercisable in the future. Since property rights affect third parties directly, the characterization should be objectively determinable by third parties.

This means that we need to define the essential elements of property in order to identify when a bona fide, enforceable transfer of a property interest has occurred. My Hegelian approach argues that there must be an element of possession (objectification), as well as the elements of enjoyment and alienation, for a legal interest to be considered a full property. What the court labeled "dominion" in *Benedict v. Ratner* might be reinterpreted as an attempt to identify what it means to have a property interest in an intangible. Did the purported assignee have any publicly recognizable right to possess, enjoy, or alienate the accounts? It may be that an effective assignment of the accounts had not been made because the assignee's rights to the account were not "possessory" in the Hegelian sense: they were totally subjective, in the sense of private, and not objective, in the sense of publicly recognizable. Possession is the logically first, most primitive element of property. Since there was no "possession," the creation of a property interest was never completed. As the arrangement was private between two persons, and was not recognizable by third persons, any rights which the assignee had should be considered contractual in nature. Under this reasoning, one does not need to invent theories of constructive "fraud" in order to refuse to enforce an inchoate transfer which was never consummated.[103]

The drafters of the U.C.C. claim to have rejected the rule of *Benedict*

---

102. Parties often try to characterize security interests as leases because leasehold interests often receive more favorable treatment under bankruptcy and tax law, and under generally accepted accounting principles.

103. This interpretation is consistent with some of the language of *Benedict v. Ratner.* Although the Court held that failure of an assignment constituted fraud in law, it found that "[i]t does not raise a presumption of fraud. It imputes fraud conclusively *because of the reservation of dominion inconsistent with the effective disposition of title and creation of a lien.*" 268

v. Ratner.[104] In my reinterpretation, this is an overstatement. The drafters contradict *Benedict v. Ratner* in the sense that the Supreme Court voided nonnotification assignments of accounts which are not sufficiently policed by the assignee, while the U.C.C. expressly provides that they can be valid and enforceable as Article 9 security interests. The U.C.C. does not, however, reject the underlying concept that to be an enforceable present property interest in accounts, rather than a mere contract right to future assignment of accounts, an assignment must be possessory in the Hegelian sense. They merely require a different form of objectification. The *Benedict v. Ratner* court required the assignee to objectify his property interest by notifying the account debtors and otherwise to obtain the direct power to deal with the collateral. In contradistinction, Article 9 provides that most assignments of accounts fall within the defined term "security interest" whether or not the assignment is an outright sale or only an assignment as security.[105] Security interests are not enforceable against most third parties (i.e., are not legally recognizable as full property interests) unless they are perfected.[106] The formality[107] required for perfection of assignments of accounts is public filing.[108]

U.S. at 363 (emphasis added). Later they characterize the precedent as pointing "out that a reservation of full control by the mortgagor might well *prevent the effective creation* of a lien in the mortgagee." *Id.* at 364 (emphasis added). They also speak of "reserving dominion" as being "inconsistent with the effective disposition of title." *Id.* By "dominion," the Court can be read to mean one of the bare-minimum elements of property. Failure of a secured party to take dominion would be inconsistent with the creation of a security interest by definition if a security interest is a property interest and dominion is a necessary element of property. The Court may have intuitively required dominion not merely to prevent fraud in the sense of misplaced reliance—the concern of traditional perfection policy. It may also have found dominion necessary to change the subjective contractual relationship between a debtor and secured party into an objective legal interest which falls within the definition of property—the concern of my neo-Hegelian perfection analysis.

That is, in order for the assignee to take on his paternal role, it was necessary that he possess the *Phallus* of property.

104. [T]his section [9-205] provides that a security interest is not invalid or fraudulent by reason of liberty in the debtor to dispose of the collateral without being required to account for the proceeds or substitute new collateral. [Article 9] repeals the rule of *Benedict v. Ratner* . . . and other cases which held such arrangements void as a matter of law because the debtor was given unfettered dominion or control over the collateral.

U.C.C. § 9-205 cmt. 1.

105. U.C.C. § 1-201(37), 9-102.

106. U.C.C. § 9-301.

107. In addition to satisfaction of all of the elements of attachment. U.C.C. §§ 9-203, 9-302.

108. U.C.C. § 9-302. There is a *de minimis* exception which allows automatic perfection. This is not to imply that the objectification formalities of the *Benedict* rule and the

In other words, even as the U.C.C. rejected the specific holding of
Benedict v. Ratner, Article 9 also arguably adopted its inchoate general
principle—security interests should not be enforceable against third parties (i.e., be recognized as property) unless they are made objectively recognizable by third parties. The proposed revisions to Articles 8 and 9 adopt
a variation of dominion as the most adequate mode of objectifying a security interest when the collateral consists of investment property. That
is, the highest priority is granted by the secured who obtains "control"—
the power to deal in the collateral.

The ostensible-ownership doctrine dimly recognizes that property interests need to be possessory, in the Hegelian sense, but confuses the general concept with a specific example—physical custody of tangible things.
Lacanian theory reveals why this doctrine is both erroneous and seductive. Hegelian theory enables us to identify the function which ostensible-
ownership doctrine unsuccessfully tries to address. Used together, they enable us to get beyond the phallic metaphor to rewrite property doctrine.

III. THE BUNDLE OF STICKS:
THE NEGATIVE VERSION OF THE
MASCULINE PHALLIC METAPHOR

A. Chix Nix Bundle-o-Stix: A Critique
of the Attempted Negation of Physicality

1. PROPHECIES The most eloquent prophet of the death of property
is Thomas Grey. In his justly famous 1980 essay "The Disintegration of
Property,"[109] Grey argued that by reconceptualizing property as a bundle
of sticks, modern jurisprudence had undermined its very foundation. As
a result, property is doomed to disappear as an important category of law.

U.C.C. completely eliminate the opportunities for sham transactions. A security interest is
a form of property and, therefore, requires that the secured party have certain rights of enjoyment and alienation as well as possession. In addition, as creatures of contract, security
interests must fulfill the attachment requirements of U.C.C. § 9-203. I am merely arguing
that objectification is a necessary, not a sufficient, requirement for enforceability of a claim
that purports to be a security interest.

109. *See* Thomas Grey, *The Disintegration of Property* [hereinafter Grey, *Disintegration
of Property*], *in* Property 69 (J. Roland Pennock & John W. Chapman eds., 22 Nomos, 1980)
[hereinafter Nomos, Property].

Unfortunately, despite the undeniable elegance and influence of this essay, Grey's analysis could not be more erroneous and his conclusions more wrong. In the name of rejecting the physicalist, phallic metaphor for property as object, Grey restates it apophatically through simple negation.

Grey claims a dichotomy between the idea of property held by the general public and the idea held by "specialists" such as lawyers and economists. The former, according to Grey, thinks of property as *"things* that are *owned by persons."*[110] The latter "tends both to dissolve the notion of ownership and to eliminate any necessary connection between property and things. . . . The specialist fragments the robust unitary conception of ownership into a more shadowy 'bundle of rights.'"[111] That is, laypeople see the fasces of property as an axe, but specialists know that the fact that it can be untied and broken into its component parts means that it is really only a bundle of sticks. At best, property is a label for a legal conclusion. Grey concludes that "the substitution of a bundle-of-rights for a thing-ownership conception of property has the ultimate consequence that property ceases to be an important category in legal and political theory."[112] Moreover, the concept of property is incoherent, as evidenced by the many different ways the word is used in both legal and colloquial discourse.[113]

110. *Id.* at 69.
111. *Id.*
112. *Id.* at 81.
113. Supposedly inconsistent uses of the word "property" identified by Grey include: (i) the rules of conveyancing of real property taught as a first-year course in law school; (ii) the legal and economic distinction between *in rem* rights as opposed to *in personam* rights; (iii) the economist's notion of property as those entitlements that should be recognized for the sake of efficiency; (iv) the contemporary legal theory whereby property is a means to protect certain public-law entitlements, as with the "new property" identified by Charles Reich; (v) the constitutional concept of what may not be taken by the government without a public purpose and just compensation—a concept often reified as things or pieces of property, as opposed to other rights (as in the Ackerman "Ordinary Observer's" view); and (vi) Guido Calabresi and Douglas Melamed's concept of property remedies, as opposed to liability remedies. See Grey, *supra* note 109, at 71–72 (citing Charles A. Reich, *The New Property,* 73 Yale L.J. 733 (1964)); Calabresi & Melamed, *supra* note 7.

Unfortunately, Grey's list shows neither that property lacks meaning or has inconsistent meanings nor that any of these views of property reflect a break from the objective view of property. Rather, these different uses of the word merely reflect discussion of the scope of property in the sense of identifying the proper objects of property—for example, whether property rights should be identified with respect to all conceivable external objects, including entitlement against the government, or merely certain traditionally recognized objects, such as parcels of real property—and the different functions that property can or should serve— as in the economic-efficiency argument, the new-property argument, and the Calabresi-Melamed remedies argument. I criticize Calabresi and Melamed's choice of terminology elsewhere. Schroeder, Three's a Crowd, *supra* note 7.

The intended implication of Grey's description is that the specialist's definition is more sophisticated and more accurate than the layperson's.[114] The former will, therefore, eventually supplant the latter. By deemphasizing the objective aspect of property and emphasizing the intersubjective aspect, the specialist's definition breaks down the traditionally recognized distinction between property and other forms of legal relations. Accordingly, as property is shorn of its uniqueness, it will cease to play its traditional inspirational and political role in American society.

Grey gives a historical gloss to his analysis. He argues that the lay definition of property as "thing-ownership" is consistent with the eighteenth-century concept of property both as expressed by William Blackstone and, presumably, as adopted by the Framers of the Constitution.[115]

> The conception of property held by the legal and political theorists of classical liberalism coincided precisely with the present popular idea, the notion of thing-ownership. . . .
>
> It is not difficult to see how the idea of simple ownership came to dominate classical liberal legal and political thought. First, this conception of property mirrored economic reality to a much greater extent than it did before or has since. . . .
>
> Second, the concept of property as thing-ownership served important ideological functions. . . . A central feature of feudalism was its complex and hierarchical system of land tenure. . . . On the other hand, property conceived as the control of a piece of the material world by a single individual meant freedom and equality of status. . . .
>
> Third, ownership of things by individuals fitted the principal justifications for treating property as a natural right.[116]

In other words, Grey argues that the lay-traditional concept of property might have, in fact, cohered with the economic reality of property practice in the early capitalist period. The feudal period was characterized by highly complex, overlapping, and interrelated ownership rules, whereby the same object was subject to the property rights of numerous persons.

---

114. A variation on Grey's analytical approach is Bruce Ackerman's dichotomy between the conception of property held by the "Ordinary Observer" and that held by the "Scientific Policymaker." Ackerman argues that the Supreme Court's takings jurisprudence often seems incoherent to the Scientific Policymaker because it does not use sharp definitions or follow a rigid logic. It becomes quite comprehensible, however, if viewed from the perspective of the Ordinary Observer who applies more fluid concepts of practical reasoning and cultural understandings. Bruce Ackerman, Private Property and the Constitution 26–29, 100–16 (1977).

115. Grey, *supra* note 109, at 73–74.

116. *Id.*

These rights were themselves intertwined with a complex system of mutual obligation and social, political, and religious status. The early capitalist era was, in contradistinction, characterized by the consolidation and simplification of property interests and the separation of property interests from obligation and status. Consequently, *when compared with feudal property,* capitalistic property seemed to be characterized by unitary interests in tangible objects epitomized by sensuous contact.[117] According to Grey:

> We have gone, then, in less than two centuries, from a world in which property was a central idea mirroring a clearly understood institution, to one in which it is no longer a coherent or crucial category in our conceptual scheme. The concept of property and the institution of property have disintegrated. . . .
>
> My explanatory point is that the collapse of the idea of property can best be understood as a process internal to the development of capitalism itself. . . . [I]t is intrinsic to the development of a free-market economy into an industrial phase. . . . The decline of capitalism may also contribute to the breakdown of the idea of private property, so that the two phenomena mutually reinforce each other. . . . [118]

How does Grey leap from the observation that contemporary legal scholarship tends to describe property as a bundle of rights to the conclusions that the connection between property and things has disappeared and that the concept of property is losing its significance in our economy? He does so by repeating an error made by Wesley Newcomb Hohfeld: he conflates the concept of the object of property and tangibility. He states, for example:

> What, then, of the idea that property rights must be rights in things? Perhaps we no longer need a notion of ownership, but surely property rights are a distinct category from other legal rights in that they pertain to things. But this suggestion cannot withstand analysis either; most property in a modern capitalist economy is intangible.[119]

That is, Grey cannot grasp the concept of a thing that he cannot grasp.[120] But the concept of the object of property always included, and continues

117. *Id.*

118. *Id.* at 74–75.

119. *Id.* at 70.

120. This is a very common move in American legal scholarship. For example, Felix Cohen assumed that because Blackstone and Hegel referred to external objects of property, they had to be referring to the physical relations between men and tangible things.

to include, intangible *things*. Neither the concept of property as an inter-relationship between subjects nor the concept of intangibility implies the elimination of the object from property jurisprudence. Grey's confusion does illustrate, however, how the archetypical image of property as physical custody of a tangible object is a misleading starting point for analyzing property interests generally. Yet it is this image that Grey implicitly keeps in his mind and that leads him to believe that modern concepts of property are becoming incoherent.

In support of this so-called lay-traditionalist/specialist-modern di-

---

See Felix S. Cohen, *Dialogue on Private Property*, 9 Rutgers L. Rev. 357, 361–63 (1954). To do so, Cohen had to ignore both the definitions and the examples of external things expressly provided by both writers.

Kennedy tars the conceptualization of intangibles as objects of property with the pejorative "reification." See Kennedy, *supra* note 34, at 335. Kennedy's approach presupposes that tangibles are naturally, essentially, prelegal, real things and that intangibles have some sort of preexisting, prelegal, unthinglike essence, so that thinghood is inauthentically and illegitimately thrust upon them. If one defines "thing" or object as merely the correlate of the self-conscious subject, then everything that is not a subject is, by definition, an object or thing. Consequently, intangibles do not have to be "thingified" but merely fall within a definition of object. Kennedy seems to be using the word "thing" to refer to the object of property rights—that is, a *res*. In this context, a thing is not a natural object but a symbolic one. The declaration that an object can serve as a *res* is reification. In other words, by recognizing property, we reify tangible as well as intangible objects.

I believe Kennedy has a good point that gets lost because of unacknowledged acceptance of the masculine phallic metaphor for property. The good point is that it is not necessary, and is perhaps misleading, to analyze property interests in intangibles by analogy to the properties of tangibles. Because Kennedy implicitly thinks, however, that the only real things are tangible things one can see and hold—the phallic metaphor—he incorrectly conflates comparing intangibles and tangibles with making intangibles into things—a process he incorrectly calls reification.

Even the most sophisticated analysts often cannot completely resist the phallic lure of tangibility. For example, in his excellent recent article, J.E. Penner makes a point very similar to mine that "things" is not a category that exists outside of property. Penner, *supra* note 6, at 807. He also criticizes Hohfeld for confusing traditional property with the right to "tangible objects." *Id*. at 712. And yet when Penner discusses the categories of *res* of property, he occasionally distinguishes intangibles from "true objects." *Id*. at 811. For example, although he realizes that debts are "undoubtedly property, [they] are close to the line because they are just barely things . . . ." *Id*. at 802. Consequently he conflates the concept of a debt as the right against someone for the payment of money, with the money paid. *Id*. at 811.

Similarly, in an otherwise cogent discussion of property rights in intangibles, Stephen Munzer comes to the extraordinary conclusion that the only way that "embodied entities such as human persons can have property in nonmaterial things . . . [is] through some physical manifestation." Munzer, *supra* note 60, at 72. As I discuss in Section II.B.3 of this chapter, this is because Munzer is conflating the requirement that property be objectified (i.e., possessory) with the necessity that it be physicalized.

chotomy of property, Grey contrasts the definitions of property expounded by Blackstone and Hohfeld. In order to analyze this dichotomy, it is useful to take an extended side trip through a lesser-known article—published the same year as Grey's—by Kenneth Vandevelde that more thoroughly, but succinctly, sets forth many of the assumptions about property theory that underlie Grey's work. I will then consider certain other examples Grey identifies of simplistic "thing-ownership" theories. Finally, I will explore the political context in which Grey's analysis is located. I will argue in contradistinction to Grey that the laity are not less sophisticated about property. Rather, they are much *more* sophisticated than the self-styled experts of academia, easily adopting and inventing fluid concepts of multiple and intangible property concepts. Property doctrine and scholarship lag far behind property practice. Grey incorrectly accuses the general public of making a mistake which is more accurately attributed to Waldron—reducing property to the single element of sensuous possession. Yet Grey himself ends up reducing property to a single element—this time the masculine element of intersubjective exchange—precisely because he conflates possession with sensuous grasp.

2. VANDEVELDE'S ANALYSIS   Back in the high and palmy days of Critical Legal Studies, a recent law-school graduate published an ambitious article that cogently presented the common contemporary account— or, as I would argue, misconception—of the differences between the property jurisprudence of the nineteenth and twentieth centuries. In *The New Property of the Nineteenth Century: The Development of the Modern Concept of Property,*[121] Kenneth Vandevelde argued that certain common assumptions of property law are not universal but reflect a paradigm that developed with early capitalism and peaked in the nineteenth century. The nineteenth-century paradigm—exclusive, unitary, objective property expressed through the sensuous grasp of tangible things—was arguably appropriate to the early capitalist economy, according to Vandevelde, but this paradigm began degenerating in the twentieth century, as the capitalist economy became more complex. This demonstrates that in our current "information age" the old paradigm is ripe for replacement with a new paradigm that better explains contemporary property relations.

Unfortunately, the material Vandevelde presents does not support the dichotomy he (like Grey) wishes to set up. Vandevelde insists on a radi-

---

121. Kenneth Vandevelde, *The New Property of the Nineteenth Century: The Development of the Modern Concept of Property,* 29 Buff. L. Rev. 325 (1980).

cal purist version of the nineteenth-century paradigm of property, which he attributes to Blackstone, and contrasts it with an equally radical purist negation, which he attributes to Hohfeld. This is precisely the same move which Grey makes in his article, albeit in lesser detail.

My point is not to criticize Vandevelde or Grey for using abstract, simplified models as tools for analyzing messy empirical reality. Rather, I will argue that their specific models do not serve the purpose for which they were invented. In the name of burying Blackstone and praising Hohfeld, Grey and Vandevelde actually imply that the Blackstonian paradigm is correct and that the Hohfeldian paradigm is not property!

Indeed, neither Hohfeld, Grey, nor Vandevelde can even imagine property other than as an ultra-"Blackstonian" phallic construct. Whereas Grey and Hohfeld present Blackstone as seeing only the object of property, Hohfeld and his progeny see only its subjects. Yet it is the Hohfeldians who are obsessed with the phallic physical object itself; their primary concern is its presence or absence in the discourse of property. In their insistence on denying castration by trying to forget the *Phallic* barrier to intersubjective relations, they not only seek to deny the mediating object—they deny all sophistication to Blackstone.

I do not deny that there has been evolution in the dominant legal conception of property. As I shall discuss below, Blackstone was a man of his time who could not entirely escape the masculine phallic metaphor. What I do argue is that the specific Hohfeldian criticism of Blackstone made by Grey and Vandevelde misses its mark. Moreover, the Hohfeldians have not made the paradigm shift or reconceptualization of property law they claim. At most they identify a crisis within the existing paradigm. The positive masculine phallic paradigm is inadequate precisely because it privileges one element of property—possession conflated with sensuous grasp—over the other two. Consequently, in order to make their argument, the Hohfeldians must repress and deny those aspects of Blackstone's theory that either implicitly or explicitly recognize the intersubjective nature of property. Conversely, they repeat Hohfeld's confusion as to the objective aspect of property rights. In an attempt to avoid the phallic metaphor, they privilege one masculine element of property—in this case alienation in the form of intersubjective relations—and repress the others. And, as any student of psychoanalysis knows, "repression and the return of the repressed are one and the same thing."[122]

122. Lacan, Seminar II, *supra* note 2, at 46.

a. The Hohfeldian Attribution of the Phallic *Metaphor to Blackstone.* The contrast Vandevelde sets up is as follows: "At the beginning of the nineteenth century, property was ideally defined as absolute dominion over things."[123] Vandevelde calls this the absolutist and physicalist conception of property and names Blackstone as its spokesman.[124] This conceptualization became more and more unworkable throughout the nineteenth century as more and more intangible assets became subject to the property-law regime and as more and more exceptions to the absolutist nature of property rights were recognized. Finally, in the early twentieth century, Hohfeld created a new vocabulary to describe the new property interest: "This new property was defined as a set of legal relations among persons. Property was no longer defined as dominion over things. Moreover, property was no longer absolute, but limited, with the meaning of the term varying from case to case."[125] This disaggregation of property, according to Vandevelde, threatens to undermine the traditional legal regime:

> Once property was reconceived to include potentially any valuable interest, there was no logical stopping point. Property could include all legal relations. . . .
> Such an explosion of the concept of property threatened to render the term absolutely meaningless in two ways. First, if property included all legal relations, then it could no longer serve to distinguish one set of legal relations from another. It would lose its meaning as a category of law. Second, the greater the variety of interests that were protected as property, the more difficult it would be to assert that all property should be protected to the same degree.[126]

At first blush, there seems to be great power in this argument. Unfortunately, it rests on a misreading of Blackstone.

Vandevelde, following Grey, quotes Blackstone's well-known definition of property as "that sole and despotic dominion which one man claims and exercises over the external things of the world, in total exclusion of the right of any other individual in the universe."[127] According to Vandevelde, "Blackstone's definition contained essentially two elements: (1) The physicalist conception of property that required some 'external thing' to serve as the object of property rights, and (2) the absolutist concep-

---

123. Vandevelde, *supra* note 121, at 328.
124. *See id.* at 329.
125. *Id.* at 330.
126. *Id.* at 362.
127. 2 Blackstone's Commentaries, *supra* note 34, at 2, cited in Vandevelde, *supra* note 121, at 331 *and* Grey, *supra* note 109, at 73.

tion which gave the owner 'sole and despotic dominion' over the thing."[128] Vandevelde, of course, considers this to be a notion of "property" as physical custody of a thing, with "thing" meaning "tangible thing"—property as possession, and possession as sensuous grasp. But Blackstone's own language, standing on its own, does not support this analysis.

First, Blackstone's definition of property emphasizes its intersubjective nature in addition to its objective nature. That is, he does not, as Vandevelde suggests, present property as an immediate, binary subject-object relation. Blackstone not only is aware but expressly states that the concept of dominion can only be understood as the right of one individual in relation to other individuals. Blackstone recognizes property as objective, not only in the sense of relating to an object but also in the sense of being generally enforceable against the relevant community of legal subjects.[129] That is, Blackstone does not merely describe property as power over a thing, as Vandevelde suggests. This is reflected in Blackstone's very careful language. He speaks of property as a *claim* to dominion and of the *exercise* of that claim vis-à-vis *any other individual in the universe*. As we shall see, "a claim enforceable against the world" will be precisely Hohfeld's definition of *in rem* (that is, property) rights. Blackstone is scrupulous in his *Commentaries* to refer to "property" only in the sense of the legal right and never in the sense of the object with respect to which the right exists.[130] He speaks of having "a property in" certain things but does not refer to owned objects as "property."

Second, although it is true that Blackstone recognizes that property is objective in that property rights among subjects always relate to an ex-

128. Vandevelde, *supra* note 121, at 331. David Frisch similarly misreads Blackstone: "If the world were inhabited by one person, Blackstone's description of property . . . might make sense." David Frisch, *Remedies as Property: A Different Perspective on Specific Performance Clauses,* 35 Wm. & Mary L. Rev. 1691, 1702 (1994).

129. This is similar, of course, to my argument that property interests must be objectified as a condition of enforceability. Hohfeld similarly recognizes what I have called the "Community Objective" nature of property but does not recognize the "Philosophical Objective" nature. I set forth my taxonomy of objectivity in Jeanne L. Schroeder, *Subject: Object,* 47 U. Miami L. Rev. 1 (1972) [hereinafter Schroeder, *Subject: Object*].

130. Blackstone does occasionally speak of a person's property, but I believe that in each case the context makes it clear that by this he is referring to the person's rights and not to the underlying thing to which the rights relate.

Kennedy criticizes Blackstone for not discussing the ambiguity of property as rights and property as thing. See Kennedy, *supra* note 34, at 318–19. This criticism is anachronistic. The use of "property" to denote the underlying thing was novel at the time Blackstone was writing. Charles Donahue, Jr., *The Future of the Concept of Property Predicted from Its Past, in* Nomos, Property, *supra* note 109, 28, 34. MacPherson gives a similar account of the development of the meaning of the word "property." *See* MacPherson, *supra* note 33, at 6–9.

ternal object, nothing indicates that Blackstone's definition of property is necessarily limited to rights to physical things. He merely speaks of "external things."[131]

Indeed, Blackstone makes it very clear that he uses the word "things" not in the sense of *physical things* but as the objects of property. Such objects are defined in the negative—as that which are not human. Blackstone defines the things that are the objects of property as follows: "The objects of dominion or property are things, as contradistinguished from *persons*. . . . "[132] This is the traditional definition of *object* or *thing* used in philosophical discourse—including the discourse of Blackstone's day. This is, of course, the definition adopted by Hegel a little over fifty years later. An "object" is external to—in the sense of other than—the "subject."[133]

Moreover, Blackstone not only is aware but absolutely insists that "things," as so defined, are not limited to the corporeal and the tangible. As Vandevelde admits, Blackstone divides the class of the types of realty that could serve as the objects of property into "corporeal hereditaments—things which could be detected by the senses, and incorporeal hereditaments—things which existed only 'in contemplation.'"[134] Blackstone expressly tries to wean his readers away from the physicalist notion of the objects of property:

> An incorporeal hereditament is a right issuing out of a thing corporate (whether real or personal) or concerning, or annexed to, or exercisable within, the same. It is not the thing corporate itself, which may consist in lands, houses, jewels, or the like; but something collateral thereto, as a rent issuing out of those lands or houses, or an office relating to those jewels. In short, as the logicians speak, corporeal hereditaments are the substance, which may be always seen, always handled: incorporeal hereditaments are but a sort of accidents, which inhere in and are supported by that substance; and may belong, or not belong to it, without any visible alteration therein. Their existence is merely an idea and abstracted contemplation; though their effects and profits may be frequently objects of our bodily senses. And

131. The title of the second volume of Blackstone's *Commentaries* may seem curious to the contemporary American reader: "The Rights of Things." Obviously, in this context the word "of" is being used in the sense of "concerning" rather than in the sense of "owned by."

132. 2 Blackstone's Commentaries, *supra* note 34, at 16.

133. *See* Schroeder, *Subject: Object, supra* note 129. Nevertheless, Grey and Vandevelde assertorially insist that Blackstone is wrong. Similarly, Frisch ignores Blackstone's express language to the contrary and declares that according to Blackstone's conception of property, "property can only exist in tangible things." Frisch, *supra* note 128, at 1702 n.38.

134. Vandevelde, *supra* note 121, at 331 (footnotes omitted).

indeed, if we would fix a clear notion of an incorporeal hereditament, we must be careful not to confound together the profits produced, and the thing, or hereditament, which produces them. An annuity, for instance, is an incorporeal hereditament: for though the money, which is the fruit or product of this annuity, is doubtless of a corporeal nature, yet the annuity itself, which produces that money, is a thing invisible, has only a mental existence, and cannot be delivered over from hand to hand.[135]

Similarly, the types of personalty that could serve as the objects of property

also [were] divided into two categories: in possession and in action. Chattels personal in possession consisted of actual possession of some thing while chattels personal in action, or choses in action, consisted only of the right to hold the thing in possession at some future time. As Blackstone put it, a chose in action was a "thing rather in potential than in esse."[136]

As I shall point out when I discuss Vandevelde's reading of Hohfeld, Vandevelde—and, as we shall see, Hohfeld—not Blackstone, assumes that the word "thing" means tangible thing. In so doing, he ignores not only Blackstone's own express definition but hundreds of years of Western tradition. As we will see, in making this error, Vandevelde is in good company.

b. The Lacanian Argument for Locating the Phallic *Metaphor in Blackstone.* Vandevelde and Grey grossly misinterpret Blackstone's theory. But to defend Blackstone from the fallacious charges leveled at him by the Hohfeldians is not to assert that his is a postmodern or philosophically adequate account of property. Although Blackstone recognized the intersubjective as well as the objective aspect of property and understood that

135. 2 Blackstone's Commentaries, *supra* note 34, at 20. Blackstone wrote, of course, in a time when money was usually represented by coins. Even the concept of paper money was new. The case of Miller v. Race, 1 Burr. 452, 97 Eng. Rep. 398 (King's Bench, 1758), which established the rule of negotiability by which promissory notes issued by the Bank of England could freely circulate as currency, had only recently been decided when the *Commentaries* were published. Consequently, from the perspective of the late eighteenth century, there was little reason to distinguish the concept of money from the coins that are money's token, so money itself seemed to be a tangible thing.

Today, of course, most money is not represented by any physical token—whether metal or paper. Rather, it consists of unsecured debt obligations of banks to their customers evidenced by entries on the banks' books. Even the expression "book" entry adds an inaccurate tangible aura to the transaction, as most of these records are, in fact, maintained in electronic form. Consequently, from the perspective of the late twentieth century, money seems to epitomize incorporeality.

136. Vandevelde, *supra* note 121, at 332 (footnotes omitted).

the objects of property could not be limited to the tangible, by defining property as the claim to a thing enforceable against others he followed the masculine tendency of reducing property to the single Hegelian element of possession and of repressing the element of enjoyment.

Moreover, Blackstone's treatment of personal property, generally, and intangible property, specifically, is sketchy when compared with his treatment of real property. This reflects the fact that this "branch of the law . . . was, in Blackstone's time, relatively less developed than that of real property. . . . "[137] As A.W.B. Simpson notes, the *Commentaries* "smells of the countryside; the law is the law of the country gentry, not Cheapside. The *Commentaries* reflects the essentially rural character of the high civilization of the eighteenth century."[138] Blackstone does include among the forms of *choses in action* a few of the most important objects of modern intangible property: insurance, copyrights, and debts. But many, or most, of the forms of intangible personal property that constitute a significant proportion of the wealth in contemporary society are "essentially emanations of the urban commercial world of merchants, principally though not exclusively taking the form of offshoots of commercial contract law."[139] They were, therefore, still relatively new and exotic—or perhaps even not yet invented—in Blackstone's time and, therefore, are not discussed.

Finally, Blackstone's discussions of the modern forms of intangible objects of property are hardly satisfactory. Simpson notes in particular that Blackstone's attempt, reflecting the custom of his time, to distinguish intangibles from tangibles as those things that are "recoverable by legal action, as opposed to being in the actual possession of the owner," and his proposition that all intangibles are created by contract seem particularly defective.[140] But even this analysis is inaccurate in that it adopts the phallic metaphor and assumes, like Waldron, that real property is tangible. I have already raised in my discussion of Waldron's theory in section II.A of this chapter how the traditional understanding of estates in land cannot be reduced to the land itself. Moreover, following eighteenth-century taxonomy, Blackstone includes as real property several of the incorporeal hereditaments that are forms of intangible property and might even be considered forms of personal property in contemporary parlance: advowsons, tithes, offices, dignities, some types of franchises, pensions,

137. Simpson, *supra* note 34, at xii.
138. *Id.*
139. *Id.* at xii–xiii.
140. *Id.* at xiii.

and annuities.[141] These discussions are quite well developed but are only of passing interest to the modern commercial lawyer concerned with problems of contemporary forms of intangible property.

In other words, although Blackstone understood as a matter of theory that property rights were not limited to rights concerning those objects that can be seen and sensuously possessed, as a matter of practice he did not derive a convincing account of property rights in modern intangibles. This may have been in part because of one reason offered by Grey and Vandevelde. During the early capitalist era when Blackstone was writing, absolutist, possessory rights in corporeal objects had become relatively more important than divided rights in incorporeal objects, which characterized the previous feudal system of societal organization. Consequently, it may have become analytically convenient to view these newly developed forms of property as the epitome of liberal legal and political rights. Blackstone's vocabulary was sufficient for his time—as shown in his exhaustive discussions of eighteenth-century intangible "real" property. In other words, although the physical, unitary paradigm of property is technically inaccurate, a legal vocabulary which spoke of property as a unitary right may have been adequate to the task of analyzing most eighteenth-century property issues in precisely the same way that the eighteenth-century paradigm of Newtonian physics seemed adequate to describe the macroworld it measured, despite its inaccuracy.

To restate this argument in my Lacanian terminology, whether or not the historic Blackstone recognized that the positive masculine phallic paradigm of property was inaccurate, he did not need (and, perhaps, was unable) to construct an adequate substitute paradigm. Although on one level he recognized that property was a symbolic function, his vocabulary may indicate that he did not totally resist the temptation to collapse the symbolic into the real.

But even this goes too far if it infers from the fact that Blackstone adopted the unitary property vocabulary of his time that Blackstone—or his contemporaries—thereby did not recognize multiple property rights.

3. ATOMS V. MOLECULES Specifically, Vandevelde and Grey accuse Blackstone of adopting a unitary picture of property,[142] as contrasted with the modern "bundle of sticks" approach. This is, once again, not strictly

141. 2 Blackstone's Commentaries, *supra* note 34, at 20–43.

142. Frisch similarly declares that according to Blackstone's conception of property, "all property is absolute." Frisch, *supra* note 128, at 1702 n.38.

accurate. Blackstone does not by any stretch of the imagination argue that ownership always consists of the complete and inviolable rights to possess, use, and alienate the object of the right. Indeed, the common-law concept of estates in land that Blackstone explicates in excruciating detail is an elaborate system of dividing and limiting these rights. The majority of Blackstone's volume on property concentrates precisely on the myriad ways in which these estates may be transferred and on the different limitations inherent in different property rights.

The difference is that Hohfeldian analysis focuses on the components of property, rather than on the various ways these components combine to form recognizable property interests. In contradistinction, Blackstone's common-law approach concentrates on identifiable combinations of property rights—with each combination given a specific name as a different estate or hereditament—rather than on the constituent components. Therefore, although in the Blackstonian paradigm the owner of each estate has all the unfettered rights, duties, and liabilities of that estate, the various estates themselves contain a wide variety of combinations of rights and liabilities. To put it another way, the Hohfeldian vocabulary describes the atoms of property; the Blackstonian vocabulary describes the molecules formed from these atoms.

This interpretation suggests that the Blackstonian *unitary* approach is neither less sophisticated than nor necessarily inconsistent with the Hohfeldian *disaggregated* approach toward property in theory. It might, however, suggest that application of the two approaches might be likely to lead to different results in practice.

The Hohfeldian atomic analysis might have an advantage in flexibility and creativity in that it highlights the possibility of crafting a seemingly infinite combination of legal rights in response to changing market needs. The Blackstonian molecular approach, highlighting specific, traditional combinations of rights, might not encourage the same degree of experimentation and adaption to changing circumstances. To switch metaphors, Hohfeldian property is made to order; Blackstonian property is off the rack. It might not be possible to alter Blackstonian property to "fit" all legal situations as well as Hohfeldian property could.

Duncan Kennedy has identified another related disadvantage of what I call the Blackstonian approach.[143] The identification of molecules of property, rather than atoms, can make the identified molecules look natural or inevitable and thus hide the political choices inherent in any prop-

143. *See* Kennedy, *supra* note 34, at 335–37, 348.

erty regime. Accordingly, the molecular approach can be used as a tool of the status quo.[144]

But Blackstonian property might have relative advantages that could outweigh these disadvantages. Pret-a-porter is considerably cheaper than couture and may fit well, if not perfectly, and look good enough. As I have already suggested, and as I shall explore at greater length below, the Hohfeldian analysis risks losing sight of the necessity of an object of property and the common elements of property, as well as the significance of specific combinations of seemingly disparate property rights. It may, therefore, lack not only intuitive attractiveness but analytical strength when used as a tool for describing existing social and economic institutions and legal practices.

Leaving fashion and returning to chemistry, the Hohfeldian conclusion that property is merely a bundle of sticks and is indistinguishable from other types of legal rights is a non sequitur similar to concluding from the identification of elements either that there are no such things as compounds or that the distinction between different compounds is inessential. It may be technically correct, and analytically useful for some purposes, to recognize that both glucose and petroleum are made of oxygen, carbon, and hydrogen atoms and to understand that new combinations of these atoms could be identified or created. When I bake a cake or drive a car, however, I care little about the similarity and separability of the component atoms and a lot about being able to tell a sugar bowl from a gas tank.

a. Hohfeld's Attempt to Deny the Object. If Grey and Vandevelde do not acknowledge Blackstone's insistence on the intersubjective aspect of property, it may be because they too quickly accept Hohfeld's dismissal of the objective aspect of property rights. They thereby attribute to Blackstone a lack of philosophical sophistication that is more properly ascribed to Hohfeld. According to Vandevelde, one of the distinctions between Blackstone and Hohfeld was

> [w]hether property was the thing or the right over the thing[.] Blackstone had made clear that property could exist only in relation to some thing. Hohfeld rejected even this minimal association with tangible objects, arguing that property could exist whether or not there was any tangible thing to serve as the object of the rights.[145]

144. *See id.* Kennedy reaches this conclusion but does not use my molecular-atomic vocabulary.

145. Vandevelde, *supra* note 121, at 360.

As we have seen, this statement is not just misleading but outright erroneous. Vandevelde assumes that because Blackstone insisted that property rights must relate to an object, Blackstone believed (i) that the object of property must be tangible and (ii) that property rights are not also intersubjective. Vandevelde assertorially denies Blackstonian intangibles through the extraordinary means of denying the existence of intangible *things*. Despite hundreds of years of Western philosophical and jurisprudential understanding to the contrary, Vandevelde denies the possibility of any type of thing except physical things.

> Calling a right a thing did not make it one. Furthermore, if rights were things, then all legal rights could be considered property and Blackstone's fundamental distinction between rights over persons and rights over things was destined to evaporate.[146]

Thus, with a stroke of a key, Vandevelde repeals modern commercial law—large chunks of Articles 3, 4, 5, 7, 8, and 9 of the U.C.C. disappear in a flash![147] He does not recognize that a right can be, and is on a regular basis recognized as, a *thing* and the object of property when it is a right against a third party to a transaction.

That is, if X buys a good from Y on credit, X's obligation to pay Y is called an "account."[148] If we are only concerned with the two-party relationship between X and Y, we call this "contract" rather than "property," even though the account can be analogized as an "object," in the philo-

146. *Id.* at 332.

147. Under the U.C.C., debts can take the form of general intangibles, accounts, chattel paper, instruments, or various types of investment property. Certain other types of intangibles, such as deposit accounts and insurance policies, are recognized but expressly excluded from the U.C.C. Articles 3 and 4 govern certain property issues concerning those debts and other intangible rights which are reified into negotiable instruments; Article 5 governs those which take the form of letters of credit; Article 7 governs those which take the form of documents, and Article 8, those which take the form of investment property. All forms of debt and intangibles (whether or not reified into an instrument, letter of credit, document, or certificate) can be conveyed as property and can serve as collateral for security interests under Article 9 or the common law. Such intangibles are also property of the debtor for the purposes of the Bankruptcy Code. *See* 11 U.S.C. 541(a)(1) (1988). Indeed, bankruptcy law reflects the traditional philosophic and jurisprudential understanding that things are not limited to tangibles but potentially include all external objects. Bankruptcy cases are customarily denominated by the heading "*In re* . . . " This is frequently translated as "in the matter of . . . " But the word *res* is also used in law to designate the object of a property right in the sense of the object in which the property right is asserted. This is because the original Latin word *res* means both "the matter in dispute" and "thing," or what I have been calling the object.

148. U.C.C. § 9-106 (1990).

sophical sense of something external to the two legal subjects. This is because the property aspect adds nothing to the legal analysis of the two-party relationship between X and Y *at this point*.[149] If, however, Y sells the X account to Z, it becomes meaningful to recognize the object nature of the account and to conceptualize the assignment of the account as a transfer of a property interest in an object—that is, the X account—from Y to Z pursuant to personal-property conveyancing principles. Indeed, it is in precisely this sense that Blackstone correctly included debts within the category of choses in action that can serve as the object of personal property. Moreover, it is the approach to debt taken in Article 9 of the U.C.C. This characterization does not, as Vandevelde suggests, break down the distinction between rights over persons—contract—and rights over things—property. Y's contract rights against X to enforce the account remain distinguishable from Y's property rights vis-à-vis Z and the rest of the world to transfer Y's rights in the account to others. Consequently, modern commercial law and economic practice correctly recognize debts as objects of property.[150]

Vandevelde and Grey come by their misconception honestly in that Hohfeld makes a similar conceptual error. Hohfeld may have been a great jurisprude, but he was an indifferent philosopher and no psychoanalyst. In his zeal to emphasize the intersubjective nature of legal rights, he adopted a radically physicalist conception of the object. In his attempt to identify intersubjective relations, he tried to deny that all relations are mediated.

Hohfeld's precise taxonomy of legal rights and liabilities was motivated by two closely related goals: (i) to avoid ambiguity and (ii) to differentiate between "legal relations [and] the physical and mental facts that call such relations into being."[151] One of the areas that he thought particularly exhibited latent ambiguities is the concept of property.[152] He

149. It may be relevant to the philosophical analysis, however. For example, because Hegel wants to distinguish the concepts of abstract personality and objects, he analyzes all contracts as involving property. *See* Hegel, The Philosophy of Right, *supra* note 23, at 71–72.

150. Kennedy criticizes Blackstone's treatment of debt as property in a way that is similar to Vandevelde's criticism of Blackstone. *See* Kennedy, *supra* note 34, at 338–39. Like Vandevelde, Kennedy correctly identifies the contract aspect of the two-party debt relationship, but he fails to see that debt also takes on a property aspect when the obligee's rights against the obligor become the object of a legal relationship or dispute with a third party.

151. Wesley Newcomb Hohfeld, Fundamental Legal Conceptions as Applied in Legal Reasoning 23, 27 (W. Cook ed., 1919). For a particularly useful exegesis on how Hohfeld's taxonomy fits into a specific jurisdictional tradition analyzing the nature of legal rights, see Joseph William Singer, *The Legal Rights Debate in Analytical Jurisprudence from Bentham to Hohfeld*, 1982 Wis. L. Rev. 975 (1982).

152. Hohfeld, *supra* note 151, at 29.

specifically criticized Blackstone's division of hereditaments into the corporeal and the incorporeal.

Since all legal interests are "incorporeal"—consisting, as they do, of more or less limited aggregates of abstract legal relations—such a supposed contrast as that sought to be drawn by Blackstone can but serve to mislead the unwary. The legal interest of the fee simple owner of land and the comparatively limited interest of the owner of a "right-of-way" over such land are alike so far as "incorporeality" is concerned; the true contrast consists, of course, primarily in the fact that the fee simple owner's aggregate of legal relations is far more extensive than the aggregate of the easement owner.[153] Hohfeld's general proposition that all legal relations—including property—are relations among subjects and not relations between a subject and an object seems self-evidently correct today. Unfortunately, he missed the point that property is a relationship between subjects that is mediated through an object. This is because the only way Hohfeld could conceive of objectivity was through the phallic sensuous grasping metaphor. Hohfeld's ostensible rejection of the phallic metaphor was merely a repression and therefore a reflection and reinstatement of tangibility as the only possible way of thinking about the object. Simple negation is restatement. What is repressed in the symbolic always returns in the real.[154]

The Hohfeldian approach seems attractive because at first blush it appears to offer a way of satisfying the insatiable human desire to achieve impossible immediate intersubjective relations. By showing that specific tangible things cannot adequately serve as a mediator between subjects, it seems, for a moment, to disprove the necessity for, and the fact of, mediation. Yet Hegel and Lacan argue that mediation always remains necessary for the creation of subjectivity and intersubjective relations. The inadequacy of the physical (i.e., seemingly real) objects chosen to stand in for the mediating *Phallic* object of desire does not mean that the necessity for mediation disappears. Rather, it makes it all the more necessary.

Hohfeld's denial of the objective mediating aspect of property can be seen in his discussion of the related subject of the distinction between *in personam* and *in rem* rights. First, Hohfeld warns that a simplistic, literal translation of the Latin terms implies that

> if a right *in personam* is simply a right against a person, a right *in rem* must be a right that is not against a person, but against *a thing*. That is, the ex-

153. *Id.* at 30.
154. Lacan, Seminar III, *supra* note 5, at 86.

pression right *in personam,* standing alone, seems to encourage the impression that there must be rights that are *not* against persons. . . . Such a notion of rights *in rem* is, as already intimated, crude and fallacious; and it can but serve as a stumbling-block to clear thinking and exact expression.[155]

So far, so good. At this point, however, Hohfeld makes a move that his argument does not require. He continues:

A man may indeed sustain close and beneficial *physical* relations to a given *physical thing:* he may *physically* control and use such thing, and he may *physically* exclude others from any similar control or enjoyment. But, obviously, such purely *physical* relations could as well exist quite apart from, or occasionally in spite of, the law of organized society: physical relations are wholly distinct from jural relations.[156]

Even now, Hohfeld goes too far. His strong point is that *legal* relations are by definition *social* relations, which only exist between and among subjects. The legal symbolic relationship of property is not identical with the physical relation that exists between an owning subject and an owned object. It does not follow from this, however, that "physical relations are *wholly* distinct from jural relations." The different orders of experience overlap to form a Borromean Knot so that the same object can simultaneously perform functions in more than one order. Jural relations with respect to tangible objects, for instance, govern, among other things, who of a number of rival subjects is entitled to enjoy sensuous relations with the objects.

This physicalist confusion also leads Hohfeld to make the unnecessary assertion that not only are rights *in rem* rights against subjects as opposed to rights against objects, but they are not even rights among subjects *with respect to objects*—or, to put it in Hohfeld's vocabulary, rights "to a thing": limiting *in rem* rights to rights to a thing "would exclude not only many rights *in rem,* or multital rights, relating to *persons,* but also those constituting elements of patent interests, copyright interests, etc."[157] Elsewhere, he writes:

[I]t must now be reasonably clear that the attempt to conceive of a right *in rem* as a right *against a thing* should be abandoned as intrinsically unsound, as thoroughly discredited according to good usage, and, finally, as

---

155. Hohfeld, *supra* note 151, at 75.
156. *Id.*
157. Hohfeld, *supra* note 151, at 78. As I explain below, Hohfeld unsuccessfully proposed that the traditional dichotomy between *in personam* and *in rem* rights be replaced by his new dichotomy of paucital and multital rights.

all too likely to confuse and mislead. It is desirable, next, to emphasize, in more specific and direct form, another important point which has already been incidently noticed: that a right *in rem* is not necessarily one *relating to,* or *concerning* a thing, i.e., a tangible object. Such an assumption, although made by Leake and by many others who have given little or no attention to fundamental legal conceptions, is clearly erroneous.[158]

That is, to Hohfeld the word "thing" can only mean "*tangible* thing." This seems at first blush to contradict his and Vandevelde's contention that Blackstone was wrong to divide hereditaments between the corporeal and the incorporeal because they are in fact all incorporeal. I believe, however, that these passages are merely confusing, not contradictory.

Hohfeld tries to identify the minimum distinguishable elements of property rights. He argues that Blackstone's insistence on distinguishing between tangible and intangible property—that is, hereditaments—is not only unnecessary or irrelevant to scrutiny at the atomic level but actually pernicious insofar as it complicates the analysis. Hohfeld also tries to wean lawyers away from positive masculine phallic metaphor for property as sensuous grasp. As I have argued, the attempt to locate the elements of property through the use of a tangible archetype must be ultimately unsuccessful in that it requires the use of legal fictions that intangible objects constructively have characteristics that they could not possibly have. I also agree that not only in colloquial speech but also in judicial opinions and jurisprudential discussions, many lawyers conflate the word "thing" with physicality, despite a long intellectual history to the contrary.

It does not follow from any of this that property relations between subjects do not relate to an external object.

b. Subjectivity, Objectivity, Intersubjectivity. The word "objectivity" has many different meanings.[159] I have so far generally used it in the sense I have elsewhere termed "Philosophical Objectivity"—that is, the relationship of *subjects* (conscious legal actors) with respect to *objects* (everything else). Another way of defining objectivity is to contrast it with its negative of subjectivity conceived as the viewpoint of a single individual subject; I term this "Individualistic Subjectivity." Consequently, what I have named "Community Objectivity" refers to the intersubjective agreement of a community of subjects. My earlier suggestion that the Hegelian element of possession might better be termed "objectification" reflects the

158. *Id.* at 85.
159. Schroeder, *Subject: Object, supra* note 129.

concepts of both Philosophical Objectivity and Community Objectivity. Possession is objective in that it is the way the abstract subject takes on individuating characteristics by investing its will into objects. It is Community Objective in that in order to serve property's function of recognition, possession must also include the exclusion of others in a way that is recognizable by the relevant community.

Hohfeld himself instinctively recognizes the need to identify an *objective* aspect of property or *in rem* rights to contrast with the subjective aspect of contract or *in personam* rights. To Hohfeld, *in personam* rights are rights that are Individualistically Subjectively enforceable. In Hohfeld's terminology:

> A paucital right, or claim (right *in personam*), is either a unique right residing in a person (or group of persons) and availing against a single person (or single group of persons); or else it is one of a few fundamentally similar, yet separate, rights availing respectively against a few definite persons.[160]

Conversely, *in rem* rights are rights that are Community Objectively enforceable: "A multital right, or claim (right *in rem*), is always *one* of a large class of *fundamentally similar* yet separate rights, actual and potential, residing in a single person (or single group of persons) but availing respectively against persons constituting a very large and indefinite class of people."[161] In other words, a contract right is *in personam* because in most cases I can only enforce the contract against the specific person or persons who are parties to the contract. My property right in my apartment is *in rem* because I have the right to exclude not only specific persons from my apartment but the "whole world."

Notice that despite his denial, Hohfeld has come full circle to Blackstone's definition of property—a right is a property if it is dominion claimed and enforceable *against the world*. In explicating his theory of multital rights, Hohfeld by illustration tries to show that they do not all necessarily involve a thing. He lists five categories of multital rights:

> 1. Multital rights, or claims, relating to a definite *tangible object*. . . . 2. Multital rights (or claims) relating neither to definite tangible object nor to (tangible) person [such as patentee's rights] . . . ; 3. Multital rights, or claims, relating to the holder's *own person* [in the sense of one's body] . . . ;

160. Hohfeld, *supra* note 151, at 72.

161. *Id.* Colloquially, we tend to say that an owner has rights enforceable "against the whole world." This is, of course, not literally true as a legal matter. The expression "whole world" should be considered as an idiomatic expression for Hohfeld's "large and indefinite class."

4. Multital rights residing in a given person and relating to *another* person, e.g., the right of a father that his daughter shall not be seduced, or the right of a husband that harm shall not be inflicted on his wife so as to deprive him of her company and assistance; 5. Multital rights, or claims, not relating directly to either a (tangible) person or a tangible object, e.g., a person's right that another shall not publish a libel of him, or a person's right that another shall not publish his picture,—the so-called "right of privacy" existing in some states, but not in all.[162]

On one level, one could try to argue that all of these are examples of rights with respect to things *if* anything external to the abstract subject (self-consciousness as free will) can potentially serve as the object of property. This includes our bodies (Hohfeld's third example), other persons (Hohfeld's fourth example), and our talents, qualities, and reputation (Hohfeld's fifth example). But even for Hegel, this is only true at the level of Abstract Right and may not be the case in the more developed realms of human relations: morality and ethical life. Moreover, even at the level of Abstract Right, Hegel argues that it is incorrect to analyze our relations to objects that become part of a person's personality in terms of property. Those objects of personality which are necessary for recognizability (the logical goal of property) should be inalienable—that is, not fully subject to the property regime. To Hegel, Hohfeld's fourth category—rights over other persons—cannot be properly analyzed as property because persons are capable of subjectivity and, therefore, cannot rightfully be treated as the objects of property. Similarly, Hohfeld's fifth category—reputation—may or may not come within Hegel's category of objects which become so internalized as personality that they should be inalienable.

In any event, whatever its philosophical integrity, I think that the characterization of all of Hohfeld's examples of multital rights as property has little specific utility in a discussion of American law. Rather, I would argue that Hohfeld's very examples reveal the weakness of his decision to reject the object. He lumps together legal relations which are fundamentally diverse. It also explains why, despite Hohfeld's influence over legal scholarship, his "paucital-multital" terminology has never been adopted and sounds as awkward today as it no doubt sounded in 1918.

The first two examples Hohfeld gives fall under the generally understood rubric of property law. Both of these relate to objects—tangible and intangible. But the last three examples fall under the generally understood rubrics of tort and civil-rights law, although it is both evocative and con-

162. *Id.* at 85.

sistent with my analysis that Hohfeld sees a man's claim to a woman's sexuality (his fourth example, which includes a father's interest in his daughter's virginity and a husband's in his wife's consortium) as indistinguishable from property. As we have seen, Vandevelde accepts Hohfeld's contention that there is no meaningful distinction at face value between property and other rights good against the world, and he concludes that property analysis has, therefore, lost its meaning. Grey also agrees with the Hohfeldian analysis and suggests that, accordingly, property will lose its inspirational role in political theory. Jennifer Nedelsky concludes from a Hohfeldian analysis that property is a myth that cannot fulfill its constitutional function of serving as the barrier between the private realm of individual freedom and oppression from the state.[163] I would argue to the contrary. The fact that Hohfeld cannot distinguish between property and tort suggests more about the weakness of Hohfeld's analysis than it does about the incoherence of property.

Hohfeld asserts more than argues his conclusion that these traditionally disparate areas of law do not differ from each other. As an empirical matter, American legal discourse recognizes a distinction between property and tort. This distinction is so familiar as to seem natural to most Americans. Hohfeld may be correct that both property and tort differ from contract in that the former two are rights against the world and the latter consists of rights against an individual. It does not follow from this, however, that no relevant distinction exists between the concepts of property and tort. This may be true even if the empirical reality of legal practice in property and tort does not display the sharp lines of the theoretical, analytical distinctions, and even if certain rights are hybrids containing elements of both property and tort.[164] Hohfeld at most points out a common element between property and tort, but two things that share a common element are not necessarily the same. In order to make a convincing case that it is not meaningful to distinguish between rights among persons with respect to an external object and other types of rights enforceable generally against the world, one must identify the perceived difference and the function it serves and then argue why this is misleading or useless.[165]

For example, a significant jurisprudential question concerns whether

163. Jennifer Nedelsky, Private Property and the Limits of American Constitutionalism: The Madisonian Framework and Its Legacy 9–10, 224–25, 239, 253–54 (1990).

164. For example, wrongful interference with the property rights of another is the tort of conversion.

165. Of course, at some level of generality, everything is the same, and at some level of specificity, no two things are the same. Legal argument consists in large part in establish-

Hohfeld's third example of multital rights—one's rights vis-à-vis one's body—should be analyzed in terms of property law, tort law, or otherwise. Much of the Law and Economics analysis of tort law is an attempt to reconceptualize tort law in terms of property and contract doctrines. Those who take this point of view to its logical extreme, including Richard Posner, argue that because we have a property right in our bodies, we should be able to buy and sell our body and body parts, as well as our infants.[166] On the other side of the political spectrum, Radin agrees that we have a property right in our bodies, but she comes to the opposite conclusion as to the permissibility of rights of market alienation.[167] To Radin, although the body may be property, market alienability of female sexuality, in the form of either prostitution or surrogate motherhood, should be restricted as destructive of human flourishing. A neo-Hegelian might agree with Radin's policy recommendations on specific issues such as prostitution, but on the grounds that it is a category mistake to analyze body relations in terms of property relations.[168]

4. THE REINSTATEMENT OF "BLACKSTONIAN" PROPERTY Now it should be apparent why I said that the Grey-Vandevelde-Hohfeldian ostensible denial of traditional Blackstonian property is, in fact, a reinscription of it. Their "denial" of Blackstone is, in effect, a "super-Blackstonian" approach that insists more firmly on a physical, unitary concept of property than the historical Blackstone ever did.

---

ing consensus as to the correct level of generality in specific situations: is this case distinguishable from another? If a distinction can be drawn, is it relevant, or is it a distinction that makes no difference?

Penner similarly takes Hohfeld to task for not thoroughly analyzing his categories. It was not sufficient to note, as Hohfeld did, that property rights are enforceable generally and contract specifically. To make this a meaningful analytical distinction, one needs to ask "why" some rights are generally enforceable and others specifically. Penner, like me, concludes that what those categories of rights which are traditionally called "property" have in common is that they concern a thing. Penner, *supra* note 6, at 727–30. Consequently, Penner believes that the bundle-of-sticks approach does not, in fact, get beyond the simplistic "person-thing" analysis. *Id.* at 733.

166. Richard A. Posner, Economic Analysis of Law 151–54 (4th ed. 1992); Richard A. Posner, Sex and Reason 409–17 (1992); Elizabeth M. Landes & Richard A. Posner, *The Economics of the Baby Shortage*, 7 J. Legal Stud. 323, 344 (1978).

167. Margaret Jane Radin, *Market-Inalienability*, 100 Harv. L. Rev. 1849, 1921–36 (1987); Margaret Jane Radin, Reinterpreting Property, 40–43 (1993) [hereinafter Radin, Reinterpreting Property].

168. Munzer comes to a similar conclusion. He believes that property necessarily includes alienability. Consequently, he argues that, although we may have some property rights in our bodies, it is misleading and confusing to analyze all body rights in terms of property. Munzer, *supra* note 60, at 37–58.

The Hohfeldian analysis of property does not, in fact, offer an alternate paradigm to the physicalist, phallic paradigm. It accepts the notion that the only possible definition of property is a unitary notion which privileges possession reduced to the sensuous grasping of physical things. Hohfeld, Grey, and Vandevelde believe that their analysis shows that the unitary, physical paradigm does not adequately describe actual jural relations. They observe anomalies that the paradigm does not explain.

As the theory of sophisticated falsifiability reminds us, we cannot as a psychological or logical matter reject a paradigm merely because we find that it is inconsistent with empirical observations. Rather, it remains as the paradigm until a new paradigm is developed. Vandevelde and Hohfeld are left with the existing paradigm in its purest form, without its protective belt, and argue that it is the only paradigm of property. They recognize that those relations we call property always include an expressly intersubjective element (i.e., alienation in the form of exchange) which cannot be comprehended by an impoverished conception of property as sensuous grasp. Because this paradigm does not accurately describe our empirical legal world, they conclude that no examples of property in fact exist. The definition of property remains, but examples of property form a null set. The old paradigm remains, but it is declared moribund.[169]

Unfortunately for this approach, property as an economic and legal practice continues to flourish. Property concepts have not come crashing down in the face of this arid and acontextual legal argument. As J.E. Penner has so succinctly put it in a recent article, the dominant bundle-of-sticks paradigm championed by Grey "is really no explanatory model at all, but represents the absence of one."[170] The Hohfeldian approach refuses to analyze contemporary property qua property on the grounds that property is dead as an analytical category. The marketplace, however, has proved indifferent to this development.

5. THE SUPPOSED DISAGGREGATION OF PROPERTY IN CONSTITUTIONAL AND PRIVATE LAW   In addition to their analytic argument as to why property should die, Grey and Vandevelde also make an empirical claim that property is in fact in the process of disintegrating. This is based in large part on a consideration of constitutional law

169. Penner arrives at a very similar critique of Grey's theories. "In other words, the bundle of rights picture adopts a Classical view of the meaning of terms, and thus in light of the difficulty of generating a Classical definition holds that 'property' is somehow degenerate or useless." Penner, *supra* note 6, at 769.

170. *Id.* at 714.

and, to a lesser extent, on the history of twentieth-century commercial-law reform.

a. Physicality and the Federalists. In addition to Blackstone, Grey describes the Framers of the U.S. Constitution as holding the so-called traditionalist-lay conception of property as "thing ownership." This relates to Grey's implicit political agenda. He fears that oversolicitousness toward the Takings Clause of the Constitution may hinder progressive legislation. He hopes that, once the definition of property is shown to be meaningless or, at least, unworkable in our modern economy, even originalist Supreme Court Justices will have to adopt an alternate interpretation of the Fifth Amendment more amenable to liberal political goals.

Unfortunately, even a cursory analysis of the theories of the Framers suggests that the vision of property reflected in the language of the Constitution is far more sophisticated than the crude view attributed to them by Grey. Moreover, Grey's proposed disaggregated "bundle of sticks" concept of property, which covertly reinstates the phallic metaphor, actually could lead to a stricter, less progressive reading of the Constitution.

b. The Objects of Property. In her illuminating book *Private Property and the Limits of American Constitutionalism: The Madisonian Framework and Its Legacy*,[171] Jennifer Nedelsky parses the writings of the Federalists in order to explicate their theory of property and the fundamental role it played in their notion of political freedom. She emphasizes, as Grey does, that for the most part, the Federalists thought the concept of property was so self-evident that it did not need defining.[172] Nevertheless, the examples they used of the potential oppression of property rights by an unjust political system provide strong evidence that their concept of property was not limited to the physical thing–sensuous grasping model Grey posits. They spoke of property rights not only in connection with land and the means of production—stock-in-trade, manufacturing plants, and so on—as one would expect in a thing-holding regime. They also spoke of property in moneylending and investment.[173] They were not only concerned with the state's wresting of physical things from their owners' grasp. They were also concerned with more subtle "takings" that destroyed the value of intangible property such as inflationary monetary policies, the

171. Nedelsky, *supra* note 163.
172. *See, e.g., id.* at 36–37.
173. *See, e.g., id.* at 30.

printing of paper money, and bankruptcy legislation.[174] That is, they feared government interference with the rights of enjoyment and alienation as well as possession.

My colleague, John O. McGinnis, who explores the natural-law aspects of the Framers' political theory, goes even further.[175] According to McGinnis, both the Federalists and the anti-Federalists recognized property as the natural right of man.[176] Related to this is the fact that other essential rights necessary for human liberty were justified precisely because they were forms of property rights. For example, James Madison argued for the freedoms of speech and religion on the express ground that each man has a natural property in "his opinions and the free communication of them" and in "the free use of his faculties and free choice of the objects on which to employ them."[177]

In other words, although the Framers of the Constitution were not Hegelians, their writings clearly reflect the Western philosophical tradition which does not limit the potential objects of property to physical objects or property relations to the satisfaction of physical, or real, needs. Rather, the objects of property include everything other than the self. In the words of John Lilly, an eighteenth-century popularizer of Locke, "Every Man . . . hath a Property and Right which the Law allows him to defend his Life, Liberty, and Estate. . . . "[178] And property relations are necessary in order for humans to constitute themselves as subjects who can seek to actualize their freedom. In other words, *property* relates to all that is *proper* to mankind.[179]

c. Conceptual Severance, or "Rights Chopping." The problem that Grey and Vandevelde may really see is not that the disaggregation of property is

174. *See, e.g., id.* at 71–75.

175. *See* John O. McGinnis, *The Partial Republican,* 35 Wm. & Mary L. Rev. 1751 (1994) (reviewing Cass Sunstein, The Partial Constitution (1993)).

176. *Id.* at 1758–66.

177. *Id.* at 1760 (quoting Madison). Munzer asserts that "virtually no one thinks of free speech as a property right." Munzer, *supra* note 60, at 46 (citing Wesley J. Liebeler as an exception to this general rule). Although this is no doubt empirically correct today, it may not have been true in the past.

For a further discussion of the broad way in which property rights were conceived in the eighteenth century, see MacPherson, *supra* note 33, at 7–8.

178. Aylmer, *supra* note 32, at 95 (quoting John Lilly, The Practical Register; or, A General Abridgement of the Law (London, Eliz. Nutt & R. Gosling for T. Ward 1719)).

179. This is reflected in the etymology of the English word "property," which derives from the Latin *proprius,* which means "proper," or "peculiar to a person or thing." 12 The Oxford English Dictionary 639 (2d ed. 1989); D.P. Simpson, Cassell's New Latin Dictionary 482 (1968).

killing property but that it is giving property new life. Disaggregated property, like the dismembered god Osiris, threatens to fill the world with its power.

As other left-leaning critics have lamented, the trend under the Rehnquist Court has not been toward the withering or even the diminution of the traditional view of property—the exclusive rights to possess, enjoy, and alienate objects—but toward its *strengthening*.[180] Moreover, this trend has been abetted, not hindered, by the disaggregation of property.

Margaret Radin has identified a tendency of certain Justices to find that any governmental interference with any one of the many disaggregated rights associated with property may be a "taking."[181] This approach, which Radin critiques under the awkward name "conceptual severance,"[182]

> consists of delineating a property interest consisting of just what the government action has removed from the owner, and then asserting that that particular whole thing has been permanently taken. Thus, this strategy hypothetically or conceptually "severs" from the whole bundle of rights just those strands that are interfered with by the regulation, and then hypothetically or conceptually construes those strands in the aggregate as a separate whole thing.[183]

Believing that short and common Anglo-Saxon words are better than complicated heptasyllabic, Latinate neologisms, I accept a suggestion made by Frank Michelman and call this process "rights chopping."[184] Radin condemns this approach as incorporating a conservative political and jurisprudential philosophy.[185] It puts governmental regulation she deems progressive at risk of being invalidated as unconstitutional under the Takings Clause—precisely the harm which Grey wished to avoid.[186] If one recognizes for constitutional-law purposes that property consists of a bun-

180. Radin, Reinterpreting Property, *supra* note 167, at 123–35.

181. The cases Radin particularly discusses are Loretto v. Teleprompter Manhattan CATV, 458 U.S. 419 (1982); Nollan v. Cal. Coastal Comm'n, 483 U.S. 825 (1987); and First English Evangelical Lutheran Church v. County of L.A., 482 U.S. 304 (1987). *Id.* at 123–30.

182. *Id.* at 127. To be slightly more accurate, Radin does not maintain that Chief Justice Rehnquist has been caught embracing conceptual severance but that he flirts with it in some of his opinions.

183. *Id.* at 127–28.

184. Actually, Michelman calls it "entitlement chopping." Frank Michelman, *Takings 1987*, 99 Colum. L. Rev. 1600, 1601 (1988). But as long as I'm wielding the phallic axe, I'll cut the four-syllable word "entitlement" down to size as well.

185. Radin, Reinterpreting Property, *supra* note 167, at 126–30.

186. *Id.* at 176–78.

dle of severable sticks, it is "an easy slippery slope" to the conclusion that "every regulation of any portion of an owner's 'bundle of sticks' is a taking of the whole of that particular portion considered separately."[187]

Implicitly, she criticizes the Court precisely for adopting a bundle-of-sticks analysis in lieu of a unitary notion of property.[188] In other words, Grey argues that Hohfeld's revelation that property rights are severable and indistinguishable from other legal rights meant that property does not exist. If property is everything, then property is nothing. Radin shows how a libertarian can come to the opposite conclusion. Consequently, as I shall discuss in chapter 3, she rejects the Hohfeldian intersubjective account of property in favor of a radically objective account. I shall return to, and partially defend, rights chopping as inevitable from both an empirical and logical standpoint in chapter 4.

d. Property as the Public-Private Distinction. Grey and other property critics may feel the need to adopt such sharp, either-or, clear, visible, and absolute distinctions between property and nonproperty because they analyze property primarily for the instrumental purposes of public law. It is traditional in legal political and jurisprudential theory to view property as one of the barriers between the individual and the state. In chapter 4, I will argue that the necessity of rights chopping means that it is logically impossible for the institution of property to serve the barrier function assigned to it by the Founders. Nevertheless, the fact that property cannot serve this political function carries no necessary implication for the continued validity of property notions generally.

Most property relations, however, take place in the context of so-called private law—commercial and real-property transactions between legal actors. In the fluid and intersubjective world of the market, fluid and intersubjective notions of property arguably function more, not less, adequately than rigid and absolutist notions. That is probably why they have developed. Thus, one of the problems with contemporary property scholarship may be precisely that we still try to use one concept—property—for at least two very different functions: first, to allow legal actors to re-

187. *Id.* at 129.
188. To date, Radin argues, this risk is more potential than actual. This is because the Court has concentrated primarily on the "exclusive occupation" element of property. *Id.* at 130. She believes, however, that the Court has been moving closer toward the constitutionalization of what she sees as the full, traditional liberal trinity of possession, use, and alienation. It is the constitutionalization of commercial enjoyment and alienation that could have a devastating effect on regulation. *Id.* at 136–37.

late with each other as subjects in the marketplace, and second, to serve as the line between the public and the private. Whether or not property ever successfully fulfilled this dual function in the past, it may no longer be able to do so if the market moment of property requires fluidity and the political moment of property requires rigidity.

In arguing that property law never could bear the full weight of serving as the constitutional public-private boundary between citizen and state, Grey makes another brief, but clever, argument. Grey tries to claim that property died for commercial law purposes and, therefore, is doubly dead for constitutional-law purposes. Property's murder in private law was supposedly the work of the legal realists.

In the next section I shall show that Grey's claim that the legal realists' "bundle of sticks" imagery challenges the phallic metaphor of property as thing ownership is simply incorrect. In fact, the greatest monument to legal realism, the Uniform Commercial Code, adopts an ultraphysicalist, phallic, unitary paradigm of property that out-Blackstones Blackstone.

B. Musings on the Myth that the Uniform Commercial Code Disaggregated and Killed Property

1. THE GATES OF IVORY AND HORN

> *Circumspect Penelope said to him in answer: "My friend, dreams are things hard to interpret, hopeless to puzzle out, and people find that not all of them end in anything. There are two gates through which the insubstantial dreams issue. One pair of gates is made of horn, and one of ivory. Those of the dreams which issue through the gate of sawn ivory, these are deceptive dreams, their message is never accomplished. But those that come into the open through the gates of the polished horn accomplish the truth for any mortal who sees them."*[189]

Private-law doctrinalists, like public-law theorists, tell a myth about the death of property. Grey asserts that these myths are fundamentally the same. They both speak of an evil demon worshiped by our ancestors—unitary physical property—and slain by academic demigods who then bring about a new age of truth and justice. Grey seeks to convince us that the concept of property *should* fade away in constitutional discourse because it has already been killed off in private-

189. Homer, The Odyssey of Homer, 296–97 (Richard Lattimore trans., 1965).

law doctrine. I agree that there are similarities between the two myths but believe that they convey different messages. The account of the death of property turns out to be mythic in the pejorative sense of illusory and misleading. Private law only claims to have killed off unitary physicalist property. The murder of the *Phallic* god is always the prelude to his resurrection.

The creation myth, or "just-so" story, of commercial law doctrine tells how in ancient times our benighted legal ancestors worshiped a metaphysical concept known as "Title." The lionlike Llewellyn and his fellow legal realists fulfilled the prophecies of Hohfeld by killing "Title." They shattered or disaggregated it into a bundle of sticks. Their deeds are enshrined in their holy book—the Uniform Commercial Code.[190]

Specifically, the code drafters declared that the different legal questions

---

190. This myth pervades E. Allan Farnsworth & John Honnold, Cases and Materials on Commercial Law (4th ed. 1985). (The Fifth Edition, which is also edited by Steven L. Harris, Charles W. Mooney, Jr., and Curtis R. Reitz, has dropped some, but not all, of these references.) For example, Farnsworth and Honnold laud the revolutionary nature of the U.C.C.'s "virtual abandonment of 'property' (or 'title') as a vehicle for deciding sales controversies." *Id.* at 480. They quote Williston, who said that this step was "the most objectionable and irreparable feature" of the new Code. *Id.* (quoting Samuel Williston, *The Law of Sales in the Proposed Uniform Commercial Code*, 63 Harv. L. Rev. 561, 569–71 (1950)). Farnsworth and Honnold also praise the drafters for "exorcising 'title' from sales controversies and banishing the 'lien'" in favor of "down-to-earth language." *Id.* at 720.

Notice that in their rush to praise the code drafters, they fail to mention that this replacement of legal terminology with "down-to-earth" language does not exclude using many other words in their technical legal sense as opposed to their familiar colloquial meanings. For example, "purchaser" is given a technical meaning as a transferee in any voluntary transaction, rather than its colloquial meaning as "buyer." See U.C.C. § 1-201(32)–(33) (1987).

Farnsworth and Honnold defend the provisions of U.C.C. § 2-501, which gives a buyer a "special property" in goods identified to a contract:

> The Code (with good reason) discarded the traditional concepts of "property" and "title" as tools for deciding a wide variety of issues . . . . Nevertheless, to cope with problems posed by claims against third persons it seems necessary to follow a line of thought that resembles the "property" concept. Happily, this process is not subject to the vice that led to the rejection of "property" as a general solvent, for we are taking on only one problem at a time—as contrasted with the confused, cross-eyed pre-Code approach of using one general concept for a wide variety of different problems.

Farnsworth & Honnold, *supra* at 718. This statement, unfortunately, begs the question as to what "is" a property interest at all. If, as Hohfeld suggests, a property right is what he calls a multital right—that is, a right against the world—then problems posed by claims against third persons do not resemble property; rather, these claims are property by definition. Conversely, Farnsworth and Honnold seem to be assuming that the issues our legal ancestors decided under the rubric of "property" were a "wide variety of different problems," *id.*, even though the question of property's coherence hinges precisely on whether the differences or similarities of different problems are essential.

supposedly answered by "Title" analysis were just that—different legal questions. These differences had been obscured by the fact that the single term "Title" was used as shorthand for a bundle of separate rights. Common lawyers were idealists who assumed that unity of terminology reflected a unitary essence. The legal realists were nominalists who sought to examine the reality of practice that words obscured. Title, they declared, was a chimera, initially frightening until one realizes that it is an illusion or, in the words of Llewellyn, an "intangible something."[191]

According to Homer, the faithful Penelope learned the hard way that one should not place one's trust in dreams. Those myths (the collective dreams of a people) that originate at the gate of horn present a simplified and idealized image of those ideals which give structure and meaning to a culture. They can, therefore, claim a truth which is beyond literal empirical fact. Most myths, however, come through the gates of ivory and are mere fairy tales, delusions, or outright lies.

A cursory examination may lead one to believe that the U.C.C. creation myth is horny in the Homeric sense. It seems to be an accurate, albeit simplified, account of trends in twentieth-century commercial law. I shall show, however, that the myth of the bundle of sticks is, in fact, merely a lovely, but deceptive, ivory dream. The analysis that the U.C.C. killed or even weakened property is, in fact, a classic "academic" argument, in the pejorative sense of that term. It concentrates on the aesthetics of Hohfeld's admittedly elegant taxonomy and ignores the economic, social, legal, and political practice of property, as well as the language of the U.C.C. itself, and the writings of its chief reporter, Llewellyn.

2. PRACTICAL MEN AND THEIR TANGIBLE THINGS

> *The purpose is to avoid making practical issues between practical men turn upon the location of an intangible something, the passing of which no man can prove by evidence and to substitute for such abstractions proof of words and actions of a tangible character.*[192]

A revisionist view of this history is both less and potentially more earthshaking than the bundle-of-sticks myth. The U.C.C. neither abandoned nor disaggregated property. The U.C.C.'s drafters did

---

191. Karl Llewellyn, Chief Reporter of the U.C.C., called "Title" a "mystical something." Karl N. Llewellyn, Cases and Materials on the Law of Sales 561 (1930) [hereinafter Llewellyn, Sales].

192. U.C.C. § 2-101 cmt. (1962). This comment, probably penned by Llewellyn, bears a family relationship to his scholarly writings:

try to deny title or wish it away, but they also enacted a property concept containing a unity of certain minimal rights. Moreover, and most significantly for the present purposes, the drafters did not even try to replace the common-law phallic paradigm, which identified property with sensuous grasping of *physical* things. They embraced it wholeheartedly. The U.C.C. represses title, and what is repressed in the symbolic always returns in the real.

As the quotation at the head of this section indicates, the legal realists rejected the common-law terminology of "Title" not because it was unitary or objective but precisely because it was insufficiently *tangible*. These self-proclaimed "practical men" found elusive, feminine intangibility to be seductive, but also dangerous because elusive. Intangibility is metaphysical and flaccid. They longed for that determinate masculine firmness which is so hard to achieve and so easy to lose.[193] They demanded that not only goods but also *acts and words* must become tangible. In the legal imaginary of the U.C.C., not only property but the entire symbolic realm of law must be collapsed into the real. Like Odysseus, the drafters heard the Sirens' song, but in order to prevent their own destruction, they bound themselves to the mast of tangibility—binding themselves like a bundle of sticks, turning themselves into fasces. The realists turn out to have been "real-ists."

Thus, on the one hand, my analysis suggests that, rather than a radical escape from the past, the U.C.C. can be seen as a reactionary embrace of its most simplistic, physicalist aspects. As in public law, the adoption of the bundle-of-sticks metaphor in private law is not a challenge to, but a strengthening of, the masculine phallic property paradigm.

3. ARTICLE 2 AS TEXT

a. Evidence for the Disaggregation of Property. To determine whether either the U.C.C. or contemporary commercial legal practice actually adopts such a disaggregated concept of property, we must look at the

---

They want law to deal, they themselves want to deal, with things, with people, with tangibles, with definite tangibles, and observable relations between definite tangibles—not with words alone; when law deals with words, they want the words to represent tangibles which can be got at beneath the words, and observable relations between those tangibles.

Karl N. Llewellyn, *Some Realism About Legal Realism—Responding to Dean Pound,* 44 Harv. L. Rev. 1222, 1223 (1931) [hereinafter Llewellyn, *Realism*].

193. Llewellyn called "Title" in chattel "mythical" or "mystical" and complained that it

language of the U.C.C. itself. The strongest argument for the supposed rejection of title is contained in the opening sentence of U.C.C. § 2-401:

> Each provision of this Article with regard to the rights, obligations and remedies of the seller, the buyer, purchasers or other third parties applies irrespective of title to the goods except where the provision refers to such title.

This ostensible denial of title and freedom of contract also seems to be reflected in the first subsection of U.C.C. § 2-401, which reads in relevant part:

> Any retention or reservation by the seller of the title (property) in goods shipped or delivered to the buyer is limited in effect to a reservation of a security interest.[194]

One might also find evidence of the rejection of traditional notions of "Title" and the disaggregation of property in several of the substantive provisions of Article 2. Consistent with the language of U.C.C. § 2-401, the location of title is irrelevant to the risk-of-loss rules of U.C.C. §§ 2-509 and 2-510 and the good-faith-purchaser rules of U.C.C. § 2-403.

And yet the rest of Part 4 of Article 2, including U.C.C. § 2-401, consists of conveyancing rules which govern when title passes, and when title is "good" or "voidable." Indeed, U.C.C. § 2-106(1) defines "sale"—the very subject matter of Article 2—as "the passing of title from the seller to the buyer for a price" even as it cross-references U.C.C. § 2-401—the U.C.C.'s famous denial of title.

What is going on here? Is property a secret mistress which commercial law publicly repudiates, yet privately embraces?

---

cannot be seen—unlike title in real property, which can be seen in the form of a chain of recording documents. *See* Karl N. Llewellyn, *Through Title to Contract and a Bit Beyond,* 15 N.Y.U. L.Q. Rev. 159, 165 (1939) [hereinafter Llewellyn, *Through Title to Contract*]. He called for a "firm, objective basis for allocating title." *Id.* at 166.

194. This corresponds to U.C.C. § 9-202, which states that "[e]ach provision of [Article 9] with regard to rights, obligations and remedies applies whether title to collateral is in the secured party or in the debtor." Further, U.C.C. § 9-201(37) provides in relevant part that

> "[s]ecurity interest" means an interest in personal property or fixtures which secures payment or performance of an obligation. The retention or reservation of title by a seller of goods notwithstanding shipment or delivery to the buyer (Section 2-401) is limited in effect to a reservation of a "security interest."

b. Article 2's Clandestine Affair with Title. A legal-realist statute is supposed to reflect actual practices rather than legal abstractions. The institution of private property is the sun about which our capitalistic solar system revolves. It would be shocking indeed if the primary legal-realist artifact—the Uniform Commercial Code—denied property on the grounds of any supposed theoretical incoherence.

Just as bumblebees continue to fly in derogation of aerodynamic theory,[195] the continued viability of private property is strong evidence that the so-called Hohfeldian attempt to describe property was not a successful new "revolutionary" paradigm of property but merely another failed attempt to add auxiliaries to the existing degenerating paradigm. Or more accurately, truth is, if not stranger, then more complex, than fiction.

Llewellyn and his fellow code drafters were tremendously influenced by Hohfeld's work. But the myth of the death of property fails to reflect that Hohfeld's project had two distinct and separable parts which I discussed in the immediately preceding section of this chapter. Llewellyn and the realists adopted the better-known part of Hohfeld's project: his taxonomy of jural conceptions or lowest common denominators of legal rights. However, Llewellyn expressly rejected his other part discussed at length in that section: the definition of property without an object. The U.C.C. reflects the traditional "Blackstonian" conceptualization of property as a legal relation among subjects with respect to objects.

First and foremost, U.C.C. Article 2, which governs sales of goods, cannot reject property because the very nature of a sale *presupposes* property rights in a good. Nor can it reject the traditional concept of property as rights with respect to an object because sales transactions, by definition, involve a specific class of objects known as "goods." The conveyance of property in specified goods is the *raison d'être* of sales. A sales transaction is based on the proposition that the seller has some valuable rights in an identifiable good which can be conveyed to a buyer. Unless the prior claimant (i.e., the seller) has an enforceable right of possession (i.e., exclusion) in the good, the subsequent claimant (i.e., the buyer) does not have to buy the good; she could just try to take it. Moreover, a buyer will have little reason to give value to buy a good unless she can be assured that she will obtain security of possession. To induce a buyer to pay for a good, she must obtain the right of enjoyment—i.e., the right to consume, collect, or otherwise use the good.[196] Finally, it is obvious

195. Apparently, aerodynamics has finally capitulated to the bees. Warren E. Leary, *Aerodynamic Secrets of Insect Flight,* N.Y. Times, Dec. 24, 1996, at C1.

that unless the seller has the power of alienation, the sale cannot occur.[197]

4. THE WIT AND WISDOM OF KARL LLEWELLYN Despite this, some of Llewellyn's most stinging vituperatives are launched at title concepts in sales law. Sometimes he railed against "the property"—the British equivalent of the American term "title." He described the drafters of Article 2 (of which he was the most prominent) as having "deemed it imperative to abandon title as the focal point of a sales contract. . . . "[198] But by attacking "title" Llewellyn was not attempting to attack or disaggregate "property" per se. And the fact that Llewellyn referred to that package of "Hohfeldian desirabilities [which] we know together as 'property in specific goods'" does not imply that he believed that property was a random bundle of Hohfeldian sticks. Rather, Llewellyn was trying to rescue property from distortions caused by a specific common-law doctrine known as "Title." For clarity, I shall capitalize the word "Title" when referring to the grandiose common-law sense, to distinguish it from the more modest or "cheerful" use adopted in the U.C.C. In addition, Llewellyn intuitively understood the necessity of distinguishing between the elements of possession (identification of object to subject) and exchange (conveyance).

Llewellyn had two closely related critiques of the common law of "Title." First, by analyzing substantially all sales issues through the loca-

196. This is the case even when the buyer is herself a merchant who does not intend personally to enjoy the good. The exchange value of a good is dependent on obtaining the ability to convey the right of enjoyment to a theoretical ultimate buyer who will purchase the good for its use value.

197. I am using Hohfeldian terminology. Although the seller must have some *power* of alienation, a *right* of alienation is not necessary. For example, U.C.C. § 2-403(2) provides that certain entrustees have the power to sell a good to a buyer in the ordinary course of business even when they do not have such a right. In this book, unless I indicate otherwise, I use the word "right" in the more general sense which can include any and all of the Hohfeldian desirabilities, rather than in the specific Hohfeldian jural correlative which he called a "right" (as opposed to a power, privilege, etc.).

Less obvious, although a right of further alienation in the buyer may not be minimally necessary for a sale to occur, it does encourage sales in that it preserves the exchange value in the hands of the buyer.

198. Karl N. Llewellyn, *Why a Commercial Code?* 22 Tenn. L. Rev. 779, 786–87 (1953) [hereinafter Llewellyn, *Why a Commercial Code?*]. Accordingly, in an early broadside published in the *Harvard Law Review,* Samuel Williston declared that

the Code's departure from the long-established tests for determining title and the consequences of title or lack of it . . . [is] the most objectionable and irreparable feature of the part of the Code relating to sales.

Williston, *supra* note 190, at 570–71.

tion of "Title," the common law had inappropriately allowed contract to be subsumed into property. Second, "Title" analysis reflected an obsolete paradigm of the sales transaction—a premodern agricultural model of a sale as an *event,* as opposed to a modern mercantile model of a sale as a *process.* Llewellyn also had a third, implicit, critique of the common law. He thought that "Title" was *too* obviously symbolic, and not sufficiently physical or real.

a. Differentiating Property from Contract. In Llewellyn's words, "Title-thinking [is] Sales law viewed as property law. . . . "[199] In contradistinction, he characterized his analytical approach as being rooted "in the proposition that the modern law of Sale is a law of contract for future delivery; that the present sale plays little part today in litigation; and that most problems commonly dealt with under the heading of 'title' are obscured rather than clarified by that dealing."[200]

In other words, although sales, by definition, involve the conveyance of property, modern mercantile transactions cannot be reduced to conveyancing. There are aspects of sales relations which are purely contractual in nature—such as terms relating to production specifications, requirements, warranties, credit, transportation, storage, and so on. They should, therefore, be left to the general principle of freedom of contract.

Unfortunately, according to Llewellyn, the common law tended to assume that *all* legal issues relating to sales were property issues and that all property rights could be reduced to possession. This is why he entitled one of his critiques *Through Title to Contract and a Bit Beyond* and began it with the reminder that "[t]he law of Sales, as is well known, is in one

---

199. Llewellyn, *Through Title to Contract, supra* note 193, at 191.

[T]he property concept is repeatedly used by courts as a device to settle various issues which in themselves are contract and not "property" issues: *i.e.,* they are matters which the parties have power to arrange at will by express contractual clauses, if they want to, and think about it.

Llewellyn, Sales, *supra* note 191, at 64.

Llewellyn first developed his critique of the common law in terms of a conflation of the concept of the sale (i.e., the conveyancing of a property interest in a good) and the contract for future sale in his great casebook on sales. *Id.* at xii–xiv. Hegel also makes a distinction between an executory contract and the performance of the contract and compares it to the parallel distinction between property and the possession. In both dyads, the former is potentiality and the latter is its actualization. Hegel, The Philosophy of Right, *supra* note 23, at 108.

200. Llewellyn, Sales, *supra* note 191, at xiv.

phase part of the law of contract, in another phase part of the law of property."[201] The common law of sales repressed contract and subordinated the contract aspects of sales to the property aspect.[202]

> The approach of prevailing Sales doctrine . . . is this: Unless cogent reason be shown to the contrary, the location of Title will govern every point which it can be made to govern.[203]

In other words, Llewellyn denied neither the coherence or unity of the concept of property, generally, nor the property aspects of sales, specifically. But he condemned common-law property analysis for making the grave category mistake of trying to analyze contract issues in terms of property principles. He hoped that he could avoid this error by concentrating on the contract aspects of sales and deemphasizing the property aspects and by developing new language for the analysis of sales.[204]

---

201. Llewellyn, *Through Title to Contract, supra* note 193, at 159.

202. Perhaps out of pure inertia, perhaps because one of the traditionally central problems of the field is whether a given agreement operates at the very instant of its making as a transfer, nobody has yet tried very hard to take the Contract parts of the "field" out of Sales, and to locate them over in Contracts.

Karl N. Llewellyn, *Across Sales on Horseback,* 52 Harv. L. Rev. 725, 728 (1939) [hereinafter Llewellyn, *Across Sales on Horseback*].

Oddly enough, Llewellyn argued against moving contract law out of sales entirely so that the contract of sales would be analyzed under the general law of contract. He thought it was analytically necessary for there to be a separate law of sales, but wanted the contract aspects of the law of sales to be analyzed in terms of contract concepts rather than property concepts. This concern with identifying separate identifiable "fields" of law seems strangely archaic today. Nevertheless, it is reflected in Article 2 of the U.C.C., which governs contracts only insofar as they relate to the sales of goods.

203. Llewellyn, *Through Title to Contract, supra* note 193, at 169.

204. Llewellyn hoped to encourage a latent, but faltering, trend in early-twentieth-century judicial reasoning. Llewellyn acknowledges that new sales concepts were emerging in his day but thought that "the process is as groping and uncertain as it is stubborn; and . . . is often obscured, still more often hindered or twisted, by the traditional language used in discussing the situations." Llewellyn, Sales, *supra* note 191, at 562. This is related to Llewellyn's second critique of the obsolete imagery reflected in the common law.

> To get along without the title concept, to get along without learning to use it, reason with it, argue from it, is impossible. But to accept it blindly as the basis of all sales discussion . . . is to lose perspective on modern developments, to cripple one's drafting technique and to load one's self up with a baggage of useless confusion. The courts have spent a century struggling through to recognition of issue after issue as severable from title. Surely the student should start with such clarity as is available today; not shackle his thinking with the very over-generalization from which the law is working free.

Id. at xiv–xv.

b. The Common-Law Sales Paradigm.

(1) Horsing Around with Karl.

> *Anyway . . . after much screaming and yelling and horsing around, . . . we had a Uniform Revised Sales Act.*[205]

Llewellyn's other related critique of the common law of sales was that it did not and could not deal with modern commercial transactions because its underlying imagery was obsolete. According to Llewellyn, the legal analyst is informed by "his problems, his illustrations, the tacit and often unconscious fact-pictures against which he tests the meaning and bearing of words, the whole stock of implicit orientations to solution which are the life of active work with law. . . ."[206] For there to be a significant change in the law it is necessary for "the facts and their connotations of practice, need and context [to be] effectively iterative, cumulated without interruption, . . . so clustered as to become moderately familiar to the run of relevant lawyers."[207] This is because "[o]ur fields of law, our patterns of legal thinking, our legal concepts, have grown up each one around some 'type' of occurrence or transaction, *felt* as a typical something, *seen* in due course as a legally significant type, and, as a type-picture, made a standard and a norm for judging."[208]

To translate Llewellyn's point into Kuhnian-Lakotosian language, Llewellyn thought that law is governed by specific, implicit images of the typical transaction which are shared by the legal community—a paradigm.[209] Under the theory of sophisticated falsification as developed by Imre Lakatos,[210] paradigm shifts do not occur merely because the community observes inconsistent empirical evidence which falsifies the original hypothesis. Rather, the community formulates an "auxiliary" hy-

205. So Soia Mentschikoff described the process of drafting the U.C.C. under the supervision of her husband, Karl Llewellyn. Soia Mentschikoff, *Reflections of a Drafter,* 43 Ohio St. L.J 537, 538 (1982). Apparently, equine metaphors were popular in the Mentschikoff-Llewellyn household. She uses this expression at least three times in her short reminiscence.

206. Karl N. Llewellyn, *The First Struggle to Unhorse Sales,* 52 Harv. L. Rev. 873, 874 (1939) [hereinafter Llewellyn, *The Struggle to Unhorse Sales*].

207. *Id.* at 875.

208. *Id.* at 880.

209. Needless to say, Llewellyn was writing more than thirty years prior to the publication of Kuhn's seminal work and could not have been influenced by Kuhn's theory. Nevertheless, I believe one can find certain similarities between Llewellyn's and Kuhn's ideas.

210. Lakatos preferred the more modest "research programme" to Kuhn's "paradigm." Imre Lakatos, *Falsification and the Methodology of Scientific Research Programmes, in* Criticism

pothesis to explain away the apparent anomaly. Paradigms eventually degenerate when they become so encrusted with "protective belts" of auxiliaries that they begin to explain less and less as more and more empirical evidence is explained away as exceptions which prove the rule. Although degenerative paradigms are ripe to be overthrown, this cannot occur until a revolutionary paradigm is devised.

Llewellyn posits that significant changes in the law only occur when a new image (paradigm) of the typical transaction becomes dominant in the profession. The early-twentieth-century paradigm of sales was what Llewellyn called a "farmer's transaction."[211]

In the traditional agrarian economy, an individual seller sells a readily identifiable and unique good to an individual buyer whom he already knows, in an isolated face-to-face cash transaction, probably for the buyer's personal consumption or use.[212] The quintessential "good" in this picture was a horse.[213]

In this archetypal sale of a horse between farmers, property rules are very simple.[214] Old MacDonald and Mr. Greenjeans know each other and have a basis to make a judgment on their relative honesty and creditworthiness. MacDonald shows Dobbin to Greenjeans. Greenjeans has ample opportunity to look the horse in the mouth at the MacDonald farm or at a public market established for this purpose and, therefore, has no need for MacDonald to warrant Dobbin's qualities. If Greenjeans decides to buy Dobbin, he will hand cash to MacDonald. MacDonald will take the cash and hand the reins over to Greenjeans, who will then ride Dobbin home. The contract and the conveyance happen simultaneously. The time of the sale and the time of the passing of "Title" are clear. MacDonald had all rights in Dobbin until Greenjeans paid the purchase price, and

---

and the Growth of Knowledge 91 (Imre Lakatos & Alan Musgrave eds., 1970). *See* Jeanne L. Schroeder, *Abduction from the Seraglio: Feminist Methodologies and the Logic of Imagination,* 70 Tex. L. Rev. 109, 168–71 (1991) [hereinafter Schroeder, *Abduction from the Seraglio*].

211. So also of the peculiar problems of case-law in remodelling its concepts and its rules; for by what is an extraordinary series of accidents this branch of our mercantile law took off with farmer's eyes and farmer's tools; and though it has shown something of a farmer's handiness in effective tinkering (albeit with poor equipment) it retains to this day the old-time farmer's unreadiness to follow a leader in his theory as distinct from his practice.

Llewellyn, *Across Sales on Horseback, supra* note 202, at 727.

212. "The picture begins in terms of a community whose trade is only one step removed from barter. . . . " Llewellyn, *Sales, supra* note 191, at 204.

213. Hence the punning names of two of Llewellyn's articles—*Across Sales on Horseback, supra* note 202, and *The Struggle to Unhorse Sales, supra* note 206.

214. Llewellyn, *The Struggle to Unhorse Sales, supra* note 206, at 881–82.

Greenjeans had all rights thereafter. Risk of casualty loss was also perfectly correlated with the sale and therefore seemed to be a function of "Title." If Dobbin was killed in a barn burning the night before the sale, that was MacDonald's problem. If Dobbin fell and broke his leg when Greenjeans rode him home, it was Greenjeans's loss. In the life of a farmer, a sale is an event.[215]

The agricultural imagery of "Title" analysis reflects the solid physical metaphor which imagines that archetypical property relationship is possession reduced to the sensuous grasp of a solid, physical thing. The correlative imagery of a conveyance or transfer of property is the handing over of a solid object from one person to another, such as the passing of a baton from runner to runner in a relay race or the passing of the reins of a horse from farmer to farmer. Such a transfer of a solid thing takes place instantaneously. Accordingly, this imagery reflects the longing for the real. The real is the collapse of all castrating distinctions of time and space into an ideal, immediate uterine unity. The real is, therefore, an event, not a process.

Although this imagery conflates the property right in the thing with the thing-in-itself, this theoretical confusion arguably causes few practical problems in an agricultural economy where most property transactions in fact concerned tangible objects such as horses, when all property interests in the object tended to reside in the person who had actual physical custody of the object, and where conveyances of property tended to be accomplished through transfer of physical custody of the tangible objects.

This premodern agricultural imagery is poorly suited to the commercial reality of twentieth-century mercantilism.[216] Llewellyn was not im-

---

215. This imagery also determined the common law of warranty. In the farmer's transaction, not only do the buyer and seller know each other, the buyer had the chance to inspect a preexisting good before the sale. In such a world, warranties have little place. See, e.g., Llewellyn, Sales, *supra* note 191, at 204.

> [C]ontract, payment, and delivery will be as close to simultaneous as man can make them. And [the Buyer] can then walk away with the chattel—it is his—title has leaped into him. No one saw it leap; but that occasions no confusion. Bargain, payment and delivery have occurred; the deal was single; and it is unambiguously closed.

Id. at 561.

216. And until merchant-to-merchant sales of wares are *seen* as the focus of a particular body of law (*which they already largely are, in fact and in the decisions*) we go on lacking clear, neat doctrine to distinguish from them, where needed, sales *by* nonmerchants, or to distinguish, where needed, sales *to* nonmerchants (the ultimate consumer) from both.

Llewellyn, *The Struggle to Unhorse Sales, supra* note 206, at 879.

plying that the common law was totally blind to the mercantile nature of many sales.[217] His point was that the common law continued to treat the agricultural transaction as the norm upon which exceptional mercantile rules were layered—that is, a protective belt of auxiliary merchant rules was added to the basic agricultural paradigm.[218] In Llewellyn's metaphoric words:

Llewellyn might be seen as trying to complete a development in commercial law which began in the previous century. As explained by Richard Sauer in an elegant article, the controversy concerning adoption of the Bankruptcy Act of 1898 can be seen as a struggle between a traditional agrarian model of commercial relationships—which still characterized the economy of the South—and a "modern" mercantile model—which increasingly characterized the economy of the North. Richard C. Sauer, *Bankruptcy Law and the Maturing of American Capitalism,* 55 Ohio St. L.J. 291 (1994). Sauer's description of the agrarian economic paradigm is strikingly similar to Llewellyn's.

> Farmers have historically regarded property as something tangible to be physically held and used—primarily land and its products—its value deriving from its utility in possession. Naturally, some portion of the farmer's product will be taken to market and become temporarily property in exchange. But this process was seen as little different than straightforward barter between producers, closely circumscribed in time. . . .
>
> To the commercial classes, on the other hand, tangible assets exist for the very purpose of exchange.

Id. at 304–05.

217. Llewellyn briefly traces the development of mercantile law starting from Coke. His point is not that these great judges were unable to develop rules which addressed the unique needs of mercantile transactions, but that they developed them as exceptions to or special circumstances of a law designed for agricultural transactions. Llewellyn, *Across Sales on Horseback, supra* note 202, at 732–46.

218. Since at least the eighteenth century, smart judges would occasionally arrive at decisions which were better adapted to mercantile practice. Yet, because the underlying agricultural paradigm remained in place, these decisions were interpreted as exceptions to the general rule unique to specific and unusual fact situations rather than broadly applicable precedent. Llewellyn, *The Struggle to Unhorse Sales, supra* note 206, at 876.

> The half-analysis made, painful to make, more painful still to carry forward, loses impetus. The courts lapse back into the farmer's simple concept; not every court, but too many courts; not every time, but too many times. The thread of the growth is broken. The job of making merchants' law fit merchants' work must be re-begun.

Id. at 894.

> *Unless* the *stock* intellectual equipment is apt, it takes extra art or intuition to get proper results with it. Whereas *if* the stock intellectual equipment is apt, it takes extra ineptitude to get sad results with it. And the work of the artist, accomplished with poor intellectual equipment, is not clearly intelligible to the inept reader. . . . [I]t does not help him focus issues.

Id. at 876. If the basic paradigm is inapt, good opinions are seen as uncharacteristic and not controlling. "*They do not cumulate into stock equipment* . . . . The getting of such stock equipment is a struggle." *Id.*

The mercantile rules of law—and they are solid—which I have been describing make their way through this like ivy through a wall, live, growing, spreading, finding cranny after cranny. But the wall is still there, it is still in the way.[219]

(2) The Process of Mercantile Sales.

The agricultural imagery sees sale as an event—a single, definitive, unique moment of time at which all aspects of the transfer of "Title" occur. In contradistinction, mercantile imagery sees sale as the process by which ownership rights are conveyed and other legal rights and obligations are created.[220] It concentrates on exchange—the process by which possession changes. Unlike an event, which occurs instantaneously and, therefore, "in no time at all," a process takes place in time. The legal issues which arise during a mercantile sale involve how this process works over time. The agricultural paradigm is inadequate precisely because it does not include a concept of time.[221] The agricultural paradigm is real, but legal relations are symbolic.

219. Llewellyn, *Across Sales on Horseback, supra* note 202, at 736.

220. [In] a credit and industrial economy [o]verseas trade in seaports introduces cargo-lot dealing, and dealing in goods at a distance, before they can be seen. Markets widen with improved transportation—internal water ways, railroads. This means reliance on distant sellers. Middlemen's dealings mean, sometimes, the postponement of inspection; always they mean some ignorance in the seller of the history of the goods. Industrialization grows out of and produces standardization, grading and sizing of lumber, grading and branding of flour or hardware, a certain predictability and reliability of goods. Contracts made by description, or by sample, which is a form of description, or by specification, which is an elaborate description, become the order of the day. Contracts come increasingly to precede production. Sellers begin to build for good will, in wide markets, to feel their standing behind goods to be no hardship, no outrage, no threat to their solvency from a thousand lurking claims, but the mark of business respectability and the road to future profit. The law of seller's obligation *must* change, to suit.

Llewellyn, Sales, *supra* note 191, at 204.
    Elsewhere, Llewellyn illustrates this in detail by following the history of the institution of "factoring" in sales practice and the struggle of sales law to adapt to it. Llewellyn, *The Struggle to Unhorse Sales, supra* note 206, at 883–94. Llewellyn's specific examples are now perhaps only of historic interest since sales practice (and, in large part due to Llewellyn, law) has changed considerably in the last fifty-eight years.

221. Our concern is to observe that we have here *complex structures of certain part-way stages* occurring so frequently between the time when property was just "in the seller" and the time when property is finally just "in the buyer" that we have special and complex rules about the part-way stages as such. Evidently this *"passing"* process can be quite a process. Evidently it is not always a matter of one terrific stroke of the hydraulic press of law: here a fine sheet of steel, "property in the seller"; the Law plunges, rises; lo, a car-body, "property in the buyer"—take it away.

This does not mean property or "Title" analysis is always useless in mercantile paradigm.[222] One can successfully use a paradigm which lacks an account of time to analyze those static legal issues which do not take place over time. But applying common-law "Title" analysis to the property issues which arise *during* a sale begs the question by assuming that the ongoing process to be analyzed—the passing of property—has already been completed: title has passed. A sale is the temporary disruption of "Title."[223]

> The precise situation to which "the property" is the key is *not* suited to the situation of commerce-in-action, the situation in which "the property" is not static but in motion, not in one fist, but in the spread interlocked fingers of at least two different hands; not lumped and obvious with its history a firm key to its location, but scattered and divided, with its history showing only where it is *not* to be at the end.[224]

To give an analogy, suppose I, who live in New York City, wished to visit my in-laws in Irvine, California. Until we invent a teletransporter like the one in *Star Trek,* this trip will not be an event but a process that can take hours or even days, depending on the mode of transportation. If we were to analyze my trip in terms of "Title" concepts which analyze changes as instantaneous events, we would declare that I was either "in New York" or "in California" when certain conditions were met. If, for example, this were analogized as an FOB point of shipment contract, then I would "leave" New York, and "arrive" in California, when I had hailed the cab to the airport. This proposition is so intuitively ludicrous that it is virtually incomprehensible. Obviously, during the trip one can speak meaningfully of my speed, my direction, my estimated time of arrival, and my relative position with respect to my home and my destination. But it is nonsense to say that I am at either location during my journey. Nevertheless, it does roughly describe the problems with the law of "Title" in

---

Llewellyn, *Across Sales on Horseback, supra* note 202, at 730–31.

222. "Title" analysis is perfectly appropriate and useful to a wide variety of issues such as "when (a) there is no question who has the property in the chattels, and when (b) the absence of doubt lies between the obvious man who is concerned and his neighbor who is obviously not." *Id.* at 731.

223. Now this [i.e., title analysis] would be an advisable way to go at it if the Title concept (or other basic integrated concept used) had been tailored to fit the normal course of a *going or suspended situation during its flux or suspension.* But Title was not thus conceived, nor has its environment of buyers and sellers had material effect upon it. It remains, in the Sales field, an alien lump, undigested. It even interferes with the digestive process.

Llewellyn, *Through Title to Contract, supra* note 193, at 169.

224. Llewellyn, *Across Sales on Horseback, supra* note 202, at 732.

the sense of an instantaneous moment in which all rights in property are deemed transferred.

Notice that the obverse side of this is that before and after my journey it is meaningful for me to speak of being in New York or in California. And so, before and after a sales transaction it remains meaningful to speak of one party or another as having "title" in (i.e., in the sense of ownership of) the good. As I shall discuss in the last chapter of this book, in the context of the Takings Clause of the U.S. Constitution the fact that the change from being the owner to not being the owner (when viewed from the position of the seller), or from not being the owner to being the owner (when viewed from the position of the buyer), is gradual does not in itself mean that the concept of property or ownership is incoherent. Rather, in Hegelian terms, having and not having ownership are qualitatively different. Having more and having fewer indices of ownership, however, are quantitatively different. Changes in quantity eventually become changes in quality through sublation. As we shall see, the pragmatic problem for the lawyer and the judge is that it is logically impossible for there to be an exact point at which this change happens.[225]

c. Llewellyn and Hohfeld. Llewellyn frequently used Hohfeld's taxonomy of jural conceptions as an analytic tool. A Hohfeldian analysis can be used to show that traditional "Title" analysis is backward. The common law purported first to locate property and then to allocate its constituent rights. But this is impossible if (as Hohfeld suggested) property can only be identified as the sum of its constituent rights. This means that one must first locate those rights which constitute property, and only when one has assigned all of these to one party can one then identify "title"

---

225. This causes an insuperable problem for a bankruptcy analysis for an important financing device called "securitization." To oversimplify, in a securitization a debtor assigns accounts or other intangibles to a financing party in a transaction similar to that voided in the case of *Benedict v. Ratner.* Under Bankruptcy Code § 541(a)(1), the debtor's estate includes "all legal or equitable interests of the debtor in property as of the commencement of the case." This raises the question as to whether a financer must turn over to the debtor's trustee the assets transferred in a securitization. Most analysts who have studied this issue have presumed that the answer turns on whether or not the securitization was a true sale. They presume that, if the transaction is a true sale, then the assignor no longer has any interest in the assets transferred. In my analysis, this is a red herring because it assumes that a sale is an event. If, instead, a sale is a process, a seller can retain interests in assets for a considerable period of time. *See* David Gray Carlson, *The Dubious Foundations of Securitization* 39 Wm. & Mary L. Rev. (forthcoming 1998).

or ownership (i.e., as the sum of these rights).[226] The implications for sales law is that one can, therefore, locate "title" (ownership) in the seller before the sale, and "title" (ownership) in the buyer after the sale, but it is meaningless to speak of the location of "Title" during the sales process.[227]

But, although Llewellyn was influenced by Hohfeld's taxonomy, he rejected the other half of Hohfeld's analysis which held that property, as a legal relation between subjects, does not also require an external object or *res* which is the subject of these relations. Llewellyn is clear that property relations are "with respect to a particular thing."[228] He maintained that

> [p]roperty rights in non-existing goods are either impossible, or of no importance as long as the goods in question remain non-existent. The problem becomes a real one only when, following yesterday's apparent attempt to create property in non-existing goods, the goods today come into existence and become a subject of dispute.[229]

---

226. Indeed, Llewellyn suggested that despite its protests to the contrary, the common law, in fact, frequently allocated "Title" by reference to the location of its constituents, rather than the other way around.

227. In Llewellyn's words:

> Under [Hohfeld's] view "title" is not the designation of a mystic condition or relation from which observable legal consequences "flow," but is a lump-designation for the conjunction in one person of a large number of particular legal relations with respect to a particular thing. . . . The sum of these and similar legal relations to Hohfeld, *is* title. And only one of such relations is in issue in any dispute between B and S. . . . But where the "ordinary" aggregate of relations is impaired, as where B carries risk (duty to pay, despite destruction) and perhaps (as in installment sales) liberty as against S to use, but has no liberty to destroy or remove without notice, and is without power to give a good title by sale—in such a case the Hohfeld analysis would require some new designation for B's interest and for S's, both as distinct from "full ordinary title." Because a single label for several aggregates of divergent constitution is bound to lead to confusion (by way of ambiguous middle) if major and minor premises of a syllogism use the one label, though referring to different aggregates. Indeed the discrepancy in the aggregates may be precisely in regard to the one legal relation which is in issue.

Llewellyn, Sales, *supra* note 191, at 572. He continues:

> It is clear that Hohfeld's analysis lies at the foundation of the narrow-issue analysis discussed above; such difference as there is, is only one of emphasis, of stressing narrow issues purely (Hohfeld) in terms of the single legal relation concerned, or (above) chiefly in terms of the economic significance of the issue. The Hohfeld approach is almost indispensable to clear statement of a narrow issue in its legal aspects.

Id.

228. *Id.* at 572, 575.

229. *Id.* at 575.

Llewellyn's analysis is enshrined in Article 2, which provides that

> [g]oods must be both existing and identified before any interest in them can pass. Goods which are not both existing and identified are "future" goods. A purported present sale of future goods or of any interest therein, operates as a contract to sell.[230]

In other words, an agreement which purports to transfer goods not yet owned by the seller is a mere contract relationship, and cannot operate as a present conveyance of a property interest until the parties identify a specific *res* to serve as the object of the relationship.[231] Consequently, contrary to Thomas Grey's analysis, property remains a distinct, distinguishable legal category under the U.C.C.

5. TWO EXAMPLES: CONDITIONAL SALES AND RISK OF LOSS

Let us look more closely at two supposed examples of the abandonment of title and the disaggregation of property in Article 2 of the U.C.C.—the treatment of conditional sales and risk of loss.

a. Conditional Sales as Substance over Form. U.C.C. § 2-401(2) states, in effect, that even if a seller and buyer expressly agree that the passage of title in a good which is sold on credit is conditioned upon the buyer's payment in full of the purchase price, the U.C.C will treat the transaction as though title vested in the good to the buyer immediately. The seller will only have a purchase money security interest in the good, subject to the perfection and other requirements of Article 9. This can be read, at first blush, as not merely a rejection or disaggregation of "Title" analysis but an abrogation of freedom of contract. These impressions are inaccurate.

---

230. U.C.C. § 2-105(2).

231. This idea of property as legal relations with respect to an external object or *res* is also included in the requirements of Article 9 and the Bankruptcy Code that a security interest cannot attach until the debtor obtains "rights in the property." U.C.C. § 9-203(1)(c) and Bankruptcy Code § 547(e)(3). It is meaningless to speak of the property right known as a security interest without an object called collateral because the rights conveyed by the debtor to the secured party include precisely the rights to take possession (U.C.C. § 9-503), and realize value by either alienating (the basic remedy under Article 9 is to sell the collateral in a foreclosure sale, U.C.C. §§ 9-504 and 505) or enjoying identifiable collateral. If the collateral consists of a right of payment, the secured party has the alternate remedy of collecting the payment rather than selling the collateral. U.C.C § 9-502. A secured party may also, under some circumstances, exercise the right of strict foreclosure under which it can become the "owner" of the collateral with full rights of possession, enjoyment, and alienation. U.C.C. § 9-505(2).

U.C.C. § 2-401(2) can only be understood in context. U.C.C. § 9-102(1)(a) provides that Article 9 applies "to any transaction (regardless of its form) which is intended to create a security interest in personal property or fixtures. . . . " U.C.C. § 2-401(2) is not, therefore, a rejection of property or freedom of contract per se but merely a restatement of the general U.C.C principle that substance should prevail over form.[232] A self-serving *statement* as to the location of "Title" standing alone should not necessarily determine all property-related issues for all commercial-law purposes. This is a corollary to the proposition which I discussed in section II.B of this chapter that conveyances of property, which affect third-party rights, should be "objectively" recognizable and verifiable by third parties. Among themselves (i.e., contract), the two parties may characterize their relationship according to their private, subjective, idiosyncratic will. But if they wish to bind third parties (property), their actions must be public, objective, and recognized by the community. In other words, if possession (title) must be objectified and if exchange (conveyancing) is the process by which possession is altered, the contract of conveyance should also have a Community Objective aspect.

In contradistinction, common-law "Title" doctrine raised form over substance. The (subjective) declaration of the location of "Title" determined property issues despite, not because of, the allocation of the (objective) substantive rights constituting property. Llewellyn called such

232. As emphasized by Arthur Corbin in an early defense of the then proposed Article 2, the article on sales does not even eschew the term "title." What it did do is avoid using it in the rigid and totemic fashion of the common law. Rather, it reflects a decision that since the word "title" is such a variable term—one that can create an illusion of certainty—the code drafter should use it

> in a cheerful spirit, without fear and without reproach—without fear that others will give it any specific meaning that will cause misunderstanding, and without the reproaches that are sure to follow if he tries to require his readers to accept it with a specific and limited meaning.

Arthur L. Corbin, *The Uniform Commercial Code—Sales, Should It Be Enacted?* 59 Yale L.J. 821, 825 (1950). Consequently,

> no attempt is made to define the term "title". . . : [T]he Code adopt[s] the "cheerful" alternative that is listed above; . . . [it] does not attempt a definition. . . . [The primary difference between Article 2 and the earlier Uniform Sales Act is that] the Code everywhere puts more emphasis upon the operative facts on which stated legal results depend and warns us that those legal results are not determined by such undefined concepts as "title" or "property in the goods." By such emphasis and warning, the attention of both merchant and lawyer are focussed on the vitally important factors and not on the undefined and inoperative concepts.

Id. at 826–27.

declarations of the form of "Title" over the substance of property "paper thunderings."[233]

Formal declarations of "Title" become even more troublesome when one examines the substance of the typical mercantile transaction. During the sales process, "Title" (understood as the totality of all incidences of property) by definition cannot be definitively located because it is a moving target. It cannot, therefore, be fixed through the subjective intent of the contracting parties.[234] This was precisely Llewellyn's criticism of the common law of conditional sales in which

> the papers . . . make clear that it is *not* to be a sale, that "property" is not to pass. Something is to pass: The "buyer" is to get possession, and privileges of user, and come under a solid debt for the price; but "property" he is not to get.[235]

In other words, in a so-called conditional sale the transferee has conditionally acquired significant elements of ownership—the right to immediate physical possession and use. Although the transferee in these transactions may not immediately have the third traditional right of alienation, it is anticipated that she will obtain this right as well upon the payment of the purchase price.[236] Indeed, even when the further alienation of the entire property interest in the collateral by the buyer-debtor is wrongful under the terms of the contract, the debtor always has the *power* to convey her equity in the collateral.[237]

The seller–secured party also has some property rights in the good. In section II.B of this chapter I discussed how a secured party has rights to repossess the good, and to alienate it in a foreclosure sale or to use it through collection or, less often, in strict foreclosure. Since buyer and seller can both be said to have some form of property rights in a conditionally

---

233. Llewellyn, *Across Sales on Horseback, supra* note 202, at 733.

234. "Now when the location of 'the property' in the wares thus gets far enough away from homely fact to need a lawyer to decide about it, but is supposed to be determined by the intentions of parties who are not lawyers, that is not so good." *Id.*

235. *Id.* at 729. He makes a similar analysis of trust receipts and reservation of title.

236. These transactions can, for all their surface strangeness, claim as of right to be included in the law of Sales, because if carried to intended completion and fruition they will result in passage from a seller to a buyer of all those rights and other Hohfeldian desirabilities we know together as "property in specific goods."

Id. at 730.

237. U.C.C § 9-311. Moreover, in some cases she can even convey the secured party's interest in the collateral as well. For example, in some circumstances, a buyer of goods in the ordinary course takes free of the claims of security interests created by his seller. U.C.C. § 9-307(1).

sold good, we cannot say that either party owns the good free and clear—that is, full "Title." Nevertheless, in our legal system, when property rights are divided, we customarily say one party "owns" the property, subject to the rights of the other party. Consequently, we need to make a pragmatic decision as to which of the parties—the conditional seller or the buyer—will be called the "owner."

If property should be "objective," then all transactions structured in the same way should be given the same legal treatment. The drafters of the U.C.C. made a pragmatic decision that the division of the significant incidences of property in a conditional sale is substantially identical with the division in a hypothecation.[238] We are accustomed to call the debtor's present rights in a hypothecation "ownership." These rights consist of the residual value in the collateral after payment of the secured transaction. As a buyer in a conditional sale similarly acquires the residual upon payment of the purchase price, it seems consistent also to call the conditional buyer the "owner."[239]

In contradistinction, the common law allowed the private, subjective intent or opinion of the contracting parties to override the public, objective analysis of the transaction—that is, form governed over substance.

238. In both a conditional sale and a hypothecation, the buyer-debtor's rights of possession and use, and her power of alienation, are immediately exercisable. The seller–secured party's rights are subject to a condition precedent—the buyer's default under the sales contract, or the debtor's default under the secured obligation.

239. I am not arguing that there is any a priori reason why the debtor-buyer need be deemed the "owner." Actual decisions such as when property interests are deemed sufficiently objectively manifest as to be granted legal recognition, or how to allocate property interests, are matters of positive law, not jurisprudence, and can only be decided by practical reasoning rather than strict logic. I believe that in this specific case, the drafters of the U.C.C. made a pragmatic decision that although conditional sales and hypothecations are not identical, their objectively determinable allocation of certain important incidences of property are so similar that they should be given similar legal treatment.

I am also not arguing that property theory demands that at any one time there must be a party designated as the "owner" of the property. It is merely the historically contingent fact in our legal system that we do so. One could imagine alternate approaches when property interests in the same *res* are divided, as in the cases of hypothecations and conditional sales. For example, we could have developed something similar to the common-law estates. Under such an analysis, neither the debtor nor the secured party would be deemed to be the "owner" of the collateral in the sense of being the holder of the equivalent of fee simple absolute, but rather, they would have some limited interest or "estate" in the good. Actually, for some purposes we do so. We sometimes speak of the debtor owning the "equity" in collateral, to distinguish this from ownership free and clear. Similarly, even in states which have traditional mortgages rather than deeds of trust, consumers often colloquially speak of their mortgage bank as "owning" their houses. This reflects an intuitive understanding that a debtor's "ownership" of collateral subject to a security interest is not, substantively, equivalent to fee simple absolute.

This is inconsistent with the competing common-law doctrine of ostensible ownership—property interests which are not open and notorious are constructively fraudulent against creditors.[240]

In other words, the concept of location of "Title" as a matter of subjective intent is inadequate in theory and practice to the lengthy processes of mercantile sales which require property to be determinable by objective evidence. Accordingly, Llewellyn described Article 2's treatment of title as follows:

> [A]n objectively manifested act becomes the title-passing point without regard to the intention of the parties to pass or retain title. Such intention is controlling under present law.[241]

This is why U.C.C. § 2-401 provides that the objective rules of Articles 2 and 9 apply *despite* subjective declarations of the location of "Title" to the contrary.[242]

---

240. Specifically, as Llewellyn noted, such common-law terminology as "trust receipt" and "reservation of title" merely "perfumed what might otherwise have smelt like 'secret lien' or that rat in Denmark: 'secret chattel mortgage on a stock in trade.'" Llewellyn, *Across Sales on Horseback, supra* note 202, at 730. Llewellyn had earlier raised a similar point in his casebook. Llewellyn, Sales, *supra* note 191, at 705. Elsewhere in this casebook, Llewellyn raised the question of form and substance in the opposite case where the form of the contract purports to transfer title to the buyer, but the substantive elements of property remain in the seller:

> We turn now first of all to the more primitive situation where the dicker deals with existing goods, where the parties used language that looks like a present sale, and the question is: whether they have accomplished their apparent purpose. Here, as always, the first question is: Is this a present sale or a contract for sale. Only after that question is settled for the second of these alternatives, does the question arise: what obligation rests on S? And: what is the effect, under the contract, of S's acts of purported performance?

Id. at 574.

If the common-law "Title" analysis is inadequate in those cases where the parties actually subjectively allocate title in a conditional sales contract, it is absurd in those cases where the parties do not actually expressly contract as to the location of title. In this case the courts looked to other aspects of the contract to determine the parties' constructive intent. But this approach often resulted in different determinations of the parties' "intent" based on what questions were asked and which parts of the sales contract were examined.

> And when . . . "the property" bounces around from party to party according to the issue, it begins to look as if "the property in the goods," as an issue-determiner, were in the mercantile cases a farmer far from the dell, and none too well adjusted to the new environment.

Llewellyn, *Across Sales on Horseback, supra* note 202, at 733.
241. Llewellyn, *Why a Commercial Code? supra* note 198, at 787.
242. An earlier version of Official Comment 1 to this section reflected the Llewellynesque reasoning even more clearly than the final version of the comment. It originally read:

b. Risk of Loss and the Movement of the Indicia of Ownership. The risk-of-loss rules of Article 2 are another familiar example of the supposed disaggregation of property. Risk of loss is not one of the three traditional elements of property—unless one masochistically believes risk to be the dark side of enjoyment. Nevertheless, it has traditionally been considered closely related to property because it deals with certain obligations of contract parties with respect to specific objects of property. In the great majority of cases, simple unitary property concepts (i.e., "Title") still determine who bears the loss from casualty to a good—the "owner."[243] This is the farmer's world, where "use and control and possession and risk and power of disposition sit comfortably in the same fist. . . . "[244] In this paradigm, risk of loss passes at the same time as "Title" (in the sense of the totality of ownership) not because risk of loss is related to "Title" per se but because all aspects of the sale—contract as well as conveyance—are consummated simultaneously. What the drafters of Article 2 questioned was whether this simple rule results in an appropriate answer during the ambiguous period when the ownership of the good is *itself* in flux—during the sales process.[245]

This article . . . deals with the issues between seller and buyer in terms of step-by-step performance or nonperformance under the contract for sale and not in terms of whether or not "title" to the goods has passed. Similarly the presence or absence of *externally observable and determinable facts* and not the location of "title," controls the rights of the seller's creditors and of good faith purchasers from either the buyer or the seller.

Quoted in Williston, *supra* note 190, at 568 (emphasis added).

243. Llewellyn makes precisely this point that it does not follow that because the risk of loss normally falls upon the "owner" when ownership is not in dispute or in a state of transition, risk of loss is itself an incidence of property which must follow "Title."

We should know what we meant by saying "owner." We should think in comfort as we can think about two neighboring farmers and their hay stacks. If lightning strikes one stack, it is plain whose is the loss.

Llewellyn, *Across Sales on Horseback, supra* note 202, at 731.

244. *Id.* at 732. For example, if I were to spill a fine burgundy on the couch in my living room, it would be my loss. Why? Because of the truism that I am the owner of both the wine and the couch. You will not have any financial loss, although if you are my guest you might suffer in the sense that you were looking forward to drinking the burgundy which is now seeping into my Chinese rug. But in that case, you suffer because you anticipated that you would soon have a property interest in the wine (the right to enjoy in the form of consumption) as a result of my gift. The U.C.C. approach does not change this simple and intuitive common-law rule when ownership is clearly and definitely located. American law tends to favor the status quo. The law will leave the unfortunate diminution of the value of the coach with me as owner, absent an exceptional rule which would shift the loss (e.g., if I could prove that you were at fault for the spill).

245. A similar question arose recently when the drafters of Article 2A had to consider application of the rule in one common situation when property rights are divided in a good—

Since the elements of property are dispersed during the sales process, contractual statements of the location of "Title" confuse, rather than aid, the analysis of property issues during the transition period. Recognizing that property is temporarily dispersed places us in the position to ask which, if any, incident of property is related to risk of loss. Llewellyn's analysis reveals that during the pendency of the sales process, risk of loss can always be reduced to a pricing term of the sales contract. The cost of the risk (monetized into the cost of insurance) can either be included in the price quoted by the seller (i.e., the seller bears the risk of loss) or be an additional cost charged to the buyer over and above the purchase price (i.e., the buyer bears the risk of loss). Consequently, risk of loss is not an incident of property (conveyancing) at all. It is just another two-party contract term which does not directly affect third-party rights. Its allocation should, therefore, be governed by the U.C.C.'s general principle of freedom of contract. The U.C.C., therefore, merely needs to set forth "default" rules which apply when a contract is silent.

6. THE CONTINUING PRIMACY OF PHYSICALITY IN THE U.C.C.
Nothing we have seen so far about the supposed disaggregation of property by the U.C.C. has involved a rejection of the traditional identification of property with the physical custody or sensuous grasp of tangible things in favor of an adoption of a Hohfeldian notion of property which does not necessarily require an object of the property rights. Even a brief examination of the conveyancing rules of the U.C.C. will show that its property paradigm continues to be imagined as the real relationship of a person with a physical object, not a symbolic relationship among persons.

a. The Primacy of Physical Custody. The basic rule of property conveyancing is that upon a transfer of an object of property, the transferee receives only the transferor's interest.[246] Elsewhere, I have referred to this as a "derivation" rule, because the transferee's rights "derive" from the

---

that is, in leases when one party, the lessor, has title in the goods, the right to use the good in the sense of receiving rents, the right to alienate the good in the sense of selling his ownership, and the right to physically possess the good at the end of the lease term and earlier upon default of the lessee; and the other party, the lessee, is not deemed owner of the good itself, but has the property rights to physically possess and use the goods during the lease term, but conditioned on the payment of rent, and may have the right to alienate his leasehold through assignment or sublease.

246. This general rule is set forth in U.C.C. §§ 2-403(1) (goods), 3-203(b) (instruments), 7-504(1) (documents), and 8-301(1) (investment securities).

transferor's.[247] This is, of course, a corollary of the basic property priority rule of "first in time, first in right." It relates both to the very definition of possession (i.e., the rightful claim to ownership with the power to exclude others) and to the liberal concern for autonomy (the first claimant's property rights cannot be abrogated without her private consent).

Nevertheless, there are many instances in which a transferee can acquire greater rights than her transferor possessed and cut off the property claims of a prior owner or other claimant. I refer to these rules which promote the property element of alienation and the liquidity of the market by favoring certain preferred purchasers, as "negotiability" rules.[248] In most American property regimes,[249] the derivation principle is the default rule. In other words, the first-in-time claimant prevails unless the second-in-time can establish the elements of an appropriate negotiation exception.[250] The availability of the negotiation exception is based in large part, either expressly or implicitly, on physical custody of the object of the property right.[251]

This is self-evident in the case of negotiable instruments and negotiable

247. *See* Schroeder, *Is Article 8 Finally Ready? supra* note 97. This is the terminology adopted by Baird & Jackson in their security interests casebook. Baird & Jackson, Security Interests, *supra* note 41 at 4. The principle is sometimes known as the rule of *nemo dat quod non habet*. E. Allan Farnsworth et al., Commercial Law: Cases and Materials 28 (5th ed. 1993).

248. Once again, this is the Baird & Jackson terminology. Baird & Jackson, Security Interests, *supra* note 41, at 6. Farnsworth et al. refer to this principle as the rule of *possession vaut titre*. Farnsworth et al., *supra* note 247, at 28. The term "negotiability" is also used more narrowly to refer specifically to the regime of negotiable instruments, documents, and certificated securities in which obligations are reified into pieces of paper which must be literally grasped by the prevailing party.

249. Including every article of the U.C.C. other than the 1994 revisions of Article 8.

250. As I discuss in Schroeder, *Is Article 8 Finally Ready? supra* note 97, the 1994 amendments to Article 8 reverse the usual conveyancing regime when the property in question is securities or other investment properties held indirectly through brokers and other securities intermediaries. In what I have called a "super-negotiability" regime, the negotiation principle will, in fact, be the default rule. That is, the second-in-time claimant will prevail over the first-in-time claimant unless the original owner can establish the derivation exception by showing that the second-in-time claimant colluded with the intermediary in violation of the first-in-time claimant's rights. As of the date of this book, not all states have adopted these amendments. The version of Article 8 still in effect in these jurisdictions reflects the traditional structure whereby derivation is the default rule and negotiation the exception.

Of course, the fact that the U.C.C. is generally structured so that the derivation rule is the default rule and the negotiation rule the exception does not mean that as an empirical matter the former is the norm and the latter is rare. For example, the holder-in-due-course negotiation rule of Article 3 probably governs the great majority of conveyances of checks. U.C.C. § 3-306. Moreover, in some cases (such as the priority rule with respect to unperfected security interests) the negotiation "exceptions" all but eat up the derivation "norm."

251. Other typical elements of negotiation rules are some favorable mental state (such as good faith and/or lack of notice) and participation in appropriate market transactions

documents where the intangible claim evidenced by the instrument or document is actually reified into a piece of paper. Consequently the favored claimant who has the right to enforce the rights reified in the paper is actually called the "holder" because she must literally have physical custody of the paper and tender physical custody to the obligor to satisfy the requirements of presentment.[252] These negotiation rules are, obviously, closely related to the doctrine of ostensible ownership discussed at length in section II.B of this chapter which reduced ownership to possession and possession to sensuous grasp.

b. The Physical Metaphor in the Law of Sales. Privileging physical custody seems intuitive in the case of goods. Goods are tangible. Enjoyment of a good typically requires some form of physical custody. Frequently, the sale takes the form of the delivery of physical custody of the good from the seller to the buyer in exchange for payment—as in Llewellyn's farmer's transaction. Consequently, it might initially seem reasonable to relate claims to goods with physical custody of the good. To do so, however,

---

(such as payment of value) and, sometimes, additional formal requirements (such as negotiation by indorsement).

252. A "holder" is defined as someone "in possession" of an instrument or document either in bearer form, or payable to the possessor's order, or with all appropriate indorsements. U.C.C. § 1-201(20). The term "possession" is never defined, but in context it is quite clear that it is intended to mean physical custody by the holder, or her agent. *See* Schroeder, *Legal Surrealism, supra* note 46. Although Article 3 has been amended to permit presentment to "be made by any commercially reasonable means, including an oral, written or electronic communication," U.C.C. § 3-501(b)(1), it still provides that upon demand, the person making presentment must "exhibit the instrument," U.C.C. § 3-501(b)(2). As is common knowledge, our check-clearing system generally requires that written checks be physically transferred to the paying bank.

This is less obvious, but no less true, in the case of the law of investment securities prior to the 1994 Amendments to the U.C.C. As I discuss in exhaustive detail elsewhere (Schroeder, *Is Article 8 Finally Ready? supra* note 97, at 303–12, 323–34), most investors today do not take physical custody of security certificates. Rather, they hold their portfolios indirectly through a chain of financial intermediaries capped by a central depositary who has physical custody of the certificates. Although Article 8 contemplates totally intangible "uncertificated securities," in fact, uncertificated securities are rarely issued by private business entities and are rarely publicly traded. Schroeder & Carlson, *Security Interests in Investment Securities, supra* note 77. Nevertheless, old Article 8 assumed that physical possession of certificates was the norm and analogized not only the complex multitiered indirect-ownership system but the law of uncertificated securities to physical custody through agents and bailees. Schroeder, *Is Article 8 Finally Ready? supra* note 97, at 303–22, 328–49. In contradistinction, the 1994 Amendments to Articles 8 and 9 with respect to investment property are intended to eliminate this long-standing physical metaphor in the law of securities transfer. *Id.* at 329–30, 349–76.

risks confusing the property right in the good with the good itself—the imaginary collapse of the symbolic into the real.

More mundanely, it replicates one of the very problems Llewellyn sought to overcome. It implicitly assumes that a sale is an event. To decide a sales issue by reference to the actual contingent physical location of the good itself, Llewellyn complained, is to beg the question because property disputes in sales revolve around precisely who gets the rights in the goods during the time when property is in flux.

The very fact that we distinguish the "void title" of a custodial thief and the "voidable title" of a custodial scoundrel from the "good title" of a noncustodial owner indicates that the concept of *rightful* possession is significantly different from the contingent fact of actual physical custody.

This distinction can be seen in the conveyancing rules of Article 2. The law of sales reflects the usual regime whereby the derivation is the default rule, and negotiation the exception. An example of a derivation rule is the first sentence of Section 2-403(1), which provides that "a purchaser of goods acquires all title which his transferor had or had power to transfer." There are a number of negotiation exceptions to this rule. Pursuant to the second sentence of Section 2-403(1), a good faith purchaser of goods for value takes good "title from a person with voidable title." Moreover, if one entrusts goods to a merchant in the business of selling goods of that kind, the merchant can sell the goods to a buyer in the ordinary course of business free and clear of the entrustor's claims.[253] Similarly, when a seller (or consignor) delivers goods to a buyer (or consignee) in a transaction which is deemed to be a "sale or return," not only does the buyer-consignee, as an entrustee, have the power to sell the goods free and clear of the seller's interest to a buyer in the ordinary course, but the seller's rights are subject to the rights of the buyer-consignee's creditors.[254]

Article 9 contains a negotiation exception when the first-in-time claimant is a secured party with a perfected security interest in a good, which parallels the negotiation provision of Article 2 governing when the first-in-time claimant is the owner of the good.[255] A buyer in the ordinary

253. U.C.C. § 2-403(2).

254. U.C.C. § 2-326(2). In certain circumstances, U.C.C. § 2-326(3) permits the consignor to protect itself by taking certain actions, such as filing under U.C.C. § 9-114.

255. U.C.C. § 9-307(1). The schema of Article 9 is more complex than that of Article 2 because of the concept of perfection. U.C.C. § 9-201 provides that security agreements are enforceable not only between the debtor and the secured party but against subsequent second-in-time claimants of the collateral. In other words, the rights of subsequent transferees derive from the debtor's rights and are subject to the first-in-time property claims of

course of goods from a merchant in the business of selling goods of that kind can take free of any perfected or unperfected security interests created by the transferring merchant.[256]

All of these rules are formulated on the assumption that the transferor is physically grasping and handing over a tangible thing. The entrustment rule of Article 2 is expressly dependent on physical holding. Entrustment is defined as "any delivery and any acquiescence in retention of possession."[257] (As mentioned before, the U.C.C. uses the term "possession" not in the Hegelian sense but in the limited sense of physical custody by a party individually or through his agent or bailee.) The other Article 2 negotiation rule, permitting holders of "voidable title" to transfer "good title" to good faith purchasers for value, does not so obviously relate to physical custody.[258] The rules of Article 2 which provide when a consignment shall be treated as a "sale or return" are similarly based on physical custody.[259] They apply only "[w]here goods are delivered to a person

the secured party. Despite this, unless a security interest is perfected, the effect of the priority rules of U.C.C. § 9-301 is that the negotiation exception all but eats up the supposed derivation "norm." Perfection returns the derivation rule back to its default position by favoring a first-in-time secured party over second-in-time lien creditors, and many second-in-time secured parties and purchasers.

256. U.C.C. § 9-307(2) also contains a limited exception whereby a consumer buying consumer goods from another consumer takes free of any security interests which have been perfected by a means other than filing (i.e., automatically perfected purchase money security interests in consumer goods).

Under both Articles the transferor has the power, but not the right, to transfer ownership in the goods. What this means is that the original claimant (whether the owner or the secured party) may not replevy or foreclose on the goods "in the hands" of the transferee and has only contract or tort claims against the transferor. Where the first-in-time claimant is a secured party, in addition to this contract right it has a security interest in any proceeds from the sale in the hands of the debtor-transferor. U.C.C. § 9-306(2).

257. U.C.C. § 2-403(3). For example, if you bring your watch into a jewelry store for repair, the jewelry store sells previously owned jewelry, and the jeweler sells your watch to an innocent customer, then you probably can't get your watch back from the customer (although you may have a claim of action against the jeweler for conversion and/or breach of contract).

258. Common-law entrustment doctrine was concerned with one specific form of entrustment—consignments. In a consignment the entrustor surrenders possession in the expectation that a sale will occur, i.e., either the consignor is to sell the entrusted good to a third party as the owner's sales agent, or the consignor herself will buy the good after a tryout period. If a consignee breached the consignment contract by selling the goods in an unauthorized manner, the consignor cannot complain that a sale occurred but can only sue the consignee for breach of contract. For example, the sales agent sells the good at a price less than the one demanded by the consignor, or the consignee who was the consignor's intended purchaser transfers the good to a third party rather than buying it herself.

259. U.C.C. § 2-326(3).

for sale and such person maintains a place of business at which he deals in goods of the kind involved. . . . " Moreover, "goods *held* on sale or return are subject to such claims (i.e., of the buyer-consignee's creditors) while in the buyer's *possession*."[260] Although the provision relating to consignments is a famous example of ambiguous and confusing drafting, I believe that this language envisions that the buyer-consignee have physical custody of the goods and (in the case of true consignments deemed to be a "sale or return") that she actually keep the goods at a specific business premises.

The buyer-in-the-ordinary-course rule of Article 9 obviously parallels the similar rule of Article 2 but does not expressly speak of physical custody. Nevertheless, most commercial lawyers presumed that custody is implicitly required.

This presumption—that the grasper has the power to convey good title—was challenged in the famous case *Tanbro Fabrics Corp. v. Deering Milliken, Inc.*[261] There, Judge Charles Breitel ruled that a buyer of goods took free of a security interest even though neither the seller-debtor nor the buyer had physical custody of the goods in question. Rather, the secured party retained physical custody![262] Nevertheless, the court found that the

---

260. U.C.C. § 2-326(2) (emphasis added).

261. 350 N.E.2d 590 (N.Y. 1976).

262. In this case, the secured party was a producer of unfinished fabrics known as "greige goods." The secured creditor would sell its greige goods to fabric finishers who would further process and resell the fabric. Frequently, as in this case, these sales would be on credit with the seller retaining a purchase money security interest ("pmsi").

The parties stipulated that, since fabric finishers tend not to have storage facilities, it is customary for sellers to store and hold the greige goods on behalf of finishers and deliver them when called for on an as-needed basis. Such were the facts of this case where the first buyer and pmsi debtor left the greige goods with the seller/secured party. After having sold out its entire run of one type of greige goods, the seller–secured party was approached by a second potential buyer. The seller–secured party suggested to this second buyer that the first buyer might be willing to resell some of the greige goods which still sat in the seller–secured party's warehouse. The two buyers eventually entered into the resale agreement recommended by the seller–secured party. Once again, the new buyer stored the greige goods with the secured party. Apparently, the seller–secured party approved of the transaction since, after the sale, it obeyed the delivery instructions from the second buyer. Nevertheless, at the time the first buyer defaulted on its purchase money obligation, some of the greige goods sold to the second buyer remained in the custody of the seller–secured party. When the seller–secured party tried to foreclose on the greige goods, the second buyer claimed to be a buyer in the ordinary course of business who cut off the prior claims of the secured party. The court agreed with the second secured party.

Although Tanbro's primary business was the sale of finished goods, it also resold excess greige goods with enough regularity to be considered a merchant who deals in greige goods. The court also found that this transaction was common in the fabric-finishing business so

buyer qualified for the privileged status of a "buyer in the ordinary course of business" because the parties stipulated that the custody arrangements were customary in this industry.

This case continues to outrage commercial law scholars. Homer Kripke, who had the twin honor of having influenced the drafting of Article 9 as well as having served as a consultant to the losing party in *Tanbro*, started a public dialogue on this case which briefly threatened to become a cottage industry.[263] Kripke argued that the drafters always intended seller custody to be a necessary and inherent element of buying in the ordinary course. Moreover, he maintained that the drafters had also always intended that custodial security interests have a special position because custody has not only publicity value but also policing value. Unfortunately, the language of the U.C.C. does not expressly set forth this rule, nor does the logic of property require it.[264] Kripke suggested that this was because it was thought self-evident that a noncustodial party could not sell property out from under a custodial party.[265]

Kripke's analysis is problematic because it presupposes rather than proves the empirical facts that are supposed to be its basis. To argue that

---

that the buyer was a buyer in the ordinary course of business who took free of the possessory secured party's security interest.

One of the great mysteries of this case is why the court relied on this novel theory rather than holding that this was an authorized disposition within the meaning of U.C.C. § 9-306(2). John Dolan suggested that the manufacturer's salespeople "unwittingly invited the [buyer] to make the very purchase that triggered the dispute." John F. Dolan, *The Uniform Commercial Code and the Concept of Possession in the Marketing and Financing of Goods,* 56 Tex. L. Rev. 1147 (1978). The reported opinion suggests, however, that this invitation may have been regretted after the fact, but hardly unwitting when made. The decision states that the secured party suggested the resale, introduced the reseller to the buyer for the purpose of the resale, not merely knew of, but acknowledged, the sale, and even delivered part of the resold goods to the buyer. *See infra* note 266.

263. *See, e.g.,* Homer Kripke, *Should Section 9-307(1) of the Uniform Commercial Code Apply Against a Secured Party in Possession?* 33 Bus. Law. 153 (1977); Harold F. Birnbaum, *Section 9-307(1) of the Uniform Commercial Code Versus Possessory Security Interest—A Reply to Professor Homer Kripke,* 33 Bus. Law. 2607 (1978); *and* Samuel Gottlieb, *Section 9-307(1) and Tanbro Fabrics: A Further Response,* 33 Bus. Law. 2611 (1978). *See also* the correspondence between Kripke and Judges Braucher and Breitel reproduced in Baird & Jackson, Security Interests, *supra* note 41, at 701–02.

264. The fact that it is not *required* as a logical matter, of course, does not decide the question of whether or not we might wish to adopt such a rule for practical reasons. The American Law Institute and the National Conference of Commissioners for Uniform State Law have appointed a committee to consider amendments to Article 9. One of the issues being discussed is whether or not to continue the *Tanbro* rule or to make physical custody by the debtor-seller an express element in U.C.C. § 9-307(1).

265. Kripke, *supra* note 263, at 153–62.

the requirement of physical custody is implicit in the "ordinary" element of the ordinary-course rule is to presume that sellers ordinarily retain physical custody until sale and that buyers ordinarily take physical custody upon sale. This is an empirical question.

Realist rules are supposed to reflect actual practice, not abstract logical reasoning. In *Tanbro,* the parties stipulated that the procedures followed by the parties were customary in the fabric industry.[266] If, as an empirical matter, it is customary for buyers to resell goods prior to taking custody, then, by definition, the absence of custody is ordinary. Kripke's argument fails because it is based not on what *is, in fact,* ordinary but on what he thinks *should be* ordinary. He would make custody part of the legal definition of "ordinary" even when it is, in fact, "extraordinary." This is not legal realism but legal *sur*realism.

We insist on the real—immediate, physical—nature of property not because of, but despite, empirical evidence to the contrary.[267]

c. Llewellyn's "Real-ism." The primacy of physicality in the U.C.C. reflects Llewellyn's third, unspoken but implicit, complaint about classic "Title" law. It moved the concept of property too far away from the physical. "Title" is too obviously a legal construct—too symbolic. It makes it clear that property is a relationship between people and things which is mediated and artificial. The realists—like us all—longed for immediate, natural re-

266. Teaching in New York City, I have known many students who have been engaged in the "rag" trade before law school. These have included at least one former greige-goods merchant. These students have not only confirmed that the procedures followed in *Tanbro* were customary but also uniformly expressed the opinion that the seller–secured party was the wrongful party who was double-dealing the others. This contradicts Dolan's speculation that the secured party's actions may have been "unwitting."

267. Other exceptions to Article 9's derivation rule for perfected security interests are similarly, either expressly or implicitly, custody-oriented. Security interests in negotiable instruments and documents can only be perfected by physical custody. This is, of course, a subset of the general holder-in-due-course rules and will not be discussed here. More interesting is the super-priority rule for custodial interests in chattel paper.

I say chattel paper is "usually" nonnegotiable because, of course, chattel paper may also consist in part of a negotiable promissory note. For example, if I were to buy a car on credit, I might be required to sign a promissory note evidencing my monetary obligation to pay the purchase price, and a separate security agreement evidencing the grant of the security interest. In the case of consumer sales, FTC Rules might make it a violation of fair trade practices if the seller of the car asked me to sign a negotiable promissory note which did not bear the required legend putting subsequent holders on notice of any defenses I might have against the seller (ensuring that no subsequent holder can become a holder in due course who takes free of such defenses).

Despite this, and despite the usual rule of first-in-time, first-in-right governing rival perfected security interests, purchasers of chattel paper who give new value and take physical

lationships with the real and with each other which preexist our artificial, legal, and symbolic creations. We, therefore, envision imaginary identifications of legal rights with specific tangible objects. To put it another way, I (and Llewellyn) critique "Title" analysis of property as being inadequately "objective." Llewellyn, however, conflated objectivity with tangibility—the "real" with reality.

Llewellyn's "real-ism" is revealed in the following comment to the opening provision of Article 2, to which I have already referred. If not actually penned by Llewellyn, it is a brilliant pastiche of his distinctive writing style.

> The legal consequences are stated as following directly from the contract and action taken under it without resorting to the idea of when property or title passed or was to pass as being the determining factor. The purpose is to avoid making practical issues between practical men turn upon the location of an intangible something, the passing of which no man can prove by evidence and to substitute for such abstractions proof of words and actions of a tangible character.

Llewellyn accused legal academics of turning law "into words—placid, clear-seeming, lifeless, like some old canal. [In contrast, p]ractice rolled on, muddy, turbulent, vigorous. It is now spilling, flooding, into the canal of stagnant words."[268] Traditional academics committed the crime of revealing that law is symbolic. The realists, on the other hand,

> [w]ant law to deal, they themselves want to deal, with things, with people, with tangibles, with *definite* tangibles and *observable* relations between definite tangibles—not with words alone; when law deals with words, they want the words to represent tangibles which can be got at beneath the words, and observable relations between those tangibles.[269]

---

custody of it in the ordinary course of business have priority over two categories of rival security interests: those of secured parties who perfect by filing, but only if the custodial secured party had no knowledge of the interest in the specific piece of paper; and secured parties claiming the interest merely as proceeds of inventory, regardless of knowledge. In the first case, the metaphoric possession by filing is deemed not sufficient to trump actual physical custody. In this case the mere opportunity of the custodian to see the metaphoric possession (i.e., the possibility of seeing the metaphoric possession by searching the records) must be strengthened by actually making the custodian see it, i.e., actual knowledge. The usual way of doing this is for the noncustodial secured party to place a legend on the chattel paper. When the rival secured party tries to take custody, he will actually physically see the other parties' ownership.

268. Llewellyn, *Realism, supra* note 192, at 1222.
269. *Id.* at 1223.

Llewellyn condemns legal constructs (i.e., symbolic objects) with a realist's greatest insult—"an intangible something." That legal ideas can be proved, that they have any existence, that they are objective in a symbolic sense, is denied. Only the physical is deemed to have reality. Even language—the realm of the symbolic itself—must become real. Words must take on a tangible character.[270]

The spirit behind this comment is reflected in Llewellyn's writings. He ridiculed the concept of "Title" as "mythical—or should I say more accurately mystical?"[271] He calls "Title" a "halo."[272] Elsewhere he referred to "Title" as a "mystical something."[273] He thought "Title" was crazy because traditional sales-law issues are, "technically, silly. To a silly issue no sane answer is possible."[274] Why is "Title" supposedly so irrational? Because "[n]obody ever saw a chattel's Title. Its location in Sales cases is not discovered, but created, often *ad hoc.*" "The difficulty is plain. 'Title' cannot be seen. . . . "[275] True property, in contradistinction, is according to Llewellyn something which is "held in one's fist."

Llewellyn argues, in effect, that since title is not corporeal and not visible, it cannot exist. Because title, like all legal, "symbolic" relationships,

270. *See also* Gary Peller, *The Metaphysics of American Law,* 73 Cal. L. Rev. 1151, 1243 (1985) for a discussion of Llewellyn's assumptions concerning the difference between language and reality. Consequently, Dennis Patterson is incorrect in maintaining that Llewellyn was a Wittgensteinian. Dennis M. Patterson, *Good Faith, Lender Liability, and Discretionary Acceleration: Of Llewellyn, Wittgenstein and the Uniform Commercial Code,* 68 Tex. L. Rev. 169 (1989); *and* Dennis M. Patterson, *Wittgenstein and the Code: A Theory of Good Faith Performance Under Article Nine,* 137 U. Pa. L. Rev. 335 (1988).

Llewllyn's approach may be contrasted with Jeremy Bentham's. Although Bentham is famous (or infamous) for identifying reality only with physical existence, in his *Theory of Fictions* he distinguished between "fictitious entities" and "imaginary fabrications." The former includes legal fictions such as contracts or corporations which have a certain type of reality in that they function. The latter includes things like unicorns. Slavoj Žižek, Tarrying with the Negative: Kant, Hegel and the Critique of Ideology 85–88 (1993). Lacan was influenced by Bentham's theory of fictions in the development of his own ideas. In the words of Žižek, "Lacan was fully justified in maintaining that Bentham was the first who realized that truth has the structure of a fiction: The dimension of truth is opened up by the order of discourse which loses its consistency without the support of fictions." *Id.* at 88.

271. Llewellyn, *Through Title to Contract, supra* note 193, at 165.

272. In 1938 Llewellyn described the common-law analysis as an attempt to locate "a mythical . . . essence known as Title, which is hung over the buyer's head, *or* the seller's, like a halo." *Id.* at 165. Twenty-five years later Llewellyn used this earlier quotation approvingly in support of the schema proposed in Article 2. Llewellyn, *Why a Commercial Code? supra* note 198, at 786.

273. Llewellyn, Sales, *supra* note 191, at 561.

274. *Id.* The particular issue discussed by Llewellyn at this juncture is whether the seller can recover the price or only damages when the buyer goes back on his bargain.

275. *Id.* at 562.

does not preexist the law, but is its creature—that is, it is not "real"—Llewellyn denies that it can properly function as legal actuality.

Of course, as Llewellyn realized, the law not only recognizes property concepts but, in the case of real property, imposes a comprehensive regime of title recognition. In explaining the difference between the reality of real-property title and the unreality of chattel title, Llewellyn falls back on the imagery and metaphors of physicality. While title can't be seen "[i]n real-property matters, to be sure [title] is a meaningful concept, because a chain of documents is there for art to construe; it is possible, objectively and definitely, to determine and agree in the great run of cases where title to a disputed piece of land lies."[276]

Llewellyn imagines real-property title as being real in that it is somehow essentially embodied in the visibly recorded chain of title, whereas he imagines common-law chattel "Title" as being essentially intangible. It cannot be captured in its visible evidentiary tokens. This is because it is impracticable to subject all property transactions in chattel to a real-property–type recording regime.[277] He is making two potentially valid points—first, title, as a legal relation, is not the same as the evidentiary tokens we use to identify it, and, second, the early-twentieth-century evidentiary rules for identifying common-law chattel "Title" may have been inadequate to their task as a practical matter. From this Llewellyn draws the non sequitur that chattel title itself is necessarily unreal or incoherent.

Llewellyn is, of course, requiring that property claimants take on the masculine position of the subject who claims to have "it." This position is one of anxiety that this lie will be exposed. Consequently, the masculine subject constantly needs to reassure others (and try to fool himself) that he actually has "it" by identifying an *objet petit a*—an imaginary ob-

---

276. He considers the question as to why title law was unsuccessful with respect to chattel:

> Is there an unambiguous chain of documents which would afford a firm base line? In the common law of trust receipts such a chain has been seen and seized on, but then, repeatedly, with disregard of what the realty lawyer could offer as a tool to help the buyer out, to wit, the full interest of a mortgagor in possession. Elsewhere, as in the statutes requiring the original bill of sale to be indorsed, etc., when second-hand cars are sold, or in the shipment of goods under straight or order bill of lading, we let the chain-of-title evidence run into curious confusion with unseen intangible intention. We do so not, I repeat, in chattel matters, lay hold on a firm objective basis for allocating title when we have one—nor have we consistently utilized or remodeled the available concepts about divided interests.

Llewellyn, *Through Title to Contract, supra* note 193, at 165–66.

277. This is intuitively obvious in the case of ordinary consumer goods such as groceries (although with modern bar-code technology the day of practicability may be dawning).

ject that stands for a place in the real. He grasps the phallic substitute for the *Phallus* in his hand and wields it shouting, "See, here 'it' is!"

d. The Imagery of Destruction and the Bundle of Sticks. Combining Llewellyn's stunning insight that a sale is a process (not an event) with his traditionalist conflation of property with a physical thing in a physical metaphor does have an unfortunate side effect. It leads to the subsidiary metaphor of the bundle of sticks. The imagery of the disaggregation of property conflicts with a concept of unitary property which implicitly, but necessarily, underlies sales law.

The conclusion that a sale is a process which takes place over time implies that during the process feckless "Title" resides in neither the seller nor the buyer. The masculine phallic metaphor requires that "Title" have the firmness of the male member, not the soft elusiveness of the female body. But the identification of property with a hard thing suggests that we should be able to locate property at any given time—a thing is either here or there. The most obvious way of resolving this apparent paradox is to imagine that during the sales process, physical property is broken into pieces. Although each individual piece has location and is passed simultaneously as an event, full "Title" cannot be reassembled until all pieces have passed. This is Llewellyn's imagery. Not only did he speak of traditional property as the sensuous grasp of a single physical thing held in a "fist,"[278] he also contrasted the "modern" approach as imagining property "not in one fist, but in the spread interlocked fingers of at least two different hands; not lumped and obvious . . . but scattered and divided. . . ."[279]

Rather than the fasces being seen as one big axe, it now appears as a bundle of little sticks. A sale can now be imagined as the untying of the bundle and the passage of the little sticks separately, followed by the rebundling of the sticks at the other end. This analysis suggests, however, that there is nothing unique about the bundle—it is at most the label for the conclusion of the sales process, rather than a category of legal analysis. As the bundle starts to look contingent, the sticks take on essential characteristics. The image of the fasces breaks down into the two competing alternatives of the axe and the bundle which we must choose between. The more we look at the sticks as the essential pieces, other images are formed. Llewellyn wanted property to remain hard, but he made it brittle. To ac-

---

278. Llewellyn, *Across Sales on Horseback, supra* note 202, at 732.
279. *Id.*

count for property as a process, the realists did not so much dismantle property, they shattered it. They tied it back together like a bundle, but like Humpty Dumpty, once shattered, it is never really the same again.

Consequently, the imagery implicit in Article 2 suggests the disaggregation or disintegration of property, but it does not do so in the way supposed by Grey et al. Observing that the property paradigm is degenerating is far from saying that property itself is disintegrating. The planets did not fly off into space when the Copernican paradigm of the universe replaced the Ptolemaic, nor again when Einsteinian physics replaced Newtonian.

Llewellyn was correct that the common-law property paradigm was degenerate and ripe to be overthrown. He was incorrect, however, in identifying the basic paradigm of common-law property with its specific manifestation in the agricultural metaphor. Consequently, the substitution of mercantile imagery for agricultural imagery was not a complete paradigm shift, merely a modification of the "protective belt" which surrounds the core paradigm—the phallic metaphor.

IV. THE FASCES: AXE AND BUNDLE OF STICKS

A. Constraints

Many scholars, including not only Grey and Vandevelde but also Singer, Beermann, Balkin, and Kennedy, expressly or implicitly assume that the identification of the separate elements of property means that the elements may be freely combined and recombined in any of an infinite number of combinations and that therefore property has no essence.[280] To use my recurring terminology, they assume from the fact that the fasces can be unbundled into separate sticks that it cannot also be rebundled to serve as an axe.

For example, Jack Balkin argues that Hohfeld's theory of jural correlatives and opposites closely parallels Ferdinand de Saussure's semiotic theory of the arbitrary nature of signification in language. A Hohfeldian legal semiotic, according to Balkin, logically leads to the de-objectification

---

280. *See, e.g.,* Joseph William Singer & Jack M. Beermann, *The Social Origins of Property,* 6 Canadian J.L. & Jurisprudence 217 (1993); J.M. Balkin, *The Hohfeldian Approach to Law and Semiotics,* 44 U. Miami L. Rev. 1119, 1120–26 (1990); Kennedy, *supra* note 34.

of property and the disaggregation of legal concepts into a bundle of sticks that can be freely arranged and rearranged to suit any purpose.[281] But Balkin reveals himself to be a classical liberal sheep in postmodern wolf's clothing.[282] He implicitly presupposes an autonomous subject that creates, and therefore exists outside of, law and language. Law and language are, therefore, merely tools that can be freely changed and manipulated at will.

Lacan's theory is also by necessity a theory of linguistics, because he thought that the subject was always the subject of language. His linguistic theory relies heavily on Saussure.[283] Lacan shows, in contradistinction to Balkin's suggestion, that the logical implications of Saussure's linguistic theory are totally antagonistic to Hohfeld's—and Balkin's— jurisprudential project. The postmodern subject is not an external manipulator of language. Language and the subject are mutually constituting. This means that the subject is not only the subject *of* language. He is also *subject to* language.

Hohfeld's theory is what my colleague Arthur Jacobson calls a "correlating jurisprudence."[284] Such a jurisprudence assumes a closed legal universe in which all possible legal relationships are already captured in a complementary system of rights and obligations. This idea has been accurately conceptualized by Duncan Kennedy and Frank Michelman as a "Law of Conservation of Exposures"[285]—the only way I can increase my rights is by decreasing your rights in an equivalent manner. In contradistinction, the Lacanian-Saussurian system is a noncorrelative one.

In a Lacanian-Saussurian linguistic system, the arbitrary nature of significance means that meaning is always slipping; all language is metaphor and metonymy.[286] Consequently, true correlatives and negations of the type supposedly identified by Hohfeld are impossible or illusory. Such identification is imaginary, whereas signification is symbolic. To Lacan and Saussure, meaning is always a spurious infinity. "Each signifier refers not to any corresponding signified but rather to another signifier

281. Balkin, *supra* note 280, at 1120–26.

282. *See* David Gray Carlson, Derrida's Justice (1994) (unpublished manuscript, on file with author).

283. *See* Jacques Lacan, *The agency of the letter in the unconscious or reason since Freud* [hereinafter Lacan, *The agency of the letter*], *in* Lacan, Écrits, *supra* note 1, at 146, 149–59.

284. Arthur J. Jacobson, *Hegel's Legal Plenum*, 10 Cardozo L. Rev. 877, 881 (1989).

285. Duncan Kennedy & Frank Michelman, *Are Property and Contract Efficient?* 8 Hofstra L. Rev. 711, 759 (1980).

286. Lacan, *The agency of the letter, supra* note 283, at 156–57. Lacan identifies his concepts of metaphor and metonymy with Freud's concepts of "condensation" and "displacement." *Id.* at 160.

in a sequence or 'chain' of signifiers that Lacan describes as being like 'rings of a necklace that is a ring in another necklace made of rings.'"[287] Postmodern thought, as exemplified by Lacanian psychoanalysis, is precisely the denial of fit and complementarity; something is always missing, and something is always spilling over.

For example, although the Feminine is positioned as the negation of the Masculine, this cannot mean that if the Masculine is the positive, then the Feminine is the negative, or that woman is the complement to man. Rather, to Lacan, while the Masculine is the claim to be all, the Feminine is not nothing. She is the not-all (*pas-toute*), as in not all things are *Phallic*.[288] She is the denial of the fictional hegemony of the *Phallus*, which is the very foundation of subjectivity. Woman is not the complement to man, therefore, but a supplement.[289] The *Phallus* is the forever-lost object from which we are castrated—the lack or hole that exists at the core of Lacanian subjectivity and Hegelian totality.[290] There is always something more

287. William J. Richardson, *Lacan and the Subject of Psychoanalysis, in* Interpreting Lacan 51, 54 (Joseph Smith & William Kerrigan eds., 6 Psychiatry and the Humanities, 1983) (quoting Lacan, Écrits).

> The meaning of this chain does not "consist" in any one of these elements but rather "insists" in the whole, where the "whole" may be taken to be the entire interlude as described, whose meaning, or rather whose "effect" of meaning, is discerned retroactively.

Id. at 55.

288. "Her being not all in the phallic function does not mean that she is not in it at all. She is in it not not at all. She is right in it. But there is something more." Lacan, *God and Jouissance, supra* note 1, at 145; see also Rose, *supra* note 1, at 49–50; Žižek, Looking Awry, *supra* note 2, at 44–45.

289. "Note that I said supplementary. Had I said complementary, where would we be!" Lacan, *God and Jouissance, supra* note 1, at 144; *see also* Rose, *supra* note 1, at 51. As so clearly explained by Salecl:

> Lacan thus moves as far as possible from the notion of sexual difference as the relationship of two opposite poles which complement each other, together forming the whole of "Man." "Masculine" and "feminine" are not the two species of the genus Man but rather the two modes of the subject's failure to achieve the full identity of Man. "Man" and "Woman" together do not form a whole, since each of them is already in itself a failed whole.

Salecl, *supra* note 37, at 116.

In his most recent work, Žižek has used the word "complementarity" to describe the relationship of the Lacanian sexes. This is an uncharacteristically unfortunate and idiosyncratic choice of words by a usually eloquent scholar, albeit one for whom English is not his first, or even second, language. Žižek's conception of sexuality totally lacks the type of simple imaginary fit connoted by the word "complementary."

290. The école freudienne, *The phallic phase and the subjective import of the castration complex* [hereinafter the école freudienne, *The phallic phase*], *in* Lacan, Feminine Sexuality, *supra* note 1, at 99, 116–17; Jacques Lacan, *The direction of the treatment and the principles of its*

and something lacking that makes immediate relationship impossible. Mediation is always necessary because it is impossible.

The noncomplementarity of sexuality explains why woman is object of man's fears *and* hopes, Fury as well as Muse, Kali Ma as well as Virgin Mary. The masculine position is "all are subjected to the symbolic order." The Feminine is the denial "not all."[291] She is, therefore, on the one hand, the exposure of the lie of subjectivity and the symbol of universal castration. Woman in this aspect must be suppressed and subordinated. The Masculine tries to deny the freedom of feminine negativity by replacing her with fantasy images of femininity. On the other hand, by denying that all are castrated in the sense of subject to the law as prohibition, the feminine denial is the hope of freedom and the achievement of wholeness. She is the dream that the *Phallus* is not always already lost, but not yet found—that sexual relations are not impossible, merely forbidden. This aspect of the Feminine, like the superego, urges us "Enjoy!"

Moreover, the arbitrariness of significance does not mean that meaning or legal concepts can be freely manipulated. We do not bind ourselves to fixed linguistic and legal concepts *despite* the arbitrariness of signification but just *because* of its arbitrariness and slippage. In Lacan's metaphor, we must quilt together the shifting layers of signifier over signified.[292] Meaning and language, and subjectivity itself, consist precisely of this fiction of static significance. This is, of course, the masculine position of claiming to have "it"—to have captured that which cannot be captured. Consequently, subjectivity is a dialectic concept that is both free in that it is a fiction and bound because it is a fiction. If we change the fiction, we change ourselves. Because Lacanianism denies the naturalness or inevitability not only of the legal regime but of subjectivity itself, it holds out the possibility of the truly radical change of creating alternate sociolinguistic-legal universes. But a new alien species of subject will necessarily inhabit such new universes. The postmodern subject, unlike his liberal modern counterpart, who is at some level autonomous from the legal regime, cannot, therefore, merely "will" changes in the fundamental aspects of the legal and linguistic regime, which is the gender hierarchy. When we quilt

power, in Lacan, Écrits, *supra* note 1, at 265; Jacques Lacan, *The signification of the phallus, in* Lacan, Écrits, *supra* note 1, at 281, 288; Jeanne L. Schroeder & David Gray Carlson, *The Subject Is Nothing,* 5 Law and Critique 94 (1994) (reviewing Žižek, For They Know Not What They Do, *supra* note 1).

291. Lacan, *God and Jouissance, supra* note 1, at 145. *See also* Rose, *supra* note 1, at 49–50.
292. Lacan, Seminar III, *supra* note 5, at 258–70; Žižek, Looking Awry, *supra* note 2, at 44–45.

signification, we sew our very subjectivity. Changes in the symbolic order require a dialectical and simultaneous change in every aspect of our subjectivity and society. The problem for those of us who are both Lacanians and progressives is how to start this chicken-and-egg process in motion. How can we ever sublate masculine subjectivity and feminine objectivity to achieve the not-yet immediacy of sexual relations, without submerging into the deadly unity of the real?

Slavoj Žižek gives a wonderful illustration of the difference between the modern (Hohfeldian-Balkinian) and postmodern (Lacanian-Saussurian) concept of the subject. Near the end of the movie *Blow-Up*,[293] the protagonist passes a group of people miming a game of tennis without a ball. One of the players pretends to hit the ball out of bounds. The protagonist plays along and pretends to retrieve the ball and toss it back into the court. Modernism concludes from the observation that the "game" of society is not inevitable or natural, it has no content; content resides solely in the subject itself. Postmodernism, in contradistinction, does not deny the necessity of the object merely because it is arbitrary. Rather, it shows us the object in all its "indifferent and arbitrary character."[294] In other words, the modern subject is conceived of as autonomous from, and therefore in control of, the game. He not only can change the game or leave the game but does not even need a ball or other external object to play the game. The postmodern subject, however, is not autonomous with respect to the game of law and language. He exists as a subject only insofar as he plays the game. Consequently, there must always be a game and a mediating object of desire.

Thus, insofar as legal concepts serve functions—social, economic, psychic, or philosophical—the combinations of jural elements cannot be random or arbitrary and cannot be freely altered at will. Hegelian philosophic theory, combined with Lacanian psychoanalytic theory, indicates that the possession, enjoyment, and alienation of external objects serve necessary roles in the development of subjectivity in this society. Consequently, it is meaningful and not random for a legal regime to recognize a distinctive category of legal rights called "property" that contains all three of these elements.[295] This does not mean that all legal relationships need be full

293. Blow-Up (Bridge Films 1966).

294. Žižek, Looking Awry, *supra* note 2, at 143. Another example of the modern work of art given by Žižek is *Waiting for Godot,* in which, of course, Godot never arrives. *Id.* at 145. In a postmodern play, Godot is always there, although he may not be what you expected. *Id.*

295. Hegel can identify three elements of property precisely because he speaks at the highest levels of abstraction. A Hegelian would argue that so many discussions of property, including Grey's, wind up concluding that property is incoherent or infinitely variable pre-

property relations. Nor does it mean that all property relations must be absolute; we may want to recognize limitations on any or all of the three general categories of property rights. Indeed, as Hegel himself argued, the logic of the concept of property is both self-limiting—unlimited property rights of different subjects would be mutually inconsistent—and limited by other, more developed concerns of human development, such as morality and ethics.

Nevertheless, the Hegelian-Lacanian approach only defines the parameters of property at the most abstract level and has little or no practical use in prescribing the minutiae of specific property regimes. The specific limitations and applications of the broad and abstract concept of property to meet the needs of any given society are properly to be determined by practical reasoning and adopted into positive law—precisely as pragmatists such as Grey argue. This is why the Hegelian idealist philosophic tradition is arguably the precursor not only of Continental postmodern philosophy but also of American pragmatic philosophy. The flexibility of Hohfeldian atomic analysis arguably gives it an advantage over a molecular approach in the pragmatic enterprise of promulgating the positive law of property. But it has the danger of making us think that by fiddling with the details of the positive law of property, we can undermine the crushing hegemony of the regimes of property and gender, rather than merely replicate them.

B. The Denial of the Feminine

The imagery of the bundle of sticks—the attempt to disaggregate property—is self-defeating. It reflects the desire to capture the

---

cisely because they confuse the general concept of property with specific applications of positive law. For example, Lawrence C. Becker (following Honoré) identifies at least thirteen—or ten, depending on how one subdivides the rights—possible elements of property rights, not all of which need be present for a right to be considered property. These rights are: (i) the right (claim) to possess; (ii) the right (liberty) to use; (iii) the right (power) to manage; (iv) the right (claim) to the income; (v) the right (liberty) to consume or destroy; (vi) the right (liberty) to modify; (vii) the right (power) to alienate; (viii) the right (power) to transmit; (ix) the right (claim) to security; (x) the absence of term; (xi) the prohibition of harmful use; (xii) liability to execution; and (xiii) residuary rules. Lawrence C. Becker, *The Moral Basis of Property Rights, in* Nomos, Property, *supra* note 109, at 187, 190–91 (citing A. M. Honoré, *Ownership, in* Oxford Essays in Jurisprudence 107–47 (A.G. Guest ed., 1961)).

A Hegelian would argue that these thirteen "elements" are more accurately described as specific empirical manifestations of the three more general elements of property, or of limitations of the three elements imposed by positive law. For example, rights i, vi, ix, and x are different actualizations of the Hegelian concept of possession.

symbolic aspect of property as human interrelationships, but it denies the mediating object that permits the development of subjectivity as inter-subjectivity. In an attempt to recognize the element of exchange, it re-presses possession and enjoyment. Property as alienation reflects the failed masculine strategy of trying to attain wholeness by retroactively "con-senting" to castration in exchange for the promise of a future substitute object.

The imagery of the axe—the attempt to epitomize property as the sen-suous grasping of physical things—is the mirror image of that error and is equally self-defeating. It denies property its very nature as a legal relation—symbolic, abstract, social, and mediated—in favor of an imagined, in-fantile, immediate, real union of the subject and the object. The traditional approach taken by Waldron privileges the elements of possession and re-presses those of enjoyment and alienation. This is particularly inappro-priate in the merchant's transaction where alienation through market ex-change is of the essence. Property as possession reflects the failed masculine strategy of pretending to be whole by denying castration and the result-ing necessity for mediation.

The symbolic *Phallus* is the object of desire. Our ultimate desire is the imaginary, forever-lost union with the Other imagined as the Mother, which we place in the real world beyond interpretation. Consequently, the *Phallus*—what men are supposed to have and women are supposed to be—is paradoxically both the Feminine and the signifier of masculine subjectivity.

Men try to attain subjectivity and hold the *Phallus,* not only by having the real penis but also by trying to control women's bodies. Of course this is unsatisfactory. They can never attain the Phallic Mother. So, in frus-tration, they deny the existence of the lost Feminine. They try to pretend that they achieve unmediated relationships by denying the existence of the mediator. In Lacan's terms, "The Woman does not exist." She is real in the technical sense that she cannot be adequately described in symbolic language, but she cannot be reduced to or grasped as a real object. The Woman—the Feminine—becomes purely the imaginary object of men's fantasy; woman becomes a symptom of man.[296]

We try to explain our desire by retroactively positing a cause—the *ob-jet petit a*—which sits at the crossroads of the symbolic and the real. In the imaginary we identify the *object a* with a specific thing that is actual, biological, natural—that is, seemingly real. This is in the vain hope that

296. See Rose, *supra* note 1, at 48–51.

if we can attain the real object, then our desire will be fulfilled.[297] Or, we deny mediation entirely.

Waldron, Baird, Jackson, and Llewellyn insist that property is archetypically sensuous on the grounds that sensuous things exist, can be seen, and are easier to identify and think about. This attempt to embrace the lost Feminine by grasping tangible things is, once again, reflected in etymology. The word "material" derives from the word for "mother."[298] But property interests as a legal matter are abstract and symbolic and as an empirical matter are often concerned with noncorporeal objects. Consequently, sensuous grasping is inadequate to the role of the archetypical relation of the subject with the object of desire of property in precisely the same way as the penis and the female body are inadequate to serve the psychoanalytic role of the *Phallus*. This is the psychoanalytic position of the Masculine—the deluded, split, and despairing Lacanian subject who continues to repeat the lie that he is not castrated: he has the *Phallus* merely because he has and controls tangible property, just as he has a penis and controls women. The masculine position is not to have "it" in fact, but to claim falsely to do so.

Noncorporeal property, like feminine sexuality, is at once hidden and ubiquitous, lack and surplus. We try to deny the Feminine her role as *Phallus* precisely because she cannot be easily seen and held. Feminine sexuality must be tamed by defining her as the female body that is occupied—possessed—by the penis in heterosexual intercourse. Thus Waldron says that only the tangible, and no other form of property, exists. The noncorporeal can only be discussed if it can be analogized to the corporeal. To Waldron we possess but don't exchange, to Grey we exchange but don't possess. Neither can recognize feminine enjoyment.

Because feminine intangibility is hard to identify and think about, it

297. This strategy is, of course, always unsuccessful. Once the object is obtained, the subject merely identifies the *objet petit a* with another object. As soon as one gets that new car, one always wants another new car, a new dress, a bigger house, and so on.

In his later work, Lacan defined the objective of psychoanalysis as breaking the confusion behind this mystification, a rupture between the objet a and the Other, whose conflation he saw as the elevation of fantasy into the order of truth. The objet a, cause of desire and support of male fantasy gets transposed onto the image of the woman as Other who then acts as its guarantee. The absolute "Otherness" of the woman, therefore, serves to secure for the man his own self-knowledge and truth.

Id. at 50.

298. Joseph T. Shipley, The Origins of English Words: A Discursive Dictionary of Indo-European Roots 7 (1984); Eric Partridge, Origins: A Short Etymological Dictionary of Modern English 386 (1966).

must be denied. The Feminine and property are identified with "lack."[299] The Lacanian masculine subject insists that ~~The~~ Woman does not exist. Thus Hohfeld, Grey, and Vandevelde mirror back Waldron's psychoanalytically masculine position. They say that the *res* of property does not exist.

299. Drucilla Cornell, The Philosophy of the Limit 173 (1992); the école freudienne, *The phallic phase, supra* note 290, at 116–17.

3

The Vestal:

The Feminine Phallic Metaphor for Property

I. VIRGIN TERRITORY: PROPERTY AS THE INVIOLATE FEMININE BODY

Her vestal livery is but sick and green,
And none but fools do wear it.
Cast it off![1]

In the 1980s, Margaret Jane Radin emerged as a prominent property theorist. Radin's project is to promote legal recognition of the role that identification with objects plays in the development of personhood. Radin labeled this a theory of "property for personhood."[2] The essence of her theory is that proper object relations are necessary for the

1. William Shakespeare, Romeo and Juliet, act 2, sc. 2.
2. Margaret Jane Radin, Reinterpreting Property 41 (1993) [hereinafter Radin, Reinterpreting Property]. Radin originally formulated her theory in a series of articles, the most important of which are: Margaret Jane Radin, *The Liberal Conception of Property: Cross Currents in the Jurisprudence of Takings,* 88 Colum. L. Rev. 1667 (1988) [hereinafter Radin, *Cross Currents*]; Margaret Jane Radin, *Market-Inalienability,* 100 Harv. L. Rev. 1849 (1987) [hereinafter Radin, *Market-Inalienability*]; Margaret Jane Radin, *Property and Personhood,* 34 Stan. L. Rev. 957 (1982) [hereinafter Radin, *Property and Personhood*]. She later republished these articles with minimal changes in her book *Reinterpreting Property.* For the convenience of the reader I will usually cite to the compilation rather than to the original articles.
    Radin has since revised some of the material in these articles and incorporated it into her more recent work. Margaret Jane Radin, Contested Commodities (1996) [hereinafter Radin, Contested Commodities]. Although grounded in her earlier theoretical work, this later book concentrates on trying to counter the "law and economics" tendency of analyzing all human relations in terms of the marketplace and making "pragmatic" arguments as to why certain specific objects should be wholly or partially market-inalienable.

development of subjectivity because we identify so closely with certain objects that we cannot distinguish our property from our personhood. Consequently, human flourishing requires the recognition of certain legal rights that protect these privileged objects, which she would call "personal" property, from invasion.

Radin's theory initially seems to be a feminist jurisprudence, reflecting feminine bodily experience. Radin protects and dignifies the feminine side of personhood as object by arguing that those objects that literally or figuratively constitute the female body should be market-inalienable. Her theory of property for personhood disrupts market alienations and allows the feminine self to enjoy herself as object as means to her own ends.

The appeal which Radin's account might have for feminists is obvious. My analysis, however, reveals an intrinsic dark side to Radin's theory.[3] It is necessarily incomplete. Although she claims to account for the development of personhood *within* community, she provides no account *of* community (i.e., intersubjectivity). Community is just assumed to preexist. I will show that because Radin presupposes that persons begin as integrated members of a community, her ideal of personal property can only function to allow persons to withdraw from the community in order to enjoy a lonely autonomy. This is inconsistent with her stated goal in reinterpreting property, namely, to prevent separation.[4]

Her theory is necessarily inadequate. It never suffices for feminists merely to disrupt misogyny by exposing and withdrawing from the masculine fiction of subjectivity. Withdrawal only serves to underline the logical necessity of community. Even in denial and condemnation, we recognize masculine subjectivity and silence ourselves in feminine objectivity. Nor is it possible merely to add a feminine narrative to the masculine fiction. Rather, we must write a new myth that supersedes the masculine fiction.

In chapter 2, I showed how the triune nature of property is in danger of becoming lost in contemporary legal scholarship. Generations of legal scholars have repeated Hohfeld's faux pas that property rights do not require a *res,* or object, at all. By repressing the object (and thereby also repressing the element of possession), Hohfeld reduces property to a binary subject-subject relationship which implicitly privileges the element

3. Steven Schnably has embarked upon a similar project. *See generally* Stephen J. Schnably, *Property and Pragmatism: A Critique of Radin's Theory of Property and Personhood,* 45 Stan. L. Rev. 347 (1993).

4. As we shall see, Radin is somewhat equivocal as to whether personal property should be protected because it serves the value of connectedness or of separateness.

of alienation through exchange. Radin also adopts a binary theory of property. In contradistinction to masculinist theory, however, she centers her analysis of property on the relationship between a single subject and an object. Her dichotomy of property rights—personal property versus fungible property—is defined in terms of the nature of the owning subject's relationship with the object owned. According to Radin, the empirical process through which we develop our personality is the identification with favorite objects. In other words, we do not desire the object of personal property derivatively in order to be desired by others, but primarily as a form of narcissistic autoeroticism. Rather than seeking objects as a means of creating society, as in Hegel, Radin's person seeks objects as a means of establishing "personhood" as an inviolable refuge from a preexisting society. To Hegel, objects are the mediators between subjects which permit the establishment of intersubjective relations, but in Radin, it is the relation between subject and object which is mediated by the preestablished intersubjectivity of "society."[5]

If Hohfeld's zeal to emphasize the intersubjective aspect of property caused him to lose sight of its objective aspect, Radin's insistence on its objective aspect results in loss of its intersubjective aspect. Being intersubjective, community requires both an intersubjective and objective account of property. Consequently, a wholly objective account of property inadequately promotes Radin's stated "pragmatic" goal of developing a theory of the individual within community.

But by concentrating on the object, Radin does not merely repeat Waldron's masculine phallic error of privileging possession. Her primary concern is not with the appropriate allocation of resources among people but with a single owner's subjective, sensuous experience of the object—enjoyment. Being masculine, Waldron's and Hohfeld's accounts of property are complementary and imaginary. They seek to cure castration by holding on to, or obtaining through exchange, the object of desire that

---

5. In the preface to her compilation, Radin tries to defend herself against the criticism that she misreads Hegel. In so doing, however, she demonstrates that she has inverted Hegel's concept of the mediating roles of subject and object.

It was open for readers to think I misunderstood Hegel as holding that the property relationship is something unmediated between the person and the object, rather than always a matter of social mediation. . . . I did not mean to argue that "property" was a matter between an individual and an object alone in the universe. Instead I wanted to plug into a socially constructed understanding involving connections between persons and things that matter to them.

Radin, Reinterpreting Property, *supra* note 2, at 7–8.

fills the hole and makes the subject whole. Property is seen as an immediate binary relationship either of subject to object or of subject to subject. In contradistinction, Radin's concept of property for personhood,
being feminine, is also imaginary but seeks to be unitary and real. She
seeks to avoid castration by merging with the object of desire back into
the primordial unity that preexisted the symbolic order of law. Subject
does not relate to object; she identifies with, enjoys, and becomes object.
The ecstatic experience she calls personal property "bridge[s] the gap or
blur[s] the boundary . . . between what is subject and what is object."[6]

If traditional property theorists have adopted either a positive or a negative version of the inadequate masculine phallic metaphor for property,
Radin, in contradistinction, adopts an equally inadequate feminine phallic metaphor for property. Radin's concept of property for personhood
seeks to allow the feminine self to enjoy herself as object without also being the desired object of possession and exchange by others—that is, to
be her own end and not the means to another's ends. By seeking to reunite with the Phallic Mother, Radin calls us to obey the superego's obscene command to transgress the law of prohibition—Enjoy!

As with masculine property jurisprudence, Radin's reinterpretation
of property reflects the desire to achieve wholeness through an imaginary collapse of the three orders. Her ideal of property serves as her *objet
petit a*—the object cause of desire. She believes that if she can just enjoy
the object a, then she can achieve the integrity which she calls "personhood"; that is, the separation of the symbolic order of law will be recon-
ciled with the primordial unity of the real. In the imaginary she identifies
specific, identifiable tangible objects to stand in for the lost object of desire. She calls these favored objects "personal property." As do we all, Radin
falls "prey to imaginary lures which promise the healing of the original/
constitutive wound of symbolization."[7] As the lost object of desire is the
Phallus, Radin's imaginary personal property is phallic.

However, to Radin, the archetype of the desired phallic object is no
longer the male organ which is physically possessed and exchanged
among masculine subjects. Instead, the archetypical object of personal
property is literally the female body, as opposed to an abstract feminine
position. Property is conflated with the object of property and with enjoyment of that object. Her project is to protect this object from market

6. Radin, Contested Commodities, *supra* note 2, at 57.
7. Slavoj Žižek, The Indivisible Remainder: An Essay on Schelling and Related Matters 96 (1996) [hereinafter Žižek, The Indivisible Remainder].

intercourse. The psychoanalytic model of Radin's notion of inalienable "personal" property is, consequently, property as chastity. If masculine theorists see property as the *fasces*—an axe or a bundle of sticks—Radin sees property as the *Vestal*.

Virginity can be integrity, but it can also be sterility, isolation, loneliness—and oblivion. If the masculine desire to possess and exchange the feminine object is Eros, the feminine desire to merge back into objectivity is Thanatos—the death wish. In her attempt to escape imprisonment in the masculinist seraglio, Radin immures feminine property in a cloister, seemingly free of the masculine fiction, but only because she is walled off from community. As Hegel argued, enjoyment standing alone is addiction. Radin seeks to be "bound up with"[8] property. This violates the logic of both property and feminism as the actualization of freedom. Bound by property, woman becomes fascinated. By binding herself, the inviolate *virgo* becomes inanimate *virga*. That which is bound is a *fasces*. The *fasces* becomes *fascinus*, a curse as well as a phallus—that which is carried and displayed by men. Seeking personhood through chaste integrity, the Feminine remains the object of masculine subjectivity.

By suggesting that the favored objects of personal property should be given heightened constitutional protections against governmental takings[9] and searches and seizures, Radin replicates the traditional womanly response to her own integrity—the insistence on an inviolate realm of privacy to which she can occasionally retreat. But Radin goes further and replicates the Masculine's morbid preoccupation with feminine chastity. She fears that the sale of personal property by any person can lead to the commodification of all women. Consequently, she seeks to make the most personal objects market-inalienable as a matter of law. In other words, feminine personhood is so frail and susceptible that the reputation and

---

8. As we shall see, Radin posits that to achieve personhood one must become "bound up with" certain objects. Radin, Reinterpreting Property, *supra* note 2, at 65–66; *see also id.* at 38. This, of course, follows from her imaginary identification of personal property as the *objet petit a*. Imaginary objects are always, by definition, captivating.

9. I present Radin's analysis of takings more thoroughly in Jeanne L. Schroeder, *Virgin Territory: Margaret Radin's Imagery of Personal Property as the Inviolate Feminine Body*, 79 Minn. L. Rev. 55, 94–99 (1994). Simplistically put, Radin believes that the Constitution should be read so as to further human flourishing. Human flourishing requires healthy intimate relationships with personal property, an avoidance of unhealthy close relationships with fungible property. Consequently, the Takings Clause of the Constitution should be read to give maximum protection of personal property to avoid violation of personhood and more minimal protection of fungible property both to avoid fetishization and to enable the promulgation of progressive regulation.

integrity of the female sex generally would be injured by the promiscu-
ous intercourse of any one fallen woman. All women, therefore, need be
protected not only for their own good but for the good of all, by the forced
chastity of the veil.

And so, in her attempt to rewrite the fiction of property, Radin ends
up telling the same old story that masculinist theory told. The feminine
person merely identifies with her object of personal property, which she
enjoys in her virgin solitude. The Feminine remains the passive object
of desire—she can only claim the right to refuse her suitors, in an attempt
to deny her commodification. Feminine enjoyment—*jouissance*—remains silent, because the virgin owner never leaves her cell to have social intercourse.

Although Radin insists that the relation of person to object is always
already located within society, her concern is protecting "personal"
property from society. How do we prevent the commodification of
women through exchange? How do we prevent the loss of personhood
through the invasion of our bodies and our homes by others? That is,
to internalize and merge with objects of "personal" property is to expel
and externalize the preexisting intersubjectivity of society. Like the oda-
lisque in her seraglio or the nun in her cloister, life goes on outside without her.

Complete human development and freedom require community as well
as individuality. Radin's theory of personhood seeks to describe the individual *within* community, yet it currently has no account *of* community.
The dynamic Radin describes is the withdrawal of the individual from
community into a cloistered universe, in which the subject has nothing
to do but consume her precious objects. If the individual develops, she
develops retrogressively from an intersubjective public being into a silenced private being. The *virgo/virga* is not only bound but gagged because she is no longer located in the community of discourse.

Radin's theory of property for personhood contains the contradiction
that, although it is intended to prevent the objectification of women,[10] it
is based on the identification of personhood with objects. She seeks to
prevent the commodification of women,[11] but she has not yet understood
that the Feminine is defined as the always already commodified. The Phal-

---

10. *See* Margaret Jane Radin, *Reflections on Objectification*, 65 S. Cal. L. Rev. 341, 345–46
(1991). *See also* Radin, Contested Commodities, *supra* note 2, at 127, 154–60.

11. Radin, *Market-Inalienability, supra* note 2, at 1921; Radin, Reinterpreting Property,
supra note 2, at 137.

lic Woman is herself the archetypical and primal commodity. To be conscious and to speak is literarily, if not literally, to objectify the Feminine. This means that the feminist task cannot be to prevent the commodification and objectification of woman. It can only be to search for a way to subjectify and *de*commodify ourselves as women. Indeed, Radin's theory implicitly reflects this in that she starts out with individuals already located in society who seek to achieve personhood by removing certain objects from the preexisting market regime.

Radin's project is doomed because the feminine myth cannot be written within the masculine fiction.[12] In the masculine fiction, as retold by Lacan, feminine enjoyment—*jouissance*—must be silent by definition. But the Feminine, also by definition, cannot be totally circumscribed by the symbolic order. On the one hand, even to identify the feminine person with the object, as Radin does, is to admit the masculine fiction and to deny feminine speech. It is to engage in the masculine fantasy which purports to give positive content to the Feminine,[13] thereby depriving her of the radical freedom of her negativity. On the other hand, by insisting on speaking as a woman, one denies the objective position of the Feminine, which is the very basis of the fiction.

The fact that the feminine myth cannot be added to the masculine fiction of property does not mean that we can merely abandon either the fiction or the myth. Rather, we must write a new feminist myth that does not merely negate or modify the masculine account of the feminine position, but sublates and supersedes it in the myth of the Feminine as the not yet achieved actualization of freedom and immediate relation.

An adequate theory of the subject and the object, as expressed through our legal relations and interrelations with objects, cannot be created exclusively from the masculine position which alternately sees property as the intersubjective binary relationship of subject to subject in exchange or the objective binary relationship of subject to object in possession. Accordingly, Radin's attempted feminine objective theory of expanded bodily integrity is incomplete as written today and cannot serve as a substitute for the existing property regime. Thus, to develop a human theory of the legal person, we need to recognize that property is a necessary, but insufficient, aspect of the legal regime of object relations.

To show why Radin's theory of property cannot ground a supersed-

---

12. I say this even though I am intuitively sympathetic with many, if not most, of her specific policy proposals.

13. Žižek, The Indivisible Remainder, *supra* note 7, at 161.

ing myth of the Feminine, I begin by examining Radin's account of personal versus fungible property more thoroughly to explain how property for personhood privileges the objective aspect of property while disparaging the intersubjective. I argue that, although Radin's theory gives dignity to a concept of expanded bodily integrity, it is incomplete and offers an inadequate account of the legal institution of property, generally.[14] Radin claims that her property theory is a critique of and improvement on Hegel's. This assertion is based on a fundamental misreading of Hegel. To demonstrate this, I return to the analysis of Hegel's property theory to discover the point where Radin made a wrong turn. Finally, I conclude by examining in greater detail how Radin's theory of property for personhood relates to the psychoanalytic position of the Feminine.

A. Radin's Definition of Property

1. THE IDENTIFICATION WITH OBJECTS Radin begins her project by asking, in effect: What are the minimum material circumstances necessary to enable one to become a complete person as an empirical matter?[15] What conception of property would further "human flourishing"?[16] Radin states that human beings are, first, embodied: we relate to each other through our bodies. Consequently, it seems necessary to make some form of identification of the person with her body. Next it is necessary to compare the relationship of the individual to her body with the

---

14. Radin's most recent work indicates that she may now at least implicitly intuit this. Although *Contested Commodities* is clearly grounded in her earlier work, and even though it still purports to set forth a property analysis, it is largely concerned with the proper legal status of the body. She considers at length the sale of body parts, female sexuality (i.e., prostitution and surrogacy), and babies and critiques the Law and Economics approach to torts which analyzes personal injury in terms of a market in bodily integrity. Although she speaks generally about the importance of the relationship of subject to certain objects (such as houses), the only nonbody issue which she analyzes at any length is the implications of the metaphor of the "marketplace of ideas."

15. For example, Radin begins one of her articles by stating:

But if property for personhood cannot be viewed as other than arbitrary and subjective . . . to argue for their recognition by the legal system might collapse to a simple utilitarian preference summing. To avoid this collapse requires objective criteria differentiating good from bad identification with objects in order to identify a realm of personal property deserving recognition. The necessary objective criteria might be sought by appeal . . . to the concept of person itself. Taking the latter route, this section approaches the problem of developing a standard for recognizing claims to personal property by referring to the concept of "person" itself.

Radin, Reinterpreting Property, *supra* note 2, at 38.

16. Radin, *Market-Inalienability, supra* note 2, at 1851.

individual's relationship to other physical things.[17] A simple body/non-body dichotomy does not satisfy Radin.[18] People identify with, and are identified by, physical things other than their bodies.[19]

This argument has some empirical appeal. Human adults rarely come

---

17. Radin explains:

> [M]arket rhetoric conceives of bodily integrity as a fungible object. . . . To speak of personal attributes as fungible objects—alienable "goods"—is intuitively wrong. Thinking of rape in market rhetoric implicitly conceives of as fungible something that we know to be too personal even to be personal property. Bodily integrity is an attribute and not an object.
>
> Systematically conceiving of personal attributes as fungible objects is threatening to personhood, because it detaches from the person that which is integral to the person. . . . For someone who conceives bodily integrity as "detached," the same person will remain even if bodily integrity is lost; but if bodily integrity cannot be detached, the person cannot remain the same after loss.

Radin, *Market-Inalienability, supra* note 2, at 1880–81. Radin develops this argument in greater detail in *Contested Commodities,* but despite her denial at this point that bodily integrity is an object, she continues to analyze one's relationship with the body as an object relationship continuous with property.

18. In one of Radin's early works she expressly includes in her category of personal property the home, cars owned for personal use, and other "things" that have personal significance, such as wedding rings and furniture. *Id.* at 959–61. She discusses the body in terms of her background assumptions as to what is necessarily personal:

> On the other hand, a few objects may be so close to the personal end of the continuum that no compensation could be "just." That is, hypothetically, if some object were so bound up with me that I would cease to be "myself" if it were taken, then a government that must respect persons ought not to take it. If my kidney may be called my property, it is not property subject to condemnation for the general public welfare.

Id. at 65–66.

It is only later that Radin expressly addresses the body—specifically the female body—as an object of personal property. *See, e.g.,* Radin, *Market-Inalienability, supra* note 2, at 1921–36 (discussing alienability of female reproductive capacity). Even then there is a tension in Radin's analysis on this issue. At some moments, she recognizes the body as property, *see* Radin, Reinterpreting Property, *supra* note 2, at 41, but at other moments she expresses the concern that there is something anti-intuitive and alienating in this analysis, *see* Radin, *Market-Inalienability, supra* note 2, at 1880–81. Rather than concluding from this that her theory does not reflect traditional property categories at all but is concerned with rights of bodily integrity, Radin suggests that some things (such as the body) might be both property and inalienable. The more an object of property is located on the personal end of the spectrum of relationships, the more market-inalienable it should be. *Id.* at 1903.

> Personal property connects with inalienability, which means inseparability from the holder. Since personal property is connected with the self, morally justifiably, in a constitutive way, to disconnect it from the person (from the self) harms or destroys the self.

Radin, Contested Commodities, *supra* note 2, at 59–60. "Certain external things, for example, the shirt off my back, may also be considered personal property if they are closely enough connected with the body." Radin, Reinterpreting Property, *supra* note 2, at 41.

19. For example, Radin notes:

into contact with other humans without symbolic, concealing, identifying, medical, useful, beautifying, and other objects. Even in our most intimate moments with our lovers, we are rarely if ever truly naked. We use diaphragms, condoms, and other barriers to protect ourselves from our relationship. Radin concludes from this that we can relate to objects external to our bodies in a way that is not merely analogous to, but substantially identical with, the way we relate to our bodies. She considers this to be intuitively self-evident.

> Most people possess certain objects they feel are almost part of themselves. These objects are closely bound up with personhood because they are part of the way we constitute ourselves as continuing personal entities in the world. They may be as different as people are different, but some common examples might be a wedding ring, a portrait, an heirloom, or a house.[20]

That is, we become sentimentally attached to things. Radin argues that these nostalgic object relations can serve the same positive function as body

---

> A person cannot be fully a person without a sense of continuity of self over time. To maintain that sense of continuity over time and to exercise one's liberty or autonomy, one must have an ongoing relationship with the external environment, consisting of both "things" and other people. One perceives the ongoing relationship to the environment as a set of individual relationships, corresponding to the way our perception separates the world into distinct "things." . . . In order to lead a normal life, there must be some continuity in relating to "things."

Id. at 64. *See also* Radin, Contested Commodities, *supra* note 2, at 55. This argument seems to imply that all things one owns and perceives as part of one's continuing environment are to some degree personal. Nevertheless, Radin insists that some objects are *not* significant to self-constitution and are, therefore, fungible.

20. *Id.* at 959. I do not agree with the intuitiveness of Radin's observations. Instead, I believe such close identification with most objects is anti-intuitive—a combination of mawkish sentimentality and fetishism—as well as destructive to human freedom. Although I cannot imagine my self as separate from my body, I do not feel that my selfhood is reducible to my body. Rather than intuitive, I believe my understanding of my selfhood results from my strict Roman Catholic upbringing, which stressed the fundamental tenet of Catholicism that humans are not souls trapped in bodies—rather, we are both spirit and flesh. *See generally* Caroline W. Bynum, Fragmentation and Redemption: Essays on Gender and the Human Body in Medieval Religion (1991).

Whatever my personal identification with my body, I do not feel that I identify with other objects that I own. I have some sentimental attachment to my wedding ring in the sense that I usually wear a ring as a reminder of my husband and a symbol of my status as a married woman. I might agree that insofar as this relationship and status are intimate parts of my personality, wearing *a* ring could be considered significant to my sense of self—but I do not see how this leads to the conclusion that I identify my ring with myself. Despite what Radin says, although I would be disappointed if my ring were lost, I believe that I would feel perfectly satisfied if I received insurance or damages sufficient to purchase a replacement ring of at least equivalent value.

relations in enabling an individual to achieve personhood.[21] Indeed, we cannot draw a bright line between those objects that are our bodies and other objects:[22]

> When an item of property is involved with self-constitution in this way, it is no longer wholly "outside" the self, in the world separate from the person; but neither is it wholly "inside" the self, indistinguishable from the attributes of the person.[23]

Radin, consequently, claims that her theory is not based on a liberal notion of negative freedom, which posits "an absolute conception of property as sacred to personal autonomy," but that it reflects "an affirmative notion of an individual being bound up with an external 'thing.'"[24] Indeed, she argues that individuation and integrity require the continuity supplied by personal property object relations.[25]

2. THE ELEMENTS OF PROPERTY

a. Possession. Implicit in Radin's use of the word "property" to describe the object of property, rather than the legal rights with respect to the object, is a decision not to specify the elements which constitute property. Indeed, she condemns the attempt to articulate an enumerated set of rights as property as "naive conceptualism."[26] Thus, she criticizes the elaboration of what she calls the "liberal triad"[27] of property rights (i.e., possession, use, and alienation) as conservative, rule-like thinking.[28] Nevertheless, for Radin to speak of property, she could not avoid adopting implicit

21. *See, e.g.,* Radin, Contested Commodities, *supra* note 2, at 57–58, in which she states that things generally can further self-constitution, while noting that overconnection with certain things (fungible property) might be destructive.

22. Radin notes that although "the boundary between person and thing cannot be a bright line, still the idea of property seems to require some perceptible boundary." Radin, *Property and Personhood, supra* note 2, at 966.

23. Radin, Contested Commodities, *supra* note 2, at 57.

24. *Id.* at 957–58. More recently she cites with favor Martha Nussbaum's lists of human limits and capabilities, and circumstances necessary to live a good human life. Radin, Contested Commodities, *supra* note 2, at 66–67.

25. Radin, Contested Commodities, *supra* note 2, at 55.

26. Radin, Reinterpreting Property, *supra* note 2, at 122. Radin particularly condemns Richard Epstein for assuming there is a "real Platonic form" of property. *Id.* at 121–23.

27. *Id.* at 121–22.

28. *Id.* at 132. Radin describes the attempt to give fixed meaning to the word "property" as used in the Constitution as "semantic reductionism." *Id.* at 122. Radin discusses the three traditional elements of property only to critique a mode of constitutional analysis that would protect all three rights in all circumstances regardless of the type of object involved. *Id.* at 139–42.

definitions of property rights. That these definitions are left implicit does not mean that they do not function. To analyze fully Radin's arguments, it is necessary to make explicit these implicit definitions.

The binding of the individual to thing implies that Radin privileges use and enjoyment over alienation and even possession as the premier aspect of property. This enjoyment concept of property rights manifests itself in the specific examples of personal property that Radin offers. It is not clear that Radin even identifies "possession" per se as an essential personal property right. Because her personal/fungible dichotomy flows from an enjoyment/instrumental dichotomy, even the right of possession loses its importance and becomes conflated with, or subsumed into, the right of enjoyment. That is, possession is required only insofar it is the most primitive element of property, necessary before there can be enjoyment. For example, her discussion of whether we should recognize a constitutional right against governmental interference with possession of personal or fungible property quickly devolves into a discussion of use. Radin asks us to

> [s]tart with physical occupation—possession or the fundamental right to exclude others. . . . A normative inquiry would also be required: for what types of property interests is it ethically appropriate to permit and foster interconnection with persons? Use of property as one's residence is more closely connected to personhood than use of property as a garbage dump for one's factory.[29]

In other words, to Radin, it would seem that possession per se is not essential to property or particularly worthy of protection. Rather she would protect only that accidental possession which is necessary for specific, favored types of enjoyment—feminine sensuous experience.

Further evidence of the privilege of use over possession is the enhanced right that Radin would recognize in tenants to continue to occupy their primary residences upon the end of the lease term, limiting the right of commercial landlords to evict tenants at the end of their terms.[30] Radin makes the distinction that the apartment is personal to the tenant, because the tenant's personhood is wrapped up in her home. The same apartment is fungible to the landlord, because his relationship to it is purely financial.[31] The implication is that the favored right in personal property, as epitomized by the tenant and her apartment, is sensuous use as a primary

---

29. Radin, Reinterpreting Property, *supra* note 2, at 139.

30. *Id.* at 57–59.

31. Radin notes, however, that some landlords have "personhood" interest in their rental property, such as duplex owners who rent out one-half of their building. *Id.* at 58.

residence. Not only is the tenant not attempting to alienate the apartment, Radin would limit the tenant's power to alienate it. She suggests making all residential leases automatically renewable at the option of the lessee, thereby denying the right, power, or privilege of a tenant to enter into a nonrenewable lease (which would almost certainly entail a lower rent).[32]

b. The Fear of Alienation. Because Radin's theory is based on identification with the feminine object of desire, alienation is not merely deemphasized like possession, it is affirmatively denigrated. Indeed, to the extent pragmatically possible, market-alienation should be prohibited:

> Since personal property is connected with the self, morally justifiably, in a self-constitutive way, to disconnect it from the person (from the self) harms or destroys the self. The more something takes on the indicia of an attribute or characteristic of the self, or at least the self as the person herself would wish, the more problematic it seems to alienate it, and the stronger the inclination toward some form of inalienability.[33]

That is, she imagines that if we can just remove the object of desire from the symbolic order of law, we can more easily merge with it and reenter the real. Radin's theory of personhood as identification with the female body as object is therefore reminiscent of Lacan's psychoanalytic theory, which states that in the symbolic order, the Feminine is conceptualized as the object of desire and that the masculine subject constitutes himself through the exchange with other subjects of the object as the Feminine. If one views personhood not from the psychoanalytically masculine position of subjectivity but from the psychoanalytically feminine position of objectivity, then to be the object of commodification (exchange) is threatening. According to Radin, "[c]ommodification stresses separateness both between ourselves and our things and between ourselves and other people."[34] Sale of the female body is not a right but an un-right that should be a legal wrong.[35]

Actually, Radin is deeply ambivalent both as to the relative values of separateness and connection and as to property's role with respect to these values. In at least one place, Radin argues that her concept of personal property increases, rather than decreases, separation.

32. *Id.*
33. Radin, Contested Commodities, *supra* note 2, at 59–60.
34. Radin, *Market-Inalienability, supra* note 2, at 1907.
35. That is, in an ideal world. Radin recognizes that a different legal result might be necessary in a nonideal world, however.

It may be shown that certain functionings *can* be served by a form of private property; individual separateness, in particular, and the need to live one's life in one's very own context. When property actually serves this function in a *justifiable* way, I have called it personal. . . . [T]his form of justification of private property is "contingent and controversial," since it will collapse as a justification if someone shows, to the contrary, that the context of noninterference required for human functioning does not include private property.[36]

Following Martha Nussbaum, however, Radin considers individual separateness to be only one possible capability of humanness, and by no means the most elemental or important. Other human capabilities, which Radin seems to privilege, include affiliation with other humans and relatedness to other species and to nature.[37] She insists that "[i]n human life as we know it, self-constitution includes connectedness with other human beings and also with things in the world. . . . "[38] And so, Radin is on the one hand concerned that what she calls market-alienability or commodification of certain intimate objects will cause the over-separateness of radical individualism, and the resulting objectification and subordination of women, among others. On the other hand, since Radin concludes from the empirical fact that people are born as dependents in society that they start interconnected, she posits that we need property rights in intimate objects in order to achieve "proper" individuation.

Radin eventually comes to the conclusion I suggested at the beginning of this chapter. Feminine personhood requires the withdrawal from the intersubjectivity of society which the identification with, and enjoyment of, objects allows.

The conception of human flourishing we have been considering generates a basic requirement of "being able to live one's own life in one's very own surroundings and context." This requirement follows from the basic understanding that human beings are separate individuals; the idea is that separation from other human beings, individuation, is accomplished in part by particularized connection with things.

In other words, in this conception of human flourishing separation does not connote the idea of alienability of all of the self's attributes and possessions, but rather something like its opposite: it refers not to separation of the person from her environment, but rather to separation of one person from another person, with the premise being that for that kind of sep-

36. Radin, Contested Commodities, *supra* note 2, at 75 (emphasis added).
37. *Id.* at 66–68.
38. *Id.* at 57.

aration to be instantiated in the world, a certain kind of specific connection to one's environment may be needed.[39]

In Hegel, we seek objects derivatively in order to interrelate with others. In Radin, we seek objects in order to become disentangled from others.

3. ENJOYMENT; INTERFERENCE AS VIOLATION Radin's identification of property with the female body is most apparent in her latest work.[40] Consider two examples she discusses in detail—prostitution (which overwhelmingly involves male johns and female prostitutes) and surrogate motherhood. Her discussions of prostitution and surrogacy revolve around what she calls a "double bind"—that is, the conflict between woman's ability to enjoy her body sensuously in a personal, nonmonetary way and commercially in a fungible, monetary way.[41]

Her powerful critique of Richard Posner's attempt to analyze rape in "terms of a marriage and sex market"[42] provides an even stronger example. Radin condemns Posner's utilitarian balancing of the rapist's pleasure versus the victim's displeasure on the grounds that they are incommensurable.[43] Although she does not use my terminology, her argument in essence is that a woman's enjoyment of her body is qualitatively different from any possible enjoyment which a rapist could have.[44] She expressly argues that bodily integrity should not be thought of as an object separate from the subject that can be bought and sold.[45] Posner applies the masculine metaphor for property to rape and therefore conceives of bodily integrity as an object that one can hold in the element of possession, or exchange through the element of alienation. When one privileges the

39. *Id.* at 76.

40. *Id.*Radin discusses the sale of body parts in another article as well as in *Contested Commodities*. Margaret Jane Radin, *Justice and the Market Domain, in* Markets and Justice 165 (John W. Chapman & J. Roland Pennock eds., 30 Nomos, 1989) [hereinafter Radin, *Justice and the Market Domain*]. Although Radin calls this article a companion piece to *Market-Inalienability*, it does not expressly discuss selling body parts in terms of property law, which, in my opinion, makes it one of her stronger articles.

41. Radin, Contested Commodities, *supra* note 2, at 123–30.

42. *Id.* at 86.

43. Posner's approach is wrong because "market rhetoric conceives of bodily integrity as a fungible object." *Id.* at 87. Radin argues that "[f]ungible property is related to commensurability," *id.* at 59, and that "[p]ersonal property is related to incommensurability," *id.* at 60.

44. She chastises Posner for not citing "as an objection the idea that the purported pleasures of the rapist should not count at all." *Id.* at 86. That is, it is fundamentally wrong to even compare the rapist's enjoyment with the victim's experience.

45. Or, in the case or rape, stolen. *Id.* at 87–88.

element of possession, then interference with bodily integrity as a property right can only be analyzed in terms of castration—my valuable thing has been taken from me. Consequently, the prevention of rape is analogized to the protection of possession. When a rape does occur, Posner adopts the alternate masculine responses to castration: he pretends that it can be cured by exchange—monetary compensation. In contradistinction, unlike a market transaction, or loss of an item of fungible property, the loss of rape changes the victim because it is a loss, or destruction, of some aspect of her personhood.[46] This is because her theory holds that personhood is partially constituted by those objects which she calls personal property.

At one point in her critique of Richard Posner's analysis of rape she comes close to what I think is the stronger, Hegelian analysis, that some object relations are qualitatively different from the relation known as property. She states:

> Bodily integrity is an attribute and not an object. . . . We feel discomfort or even insult, and we fear degradation or even loss of the value involved, when bodily integrity is conceived of as a fungible object.[47]

Unfortunately, she retreats from this position. Throughout *Contested Commodities,* Radin insists that she is analyzing body relations in terms of her category of "personal property" and that her analysis is not limited to the body but includes any other thing, such as work and housing,[48] that properly serves the goal of self-constitution or human flourishing. Indeed, she insists that "[n]ot everything we might be thus [i.e., in such a way as to further proper self-constitution] connected with in the world can be property, but in a property-owning culture, some such things can be property."[49] In context, it is clear that she means that she believes that the intimate objects she discusses fall within the category of (personal) property.[50]

Radin's analysis of rape is persuasive in that, psychoanalytically, the fem-

46. *Id.* at 88.
47. *Id.*
48. *Id.* at 109.
49. *Id.* at 57.
50. At this point she notes that "[l]ots of things" are not personal property (i.e., are fungible things which cannot serve the purpose of self-constitution), *id.,* but by negative pregnant this also means that many things are personal property. That is, her analysis of the body in *Contested Commodities* is not a break from her earlier analysis of the body as personal property but a continuation of it. Indeed, for her to limit her analysis to the body would violate Radin's fundamental belief that the "the terms 'fungible' and 'personal' do not mark out a rigid binary dichotomy but rather mark the end points of a continuum." *Id.* at 58.

inine position is the identification with and enjoyment of the object of desire, and we do identify the female body with the elusive object of desire. But the significance for my purposes is that Radin presents her rape analysis as an epitome of her theory of personal property. Personal property is like the female body which we identify with and enjoy. Interference with personal property rights cannot, therefore, be analogized to castration (a taking which can be remedied through exchange) but to rape and violation, an irretrievable loss of self which cannot be replaced. It can only be acknowledged and mourned in a process which enables the self to move on and rebuild a new, but inalterably different, life. Consequently, in the latter part of her book *Contested Commodities*,[51] Radin offers a persuasive criticism of our current system of monetary damages for personal injury on the grounds that it treats the tort as a sale of a body part from the tort victim to the tort-feasor, rather than as a loss of self. In my terminology, traditional tort law adopts the masculine metaphor which perceives loss as castration (the taking of the object of desire which can be cured by the future exchange for a new object of desire) whereas Radin adopts the feminine metaphor which perceives loss as violation (the irretrievable change in both the subject and her object of desire which cannot be cured, only acknowledged and mourned).[52]

4. THE DONNING OF THE CHADOR   Although this response seems initially feminine, as I have already suggested, a closer reading will reveal that Radin might be adopting a harsh masculine approach to female virginity. In her most recent work, Radin is primarily concerned with "commodification." She is not merely concerned that loss of personal property would deprive the owner of her personhood. If this were so, she would merely advocate stronger protections of the rights of enjoyment and, therefore necessarily, possession of personal property. Rather, as she makes clear in her analysis of the law of prostitution, surrogate motherhood, rape, and personal injury, she is concerned that allowing the free market-alienability of personal property by anyone can lead to the commodification of that class of personal property and, therefore, the subordination of women generally.[53] She considers the very rhetoric of alien-

51. *Id.* at 184–205.
52. I develop at great length a similar analysis of the Law and Economics analysis of environmental nuisances first developed by Guido Calabresi and Douglas Melamed, in Jeanne L. Schroeder, Three's a Crowd: Calabresi and Melamed's Repression of the Feminine (1997) (unpublished manuscript, on file with author).
53. "If sex were openly commodified in this way, its commodification would be reflected

ation to be alienating.[54] It is not enough that I protect my personal property and that I refrain from alienating it, it is necessary that we as a society discourage market-alienability of personal property as much as practical.[55] In order for feminine subjectivity to reenter the real by merging back with the object of desire, the object of desire that is the Feminine must be rescued entirely from the symbolic order of exchange among masculine subjects. This reflects the masculine fear that feminine dignity is so delicate, and feminine will so weak, that for any woman's integrity to be preserved, it is necessary to require all women to be chaste. It is not enough that some be allowed occasionally to seek refuge in the privacy of the veil and the convent; all women must be hidden under the chador and in purdah.

5. THE INALIENABILITY OF NONBODY OBJECTS The problem with Radin's analysis is that she refuses to limit it to a consideration of a subject's proper interest in her own bodily integrity, but insists on applying it to the entire intersubjective realm of property. I have just shown how her attempt to analyze the sale of feminine sexuality in terms of property leads her to adopt imagery reminiscent of masculine control of feminine sexuality. When applied to more conventional categories of "personal" property, it leads to results which seem intuitively unattractive if not outright absurd.

What objects other than the body are personal property? Radin believes that the home is personal property, as can be seen in her analysis of automatic renewal clauses in leases and her defense of rent control. Radin also argues that the Fourth Amendment right against unreasonable searches should be extended to personal automobiles because of the close identification that Americans tend to have with their cars, as well as the

---

in everyone's discourse about sex, and in particular about women's sexuality." Radin, Contested Commodities, *supra* note 2, at 133.

54. Radin, *Market-Inalienability, supra* note 2, at 1877–87; *see also* Radin, *Justice and the Market Domain, supra* note 40, at 167–68, *and* Radin, Contested Commodities, *supra* note 2, at 79–101.

55. Radin tries to distinguish herself from idealist anti-commodifiers like certain Marxists in that, although she believes that market-alienation of personal property leads to commodification, she does not believe that this is an either-or proposition, or a slippery slope where *any* market relations lead to *complete* commodification. She believes that we can have a regime of "incomplete commodification." *See* Radin, Contested Commodities, *supra* note 2, at 102–14. More important, as a pragmatist, she believes that absolute positions cannot work in a nonideal world. In an imperfect world, ideal solutions can lead to unanticipated side effects such as the "double bind" facing poor women. This is the familiar economic notion of the problem of the second best.

right to privacy.[56] The rights which would be so protected would only be exclusive possession and quiet enjoyment but not the right to alienation or other rights to earn financial gains through the use or sale of the car.[57] Indeed, locating the primary residence and the personal automobile on the personal end of the personal/fungible property spectrum suggests not just that alienation should not be especially protected but that perhaps it should be restricted. That is, Radin argues that alienation of the most personal of property is alienation of the self. If the consumer's relationship with her automobile is entitled to Fourth Amendment protection, because the automobile is personal property, should not the market-alienability of the personal automobile be prohibited or at least restricted?

Presumably, Radin would not argue that human flourishing requires such identification with our cars that we should be limited in our ability to sell them. Such identification would be precisely what she calls "fetishism." But does this suggest that we, in fact, either do not or should not identify automobiles with our personhood and that they are not personal property within Radin's schema? If so, her position on searches and seizures concerning automobiles is defeated. Radin might respond that the automobile may be personal for some purposes and fungible for others.

As we have seen, however, in limiting termination clauses in leases, Radin *is* suggesting some limitations on alienability of homes in that she advocates mandatory renewal clauses in the case of leases of primary residences. I would suggest, however, that even Radin does not really propose this because she recognizes, or wants to encourage, identification between the apartment dweller and her apartment. This can be seen by the fact that Radin is not suggesting that I, a highly educated, well-paid lawyer, should not have the right freely to alienate my expensive New York City apartment. Rather, she wants to protect poor people from richer people (landlords) who presumably have greater bargaining power. Conse-

56. Radin, Reinterpreting Property, *supra* note 2, at 59–63. The discussion of the automobile exemplifies the problem of the "pragmatic" approach to identifying personal property. As Schnably points out, Radin's "consensus" approach in *Property and Personhood* risks degenerating into a conservative preservation of the status quo. *See generally* Schnably, *supra* note 3. I am aware that people in most of this country identify with their automobiles. Like most New Yorkers, however, I am delighted not to own an automobile. To me, an automobile is the ultimate fungible good—something to be rented on an as-needed basis. The American "love affair" with the private car strikes me as fetishistic on the individual level, but also destructive on the social level given the negative environmental effects of cars and the damage to inner cities from the commuting culture.

57. *See, e.g.,* Radin, Reinterpreting Property, *supra* note 2, at 62 n.122 (220).

quently, although we, as a society, probably want to recognize the right of consumers freely to sell and trade in their own cars so that they get the highest price, we might also decide to limit their ability to transfer their cars through hypothecation in the sense of imposing restrictions on the power of a secured creditor to repossess an automobile from a defaulting consumer. Indeed, our law imposes many such paternalistic limits on the ability of consumers to hypothecate their possessions.[58] This distinction cannot be grounded in Radin's definition of personal property as being necessarily bound up with personhood. The fact that for many purposes we consider the automobile to be fungible suggests that, despite Radin's intuitions, we do not confuse our cars with our personhood.

The problems of Radin's analysis can be seen vividly in one of Radin's favorite examples of a proper and healthy relationship with personal property—the bride who so identifies with her wedding ring that its loss would be a loss of self that could never be replaced. Fans of J.R.R. Tolkien will no doubt recognize the similarity of this relationship to that of Gollum and the Ring of Power. Poor Gollum so identified his selfhood with the Ring that he referred to both his self and the Ring by the same name, "My Precious." The loss of the Ring was such a loss of self that it drove

58. For example, the Bankruptcy Code makes most non–purchase money security interests in personal and household goods unenforceable in bankruptcy. 11 U.S.C. 522(f)(2) (1988). The Federal Trade Commission's ("FTC's") Credit Practices Rules makes non–purchase money security interests in household goods unlawful as an unfair trade practice. 16 C.F.R. 444.2 (1994). Article 9 of the Uniform Commercial Code limits the enforceability of after-acquired property clauses in security agreements covering consumer goods and imposes somewhat greater protections of the debtor in the foreclosure of security interests in consumer goods than it does in the case of other forms of collateral. U.C.C. § 9-204(2), 504(2) (1994). Personal automobiles would not fall within the protected class of collateral under the Bankruptcy Code or the FTC rule, although they can constitute consumer goods under Article 9. *Id.* 9-109 cmt. 2.

We also restrict creditors in a variety of other financial transactions out of a paternalistic desire to save consumers from themselves and others. For example, the FTC attempts to limit people's ability to alienate their money by signing promissory notes in consumer sales transactions. FTC Rule 433, 16 C.F.R. 433.2 (1994). Certainly, we do not do this to foster an intimate relationship between a fool and her money. Instead, the case law under Bankruptcy Code 522(f)(2), 11 U.S.C. 522(f)(2) (1988), suggests that Congress made most non–purchase money hypothecations of household goods unenforceable because used household goods typically have substantial use value to the consumer but low resale value (i.e., exchange value) to the creditor. *See* David Gray Carlson, *Security Interests on Exempt Property: Their Fate in Bankruptcy,* 2 J. Bankr. L. & Prac. 247, 255 (1993). Consequently, creditors take such security interests not to obtain sufficient collateral to ensure the payment of their loans but to obtain hostage power over the debtor. *Id.* Presumably, automobiles are not exempt goods like household goods because used cars retain greater exchange value than used household goods.

Gollum to utter depravity, and eventually death.[59] This is to be expected since the desire to achieve wholeness through identification with the object and submersion back into the real is *Thanatos*.

B. Pluralism, Pragmatism, and Contradiction

Radin does not believe that her intuition about personal property leads to the conclusion that all object relations are good. Some relations with some objects are inappropriate and fetishistic.[60] We need,

59. J.R.R. Tolkien, The Hobbit, or There and Back Again (1938); J.R.R. Tolkien, The Lord of the Rings (2d ed. 1965).

For those few readers who somehow escaped adolescence without having read, or seen one of the animated versions of, *The Hobbit* and *The Lord of the Rings,* Gollum was once a hobbit (or similar creature) named Smeagol. He found the cursed mystical Ring and became so obsessed with it that he became a murderous recluse who shriveled to a miserable froglike form. When we first meet Gollum in *The Hobbit,* he dementedly mumbles his thoughts out loud, addressing himself as "My Precious" and referring to the Ring as the "Birthday Present." By the end of *The Lord of the Rings,* however, his identification with the Ring has become so complete that he now also addresses the Ring as the "Precious." In the final scene, Gollum achieves the ultimate *jouissance* of identity with object and submerges back into the real. He regains the Ring and plunges to his death in the fires of Mount Doom shrieking in ecstasy, "Precious, Precious, Precious! . . . My Precious, O my Precious." J.R.R. Tolkien, The Lord of the Rings, vol. 3, The Return of the King 224 (2d ed. 1965).

60. Radin, *Market-Inalienability, supra* note 2, at 43. An interesting comparison can be made between Radin's personal/fungible dichotomy and John Ruskin's distinction between "wealth" and "illth":

Wealth, [Ruskin] concludes, is this the possession of useful things by those who can use them. Useful things are those that nurture life . . . . To the degree that possessions cause bodily harm, as in the story of the drowned man, to the degree that they incapacitate or make people ill, they are "illth."

Catherine Gallagher, *The Bio-Economics of Our Mutual Friend, in* 3 Fragments for a History of the Human Body 345, 346 (Michel Feher et al. eds. 1989). The story referred to is that of a man who drowns because he cannot let go of a bag of gold. "Now as he was sinking—had he the gold? or had the gold him?" *Id.* at 345 (quoting Ruskin). The primary difference between Ruskin and Radin is that the former seems to concentrate largely on the physical well-being of the owner whereas Radin is concerned primarily with her psychological well-being.

A seemingly more modest, but perhaps more fruitful, analysis of the apparent dichotomy between different forms of property holding is offered by Bernard Rudden in *Things as Thing and Things as Wealth,* 14 Oxford J. Legal Stud. 81 (1994). Rudden notes that people sometimes own some objects of property for their own sake, largely for sensuous enjoyment (things as things), and sometimes as a receptacle for value (things as wealth). Of course, sometimes the same object is owned for both purposes (such as one's home). Unlike Radin, he offers this as a descriptive fact, rather than as a normative judgment. He suggests that property law could be made more coherent if we were to be more express as to when we are picturing which form of property and trying to protect which function of property. He

therefore, to distinguish between the objects of property that "become justifiably bound up with the person"[61] from those that do not. Radin defines that class of objects bound up with the personhood of their owners as "personal property."[62] She describes property that people hold for purely instrumental reasons as "fungible property."[63] The way to distinguish between the fungible and personal property is by comparing

> the kind of pain that would be occasioned by its loss. . . . If a wedding ring is stolen from a jeweler, insurance proceeds can reimburse the jeweler, but if a wedding ring is stolen from a loving wearer, the price of a replacement will not restore the status quo—perhaps no amount of money can do so.[64]

Radin's work, to date, has primarily concerned identifying and distinguishing objects that are personal property from those that are merely fungible property and explicating the protections that the law should accord her favored category of personal property. Styling herself a "pluralist"[65] and a pragmatist,[66] Radin claims to reject the notion that all mar-

---

believes that his characterization is richer and potentially more useful than the obviously similar economic use value–exchange value dichotomy.

61. Radin, Reinterpreting Property, *supra* note 2, at 138; *see also id.,* at 38. The mere fact of being bound up is not sufficient to constitute an object as personal property. Radin's definition of personal property can differ between different subjects, but it is not purely subjective. *Id.* at 37. No one is more bound up with an object than a fetishist is with his fetish. Nevertheless, Radin deems this relationship to be unjustified and destructive of personhood. *Id.* at 38.

62. Radin, Reinterpreting Property, *supra* note 2, at 37. I reluctantly adopt Radin's terminology for the purposes of this chapter. The terms "personal" and "fungible" property already have very well recognized meanings in private law that differ significantly from Radin's usage. Generally, "personal" property refers to objects that are not "real" property, such as chattels and intangibles. "Fungible" property refers to objects that are practicably indistinguishable from others. In conventional terminology the same item—such as a grain of wheat—can be both personal and fungible. Indeed, under traditional equitable principles only personal property is fungible in the sense that individual parcels of real estate are thought to be so unique as to justify specific performance of real property contracts.

63. Radin, Reinterpreting Property, *supra* note 2, at 37. Radin recognizes that her dichotomy has similarities to, but is not identical with, Marx's dichotomy between objects held for use value and objects held for exchange value. *Id.* at 51, 53–55.

64. *Id.* at 37. Radin further maintains that "object-loss is more important than wealth-loss because object-loss is specially related to personhood in a way that wealth-loss is not." *Id.* at 65. Of course, in Hegelian vocabulary, "wealth" is every bit as much an "object" as physical things are.

65. Radin, *Market-Inalienability, supra* note 2, at 1857–59.

66. *Id.* at 1856, 1883.

ket relations inevitably alienate personhood.[67] She does not, however, suggest an affirmative role for the market in the development of personhood. Rather, she remains, at best, ambivalent about it. She sees

> a normatively appropriate but limited realm for commodification coexisting with one or more nonmarket realms. . . . For a pluralist, the crucial question is how to conceive of the permissible scope of the market.[68]

Yet Radin comes close to suggesting that in an ideal world, we would reject markets and commodification entirely.[69] As a pragmatist, however, she argues that in an imperfect world, markets and commodification need to be preserved as imperfect tools:

> One ideal world would countenance no commodification; another would insist that all harms to personhood are unjust; still another would permit no relationships of oppression or disempowerment. But we are situated in a nonideal world of ignorance, greed, and violence; of poverty, racism, and sexism. In spite of our ideals, justice under nonideal circumstances, pragmatic justice, consists in choosing the best alternative now available to us. . . .
>   The possible avenues for justifying market-inalienability must be reevaluated in light of our nonideal world.[70]

In other words, commodification of fungible goods is not harmful because they "have little to do with self-constitution."[71] But Radin nowhere recognizes the possibility that market (commodification) may in property circumstances be affirmatively beneficial to personhood.

By way of pragmatic compromise, Radin argues that commercial prostitution can slide down the slippery slope whereby feminine sexuality and, therefore, female personhood and human relations become commodified and women objectified.[72] But she also recognizes the "double bind" that prohibiting prostitution and criminalizing prostitutes may rob poor women of their only opportunity to make money and achieve even

---

67. *Id.* at 1857, 1870–74. Radin states, "Market-inalienability posits a nonmarket realm that appropriately coexists with a market realm, and this implicitly grants some legitimacy to market transactions, contrary to the non-commodifier's premise." *Id.* at 1875.

68. *Id.* at 1858.

69. Radin does pull back and suggest, however, that even in an ideal world the commodification of some products in market relations would continue. *Id.* at 1903.

70. *Id.* at 1915.

71. Radin, Contested Commodities, *supra* note 2, at 57.

72. Radin, *Market-Inalienability, supra* note 2, at 1922–23; *and* Radin, Contested Commodities, *supra* note 2, at 132–34.

a minimal amount of power and personhood.[73] She concludes that, although it might be unjust to discuss women's sexuality completely in terms of the market, there may be a pragmatic argument for allowing some limited commodification of sexual services, for example, by decriminalizing prostitution, but prohibiting its commercial exploitation through pimping, recruitment, and advertisement.[74] Consequently, Radin's theory fails to progress toward a complete law of property per se, in the sense of legal relationships among persons concerning external things.[75] Instead, it offers an alternative to property for a specific favored class of objects that become internalized to the owner. This is the solution proposed by Hegel, although, as we shall see, Hegel's category of things which should be inalienable as a matter of abstract right is much smaller than Radin's category of objects which should be market-inalienable to further personhood. According to Hegel, although all external things may initially be candidates for being objects of property, some objects become so internalized to the owner as to become part of the owner's personality.[76]

Perhaps most telling, Radin's disparagement of the market belies her personal/fungible property dichotomy and reveals the fundamentally solipsistic nature of her theory. As we have seen, she claims that if proper identification with personal property furthers human flourishing, then improper identification with fungible property is unhealthy fetishization. This implies that human flourishing requires that we should separate from, rather than identify with, fungible property. If, as Radin suggests, commodification and market relations (i.e., property and contract) are separating by their very nature, then human flourishing should be furthered by a market in fungible goods. Yet Radin can only grudgingly bring herself to support markets for pragmatic reasons in an imperfect world, and can imagine no intrinsic positive role for market in the development of personhood.

73. Radin, *Market-Inalienability, supra* note 2, at 1915–17; *and* Radin, Contested Commodities, *supra* note 2, at 127–30, 132.

74. Radin, *Market-Inalienability, supra* note 2, at 1934–35; *and* Radin, Contested Commodities, *supra* note 2, at 134–35.

75. In her most recent work, she tries to make a virtue out of this. As a self-identified pragmatist, she claims that her explorations are "retail rather than wholesale—sticking fairly close to the details of context and [that she is] not engaging in a search for a grand theory. In [Radin's] view, no one theory is suitable for all cases of contested commodification." Radin, Contested Commodities, *supra* note 2, at xii.

76. *See* G.W.F. Hegel, Elements of The Philosophy of Right 95–97 (H.B. Nisbet trans. & Allen E. Wood ed., 1991) [hereinafter Hegel, The Philosophy of Right].

C. Market Rhetoric

One of Radin's main arguments against the utilitarian analysis of human relations as market relations is that rhetoric has substantive effect—the rhetoric of alienation is itself alienating. Although I sympathize with Radin's condemnation of utilitarian analysis, her specific critique defeats itself. By labeling what might be more accurately analyzed as a jurisprudence of expanded bodily integrity as an account of property, Radin has all but given in to, rather than successfully challenged, the super-Benthamite claim that all human-object relations are property relations. This reduces her fundamental critique—that there is something qualitatively unique about our relationship to our bodies and certain other bodylike objects—to a relatively trivial debate over the definition and scope of property rights. For example, because Radin has chosen to analyze both bodily and commercial transactions in terms of property, she tries to downplay the role of traditional property rights in fungible property in the development of subjectivity. This strategy, however, can backfire. The super-Benthamite can agree with Radin's insistence that personal and fungible property are located on the same property spectrum, argue that market-alienability is not only necessary but appropriate for fungible property, and conclude that market-alienability is appropriate for all species of property. Radin, therefore, turns her back on her initial intuition that certain object relations are fundamentally different from commodity relations. Instead, she must make mere prudential arguments justifying limited exceptions to the market.[77]

Although Radin calls her theory "property for personhood" and insists that she is locating persons within community and that the relationship between person and object is socially mediated, she does not offer an account of property's role in community. To Radin, the property role of personal property is to remove and protect the owner from society. That is, because Radin presupposes community, property can only be seen as a means of separating from community. In an attempt to flee what she sees as the separation caused by property in community (i.e., alienation),

---

77. It is for this reason that Steven Munzer insists that, although people have some property rights in their bodies, it is inappropriate to analyze all body rights in terms of property precisely because the concept of property includes alienability. Steven R. Munzer, A Theory of Property 37–58 (1990).

This is a flaw of Radin's argument in *Market-Inalienability, supra* note 2. Although in that work she claims to take the position that alienability is not a necessary element of property, the form of her argument consists in justifying the inalienability of certain objects, i.e., alienability is implicitly assumed to be the starting point.

she necessarily returns to the ideal of the separate individual protecting her property from societal interference. Accordingly, Radin's theory risks being an account of property of nonsocial individuals, restating the traditional liberal theory of subjectivity as atomistic individuality—the precise opposite of her goal.[78] The likely result of concentrating only on the individual at this initial stage is the dilemma of classical liberalism—the individual is seen as authentic, but the community is a problem that needs to be explained. And yet, simultaneously, Radin's theory of the individual is not naturalistic but is based on an observation of individuals situated in a specific, concrete community. Such a theory can only be a tool for analyzing the positive law of property within a specific community. It cannot ground a critique of community.[79]

More specifically, to date, Radin has developed a sensuous notion of property that is limited to protecting consumption. As I have discussed, Radin's main concern is with the sensuous enjoyment of certain objects and, to a lesser extent, with the possession necessary for that enjoyment. This overriding concern evinces a solipsistic notion of subjectivity. Accordingly, she has deemphasized the possessory aspect of property, but, more dramatically, she has disparaged, and in some instances condemned, the intersubjective exchange of property.[80] Thus Radin leaves us with individuals who recognize themselves through their identification with property, yet never emerge from the walls of their self-imposed convent to interact as members of a community.

In so doing, Radin fails to consider that market alienation may encourage human flourishing in several ways. Market relations enable us to interrelate with other people and thereby become persons. Commodification frees us from overdependence on any specific objects. Market relations help us finance desirable intersubjective activities such as supporting children and other dependents. Market relations force us to become dependent on other persons. The market not only makes community possible, it makes it necessary.

Radin is concerned that too much emphasis on market rhetoric and

78. The difference between traditional liberalism and Radin's theory is that the former sees the individual property owner as *pre*-social, whereas she sees him as *post*-social. That is, property separates people and takes them out of community.

79. This may be another way of restating Schnably's critique of the inherent conservatism of Radin's theory. *See generally* Schnably, *supra* note 3.

80. Although Radin does suggest that, even in an ideal world, markets would not be abolished, her primary critique of universal noncommodification is pragmatic, not theoretical. *Market-Inalienability, supra* note 2, at 1871–77, 1903.

too much emphasis on fungible goods will cause universal commodification (commodification of people as well as things). On the one hand, she believes that this is alienating and objectifying. If all commodities are fungible (indistinguishable) by definition, this suggests that the commodification of persons causes them to lose their specific separate identities which, presumably, enable them to interact with each other on a personal level. That is, one person is as good as any other. On the other hand, she states that objectification "conceives of certain characteristics of persons—such as race, sex, or sexual orientation—as marks of lesser personhood."[81] This can result in the subordination of people who have these commodified characteristics.[82] Commodification, therefore, does *not* make all persons fungible, but gives too much importance to specific distinguishing characteristics. In other words, Radin has a confused, but intuitive, sense that treating all "objects" in the Hegelian sense as properly within the regime of property is somehow inhuman. As I have already indicated in the first chapter of this book and shall discuss below, Hegel would totally agree—some objects can become so internalized that they become part of personality and, therefore, not property. The problem is, however, that Radin refuses to make the Hegelian distinction between property and nonproperty. Because she intuits that expanded bodily integrity cannot rightly be subjected to a market regime, but insists that bodily integrity is property, she feels forced to challenge the rightness of the market regime (commodification) generally.

Although her theory of commodification as fungibility in the sense of pure interchangeability permeates her most recent work, it can most graphically be seen in her chapter on the "marketplace of ideas" metaphor, which she thinks treats one idea as being as good as any other.[83] Although a complete analysis of market theory is beyond the scope of this book, I believe that Radin is somewhat confused as to the nature of commodification because of the contradictory nature of much utilitarian writing on perfect markets. Radin thinks commodification means that all objects have the same status—we are indifferent among different objects of fungible property. It is no doubt true that Law and Economics would maintain that in a perfect market theory all objects eventually reach their exchange value and flow to the highest-valuing user—indeed, insofar as time and distance are themselves imperfections, they will always already

81. Radin, Contested Commodities, *supra* note 2, at 157.
82. *Id.*
83. Radin, Contested Commodities, *supra* note 2, at 164–83.

have done so. Consequently, all market exchange stops in the perfect market because everyone is indifferent between all objects. The perfect market is real in the Lacanian sense.

Radin is correct that much Law and Economics rhetoric constitutes an ostentatious display of indifference. But this is because its practitioners are adopting the second masculine response to castration. As we have seen, the Masculine tries to achieve wholeness by repressing the necessity for the lost object and imagining that immediate binary subject-to-subject relations are possible. But, like all masculine responses to castration, this facade of indifference is a lie. The only reason the Masculine enters into the symbolic order of exchange is *not* because he is indifferent to the lost *Phallus* but because he can think about nothing else.

Similarly, the reason why individuals enter into market exchange is *because* market participants are *not* indifferent between different objects. I exchange my money for a new pair of shoes because I recognize the shoes as different from and preferable to my money or other objects I could buy with my money. The merchant, in contradistinction, feels the opposite. That is, the very existence of exchange is the confirmation and actualization of differentiation.[84] For this reason, all real markets are necessarily imperfect.[85]

It is the exchange of properly externalized objects among persons that leads to the creation of subjectivity. As market society becomes more developed, it becomes more specialized. In the words of Shlomo Avineri, "Man produces not the objects of his own needs, but a general product which he can then exchange for the concrete object or specific objects of his need."[86] We, therefore, need to engage in transactions with others even to obtain the bare staples for survival. "The dialectics of civil society," according to Avineri, "create a universal dependence of man on man."[87] That is, prior to a market society, one was limited in persons with whom one was required to interact. One interacted personally with one's family and, perhaps, certain others like neighbors. One had to choose to interrelate with a wider range of persons and, even then, such personal interrelation may have been difficult if not impossible since one was defined generally in society by one's status rather than by one's in-

---

84. *See* Jeanne L. Schroeder, The End of the Perfect Market: A Psychoanalysis of Law and Economics (1997) (unpublished manuscript, on file with author).

85. *See* David Gray Carlson, *On the Margins of Microeconomics,* 14 Cardozo L. Rev. 1867 (1993); *and* Schroeder, *supra* note 84.

86. Shlomo Avineri, Hegel's Theory of the Modern State 91 (1984).

87. *Id*. at 146.

dividuality. The market breaks down this structure and forces us to interact as individuals.

In a recent article, J.E. Penner comes to a conclusion similar to Hegel's, albeit approaching this problem from a very different theoretical direction. Property, as a legal right, can only be understood socially. That is, he agrees with Hohfeld that property can only be understood as a relationship between and among legal persons (although, like me, he chides Hohfeld for not recognizing that the relationship of property always relates to a thing). To Penner this means that the most characteristic element of property must by necessity be its most social element. Possession and enjoyment are exclusive by nature. Their intersubjectivity is latent and negative in the sense that they require the expulsion of others. It is only in alienation that property becomes expressly and affirmatively intersubjective. Alienation is, therefore, the quintessential aspect of property.[88]

Finally, to anticipate a point I shall expand upon shortly, as an empirical matter, most of our relations with other members in our society are, in fact, the "fungible" object relations of commercial law—property and contract.[89] These are, of course, distant, formal, and abstract relationships that many of us (at least those of us who are not utilitarians) intuitively believe are fundamentally different from, and inferior to, the close, affective relationships we have with friends and family members. Although Hegel insisted on the importance of commodification and the necessity for the regime of civil society (i.e., the marketplace), he was also quite clear that a total market regime impoverishes and demeans the underclasses and that totally commodified labor alienates workers.[90] Civil society contains the contradiction that it is a regime of complete interde-

88. J.E. Penner, *The "Bundle of Rights" Picture of Property,* 43 UCLA L. Rev. 711, 747 (1996). As I discuss in chapter 1, Penner's conclusions are not identical with Hegel's. In his zeal to champion the fact that the intersubjectivity of property is actualized in alienation, he comes close to denying that possession and enjoyment are essential elements of property. Moreover, he incorrectly concludes that alienation through gift is a more social manifestation of property than alienation through contract.

89. That is, I strongly disagree on empirical grounds with Radin's assertion that "only a small fraction of everything we accept as property could possibly be justified by the conservative standard ideology [i.e., which sees all property as fungible and therefore freely alienable]." Radin, Reinterpreting Property, *supra* note 2, at 12. In contradistinction, I can think of very few objects I own—including my wedding ring—which I would not gladly trade for a price equal to one "util" above their replacement value.

Perhaps Radin has retreated somewhat from this position in that she has recently maintained that "lots of" and "many" things are fungible property which may be relatively harmlessly (if not properly or beneficially) commodified. Radin, Contested Commodities, *supra* note 2, at 57.

90. Even though Hegel does not present his analysis of poverty at length in *The Phi-*

pendence of all of its members, but it is characterized by egoism, whereby each member considers himself to be the atomistic individual of classical liberalism. Consequently, Hegel argued that it is logically necessary both to preserve and yet to limit commodification. Limitation is achieved in the family, which is characterized by particular altruism, and in the state, which is characterized by universal altruism.[91]

In other words, Radin is correct to chastise utilitarians for analyzing intimate love relations of family and friendship solely in terms of the market. But Radin herself must be chastised for criticizing all market relations for not being intimate. Indeed, it is precisely my point that it is incorrect to analyze erotic relations in terms of the traditional imagery of market relations because the latter does not recognize that even the market is erotic. In other words, Law and Economics is correct in recognizing that the market and other human relations share a fundamental essence, but incorrect in concluding from this that the latter can be reduced to the former. In contradistinction, the Hegelian would argue that the former is a primitive and inadequate aspect of the latter. It is desire for recognition by the Other, and not the accumulation of utility, that drives mankind.

D. Fungible Property

Finally, most mundanely, Radin's "property for personhood" dichotomy does not provide a tool that is useful for analyzing fungible property. Even if one accepts her self-characterization that she is developing a theory of property per se, rather than, for example, a theory of expanded bodily integrity, her theory is still inadequate to her purpose at this time. Radin claims not to be engaged in the philosophical task of positing abstract human nature. Rather, she claims to be a pragmatist analyzing concrete individuals located within a specific society—postindustrial America. This is a society built in large part around market relations and hundreds of years of property practice. An analysis of property that fails to provide tools for analyzing the market and the role

---

losophy of Right, Westphal believes that Hegel's analysis of poverty represents an important critique of the market and constitutes one of the contradictions that will lead to the sublation of civil society by the state under Hegel's theory. Merold Westphal, Hegel, Freedom, and Modernity 34–35 (1982). As Avineri explains, Hegel expounds on the idea of the degradation of the "rabble" more thoroughly in his earlier writings, and only some dim echoes of it found their way into *The Philosophy of Right.* Avineri, *supra* note 86, at 98.

91. *Id.* at 134.

the market plays in developing the personality of people in our society has limited pragmatic utility. So far, Radin's analysis comes close to a condemnation of the market generally—commodification is dangerous to personality because it causes objectification and separateness— modified by a grudging realization that some market relations must be preserved as a practical matter. In an imperfect world, total decom-modification may also be dangerous to personality because it might further disempower the weak. This analysis can be powerful if it justifies removing some human and object relations from the market and from property analysis. By labeling as "property" the objects that her theory teaches should be eliminated from the legal realm of property relations, however, she not only obscures the analysis but also leaves no tool for analysis of those object relations (what she calls relations with fungible property) that are appropriately left to the market and the traditional private law of property.

Moreover, Radin's use of the implicit feminine phallic metaphor for property, together with her disparagement of exchange, forces her to conflate property objects with physical objects, and property rights with sensuous enjoyment. This makes it an inappropriate starting place for analysis of some of the most economically important types of property in contemporary society, such as intellectual property and other incorporeals, which have no tangible existence. By justifying property solely in terms of its constituting function for the natural individual, she is left with no account of the way the largest aggregations of wealth are amassed and held in our society—collectively, but not governmentally, by private business organizations.

To put it another way, perhaps because she concentrates on the subject's identification with her objects, she does not consider the intersubjective reasons why people own *fungible* property. For example, investment property such as treasury notes and stock in publicly traded corporations would seem to be the ultimate "fungible property."[92] People often choose to forgo acquiring "personal property," such as a nicer house, car, or wedding ring, in order to purchase "fungible property" as a means to finance activities which are central to human flourishing, such as saving to pay for one's children's education. And yet Radin would give the property of the thrifty parent a lower level of constitutional protection than that of the spendthrift. She prefers the grasshopper over the ant.

Most important for the sake of this essay, Radin's focus on personal

92. As Radin recognizes. Radin, Contested Commodities, *supra* note 2, at 58.

property risks being subjective to the point of insular, if not altogether solipsistic and anti-community. That is, Radin condemns commodification as the source of separate subjectivity, as opposed to subjectivity as intersubjectivity. According to Radin:

> Commodification stresses separateness both between ourselves and our things and between ourselves and other people. To postulate personal interrelationship and communion requires us to postulate people who can yield personal things to other people and not have them instantly become fungible.[93]

In this passage, Radin admits to the existence of healthy intersubjectivity, but it is a matter of taste only for the solipsistic self. As we have seen, Radin simultaneously argues for the existence of personal property precisely because it furthers the development of separate individuality. The quoted passage shows that although gifts might be permitted or beneficial, in no sense is the gift of personal property developmentally *required*.[94] That is, properly constituted persons are capable of gift, but gift does not make them into well-adjusted persons.

But more pertinent to the point at hand, although Radin admits that the institution of private property can further the goal of separate individuality, she does not yet recognize that it also furthers the competing goal of interrelation. Radin ignores the reality that the relations most of us share with other members of our community involve fungible property—that is, commercial relationships. Every day, I interact with thousands, if not millions, of other people in society through the marketplace.

Exchange also serves relationality and community on a philosophical

---

93. Radin, *Market-Inalienability, supra* note 2, at 1907–08.

94. We have already seen that Radin believes that one of the purposes of owning personal property is the furthering of individual separateness. In contrast,

> gift takes place within a personal relationship with the recipient, or else it creates one. . . . To postulate personal interrelationship and bonding requires us to postulate people who can yield personal things to other people and not have them instantly become fungible. Seen this way, gifts diminish separateness.

Radin, Contested Commodities, *supra* note 2, at 93–94. This seems to imply that gifts of personal property actually defeat one of the primary purposes of personal property. I presume Radin would answer that separateness is only one aspect of human nature, and not necessarily the most important one. We cannot be human without also having relationships with other parties. Through a judicious combination of identification and enjoyment of personal property, on the one hand, and giving it, on the other, one can achieve the proper balance between separateness and connectedness.

basis. Radin condemns separateness but cannot do without it theoretically. For me to have a relationship with another person, I must first recognize and respect the other as a subject, not merely as an extension of
myself or as a means to my ends. Žižek explains:

> [W]e can recognize the other, acknowledge him as person, only in so far
> as, in a radical sense, he remains unknown to us—recognition implies the
> absence of cognition. A neighbor totally transparent and disclosed is no
> more a "person," we no longer relate to him as to another person: inter-
> subjectivity is founded upon the fact that the other is phenomenologically
> experienced as an "unknown quantity," as a bottomless abyss which we
> can never fathom.[95]

Intersubjectivity thus requires a mediator who simultaneously separates
us and serves as a bridge between us. Property is one such mediator.

As I have already suggested, commodification not merely enables us
to interrelate as subjects, it forces us to do so. The market, in the name
of autonomy, destroys our atomism and makes us interdependent on each
other for our very existence.

Radin is correct in arguing that it is somehow dehumanizing to analyze my relationship with my husband, family, and closest friends in terms
of market exchange.[96] But the market becomes more important to relationships as the circle of acquaintance widens. I have not always had close
personal relations with colleagues, employees, clients, opposing counsel,
or even my former law partners. Indeed, in many cases I did not want close
personal relations because of personal dislike, simple disinclination, or
snobbery. Commercial transactions are one of the ways to maintain cor-
dial relations that are productive not merely in a financial sense but in an
interpersonal and developmental sense as well. For example, I can easily
relate to the new cashier at the grocery store in terms of fungible property
relations even if I am shy, socially incompetent, or merely busy. Fungible
property serves as a mediator, enabling me to form and to maintain relationships as a member of the same community with the store's employees
and suppliers. One way in which modern industrial societies are superior
to feudal or other traditional societies is that modern commercial relations
allow us to form relationships and community far beyond our family or
clan. This is the aspect of the Hegelian theory of property that Radin needs
to reconsider if she is to account fully for property's relationship to per-

95. Slavoj Žižek, For They Know Not What They Do: Enjoyment as a Political Factor
198–99 (1991) [hereinafter Žižek, For They Know Not What They Do].
96. Even these relations are, however, mediated.

sonhood. Finally, market relations help to finance the intersubjective relation of the family. Market relations offer an important supplement to, not substitution for, the intimate relations that concern Radin.[97]

II. A RETURN TO HEGEL'S THEORY OF PROPERTY

Radin claims a debt to Hegel's theory of property while simultaneously distancing herself from it.[98] I believe Radin's desire to distance herself from Hegel stems in large part from misreading him. By misreading Hegel, Radin has forced herself into a dilemma in which she must choose between humans as atomistic, autonomous, and individually subjective and humans as victims submitted to the oppression of the objectivity of society. I suggest that to avoid Radin's dilemma and to begin to conceptualize a proper role for property in the development of both subjectivity and community, we should return to Hegel to identify Radin's fundamental misreading and, with luck, avoid her errors.

Radin's characterization of *The Philosophy of Right* is frustrating because it is highly accurate in detail but incorrect in whole. Accordingly, her account is partial and decentered. By concentrating only on certain elements of a holistic theory, Radin unintentionally achieves what Marx intentionally strove for: she stands Hegel on his head.

A. Radin's Misreading

Hegel's view of the person, Radin argues, was "the same as Kant's—simply an abstract autonomous entity capable of holding rights, a device for abstracting universal principles, and by definition, de-

---

97. As Hegel discussed, expanding market relations may reduce the scope of the family from the clan to the nuclear family and diminish the role of the family as a political unit. *See* Allen W. Wood, *Editor's Introduction* to Hegel, The Philosophy of Right, *supra* note 76, at viii, xxii–xxiii.

As Ronald Coase has emphasized (defending Adam Smith's classical liberal conception of human nature),

> [t]he great advantage of the market is that it is able to use the strength of self-interest to offset the weakness and partiality of benevolence, so that those who are unknown, unattractive, or unimportant, will have their wants served.

R.H. Coase, *Adam Smith's View of Man,* 19 J.L. & Econ. 529, 544 (1976).

98. *See* Radin, *Market-Inalienability, supra* note 2, at 1892–96; Radin, Reinterpreting Property, *supra* note 2, at 437–48.

void of individuating characteristics."[99] Radin recognizes that Hegel departed from Kantian liberalism in *The Philosophy of Right* when he argued that the abstract will and society eventually develop through higher forms until they reach the "final ideal unity of individuals and the state."[100] Radin also recognized that Hegel "implicitly claims that personhood in the richer sense of self-development and differentiation presupposes the context of human community."[101] And yet she declares that, like Kant, Hegel "treats [the Kantian abstract personality] as both logically and developmentally prior to any relationships of right arising from the person's interaction with others in society."[102]

Radin claims that her theory of property is superior to Hegel's because she bases her theory on a richer notion of the individual than the autonomous, abstract will on which Hegel relies, ignoring Hegel's later notions of the individual in community.[103] Radin argues that Hegel had a not-so-secret agenda of justifying market relations.[104] She criticizes Hegel's theory of alienability of property as arising from a strict subject/object distinction.[105] She claims that Hegel's definition of "object"

> fall[s] back on the intuition that some things are "external" and some are "internal." This answer is unsatisfactory because the categories "external" and "internal" should be the conclusion of a moral evaluation and cannot be taken as obvious premises forming its basis. . . . Hegel's solution is also unsatisfactory because (at least from our present vantage point) we can see that the external/internal distinction is a continuum and not a bright-line dichotomy.[106]

99. Radin, Reinterpreting Property, *supra* note 2, at 44. Radin notes that the Kantian person "is a free and rational agent whose existence is an end in itself." *Id.* at 39. Radin argues that Hegel accepted this Kantian view of the person as the completely abstract, autonomous, individual will. *Id.* at 44–45, 47.

100. *Id.* at 46.
101. *Id.* at 47.
102. *Id.* at 46.
103. Specifically, Radin states:

Hegel departs from classical liberalism in discussing these other kinds of property relationships. For Hegel, individuals could not become fully developed outside such relationships. They are important in comparing Hegel's theory to a theory of personal property, because *the concept of person in the theory of personal property refers to the fully developed individual.*

Id. at 46 (emphasis added).

104. Radin, *Property and Personhood, supra* note 2, at 974; Radin, *Market-Inalienability, supra* note 2, at 1888–89, 1894. She calls his analysis a "troubled apology for the market." Radin, Contested Commodities, *supra* note 2, at 38.

105. Radin, *Market-Inalienability, supra* note 2, at 1892–94.
106. *Id.* at 1908–09.

Radin contrasts her flexible personal/fungible property spectrum with what she sees as a hard-edged, either/or Hegelian dichotomy.

Very briefly, what Radin claims to take from Hegel is, first, his insistence that the autonomous individual of classical liberalism is not a satisfactory account of the free human being and, second, his recognition that personhood requires both the ownership of property and a community for complete development. She takes Hegel's analysis of the internal logic of property as abstract right to be an empirical account of actual property practices.

By comparing her theory of property for personhood within community to the Hegelian person and Hegel's initial analysis of the subject and property, Radin compares apples to oranges. As I have said, because Radin locates people originally within community, her concept of personal property can only serve to remove her from community—precisely the opposite of her goal. Instead, Radin should compare her property for personhood theory to the Hegelian notion of the fully developed individual and the role of property in the fully developed community, as embodied by the state. In the circular Hegelian dialectic, however, these fully developed concepts cannot be understood without first understanding their logically prior, more abstract, and undeveloped manifestations.

Specifically, Radin claims to agree with Hegel that the complete individual does not exist naturally but must be developed.[107] This is precisely why Radin explores the role that property plays in this development and claims to be analyzing the individual within community. But because she confuses Hegel's logical analysis of abstract personhood with an empirical account of the development of human beings, she assumes that a specific community already exists at the beginning of the analysis.[108] This assumption is problematic if, as Radin agrees, personhood (subjectivity) is not a preexisting abstraction but is a human creation, and if, as I suspect Radin would agree, community is also a human creation. As human creations, personhood and community are likely to be mutually constituting. Radin concentrates on the aspect of Hegelian property theory that relates to the creation of personhood (as subjectivity), but she ignores the

107. Radin, Reinterpreting Property, *supra* note 2, at 45.

108. In the preface of her book compiling her articles on property, Radin makes a half-hearted attempt to defend herself from the charge that she is positing a narcissistic immediate relationship between subject and object. Radin, Reinterpreting Property, *supra* note 2, at 7–8. The quotation set forth in note 5, *supra,* reveals that, rather than having an account of society, she seems to assume that society already exists. She does not understand that Hegel's account of property is an account of how the individual enters society.

aspect of property that relates to the creation of community, which then relates back to the full development of personhood (as individuality). In chapter 1, I showed how Hegel's analysis started with the abstract, pre-social person because he believed that the individual and the community were mutually constituting—developing together—and that primitive property relations were an important step in this development.

Radin presents Hegel as justifying the liberal market agenda and promoting separateness. This is a serious misstatement, in the sense of a half-truth. In fact, as I have shown, Hegel simultaneously explains, justifies, and subverts the simple, liberal market agenda;[109] it is Radin who implicitly adopts the liberal understanding of the market. Radin and classical liberalism understand or justify the market in terms of the separateness of individuals. Radin understands the utilitarian branch of liberalism as interpreting all human relations in terms of market transactions.[110] Radin argues that we should remove certain object relations from the market to prevent overseparateness,[111] but this presupposes the existence of community from which the market separates individuals. She seeks to prevent the objectification and commodification of certain privileged things,[112] but this assumes that some things start out as interrelated with subjectivity. In Radin's view, submission to the market regime inexorably leads to commodification of all human relations. Thus, despite her denials, Radin implicitly accepts the strength of the utilitarian argument that once the market is introduced, the market is the only form of analysis possible.

In other words, Radin is correct in her observation that property is the link between the concept of the autonomous individual of liberalism and the ideal of community. But because she imagines that the person starts out as an integrated member of a preexisting community, she wrongly concludes that it is property which breaks down the community into separate atomistic individuals. To Radin, person bound to object is no longer person bound to community. Hegel, in contradistinction, does not presuppose individuality or community. Rather, he explores the internal

109. *See* Westphal, *supra* note 90, at 34–35.
110. Radin, *Market-Inalienability, supra* note 2, at 1861–70, 1883–87.
111. *Id.* at 1907–08. Although Radin does see separateness as one aspect of personhood and admits that the ownership of personal property can further this function, this is only one of many aspects of personhood. Overseparateness would be destructive of human flourishing because "self-constitution includes connectedness with other human beings and also with things in the world." Radin, Contested Commodities, *supra* note 2, at 57.
112. *See, e.g., id.* at 118–28, 159–60.

logic of community itself. As we shall see, he abstracts the concept of the abstract person as a logically necessary element of the concept of community. He then asks, "If, as this suggests, autonomy is a true moment of human nature, how do autonomous persons become interdependent as members of a community?" The answer will be, through property, the *link* between individual and community which binds subject to subject rather than person to object.

Specifically, as Hegel believes that one can only understand the actualization of a concept retroactively at the end of an era, he analyzes the development of the modern liberal state of the early nineteenth century. He, in effect, asks why the enlightenment concepts of individual liberty and democracy[113] only arose simultaneously with the development of the free capitalist market. According to this analysis, the market (i.e., abstract right and civil society) simultaneously recognizes separateness and creates differentiation, allowing us to develop as autonomous free individuals, while lessening separateness by making people interdependent and thereby binding them together. In a proper Hegelian analysis, it is the Radinian person who is bound up with her things and refuses to come out to the market, thus isolating and separating herself. Such chaste virginity, perhaps initially necessary for integrity, withers over time to lonely sterility. Radin's person is not free. Like Gollum in *The Lord of the Rings,* or the genie of the lamp, she is a slave to an object—bound by the chains of property. If Radin's person is bound up with objects, Hegel's subject owns objects only so that she may become bound up with other subjects. For Hegel, although the intersubjective relation of the market is logically prior to other relations, the experience changes the subjects and enables them to have more complex moral and ethical relations.

Consequently, Radin is correct that Hegel justified the existence of the market. But whereas the utilitarian justifies all human relations in terms of the market, Hegel would justify the primitive relations of the market only in terms of their role in the development of more fully developed personality and social relations. Market relations embody the sphere that Hegel calls "civil society,"[114] but civil society does not constitute all of so-

113. Of course, the fact that the specific manifestation of the liberal state discussed in *The Philosophy of Right* is a constitutional monarchy in which people vote by estates seems one of the most problematic aspects of the book when read at the end of the twentieth century.

114. "Civil society" for Hegel includes the market, although it is not completely limited to the market. *See* Wood, *supra* note 97, at xviii–xix.

ciety, let alone the highest stage of society. Erotic relations reflect market relations, but only because market relations are themselves essentially, albeit primitively, erotic.

Before going any further, let us discuss terminology to avoid a potential source of confusion for the reader. As I have suggested, Radin and Hegel use the term "person" in two different ways that are not directly comparable.[115] Radin uses the words "person" and "personhood" to describe her concept of the fully developed, integrated, and mature human being situated in a community—that is, empirical people. She contrasts this with Hegel's use of "person" in *The Philosophy of Right*, in which Hegel began with the most minimal, abstract, and immediate concept of what a person could be: self-consciousness as absolutely free will. Radin is correct that Hegel's starting point is essentially the same as the Kantian construct. To say, however, that Hegel initially develops an inadequate concept of property based on a primitive, abstract, negative, and inadequate concept of the person is not a critique of Hegel. It is precisely Hegel's point: the initial concepts of the abstract person and the later concepts of subjectivity and private property at the level of abstract right are necessary building blocks of the full individual and full human relationships. As building blocks, however, these concepts are both necessary and inadequate *by definition*.

This minimal concept of "personality," like its liberal cousin the autonomous individual, is totally negative. But the Hegelian "person" does not stand, as Radin implies, in quite the same normative position as the autonomous individual of Kant or other liberal philosophers. Radin is confused because she purports to set forth an empirical description of how actual individuals are born into a society and become attached to objects as they grow up. She, mistakenly, assumes that Hegel is involved in a similar project. Consequently, Radin describes Hegel as believing that the abstract person is both logically and developmentally prior to the more

---

115. Radin states that "even though Hegel does not use the word person for the entity described as the person in the theory of personal property, Hegel's theory can be seen as consistent with the idea of personal property." Radin, Reinterpreting Property, *supra* note 2, at 45. This statement is inconsistent with both T.M. Knox's well-known English translation and H.B. Nisbet's more recent translation, which use the words "person" and "personality" to describe the abstract will as soon as it begins to interact with property. *See* G.W.F. Hegel, Hegel's Philosophy of Right 40 (T.M. Knox trans., 1952) *and* Hegel, The Philosophy of Right (Nisbet trans.), *supra* note 76, at 489.

Of course, Radin also criticizes Hegel's property theory because the Hegelian "person" is not fully developed. But Hegel presented the "person" as merely a logical step in the development of the "individual."

complex individual in society.[116] This is misleading because, in Hegel's view, the abstract person is not developmentally prior in any *empirical* sense. The abstract person of Hegel and Kant is not the unformed baby who eventually matures into an adult personality, and Hegel is not trying to describe the empirical process by which actual human beings acquire and become sentimentally attached to specific items of property. He is discussing the logical process of how one gets from the Kantian concept of the abstract person to the concept of the legal subject.

Hegel would agree with Radin that the economic man posited by Law and Economics theory does not accurately describe a human being. It is a caricature that grossly overemphasizes one feature. In this case, the feature may be seen as a lowest common denominator of human relations. It should not be disparaged in its proper context in that it not only allows us to have formal relations with those who are distant from us but also serves as a building block in more complex relations. Of this view of human nature, Hegel remarked that the contentions that all human actions are economically instrumental "belittle and debase all great deeds and individuals."[117] Consequently, Hegelian theory must be read as a rejection of liberal theories that see society as merely an aggregate of isolated individuals and utilitarianism that seeks merely to maximize the aggregated wealth of those individuals at the expense of the freedom of any one individual.[118] Although Hegel introduced the *Mensch* (i.e., the abstract person) early in *The Philosophy of Right,* the rest of the book logically demonstrates the inadequacy of both the abstract person and abstract right (i.e., property) standing alone and presents a theory of society that

116. According to Radin, Hegel "treats them [rights and abstract personality] as both logically *and developmentally* prior to any relationships of right arising from the person's interactions with others in society." Radin, Reinterpreting Property, *supra* note 2, at 46 (emphasis added). Radin's description of the way an individual puts her will into an object reveals that Radin actually believes Hegel's developmental priority is empirical. For example, Radin critiques Hegel for assuming that object relations development takes place "overnight," while her theory accounts for development over time. See *id.* at 111; *see also id.* at 107.

117. Hegel, The Philosophy of Right, *supra* note 76, at 152. As Avineri explains, "Hegel is aware that this tendency of civil society concepts to arrogate to themselves all other spheres of life is very strong; but he speaks against it when civil society encroaches on the realm of the family as well as when it encroaches on that of the state." Avineri, *supra* note 86, at 139.

118. *See* Wood, *supra* note 97, at xvi. Utilitarian justifications for private property are based on maximizing the happiness (or wealth) of society as a whole. Hegel, in contradistinction, based his argument solely on the logic of personhood without regard to its implications for the satisfaction of needs or the creation of happiness or wealth. *See, e.g.,* Hegel, The Philosophy of Right, *supra* note 76, at 73. As I have discussed, Hegel was well aware that the regime of abstract right in civil society may actually lead to impoverishment and alienation.

could enable the development of a full individual within community. According to Hegel, the market regime of civil society is necessary for the development of the state but is not itself the state. In other words, the *Mensch* encountered at the beginning of *The Philosophy of Right* is not what we in New York would call "a real mensch."[119]

In her critique, Radin does not grasp the implication of the circular nature of the Hegelian dialectic. The *order* of the logical presentation is important but does not have the same normative import that it has in liberalism. In liberalism, the state must be justified given the normative priority of the autonomous individual. To Hegel, the individual is prior to the state only in the sense that the individual is more primitive in a logical sense.[120] Hegel therefore discussed the individual as a temporary presupposition. Hegel expressly denied that the progression he presented, from abstract will to family to civil society to state and from abstract right to morality to ethics, is developmentally true as an empirical fact.[121] Hegel

119. This familiar Yiddishism captures Hegel's point that to be a fully developed human being is a great accomplishment. Neither the "abstract will" presented at the beginning of *The Philosophy of Right* nor the Hegelian person, the "legal subject" who is created by property and contract in the realm of Abstract Right, is yet an individual. Rather, they are merely moments in the creation of a full individual. As one scholar explained:

> Just as the individual whose behavior and attitudes are defined entirely in terms of rights is pathetically less than a real person, so the society implicit in the meeting of legal persons is abstract, immediate, formal, and false, because it is "only as owners that these two persons exist for each other."

Westphal, *supra* note 90, at 30 (quoting Hegel, *The Philosophy of Right*). Another scholar states:

> The abstract person is not yet a full person as she is severed from, among other things, all concrete family relations, the attributes of citizenship, and all roots in historical reality. Nevertheless, the abstract person who possesses an individual will and is a bearer of rights displays a sufficient identity to count as a subject of recognition.

Michel Rosenfeld, *Hegel and the Dialectics of Contract,* 10 Cardozo L. Rev. 1199, 1230 (1989) (footnote omitted).

120. As I discuss extensively in chapter 1, Hegel's procedure in each of his major works was to start with the simplest, most primitive concept and to work up to the most complex. As Westphal explains:

> Now, because property is the first embodiment of freedom (in the Hegelian sense of logical priority), his theory is also a critique of liberalism's (formalist) tendency to define freedom without paying sufficient attention to questions of morality, the family, the political community, and severe poverty. When Locke makes property rights first, it is because they are the end to which everything else is means. When Hegel puts them first it is because in their immediate form as the minimal mode of human freedom they are in radical need of correction and completion through contextualizing.

Westphal, *supra* note 90, at 31.

121. For example, Hegel wrote:

said that the "logical order" was not the "time order."[122] Thus, for example, he addressed property before the family even though we are born into
the family before we encounter property.

This does not mean that the abstract, inadequate concepts that begin
Hegel's analysis lack normative significance. I have only said that logical
priority does not have the same normative import in Hegel's philosophy
as it does in liberal philosophy.

> To call a subject matter or discussion abstract rather than concrete, im-
> mediate rather than mediated, or formal rather than substantial is to say
> that it is part of a complex whole that has been isolated from its proper
> context. In its isolation it can neither be, nor be seen to be, what it in truth
> is; for "the truth is the whole." Only in the totality of their relations to the
> whole can any of the parts (moments) either be, or be understood to be,
> what they truly are.[123]

Hegel purported to prove that the Kantian autonomous person is inadequate and contradictory and is always already becoming the individual within the state.[124] Nonetheless, the earlier moments of the dialectic
are true moments in, and necessary building blocks of, the latter. As such,

---

> But it should be noted that the moments, whose result is a further-determined form [of
> the concept], precede it as determinations of the concept in the scientific development
> of the Idea, but do not come before it as shares in its temporal development. Thus the
> Idea, in its determination as the family, presupposes those determinations of the con-
> cept from which in a later section of this work, it [i.e., the Idea] will be shown to re-
> sult. But the other side of this development is that these inner presuppositions should
> also be present for themselves as *shapes,* such as the right of property, contract, moral-
> ity, etc., and it is only at a more advanced stage of culture [*Bildung*] that the moments
> of development attain this distinctive shape of existence.

Hegel, The Philosophy of Right, *supra* note 76, at 61.

122. *Id.* at 61–62.

123. Westphal, *supra* note 90, at 29.

124. Stillman observes:

> For Locke, Kant, and Rawls, not only is the state of nature primary, in the sense of com-
> ing first in order either historically or conceptually, but conclusions derived from it are
> also primary, in the sense of coming first in predominance. Or, as Dworkin would have
> it, institutions, and ideas that come later in order than those derived from the abstract
> original condition are always to be tested against, subjected to, and vulnerable to being
> "trumped" by the principles derived from the abstract original condition.

Given the structure of Hegel's thought, his abstract right functions in exactly the opposite
way. Abstract right, being first or primary in the logical order of the major parts of Hegel's
political philosophy, is therefore the least adequate part of "objective spirit." Peter Stillman,
Hegel's Analysis of Property in The Philosophy of Right, 10 Cardozo L. Rev. 1031, 1038–39 (1980).

Rosenfeld explains Hegel's view this way:

they deserve respect and preservation. In other words, although the abstract person will be sublated into the concrete individual located within society, separateness and the need for mediation always remain. Even though Hegel claimed to prove that the abstract person is inadequate and is destined to be superseded, it simultaneously retains a moment of validity to which the system continually returns.

B. Hegel and Community

Radin repeats another common and related misunderstanding of Hegel:

> For Hegel, the properly developed state (in contrast to civil society) is an organic moral entity, "the actuality of the ethical Idea," and individuals within the state are subsumed into its community morality.
>
> Hegel's theory of the state thus carries the seeds of destruction of all liberal rights attaching to individuals (because in the state particular arbitrary will passes over into willing the universal).[125]

Radin's statement is once again incorrect because it is partial. The Hegelian concept of the state would crush the individual if Radin were correct that the dialectic "subsumed" all prior contradictions in the sense of obliterating them. But sublation preserves, as much as negates. The negative freedom of the arbitrary will and the primitive concept of property that Hegel introduced at the beginning of his political philosophy are elements of the more complex individual citizen of the state. In the dialectical logic of sublation, if the state supersedes civil society, it also preserves it. For individuals to exist who can be citizens of the state, there must be a moment when these individuals are separate from the

---

Actually, Hegel's abstract person is very much like Hobbes's individual found in the state of nature. There is, however, an important difference between the two conceptions. Hegel calls his counterpart to the Hobbesian individual in the state of nature the "abstract person," indicating that this person is a construct who has been cut off from many of the diverse concrete determinations of the real historical person. Thus, whereas the free willing subject who is the protagonist of the Philosophy of Right may at first view herself as embodying the characteristics of the abstract person, Hegel is well aware that the abstract person provides only a partial representation of the subject of legal and political relations. Hobbes, on the other hand, presents the abstract atomistic individual of his state of nature as the true representative of a universal and ahistorical conception of the human nature.

Rosenfeld, *supra* note 119, at 1209 (footnotes omitted).

125. Radin, Reinterpreting Property, *supra* note 2, at 46.

state.[126] Thus, the state must preserve these liberal elements to some extent. In other words, although it is true that Hegel thought that the individual and the state would eventually attain unity, this is *not* the presymbolic, deadly lack of differentiation of the real, or the simple identity of the imaginary. Rather, like all Hegelian totalities, the union of individual and state will have a hole—a place of unbounded freedom—at its very heart.[127]

As we have seen, Radin, the pragmatist, would grudgingly preserve some market relations for pragmatic and utilitarian reasons in an imperfect world.[128] Hegel, the idealist, would preserve market relations, even in a perfect world, because they contain an important moment in the actualization of freedom.[129]

Radin also misunderstands Hegel's theory of why it is necessary for private property to continue after the development of the state, and Hegel's thinking as to the possibility of collective property. Radin writes that "there is in Hegel's theory a foundation for the communitarian claim that each community is an organic entity in which private property ownership does not make sense. Hegel does not make this claim, perhaps because he is too firmly rooted in his own time."[130]

I believe this reflects, once again, a conflation of Hegel's account of the logic of the development of the individual and the state with empirical accounts of human biography and European history. Abstract right (including property) is the subject of the first chapter of *The Philosophy of Right,* and the state is the subject of the last. Radin assumes from this that Hegel believes that the free market develops first temporally and that then, sometime in the future, a state will develop which could at least theoretically supplant private property.[131] This is not correct. All but one of the types of intersubjective relations which Hegel identifies as being logically generated from the concept of the free individual have been around for an unspeakably long time—families of some sort (if not the monogamous nuclear family) have probably been around since man first started walk-

---

126. Hegel, The Philosophy of Right, *supra* note 76, at 283–85.

127. Žižek, The Indivisible Remainder, *supra* note 7, at 105.

128. Radin, *Market-Inalienability, supra* note 2, at 1903.

129. Avineri explains, "Since property is to Hegel the prime condition of personality, . . . the abolition of private property . . . spells for Hegel the disappearance and emasculation of personality . . . . " Avineri, *supra* note 86, at 171.

130. Radin, Reinterpreting Property, *supra* note 2, at 46–47.

131. She finds it is unclear whether Hegel thinks property and contract will continue, change, or disappear entirely in the realm of *Sittlichkeit.* Radin, Contested Commodities, *supra* note 2, at 39.

ing upright, governments have existed for thousands of years, corporations and other fraternal organizations for hundreds. What was missing was the free market regime of civil society with its related concepts of private property and freedom of contract (i.e., abstract right). That is, although abstract right is the most primitive form of intersubjectivity as a logical matter, it was the last to be actualized as a historic one. It was only when these logically necessary elements were actualized in the empirical world that the state and the individual could complete their self-actualization. If, at this stage, the government tried to abrogate these rights, it would stop the process of its own actualization dead in its tracks. Consequently, although the state is the sublation of abstract right, as is the case with all sublations, it cannot obliterate this earlier stage as unnecessary because the state only came into being at the moment that abstract right came into being. That is, as I shall explore in more detail in chapter 4, the necessity of sublation is retroactive. It is only now that we are starting to develop the state and individual freedom that we can retroactively understand that private property was necessary for this to happen.

Once the workings of sublation are understood, therefore, it is clear that there can be no communitarian claim for the total withering away of private property in Hegel's theory. A moment of private property must be preserved to allow for the constitution of intersubjective individuals as citizens. This moment of private property, however, does not preclude the possibility of collective property or limits on private property. Hegel mentioned in passing various types of collective ownership, including family and corporate ownership, throughout *The Philosophy of Right*. Hegel did not concentrate on collective ownership, however, presumably because he did not believe it serves the same logically necessary constitutive role for the family, corporation, or state that private property serves for the abstract person. This does not imply that collective property cannot or should not exist. Although collective property does not play a necessary constitutive role, collective property may be a contingent, empirical fact of life, a creature of positive law in any given society, so long as individuals hold some private property.

C. The Starting Presupposition of Personality

One of the central concerns of Hegel's theory is that the individual and society develop together, but Radin does not internalize the spiraling, retrospective nature of the dialectic. Specifically, Radin mistakenly describes the choice of the abstract will as a starting place for analysis as "assuming away" the attributes of personhood.[132] To Hegel, individual characteristics are "abstracted" away, not "assumed" away. The distinction is subtle, but crucial, as it reflects the retroactive nature of Hegel's reasoning. Abstraction is the breaking down of the complex into simple, essential components. Hegelian analysis retrospectively applies the dialectic to the individual human being in the state and abstracts to the most universal, only to circle back to show how individuating characteristics necessarily and logically develop from the abstraction. In other words, the initial abstraction does not assume away individuating characteristics but rather presupposes that individuating characteristics are always already imminent.[133] Abstraction is an attempt to explain individuation and community. For example, when an engineer considers the characteristics of a brick, she does not "assume" away the building but rather presupposes the brick's eventual function in the finished building.[134] As I shall develop at greater length in chapter 4, pursuant to Hegel's concepts of potentiality and actuality, the actualization of complex individuating characteris-

132. For example, Radin writes, "The intuitive personhood perspective on property is not equivalent to Hegelian personality theory, because that perspective incorporates the attributes of personhood that Hegel initially assumes away." Radin, Reinterpreting Property, *supra* note 2, at 47; *see also id.* at 44–45, 46.

Munzer similarly misunderstands Hegel's starting point of abstract personhood. He states:

> Hegel's conception of personhood, in the section on "abstract right," seems to presuppose an individualistic moral and political personhood. Yet perhaps there are other, communitarian views of moral and political personhood. If so, private-property rights might diminish personhood in the event that they foster the isolation of persons from one another.

Munzer, *supra* note 77, at 82 (citing Radin, *Property and Personhood*). As we have seen, Hegel does not "seem" to presuppose individualistic personhood, he expressly does so. Moreover, he does so not because he rejects a communitarian view of personhood, but because he wishes to show the inadequacy of the Kantian view of personhood and prove the necessity of a communitarian side of personhood.

133. A good expression of the retroactivity of Hegel's logic is his description of the logical ordering of civil society and the state:

> Civil society is the [stage of] difference . . . which intervenes between the family and the state, even if its full development . . . occurs later than that of the state; for as difference, it presupposes the state, which it must have before it as a self-sufficient entity in order to subsist . . . itself.

Hegel, The Philosophy of Right, *supra* note 76, at 220. This passage shows that the logically earlier stage presupposes the later stage, rather than the later presupposing the earlier.

134. To give an analogy from physics, it is incorrect to say that the Heisenberg uncertainty principle initially "assumes away" determinacy merely because it posits that exact position and momentum do not exist simultaneously at the subatomic level. Rather, as Norwood Russell Hanson explained, Heisenberg's theory of indeterminacy at the subatomic

tics of personality at the highest level of development logically requires that they were already potential at the primal level of abstract personhood. We can never know what was possible until it is actualized—possibility is abstracted from actuality.

Most fundamentally, Radin never grasps that Hegel's point is that the abstract person cannot develop subjectivity in lonely isolation but only through recognition by other subjects. Property does not, as Radin thinks, help the abstract person develop her individual separateness. Rather, the separate individual uses property to achieve the differentiation necessary for the relationship of intersubjectivity through mediation. We, therefore, seek to acquire property only derivatively to achieve our true desire—the desire of the Other.

Radin tries to explain Hegel's analysis as follows:

> Hegel also cast the argument against alienation of personhood as a "contradiction." To alienate personhood is itself contrary to personhood, in that if I can relinquish my personhood, then no "I" remains to have done the relinquishing. If I treat "the infinite embodiment of self-consciousness" as something external and try to alienate it, Hegel argued, one of two things results: if I really possess these substantive attributes, they are not external and hence not alienated; if they are alienated, I did not possess them in the first place. Hegel might have been trying to say that substantive personhood is simply not capable of objectification. The "contradiction" consists in supposing that one could give up that which, "so soon as I possess it, exists in essence as mine alone and not as something external." If this interpretation is correct, then the contradiction poses the same subject/object problems as Hegel's general view of property and alienation: Why is it that personhood cannot be objectified while at the same time person-

---

level presupposes determinacy (i.e., exact position and momentum) at the macro level. Norwood R. Hanson, Patterns of Discovery 136–49 (1965). The theory was abducted precisely to explain the logical necessity of determinacy in that one cannot explain the presence of an element at one level by reference to the presence of a factor at a lower level without devolving into a bad infinity of "turtles all the way down." It is necessary to posit a level that does not contain the element to be explained to develop a theory of the building blocks to that element. Before the uncertainty principle, determinacy at the macro level depended on determinacy at the molecular level, which depended on determinacy at the atomic level, and so on. Heisenberg posited a level at which determinacy stopped, not to argue that determinacy did not exist but to explain how determinacy comes into being. The uncertainty principle is not merely the layman's vulgarized simplification that observation affects the thing observed, making simultaneous measurement of momentum and velocity impossible. Rather, the uncertainty principle stands for the proposition, absolutely fundamental to quantum mechanical theory, that momentum and velocity do not exist simultaneously, and perhaps do not exist, unless we observe and measure them. *See id.* at 119–20, 136–49.

hood requires objectification (in things)? Exactly what items are permanently "inside" the subject and incapable of objectifications?

If the person/thing distinction is to be treated as a bright line that divides the commodifiable from the inalienable, we must know exactly which items are part of the person and which not. The person/thing distinction and its consequences seemed obvious to Kant and Hegel, but such is not the case for many modern philosophers.[135]

Radin states further:

From the view that attributes and characteristics are separate possessions, it is an easy step to conceptualize them as lying on the object side of the subject/object divide. This eliminates inalienabilities based on things internal to the person, because nothing is internal to the person. . . . It is not difficult to see them as fungible and bearing implicit monetary value.[136]

She thinks she identifies a dilemma in Hegel:

If the person/thing distinction is to be treated as a bright line that divides the commodifiable from the inalienable, we must know exactly which items are part of the person and which not. . . .

Without the bright line, arguments delineating the market realm on the basis of the subject/object distinction lose their force. If the person/thing distinction is not a sharp divide, neither is inalienability/alienability. There will be a gray area between the two.[137]

She concludes from this that maintenance of the subject/object distinction combined with a defense of the market can only lead to universal commodification. That is, since one cannot maintain the subject/object, inalienable/alienable distinction, then everything must either fall in one category or the other. If one wants a market for some things, therefore, one must require a market for everything. "[T]here is no obvious stopping place short of that."[138] This is a gross misreading of Hegel which totally ignores his insistence that the logic of philosophy could only be applied at the highest level of abstraction and that concrete empirical questions of the type which concern Radin can only be decided by pragmatic reasoning. In addition, perhaps because Radin bases her analysis of Hegel entirely on the first chapter of *The Philosophy of Right*, which cannot be understood without some grounding in his philosophical system,

135. Radin, *Market-Inalienability, supra* note 2, at 1896.
136. *Id.* at 1897.
137. Radin, Contested Commodities, *supra* note 2, at 40.
138. *Id.*

she also does not understand Hegel's notion of the relationship between qualitative and quantitative differences, which I shall discuss at length in chapter 4. As we shall see, Hegel would say that it is not merely possible but necessary for categories such as subject/object and inalienable/alienable to be both logically separate and empirically continuous.

In other words, Radin assumes that Hegel started with a sharp subject/object distinction, and from this beginning it is an "easy step" to universal commodification. She thinks it is logically inconsistent with this starting point for Hegel to conclude that some "things" become "internal" to the person and inalienable.

Radin's reasoning is the reverse of Hegel's logic. As I have discussed, Hegel defined the will as that which is an end to itself and not a means to another's end.[139] This starting definition implies a correlate: The thing that is a means to another's end — the object. At the level of abstract right, the subject/object distinction is a strictly logical truism: If the self is abstract self-consciousness as pure negation, all things not capable of self-consciousness and all things that have positive existence are objects in the sense of being other or separate from the subject. This truism would be completely banal but for its further development through the dialectic.

Radin is correct that Hegel started from a subject/object distinction and used an internal/external metaphor, but she wrongly states that Hegel's starting point is a simple intuitive sense of inner and outer. Instead, Hegel's distinction is completely *anti*-intuitive in that he claims that our bodies, opinions, and all other aspects of our personality and individuality, everything we feel to be our true selves, are logically external to ourselves as persons. This is because if the will is totally free from all contingency, all contingency is "other" with relation to the will. The will is its own end. Anything that does not have consciousness or can serve as the means to the will's end is an object. Individuating characteristics of personality start out as external to the "abstract person" by logical tautology. They are not merely "objectified," as Radin suggests, but rather are objects by definition.[140]

139. Hegel, The Philosophy of Right, *supra* note 76, at 67.

140. In chap. 2, sec. III.A, I criticized Duncan Kennedy and others for assuming that physical objects are naturally "things" whereas intangibles are artificially and inauthentically "reified" as though they were things. I stated that objectification is not a natural state — an object only takes on that status when recognized as such by a self-conscious person. I am not retreating from that position here. What I am saying here is that once one recognizes the concept of the person as self-consciousness, then the corresponding definition of an external object necessarily follows as a logical matter. Such an object is only potentially a *res*, in the sense of the object of a property relation. *This* reification requires an act of will.

Hegel's "internal/external" terminology is dictated by the German language. As H.B. Nisbet explains in a note to his translation of *The Philosophy of Right,* the English word "alienation" does not satisfactorily capture the connotations of the German equivalents *Entaeusserung* and *Veraeusserung* because these words also mean "externalization."[141] In other words, when Hegel is translated into English as saying that one cannot "alienate" that which is "internal" by nature, he may merely be stating the truisms that one cannot alienate that which is inalienable by nature or externalize that which is internal by nature. Hegel may not have intended his internal/external distinction to carry the implications of mind/body that the English translation suggests to Radin.

The inalienability of minimum personality at this stage is, therefore, merely one of definition. If the minimum definition of the person is that which is left after everything is externalized, the free will cannot logically be externalized (i.e., alienated). This does not mean that one cannot alienate one's capacity for freedom as an empirical matter—one can be enslaved, sell oneself into indentured servitude, or commit suicide. But if the goal of the will is to actualize its freedom and to have this actualization verified through the recognition of other free subjects, Hegel describes any act that destroys the will's capacity for freedom as a wrong (*Unrecht*). For the moment, it may be observed that any concrete individual empirically capable of such a wrong is far more developed than Hegel's starting point.

Of course, Hegel went beyond this logical truism that one cannot split the atom of personhood without destroying personhood. At the moment the abstract person begins to impose its will on objects, it begins to cease to be the abstract person and the subject/object distinction begins to dissolve. Among the objects that the will appropriates as part of its objectification are the individuating characteristics of personality. These characteristics started out as "objects" (i.e., external things) because they are contingent. Once these former objects are internalized, they become inalienable as a matter of abstract right, not as a matter of empirical fact, let alone morality or ethics.[142] This conclusion is based on Hegel's theory of the rationality of property—recognition by other subjects. He was posit-

---

141. Nisbet particularly bemoans that the English translation makes it "impossible to reproduce the resulting network of etymological associations." Hegel, The Philosophy of Right, *supra* note 76, at 95 (translator's note a).

142. Speaking at the level of abstract right, we must ask what is minimally necessary for this first step in the actualization of human freedom, not what is moral, ethical, or best to further human flourishing. We have not yet even developed the concepts of morality and *Sittlichkeit,* which we need in order to answer these important questions.

ing that, as a logical matter, in order to be recognizable as a specific identified person distinguishable from other persons, one must have some continuity over time. As the abstract person itself has no recognizable characteristics, this continuity must be supplied by the continued possession of specific objects of property. That is, since Radin recognizes that people start out as dependent and located in society as an empirical matter, she assumes that the continuity and individuality that comes from the inalienability of certain objects serves the function of creating separateness.[143] Hegel's point, however, is that if one starts with the theoretical proposition that the most primitive notion of what a person could be is abstract self-consciousness as free will with no pathological characteristics, then the continuity of inalienability serves the function of lessening separateness and creating intersubjectivity by making the person identifiable as a unique individual.

This means that it is logically necessary that some "internalized" objects remain inalienable for the goal of recognition to be achieved. That is, Hegel is not positing (by intuition or otherwise) that specific objects exist a priori as either internal or external to the subject. Rather, he is arguing that the logic of property (recognizability) requires that the abstract person seek to internalize *some* objects. He calls those bare minimum objects which must be continually possessed so that a person can be described and identified "personality."[144] Hegel makes pragmatic arguments as to why certain identifiable objects will likely fall within the category of personality. In other words, although Hegel does argue, as Radin claims, that

143. Radin, Contested Commodities, *supra* note 2, at 57.

144. Hegel, The Philosophy of Right, *supra* note 76, at 95. If I have one criticism of Hegel's analysis of property, it is that, although I believe he does demonstrate that it is necessary for *some* objects of "personality" to be continually owned for property to work, he does not convince me that *all* of his examples of internalized objects *necessarily* serve this purpose as a logical matter. In other words, I suspect that this is a rare case in which Hegel might confuse logical and pragmatic arguments.

Objects of personality can serve an imaginary purpose. As Lacan explains, the imaginary includes the type of simple meaning such as animals can understand, as opposed to signification, which is in the symbolic. That is, to a male bird, a red breast does not symbolize something in the sense of standing for something else. But it might *mean* that the bearer of the red breast is a rival which it must fight, i.e., red breast equals rival. Jacques Lacan, The Seminar of Jacques Lacan, Book III, The Psychoses 1955–1956, at 9–10 (Jacques-Alain Miller ed. & Russell Grigg trans., 1993) [hereinafter Lacan, Seminar III]. Similarly, one's objects of personality are those which enable others to recognize one in the sense that my acquaintances identify the person who inhabits a specific forty-three-year-old, 5'2" white female body as Jeanne Schroeder.

In contrast, the ultimate recognition achieved through a full property relationship is symbolic. To be recognized as a subject signifies that one has the dignity to bear legal rights.

there is a bright line between the qualities of alienability and inalienability, he would absolutely agree that empirical objects lie along a continuum between these categories. It is logically mandated that we make the distinction between alienability and inalienability, and we can logically derive the principles by which alienability and inalienability should be determined, but the judgment as to whether any specific object should be entirely or partially inalienable can only be made through the application of practical reasoning. Hegelian idealism requires pragmatism. This means that only at the extremes can we agree that any specific object should be inalienable.

For example, in order to be recognizable as a person, a person needs a living body.[145] An abstract person must, therefore, internalize a body — that is, treat it at least partially inalienable. Thus, suicide cannot generally be a right, which is defined as that which furthers the recognition necessary for subjectivity and the actualization of freedom.[146] Slavery is wrong because it is the legal declaration that a human being is not a person but a thing, and thereby denies the slave the human goal of recognition.[147] Any status higher than slavery that gives minimum recognition to the hu-

---

145. "[F]or others, I am in my body. I am *free for the other* only in so far as I am free in my *Existence*. . . . Violence done to *my body* by others is violence done to me." Hegel, The Philosophy of Right, *supra* note 76, at 79. Consequently, there is a real difference between physical injury to the human body and damage to other types of owned objects. *Id*. at 86–88. But note, the logical argument that the body (or bodily integrity) as a whole should be inalienable does not answer such pragmatic questions as whether certain parts or capabilities of the body should be alienable. For example, Hegel believes that within abstract right one can sell a portion of one's productive capacity as labor. Can we also rightfully sell our *re*productive capacity?

146. *Id*. at 101–02. Hegel wrote that there is no "unqualified right" to suicide, indicating that there may be a qualified right, in the case of the hero. *Id*.

147. *Id*. at 96. I find Radin's discussion of baby selling (*see, e.g.,* Radin, Contested Commodities, *supra* note 2, at 131–53) to be particularly unsuccessful, even though I am intuitively sympathetic with her policy recommendations. This is probably because of her failure to recognize the importance of mutual recognition. Like the Law and Economics analysts whom she criticizes, she analyzes the issue primarily in terms of the competing sets of parents. By comparing baby selling to a woman's selling of her body in surrogacy and prostitution, Radin shifts the focus to the effect on the mother and society generally. Only in passing does she mention the problem that "babies do not choose their own commodification." *Id*. at 161. This seems to reflect Radin's intuition that we start out connected and dependent as an empirical matter and only later develop separate individuality through property and other relations.

From a Hegelian viewpoint, however, the problem with baby selling is that since a baby has the potentiality for self-consciousness, she cannot rightfully be the object of other people's property rights. She cannot be either fungible *or personal* property. A baby cannot be rightfully sold by parents because she cannot be rightfully owned by her parents.

Of course, this logical analysis does not solve the pragmatic questions as to who should

manity of a person, as miserable as it may be, satisfies the limited goals of abstract right.[148] Hegel did not, however, purport to address the positive law of slavery or to answer the practical question as to what empirical institutions (such as, for example, serfdom, peonage, untouchability, forced prostitution) constitute slavery. Moreover, the proposition that lesser alienations of human beings that do not constitute slavery (such as exploitative employment) are permitted in abstract right does not necessarily imply that *all* such alienations should always be permitted. Even if one decides that they do not violate abstract right, they may not meet the higher standards of morality and ethics.

Thus, in contradistinction to Radin's assertion, Hegel started with, but did not maintain, a simple subject/object distinction based on intuitions of internality. Sublation overcomes and preserves the subject/object distinction in property. The distinction will continue to exist as an abstract logical moment that captures that experience of separateness and distinction which Charles Sanders Peirce calls secondness, but must break down as a logical and an empirical matter as the person becomes more determinate.[149]

Hegel's subject/object distinction also does not lead to universal commodification, contrary to Radin's assertion, even at the level of abstract right. It is true that Hegel believed that alienability is a necessary element of a full property. It is also true that the development of the person—which is the internal rationality of property—requires that certain minimum characteristics of personality be inalienable.[150] Consequently, the very rationality of abstract right necessitates that property analysis exclude

---

raise a child or whether we should allow paid adoptions. It only argues that it is wrong to conclude from the fact that paid adoptions have some empirical characteristics similar to sales of babies (i.e., money and babies change hands) that we should analyze these arrangements in terms of property and contract. Such an analysis, like the traditional analysis of marriage as contract, is not merely a category mistake, it is "shameful."

148. *Id.* at 97.

149. Radin states: "Whether Hegel did or did not reinscribe the subject/object dichotomy is a matter of serious controversy." Radin, Reinterpreting Property, *supra* note 2, at 8. Once again, this quotation reveals Radin's confusion over Hegel's concept of sublation. When the subject/object distinction is sublated, it is preserved as well as overcome. At one moment the individual cannot imagine himself as distinct from the objects which form his personality, yet at another moment he distinguishes himself from them. Although she denies it, this dialectic can be imperfectly glimpsed in Radin's own analysis. Although she continually speaks of the importance of personal property as being part of or necessary for personality, by the grammatical act of identifying specific objects as property owned by the personality she is necessarily distinguishing subject from object.

150. Hegel, The Philosophy of Right, *supra* note 76, at 95–97.

certain object relations. Property—commodification—is self-limiting by its own logic.

Despite her criticisms of Hegel, Radin bases her own theory on a presupposed internal/external distinction. Her very concern with universal commodification reflects an intuition that some objects are so internal to personhood that their market alienation is destructive. Conversely, her concern with fetishism reflects an intuition that some objects are so external to personhood that overattachment to them is destructive. Furthermore, Radin's whole analysis of expanded bodily integrity as "property"—as a form of ownership, possession, and use of objects— reflects a continuing subject/object relation. Whereas Hegel sees the subject/object distinction as a theoretical one, Radin sees it as a physical and empirical one based on literal internal/external distinctions and the empirical fact that individuals become "attached" to specific objects such as wedding rings or the old family homestead.

Indeed, Radin's argument for the affirmative role of personal property is based largely on a recognition of the need for continuity. She states:

> A person cannot be fully a person without a sense of continuity of self over time. To maintain that sense of continuity over time and to exercise one's liberty or autonomy, one must have an ongoing relationship with the external environment, consisting of both "things" and other people. One perceives the ongoing relationship to the environment as a set of individual relationships, corresponding to the way our perception separates the world into distinct "things." . . . In order to lead a normal life, there must be some continuity in relating to "things."[151]

Unfortunately, Radin attributes this longing for continuity to the person's own solipsistic sense of self and personal development, rather than to the desire for intersubjective recognition. Personal property is supposed to serve the goal of individual separateness. As a consequence, the personal property objects with which the Radinian person seeks continuity are not limited to the minimal elements of personality, such as beliefs, opinions, and, yes, the (female) body. Rather, she expands this class to include precisely those material objects which, as an empirical matter, serve as status symbols establishing one's place in the American social hierarchy—notably, the (big) house, the (fast) car, the (flashy) ring. I would argue that whether or not such object relations are relevant to eligibility for membership in a country club, they should be irrelevant to

151. Radin, Reinterpreting Property, *supra* note 2, at 64.

recognizability as a member of the human race. Consequently, whether or not this type of object relations might be appropriately privileged in a premodern society—such as feudal Europe—in which people are defined by status, they should not be given priority in a modern (let alone post-modern) society which seeks to actualize human freedom through self-definition.

D. Limitations of Positive Law

Hegel does not stop his analysis of property law at the level of abstract right. For Radin to compare her theory of property for personhood to Hegel, she must consider the role that property plays not only at the level of abstract right but also in terms of the individual in the state. Positive law and the administration of justice, as opposed to abstract right, are developments associated with the level of civil society. Hegel adds affirmative rights, such as rights for the satisfaction of needs, at this level.[152] Equity alleviates the harshness of strict application of the law. Shared ownership through the family and corporations is recognized. Limitations on property for the sake of the community may become appropriate. The Hegelian state, guided by ethics (*Sittlichkeit*) rather than abstract right, will impose further limitations on property to alleviate the degradation of the poor, which is likely to result from the laissez-faire, abstract regime of civil society.[153]

Hegel implied various limitations on rights and insisted on the development of positive freedoms and duties at the more complex levels of human interrelationships. Because he wrote at a general level, however, he did not specify precisely what these limitations would be or try to write the correct positive law of property.[154] Hegel insisted that any philosophy is a creature of its own time because *Geist* and individuals are always manifest in specific, concrete situations. Each society must develop its own specific, positive law of property.

Even though Hegel derived what Radin calls the "liberal triad" of property rights (possession, enjoyment, and alienation), his theory is not

152. Hegel, The Philosophy of Right, *supra* note 76, at 227–31.

153. *See generally* Westphal, *supra* note 90, at 26–35; Alan Brudner, The Unity of the Common Law: Essays in Hegelian Jurisprudence 77–85 (1995).

154. Munzer, unfortunately, also misunderstands this point. He chides Hegel for only tacitly recognizing the need for social and legal conventions to proscribe property law. "But the need, it may be said, merits explicit, not tacit, recognition." Munzer, *supra* note 77, at 76. As I have already discussed, positive law is the creature of practical reasoning. Rather

merely an apologia for the laissez-faire market. Hegel did not believe that the harsh, inhuman world of abstract right, in which he located his analysis of property and contract, is the be-all and end-all of human society.[155] Morality and ethics are superior to right. It is not merely impossible to speak of higher stages of social life in terms of abstract right, it is disgraceful. In the family, civil society, and the state, which are fuller manifestations of social life, restrictions on full property rights are appropriate.[156] Unlike the Lockean tradition of liberalism, the state in Hegel's view does not exist primarily to protect property rights. Rather, we protect property rights because they are necessary for the existence of the individual and the state. Nor do property rights serve the Hobbesian liberal function as the barrier that protects the individual from the state. Rather, property is the most primitive link between persons which helps to form both the individual and the state. Property is, therefore, necessary for human freedom and intersubjectivity.[157]

Hegel did not consider the great disparity of wealth and the degradation of the lower classes an accidental aspect of the market (i.e., civil society) that we could easily adjust. Rather, he considered degradation of the

---

than being implicit, Hegel expressly states in the preface to *The Philosophy of Right* that in his system, practical reasoning is completely distinct from, albeit necessitated by, philosophy. Consequently, it is beyond the scope of his book.

155. Westphal explains:

Property is the *first* embodiment of freedom because it is freedom in its immediacy, and the logic that determines the proper form of philosophical thinking. . . . The property rights of legal persons are the first embodiment of freedom, not because they are the most important form of freedom, not because they are the causal condition of other modes of freedom, but because they are the least developed, least adequate, least rational form that freedom can take without ceasing to be freedom. Hegel is very blunt about this.

Westphal, *supra* note 90, at 29.

156. Brudner, *supra* note 153, at 64–69.

157. *See* Westphal, *supra* note 90, at 28–31. Specifically, Westphal states:

Because property is the first embodiment of *freedom* for Hegel, his theory is a critique of liberalism's (naturalist) tendency to make biological survival and economic prosperity the end for which political and civil rights are the means. Now, because property is the *first embodiment* of freedom (in the Hegelian sense of logical priority), his theory is also a critique of liberalism's (formalist) tendency to define freedom without paying sufficient attention to questions of morality, the family, political community, and severe poverty. When Locke makes property rights first, it is because they are the end to which everything else is means. When Hegel puts them first it is because in their immediate form as the minimal mode of human freedom they are in radical need of correction and completion through contextualizing.

Id. at 32.

poor to be an inevitable result of laissez-faire capitalism. Hegel did not excuse this degradation but saw it as a reflection of internal contradictions within the market. To Hegel, market relations would logically develop to serve the internally rational goal of the development of human freedom but leave a section of society in a subhuman state. Moreover, although the market requires us to act as radical individualists, by coming to the market we become dependent on all others who trade in the market. Consequently, the civil society must eventually collapse and be superseded by the state, which will not replace but can harmonize the market.[158]

E. Is Hegel Useful in a Feminist Challenge to Masculinism?

Radin nevertheless implicitly makes one powerful critique of traditional Hegelian theory. This critique, when combined with Lacan's psychoanalytic theory, can form a devastating feminist-Hegelian critique of patriarchy.

Hegel was empirically writing from the masculine position. At first blush, he seems the most psychoanalytically masculine of philosophers—emphasizing the symbolic order of exchange. Perhaps reflecting traditional European-Christian misogynist theology, which identifies the body and sexuality with the Feminine and the mind and personality with the Masculine,[159] Hegel never attempted to account for sexuality per se. Specifically, he never reflected upon whether one's sexuality is so intrinsic to one's personality as to be inalienable even at the level of abstract right. One possible Hegelian argument might be that the very concept of "abstract right" deals with "abstract personality," stripped of all contingent, concrete characteristics, including sexuality. This would suggest that Hegel has postponed this issue to a later stage in the dialectic.

Indeed, Hegel did discuss sexual difference briefly in *The Philosophy of Right* and *The Phenomenology of Spirit*. Despite Hegel's claims to logic and his disdain for unsupported presuppositions, as is so often the case when men talk about women, logic flies out the window. Hegel's discussion of marriage consists largely of conclusory statements reflective of nineteenth-

158. *See* Wood, *supra* note 97, at xxiv–xxvi (explaining Hegel's vision of the state as "ultimate end"); Westphal, *supra* note 90, at 44–45.

159. *See generally* Jeanne L. Schroeder, *The Taming of the Shrew: The Liberal Attempt to Neutralize Radical Feminism*, 5 Yale J.L. & Feminism 123 (1992); *and* Jeanne L. Schroeder, *Feminism Historicized: Medieval Misogynist Stereotypes in Contemporary Feminist Jurisprudence*, 75 Iowa L. Rev. 1135, 1160–97 (1990).

century misogyny.[160] He echoes nineteenth-century sexual stereotypes and then claims that these sexual differences are rational. He does not logically prove the existence of sexual difference as a theoretical necessity. He merely declares that because these differences could exist, they do and must exist. Moreover, he assumes, without proof, that these "rational" sexual positions are inevitably assigned to the two biological sexes.[161]

A combination of Radin's legal theory and Lacan's psychoanalytic theory opens up the issue of whether the positions of sexuality are already logically necessitated, even at the levels of abstract personality and abstract right. Lacan characterizes the Hegelian theory of subjectivity as intersubjective recognition (i.e., the desire of man is the desire of the Other) as hysterical. But hysteria is not a defect, it is the paradigmatic mode of desire.[162] The hysteric's question is always one of sexual identity, "Am I a man or a woman?"[163] This is the great question which Hegel, the most

160. Women may well be educated, but they are not made for the higher sciences, for philosophy and certain artistic productions which require a universal element. Women may have insights . . . , taste, and delicacy, but they do not possess the ideal. The difference between man and woman is the difference between animal and plant; . . . When women are in charge of government, the state is in danger.

Hegel, The Philosophy of Right, *supra* note 76, at 207. Unfortunately, Hegel's viciously misogynist account of women's knowledge is frequently echoed today by many self-identified feminists who speak of women's concrete knowledge and women's ways of knowing generally.

161. Specifically, Hegel wrote:

The *natural* determinacy of the two sexes acquires an *intellectual* and *ethical* significance by virtue of its rationality. . . .

The *one* [sex] is therefore spirituality which divides itself up into personal self-sufficiency with being *for itself* and the knowledge and violation of *free universality,* i.e. into the self-consciousness of conceptual thought and the violation of the objective and ultimate end. And the *other* is spirituality which maintains itself in unity as knowledge and volition of the substantial in the form of concrete *individuality* . . . and *feeling* . . . . In its external relations, the former is powerful and active, the latter is passive and subjective.

Id. at 206.

A complete analysis of Hegel's inadequate treatment of sexuality is beyond the scope of this book. I would suggest, however, that certain aspects of Hegel's seemingly misogynist analysis may look forward to a more sophisticated Lacanian analysis. For example, Hegel's notorious assertion that women have only an unconscious intuitive understanding of ethics, as opposed to the masculine conscious understanding, G.W.F. Hegel, The Phenomenology of Spirit 274 (A.V. Miller trans., 1975), may look forward to the Lacanian concept of the feminine as the position of being and the masculine as the position of having and speaking, as well as to the Freudian analysis of the feminine and masculine superego.

162. Žižek, The Indivisible Remainder, *supra* note 7, at 167.

163. Lacan, Seminar III, *supra* note 144, at 171. *See also* Stuart Schneiderman, Jacques Lacan: The Death of an Intellectual Hero 59 (1983).

hysterical (and, therefore, the most feminine) of all philosophers, refuses to confront directly. But because he represses it, this question pervades his entire philosophy.

Consequently, when Lacan psychoanalyzes the Hegelian dialectic and brings out what has been repressed, he shows that Hegelian recognition requires a sexuated position, with the Masculine taking on the subjective and the Feminine taking on the objective role. Sexuality would, therefore, seem to fall within that category of objects of personality minimally required for recognizability as a subject and, therefore, inalienable as a matter of abstract right. Sexuality, in this view, is not contingent, but is constitutive of subjectivity. The Lacanian insight supports the feminist insistence that the Hegelian system cannot fulfill its claim to being a theory of concrete human freedom in society unless it expands to include both a theory of sexuality, generally, and a theory of property that deals with the objectification of the female body, specifically. In light of Lacan's theory, Hegelians must address whether sexuality is essential to personality at the level of abstract right.

III. THE IMPLICATIONS FOR FEMINIST PROPERTY THEORY

I began this chapter by suggesting that Jacques Lacan's psychoanalytic theory may provide an insight into Radin's insistence on the objective, and denial of the intersubjective, aspects of property. If Lacanian theory sounds depressing, that's because it is. But there is also an affirmative side of Lacan, and of Hegel. The emptiness that lies at the center of Lacanian masculine subjectivity and the lack that constitutes Lacanian feminine objectivity—like the negativity that is the essence of Hegelian abstract personality—enable desire to function. If we were full and satisfied, we would not desire. Because subjectivity is negative, personality is limitless capacity and potentiality. Moreover, it is only the Feminine in her position as lack who can serve as the radical negativity which is not only the condition precedent of freedom but the center of split subjectivity. In other words, when we look into the supposedly masculine subject, we find the Feminine. In Lacan's words, woman is the symptom of man.

The Lacanian system, written from the masculine position, includes two mediating elements—possession and alienation (i.e., exchange) of the object of desire. The element of use as enjoyment is, however, located within feminine *jouissance*.

Lacan recognized that use as enjoyment, *jouissance,* reflects the feminine position. It is a concept of enjoyment that includes not only pleasure, but obscene delight in pain and death.[164] *Jouissance* may be thought of as the fulfillment of desire in the sense of the breakdown of the subject/object distinction. It is the psychoanalytic experience of breaking out from the symbolic order of speech and the imaginary order of imagery and of achieving direct, unmediated contact with the real. Although anatomical men are capable of *jouissance, jouissance* requires one to take on the position of the Feminine[165] as speaking requires one to take on the position of the Masculine.[166] Exchange is Eros. *Jouissance* is *Thanatos.* In the masculine story of Lacanian psychoanalysis, the destruction of the subject/object distinction would be suicidal in the sense that it also destroys subjectivity, consciousness, and language.

Consequently, this part of the fiction must be retold from the feminine position. Lacan said the story so far remains untold because it is literally unspeakable in a psychoanalytic sense. *Jouissance*—the experience of the real—is by definition not symbolic. This, of course, is the untold part of the story of property that Radin glimpses but unsuccessfully attempts to tell.

Jouissance is the experience of the feminine object for herself, as opposed to the feminine object as the object of exchange of masculine subjectivity since the Feminine symbolizes the castration which men must deny in order to be masculine. It is the transgression of the law as prohibition. This understanding of *jouissance* parallels Radin's attempt to protect exclusive use of the object of personal property for the development of (feminine) personhood. It is an attempt to give dignity and meaning to the feminine person as other than the commodified object of masculine desire.

I agree with Radin's intuition that this moment of feminine selfhood as virginity—the ecstatic, unmediated relationship, and the breakdown of the subject/object distinction—is essential for an affirmative rewriting

---

164. Because enjoyment is a forbidden domain and obscene, pleasure always involves a certain displeasure. Žižek, For They Know Not What They Do, *supra* note 95, at 239.

165. Jacques Lacan, *God and the Jouissance of the Woman, in* Jacques Lacan and the école freudienne, Feminine Sexuality 137, 144–45 (Juliet Mitchell & Jacqueline Rose eds., Jacqueline Rose trans., 1985) [hereinafter Lacan, Feminine Sexuality]; Jacqueline Rose, *Introduction II* to Lacan, Feminine Sexuality, *supra* at 27, 51.

166. Elizabeth Grosz, Jacques Lacan: A Feminist Introduction 71–72 (1989).

of the Feminine as other than the negative of the Masculine. Psychoanalytic theory insists that to become "mature women," we must accept our
castration and our roles as the objects of desire and as negativity and lack.[167]
It is a grave error, however, to confuse the concept of feminine negativity with female inferiority. Lacan insisted that the masculine perspective
is a lie—a fiction. The masculine function claims to be universal—to be
a subject is to have the *Phallus* and to be a man. But the feminine function is not the simple negation of the positivity of the Masculine in the
sense of nothing (as men insist). The Feminine is not merely the negative
of not having the *Phallus*. It is the difference of being the *Phallus*. The
Feminine is "not-all"—a denial of the crushing hegemony of the false universal of the Masculine and an insistence that the masculinist story of psychoanalysis is not the truth but a fiction. The Lacanian Feminine is not
the simple negative of the masculine subject as his complement. Rather,
she is his sublation—a supplement.

This is the secret of Lacan's concept that the Feminine is a masquerade, that the *Phallus* can only function when veiled. The Woman wears
masculine fantasies of feminity as a mask. The very concept of the mask
or the veil implies that there is a true image, some positive content un-
derneath which is merely hidden from view. But this implication is itself
another mask, a feminine wile, a masculine fantasy. The moment of radical human freedom which is the Feminine rests on her total negativity—
there is nothing under the mask.[168] She is the hole, the antinomy, the contradiction which Hegel believed "appear[s] in all objects of every kind,
in all conceptions, notions and Ideas."[169] She is the space which allows
us to move.

What Radin's approach to property glimpses is the possibility of a feminine role as object that is neither passive nor silent: she does not merely
allow herself to be commodified in exchange by an active, masculine principle. The affirmative moment of the rewriting of the Feminine shows
that the masculine nightmare of castration did not occur precisely because
we never were united with the Phallic Mother. In the moment of *jouissance,* the Feminine—the unmediated relationship—is not the "forever

167. As Luce Irigaray says, criticizing Freud's theory of feminine sexual development
(and thereby implicitly criticizing Lacan's theory), the mature woman is "to have only one
desire—that of being *as much as possible like man's eternal object of desire.*" Luce Irigaray,
Speculum of the Other Woman 32 (Gillian C. Gill trans., 1985); *see also* Grosz, *supra* note
166, at 69.
168. Žižek, The Indivisible Remainder, *supra* note 7, at 158–61.
169. G.W.F. Hegel, Hegel's Logic 78 (William Wallace trans., 1975).

lost" of lack. The prohibition of the Phallic Mother that created the symbolic order moves the Feminine out of the impossible of the real and into the possible. The Feminine is messianic, the "not-all" as the "something more."[170] It is a "not yet," which might be briefly glimpsed by taking on the position of the Feminine. In this view, the Feminine becomes not the simple negation of the Masculine that reinstates the status quo but instead the creative negativity of sublation.

It is important not only to emphasize the positive moment of feminine objectivity in sexuality and property, but to overemphasize it, because it has been traditionally deprivileged. It would be a mistake, however, to forget the positive moment of masculine subjectivity. To desire and to experience the breakdown of the subject/object distinction, we must first become subjects. To function and to speak, we must submit to the symbolic order of language and take on the position of masculine subjectivity as intersubjectivity. To perceive the Feminine as possible, we must prohibit or deny her, thereby creating the temptation of transgression. It is tempting to try to get around this impasse by adopting a romantic "New Age" ideal of the ancient goddesses who were simultaneously lovers and virgins in an attempt to preserve our feminine objectivity while fulfilling our subjectivity. But like all attempts to give an affirmative image to the Feminine, this is merely another masculine fantasy.

But as we try to describe the experience of *jouissance* by speaking it, we reenter the symbolic order and lose our *jouissance*. It is impossible to sing the dream of the Feminine within the inadequate masculine speech of Lacanian and Hegelian theory, but the theory has a true moment as well in its internal contradiction. It is within this contradiction that one can locate a powerful feminist moment. Hegel argued that it is fundamentally and essentially un-right to deny another person the status of an equal human subject. It is wrong at the primitive, minimal level of abstract right, even without considering morality and ethics. Denying equal status is not merely a wrong against the person treated as nonhuman, it is a wrongful destruction of the personhood of the person who refuses to recognize the other person, because the fundamental desire to be recognized and desired by others drives persons. We accord rights to the Other precisely to give her dignity so that her recognition counts.

---

170. Drucilla Cornell, Beyond Accommodation: Ethical Feminism, Deconstruction, and the Law 13–17 (1991); Drucilla Cornell, *The Doubly-Prized World: Myth Allegory and the Feminine,* 75 Cornell L. Rev. 644, 645, 656–57, 686–87, 699 (1990). In the bi-linguistic pun, Mother is always (M)-other and "mere" is always "mehr."

Lacan argued that in our patriarchal society we identify subjectivity with the masculine position but identify the feminine position with the silent, passive role of the object of desire that active male subjects exchange. One of Lacan's most infamous tenets is that Woman is a symptom of Man—that is, the Feminine is a fiction retroactively abducted as a necessary building block in the construction of men as psychoanalytic subjects. For anatomically female humans to speak and otherwise to function in society, we must occasionally mime the Masculine. Insofar as we are recognized as feminine, we are recognized as lack of subjectivity. Accordingly, patriarchy is incapable of admitting that it recognizes feminine subjectivity. This is an abstract wrong—*Unrecht*. Within the terms of Hegel's own dialectic, as a logical matter we cannot even begin to speak of creating a moral family structure, let alone an ethical civil society or state, without establishing the minimal abstract right of feminine personhood.

Furthermore, Lacan (like Hegel) argued that the desire of man is the desire of the Other. Humans are driven by the erotic desire to be recognized and desired by an equal human being. It is only this recognition and desire that makes an abstract person into a full subject who can in turn recognize and desire others. Lacan argued that the masculine subject is constituted by constituting the feminine position as non-subject. This is not merely an abstract wrong against those of us who are positioned as feminine objectivity but renders the desire of the heterosexual, masculine subject in patriarchy impotent. He cannot accord the woman he desires the full subjectivity that would make her desire count because as soon as he did so, he would confront his own castration. Like Cybele, the Feminine can never be captured by the eunuch priests who worship her. The Phallic Mother always escapes from the subject's impotent embrace. Indeed, insofar as subjectivity is negative, and negativity is the condition of freedom, it is only the Feminine in her radical position of lack who can truly stand in the place of the subject. All claims of masculine subjectivity are thus hollow.

To put it another way: the essence of personality is freedom. The condition of freedom is the radical negativity of the Feminine. We create the possibility of the Feminine through the incest taboo which changes her from the impossible to the forbidden and, therefore, possible. The Hegelian dialectic teaches us, however, that we can only retroactively tell what is potential after it is actualized. Consequently, if man's claim to freedom is to be more than an empty boast, it is necessary for us to take on the impossible task of putting feminine freedom—including the emancipation of women—into effect.

And so, patriarchy contains its own contradiction and must go under as a logical matter. But this end is not predestined through the impersonal workings of the hypothetical *Geist*. It can only happen through the affirmative actualization of feminine subjectivity's negative potentiality.

Eros is the desire to achieve the lost Feminine. It cannot, however, serve the goal of the actualization of freedom to achieve the Feminine through a doomed attempt to negate the subject/object distinction. The lost Feminine has no positive content, she is nothing in the sense of radical negativity. Such a yearning, therefore, is the morbid nostalgia of *Thanatos*—the death wish. It is an attempt to deny castration by regressing back to a preconscious union with the M(O)ther in the real. Even if we could achieve the real of *jouissance* by denial of the symbolic, we also thereby destroy the real which does not preexist, but is constituted by, the symbolic. Desire is the attempt to achieve wholeness. Eros is the masculine position of desire—the attempt to acquire and join with the perfect complementary mate who in the imaginary will fill out the hole left by castration. *Thanatos* is the feminine position of desire—the attempt to once again become unviolated and complete within ourselves by merging back into the real.

The myth of Eurydice teaches that if we give in to the masculine desire of *Eros* and look back at the lost Feminine, we lose her forever. We can only keep her by not having her. To have her—to give the Feminine positive content—is to replace her with a masculine fantasy. Even more horribly, however, the myth of Lot's wife teaches that if we give in to the feminine desire of *Thanatos* and gaze back into the abyss of the real, we are forever silenced into inanimate objectivity, so bereft of subjectivity that even our name has been forgotten. Consequently, the obscene command to Enjoy! requires us not to look backward but to go forward on an impossible and unrealizable quest to sublate masculine subjectivity and feminine objectivity and achieve a *re*union with the Feminine as identical with and different from the Masculine.

4

The Woman Does Not Exist:

The Impossible Feminine and the Possibility of Freedom

I. NEVER JAM TODAY: THE IMPOSSIBILITY OF TAKINGS JURISPRUDENCE

"I'm sure I'll take you with pleasure!" the Queen said. "Two pence a week, and jam every other day."

Alice couldn't help laughing, as she said, "I don't want you to hire me—and I don't care for jam."

"It's very good jam," said the Queen.

"Well, I don't want any to-day, at any rate."

"You couldn't have it if you did want it," the Queen said. "The rule is, jam tomorrow and jam yesterday—but never jam to-day."

"It must come sometimes to jam to-day," Alice objected.

"No, it can't," said the Queen. "It's jam every other day: to-day isn't any other day, you know."

"I don't understand you," said Alice. "It's dreadfully confusing!"

"That's the effect of living backwards," the Queen said kindly: "It always makes one a little giddy at first—"[1]

A. Introduction

The assertion that property is not, or at least is no longer, a single coherent concept is frequently based on an analysis of the Takings

---

1. Lewis Carroll, *Through the Looking Glass and What Alice Found There*, in Alice's

Clause of the U.S. Constitution. The takings jurisprudence that has developed under the Fifth[2] and Fourteenth[3] amendments to the U.S. Constitution is a top contender for the dubious title of "most incoherent area of American law."[4] Property's critics wrongly conclude that this doctrinal incoherence is evidence of incoherence in the concept of property itself.

This is a non sequitur. In this book I have tried to show that property not only is a coherent jurisprudential concept and a flourishing economic and legal institution but is logically necessary for the actualization of human freedom. It is appropriate for pragmatic reasons, therefore, for a state's constitution expressly to recognize the fundamental importance of property and to seek to limit the state's power to limit property. The incoherence of takings jurisprudence arises because liberal jurisprudence assigns a broader role to the Takings Clause: it is supposed to be an impregnable barrier protecting the private realm from government invasion. That is, liberalism takes an instrumentalist view of property which, as I discussed in chapter 1, is bound to fail.

In this chapter, I argue that it is logically impossible for private property rights to serve this function because one cannot develop an "objective" test or algorithm of when government regulation does or does not constitute a taking. Hegelian theory explains what classical liberalism can only identify as an embarrassing paradox: private property is not itself a natural right of man but, nevertheless, is logically necessary for man's essential freedom.[5] In the retroactive logic of the Hegelian dialectic in which—as the White Queen put it—we live backwards, it is logically impossible to identify the moment at which the quantitative change of a diminution of property rights becomes the qualitative change

---

Adventures in Wonderland and Through the Looking Glass 145, 232–33 (1992) [hereinafter Carroll, *Through the Looking Glass*].

2. The so-called Takings Clause of the Fifth Amendment to the U.S. Constitution reads: "nor shall private property be taken for public use, without just compensation."

3. The Takings Clause of the Fifth Amendment applies to the states by incorporation under the Fourteenth Amendment. *See, e.g.,* Nollan v. California Coastal Commission, 483 U.S. 825, 827 (1987).

4. A LEXIS search will produce literally hundreds of recent articles attempting variously to reconcile, critique, or condemn Supreme Court takings jurisprudence or to justify, reinterpret, or reimagine the underlying theory of property. Presumably, there are many hundreds of earlier articles and notes not included on LEXIS.

5. For example, Radin calls the fact "that no one can tell with satisfactory certainty what government actions" constitute takings, a "malaise." Margaret Jane Radin, Reinterpreting Property 146 (1993).

of a destruction of property rights. Accordingly, at any given moment we can only see that a taking either has not yet occurred or has always already occurred. It is always jam tomorrow or jam yesterday, but never jam today.

This is not only consistent with, but necessary to, Hegel's conception of freedom and Lacan's concept of love. The failed encounter of property law seen in the dialectic of takings reflects a general failure and negativity that lies at the heart of subjectivity and law. And yet it is precisely this negativity that opens up room for human freedom to actualize itself by going beyond the limit. Freedom cannot be bound by a preexisting "objective" rule; we must always leave a space for subjectivity. Law requires the possibility of its own transgression. This negativity is the Feminine.

B. The Permissible Limitation on Property

If moral and ethical requirements can require the limitation of property, but the dialectic logic of sublation demands that property be preserved, then what degree of limitation of property is consistent with and necessary for the actualization of human freedom? This is the Hegelian equivalent of the liberal question of how to interpret the Takings Clause.

Hegel's answer is unfortunately, but inevitably, disappointing to the traditional constitutional-law scholar. Logic can prove why it is necessary to make this distinction between permissible limitations of property rights and impermissible takings, but it cannot develop an algorithmic logical test that can locate the line dividing the two. Rather, this determination can only be made through pragmatic rather than logical reasoning, and established through positive law. Such pragmatic reasoning and positive legislation falls precisely in the realm liberalism derides as "mere" politics.[6] Consequently, Hegel agrees with liberals that a limitation on governmental "takings" of property is necessary for freedom and a just society. But, in contradistinction to classical liberalism, Hegelian political theory cannot expect takings law to serve as a boundary function. To understand why this is the case, one needs to turn to Hegel's concepts of quality and quantity as developed in his *Greater Logic*.[7]

6. David Gray Carlson, *Liberal Philosophy's Troubled Relation to the Rule of Law,* 62 U. Toronto L.J. 257, 268–73 (1993).

7. G.W.F. Hegel's Science of Logic (A.V. Miller trans., 1969) [hereinafter Hegel, The Greater Logic].

C. The Liberal Dilemma of Takings Law

1. PROPERTY AND THE CONSTITUTION Clearly, the Framers thought that private property was essential to human liberty, or they wouldn't have given it such extraordinary protection. The Takings Clause was to stand as a barrier between politics and law, between the public and the private. As Jennifer Nedelsky says:

> The idea of boundaries and of a sharp distinction between law and politics has been central to the American conception of limited government. Property was for 150 years the quintessential instance of rights as boundaries. It has been the symbol and source of a protected sphere into which the state cannot enter.[8]

This is why Charles Reich in the 1960s thought he could protect welfare recipients from governmental caprice by redefining their entitlements as "new property."[9]

The traditional barrier role of property is most consistent with the Lockean libertarianism of the Federalists. If property is a, or even the, natural or fundamental right of man, and if man entered into the social contract in order to protect his natural rights, then, by definition, to be legitimate, a government must protect private property rights. The jurisprudential and political problem this raises is obvious. Virtually all government regulation directly or indirectly affects somebody's property.

This becomes even more problematic if one reads into the Takings

---

8. Jennifer Nedelsky, Private Property and the Limits of American Constitutionalism: The Madisonian Framework and Its Legacy 8 (1990). Vandeveld similarly claims that

> [p]roperty and its counterpart, sovereignty, have been understood as generic terms for, respectively, the collection of freedoms held by the individual and the collection of powers held by the state. In very real terms, the concept of property has marked the boundaries of individual freedom and the limits of state power.

Kenneth Vandevelde, *The New Property of the Nineteenth Century: The Development of the Modern Concept of Property*, 29 Buff. L. Rev. 325, 328 (1980). In Jeremy Paul's words, "Therefore a concept of property is necessary to render the Constitution an effective safeguard against excessive governmental interference with individual life." Jeremy Paul, *The Hidden Structure of Takings Law*, 64 S. Cal. L. Rev. 1393, 1409 (1991).

9. "The institution called property guards the troubled boundary between individual man and the state." Charles A. Reich, *The New Property*, 73 Yale L.J. 733 (1964).

Even a critic of traditional property notions such as Thomas Grey admits its traditional "sanctity" in our society. Thomas C. Grey, *The Disintegration of Property, in* Property 69, 81 (J. Roland Pennock & John W. Chapman eds., 22 Nomos, 1980). Nedelsky, also critical of the continuing viability of traditional property concepts, correctly identifies property as being "mythical" in the affirmative sense of that term. Nedelsky, *supra* note 8, at 8–9, 224–25.

Clause the Madisonian definition of property that, as we have seen, included not only rights with respect to material things (like land and cattle) and intangibles (such as debts and intellectual property) but also all things which fall within the philosophical concept of "objects" such as our bodies and minds (i.e., our talents, opinions, religion, speech, etc.). Richard Epstein[10] and Robert Nozick[11] are no doubt correct that, if one were to adopt this extreme version of the libertarian theory of property, only the most minimalist state could be justified.

Classical liberalism, broadly understood, is by far the dominant political philosophy in this country, but radical libertarians are certainly in the minority. Yet every other school of liberalism faces paradoxes when it confronts the Takings Clause. For example, it is possible to take a moderate Lockean approach that recognizes property as one, but not necessarily the only, right (natural or otherwise) which government should protect. But then, how can one balance between competing natural rights and fundamental interests? Contractarians, such as Hobbes, argue that in order to stop the war of all against all, man submitted himself to the unlimited power of the absolute sovereign who grants entitlements to citizens known as property.[12] How then can we reconcile a constitutional provision that seeks to rein in the sovereign's power over property when, by definition, the social contract has ceded absolute power over property to the sovereign? Utilitarianism protects property instrumentally as a means of achieving the greatest happiness for society as a whole.[13] Shouldn't the government then have some constitutional power to rearrange property entitlements if this would further the greater good? But how do we reconcile this with the utilitarian instinct that the best way to ensure utility (or wealth) maximization for society generally is to permit each individ-

10. Richard Epstein, Takings: Private Property and the Power of Eminent Domain (1985).

11. Nozick recognizes a natural right of property established by appropriation (either by the owner or by transfer from a legitimate owner). Robert Nozick, Anarchy, State, and Utopia 150–53, 174–82 (1974). He then asks what vision of the state is consistent with these rights. "So strong and far reaching are these rights that they raise the question of what, if anything, the state and its officials may do. How much room do individual rights leave for the state?" Id. at ix.

12. These descriptions of various schools of liberalism might be so simple as to border on caricature, but they are sufficient for the limited use to which I am putting them. For an excellent concise description of Hobbesian contractarianism, see Michel Rosenfeld, Contract and Justice: The Relation Between Classical Contract Law and Social Contract Theory, 70 Iowa L. Rev. 769, 790–98 (1985).

13. Id. at 798–802.

ual member to maximize his own utility (or wealth) in the marketplace? On the one hand, an egalitarian liberal might argue that at least some limitations on the property rights of the most wealthy could be constitutionally justified in the name of distributive justice.[14] On the other hand, an egalitarian might simultaneously recognize that the government's right to take property should be limited because it can so easily devolve into a disguised unequal and, therefore, unjust tax levied against a specific targeted individual, rather than against similarly situated people generally.[15]

In any event, our Constitution does expressly prohibit uncompensated takings of property by the government, and we lawyers need to decide what this means. Moreover, all of the major schools of liberalism recognize some fundamental liberty interest in property—either as a natural right or a right necessarily created by positive law in order to protect other natural rights such as autonomy, the pursuit of happiness, or equality. Yet all but the most extreme libertarians recognize other fundamental interests that justify at least some governmental limitations of property interests. This raises obvious line-drawing problems: when do government regulations so interfere with property rights that we say that the property has been taken?

14. My colleague Michel Rosenfeld describes egalitarian liberalism, as conceived by Thomas Nagel, as assuming that

> there is "moral equality between persons" and that each person has "an equal claim to actual or possible advantages." Moreover, besides being on the main forward-looking, egalitarianism "establishes an order of priority among needs, and gives preference to the most urgent." . . . Further, Nagel emphasizes that "the essential feature of an egalitarian priority system is that it counts improvements to the welfare of the worst off as more urgent than improvements to the welfare of the better off."

Michel Rosenfeld, Affirmative Action and Justice: A Philosophical and Constitutional Inquiry 116 (1991) (quoting Thomas Nagel, Mortal Questions (1979) (citations omitted)).

15. This, for instance, is Frank Michelman's explanation of the justifiable purpose of a takings clause. If the government wishes to create a public park, it is justified in taxing all citizens, or even all wealthy citizens and no poor citizens. But it is unjust to make one individual pay the lion's share of the cost of the park through forfeiture of his land, while other individuals of similar wealth are not required to contribute in similar ways through taxation. Frank Michelman, *Property, Utility, and Fairness: Comments on the Ethical Foundations of "Just Compensation" Law,* 80 Harv. L. Rev. 1165 (1967). The Supreme Court has on occasion adopted this as a justification for the Takings Clause. ("Fifth amendment's guarantee . . . [is] designed to bar Government from forcing some people alone to bear public burdens which, in all fairness and justice, should be borne by the public as a whole." Armstrong v. United States, 364 U.S. 40, 49 (1960).)

Interestingly enough, as is so often the case, this theory which was developed to further a progressive political agenda has been co-opted to serve other purposes. Egalitarian-type arguments are currently being used by supporters of legislation which would define certain pollution control requirements as takings which require compensation.

The need to draw lines does not, however, in and of itself make takings jurisprudence uniquely difficult. Law requires us to do this all the time. We typically do this through positive law—whether formally adopted by the legislature, promulgated through case law, or developed informally through custom and practice. The uniqueness arises under liberalism because, if the Takings Clause is the vital barrier between the public and the private, then the usual devices of positive law are inapt for this task. This is precisely because the Constitution is supposed to be above politics and positive law.

The chaotic state of the case law suggests that the Supreme Court has so far been unable to solve this dilemma. Commentators feast upon the irrationalities and inconsistencies of the precedents, and decry either the oversolicitousness toward vested interests or inattention to fundamental rights. Only a handful of critics, however, have ventured to offer a resolution.

2. THE SUPPOSED DISINTEGRATION OF PROPERTY As discussed in chapter 2, section III.A, some progressive commentators have concluded that the concept of property and the prohibition on uncompensated takings are so internally incoherent that they are disintegrating before our very eyes.[16] This conclusion is based on two observations.

First, the liberal justification for the protection of property in the Constitution is, as we have seen, that private property is a right that is either natural in and of itself or fundamental in the sense of being necessary for the protection of other natural rights, such as autonomy, the pursuit of happiness, or, to a more limited degree, equality. Yet property is also a legal right that exists only insofar as it is enforceable in a court. Specific property rights are often not merely delimited, but created, by positive law. For example, copyright is a relatively modern creature of legislation. Nedelsky, in effect, asks, "How can property both be a natural right and a right created by positive law?"[17] If it is a right created by positive law, how can it serve as a limitation on the government's power to adopt pos-

16. *See, e.g.,* Grey, *supra* note 9, at 74.

17. "Property has also carried with it the paradox of self-limiting government: it is the limit to the state; it is also the creature of the state. In property, the state sets its own limits." Nedelsky, *supra* note 8, at 8. "It is now widely accepted that property is not a limit to legitimate governmental action, but a primary subject of it." *Id.* at 231.

If property is not a "thing," not a special entity, not a sacred right, but a bundle of legal entitlements subject, like any other, to rational manipulation and distribution in accordance with some vision of public policy, then it can serve neither a real nor a symbolic function as boundary between individual rights and governmental authority.

itive laws reducing property rights?[18] To a Hegelian, the first question is not a philosophical problem, although the second remains intractable as a logical matter.

3. THE SEEMINGLY ENDLESS DIVERSITY OF PROPERTY We have seen that progressive critics such as Grey and Nedelsky fixate on the fact that empirical manifestations of property can consist of a seemingly bewildering variety of rights. For example, even though we colloquially say that an owner of a fee simple absolute estate in realty has unlimited rights of possession, enjoyment, and alienation of the object of her property, every lawyer knows these rights are in fact limited: at a minimum, her right of continued possession may be subject to the state's taxation power, her right of enjoyment is subject to nuisance restrictions, and her right of alienation is limited by antidiscrimination laws. In practice, most owners' rights are even more restricted by, for example, easements (which restrict the right of possession) and zoning restrictions (which can restrict the rights of enjoyment and alienation).[19]

How then, these critics ask, can we speak of "property" as an identifiable set of rights when we recognize such variant combinations of rights as property? I have already given the Hegelian reply: we can so long as we stay at the appropriate level of generality. It does not follow from this, however, that all *empirical* actualization of property must be full, complete, or perfect. If one grasps that the Hegelian notion of the elements of property is to be understood at the highest level of abstraction, then one can see that they can be actualized in a dizzying array of concrete manifestations. Nevertheless, all of those legal relations that we tradi-

---

Property must have a special nature to serve as a limit to the democratic claims of legislative power.

Id. at 239.

18. As explained by Paul:

In more general terms, how can government simultaneously be responsible for establishing the property rights of the citizenry and also be entrusted not to render its constituents helpless when conditions dictate defining property rights so as to benefit public officialdom? In property theory, this might be called the problem of positivism.

Paul, *supra* note 8, at 1411.

19. It is common to speak of fee simple absolute as being the most complete property right in realty. This may be true as an empirical matter, but not a theoretical one. Only the sovereign has the highest unlimited allodial estate. For an excellent discussion of the restrictions placed on "fee simple absolute" see Stewart E. Sterk, *Neighbors in American Land Law,* 87 Colum. L. Rev. 55 (1987).

tionally recognize as falling within the rubric "property" can contain some form of each of the three elements of possession, enjoyment, and alienation. The more adequate the manifestations of the three elements of property, the more likely we will label the right "ownership." If the manifestations are not as adequate, we are likely to give a different label to the right.

4. RIGHTS CHOPPING The conclusion that the abstract jurisprudential concept of property is internally coherent as a theoretical matter within Hegelian jurisprudence begs, rather than answers, the practical question posed by the Takings Clause. One approach to this Hegelian analysis is the super-libertarian position taken by Epstein and Chief Justice Rehnquist introduced in chapter 2, section III.A, which I called "rights chopping." A rights-chopping analysis recognizes as inadequate the historical takings rule, as embraced in *Loretto v. Teleprompter Manhattan CATV Corp.*,[20] that holds that a taking is most readily found when there was "permanent physical invasion of real property": it identifies property too closely with one element—possession—and further identifies possession with one of its many possible manifestations—physical custody of tangible things. That is, it adopts the positive masculine phallic metaphor. If interference with the one element of possession is a taking, then regulations that interfere with either of the elements of enjoyment and alienation should also be takings.

Super-libertarians such as Epstein would no doubt argue from this that, since property necessarily consists of manifestations of the three abstract Hegelian elements, any attempt to chop off any piece of any element in and of itself is a taking. That is, any curtailment of any empirical manifestation of any of the three abstract elements is, by definition, an interference with property rights and, therefore, a taking. Virtually all government regulations are per se takings. If one adopts the libertarian proposition that property is a natural right, then only the most minimal form of government can be justified.

We have seen that Radin suggests that the result that flows from the super-libertarian reading is so absurd as to demonstrate the fallaciousness, not the power, of the chopping argument. I agree. Indeed, because the super-libertarian approach comes close to including everything within the rubric "property," it threatens to deprive property of its analytical power as a separate, distinguishable legal category.

20. 458 U.S. 419 (1982).

But this critique can easily suggest an opposite, equally fallacious, conclusion. If property rights can be actualized in any number of empirical variations, can't we declare that a claimant still has "property" and has not been subject to a taking no matter how much of her empirical rights we chop away so long as we leave her with de minimis concrete stubs of the three abstract elements? This would, obviously, give the government great power to regulate freely without compensating persons whose property is merely diminished but not totally destroyed. Of course, the problem with this is the mirror image of the super-libertarian error—it so minimizes the essence of property that it robs it of analytical value.

Other progressives wish to preserve the traditional inspirational rhetoric of property, yet redirect it to other more "progressive" purposes. This requires that they attempt to redefine property. Prominent examples of such approaches are those of Joseph Singer, who would base property rights on reliance interests and the relative power and dependence of rival claimants,[21] and Radin, who (as we have seen) would give full constitutional protection only to that subset of the potential objects which she calls "personal property."

These new conceptualizations of property require corresponding reconceptualizations of the purpose of the Takings Clause. For example, Frank Michelman argues that the Takings Clause is designed to prevent the state from unjustly imposing tax burdens on individuals that are not generally imposed on all other similarly situated persons. Radin thinks that the Constitution should be read as a whole to further "human flourishing." Since these approaches undermine both the fundamental nature of the right of property—treating property instrumentally as a means to serve other ends—and, by extension, the barrier function of the Takings Clause, they also ameliorate the jurisprudential problem of developing a strictly logical or "objective" definition of property and takings. Consequently, Singer and Radin are both self-described "pragmatists" who advocate that courts use a situated, context-intense, case-by-case approach in deciding legal issues.[22]

21. Joseph William Singer, *The Reliance Interest in Property*, 40 Stan. L. Rev. 611 (1988).

22. Margaret Jane Radin, *Market-Inalienability*, 100 Harv. L. Rev. 1839, 1856–83 (1987); Margaret Jane Radin, *The Pragmatist and the Feminist*, 63 S. Cal. L. Rev. 1699 (1990); Margaret Jane Radin, *Lacking a Transformative Social Theory: A Response*, 45 Stan. L. Rev. 409 (1993); Joseph William Singer, *Book Review: Should Lawyers Care About Philosophy?* (reviewing Richard Rorty, Contingency, Irony and Solidarity (1989), and Elizabeth V. Spelman,

5. METONYMY An interesting variation of this critique has recently been offered by Louise Halper.[23] She upbraids Justice Scalia for his opinion in the most prominent rights-chopping case, *Lucas v. South Carolina Coastal Commission*.[24] In this case the Supreme Court held that a regulation which diminishes the value of a parcel of realty by limiting its commercial development can be a taking. She characterizes this as a metonymy.[25] In her view he is confusing a part—value—for the whole—the land.[26]

I would agree that this is indeed a metonymic trope, but not the one Halper identifies. The whole of property can never be the land itself, but only the claimant's rights with respect to the land. The land is only the object of these rights. Consequently, the metonymy that Scalia did make was to substitute a manifestation of one of the three elements of property—enjoyment manifested in the form of the right to development for monetary purposes—for the whole of the element of enjoyment, and to substitute the element of enjoyment for the entirety of property.

This analysis is particularly apt because Lacan identified metonymy as the feminine slippage of meaning, as opposed to the masculine slippage of metaphor.[27] A threat to the feminine aspect of property causes Scalia modestly to avoid violation through a feminine trope.

Inessential Women: Problems of Exclusion in Feminist Thought (1988)), 1989 Duke L.J. 1752; Joseph William Singer, *Property and Coercion in Federal Indian Law: The Conflict Between Critical and Complacent Pragmatism*, 63 S. Cal. L. Rev. 1821 (1990); Joseph William Singer, *A Pragmatic Guide to Conflicts,* 70 B.U. L. Rev. 731 (1990).

23. Louise Halper, *Tropes of Anxiety and Desire: Metaphor and Metonymy in the Law of Takings,* 8 Yale J.L. & Human. 31 (1996).

24. 505 U.S. 1003 (1992).

25. Halper, *supra* note 23, at 32, 35, 46. Specifically, it is a synecdoche. A metonymy is generally the substitution of an attribute of a thing for the thing. A synecdoche is a subset of metonymy—a part for the whole. Halper, like me, is influenced by Lacan, who thought that all linguistic meaning consisted of the slippage of meaning of metaphor and metonymy. Although the example he gives of a metonymy is arguably a synecdoche (*see* Jacques Lacan, *The agency of the letter in the unconscious or reason since Freud, in* Jacques Lacan, Écrits 146, 156 (Alan Sheridan trans., 1977) (1966)), it is clear from his analysis that he was not so limiting his definition. Lacan thought of metonymy as a substitution of *"word-to-word,"* as opposed to metaphor which is the substitution of *"one word for another."* *Id.* at 157. *See* Jean-Luc Nancy & Phillipe Lacoue-LaBarthe, The Title of the Letter: A Reading of Lacan 71–76, 96–97, 139–40 (F. Raffoul & D. Pettigrew trans., 1992).

26. Halper, *supra* note 23, at 46–51.

27. In Freudian terms, metonymy is displacement and metaphor is condensation. Jacques Lacan, The Seminar of Jacques Lacan, Book III, The Psychoses 1955–1956, at 221 (Jacques-Alain Miller ed. & Russell Grigg trans., 1993). *See also* Jane Gallop, Reading Lacan, 24–32 (1985).

In any event, whatever the form of the metonymy, Halper's argument is that one does not destroy the whole of property by merely interfering with its parts. The libertarian should (correctly) counter that since property is by definition a unity of constituent rights, the only way to destroy property is by destroying its parts. Indeed, if property logically consists of the unity of the three classic elements, the destruction of any one of the three elements by definition destroys the status of a claim as property.

Part of the problem, of course, arises because the very terminology of the Constitution reflects the positive masculine phallic metaphor. Property is a thing that can be taken away. All interferences with property rights are described in terms of castration—someone has taken my object of desire. My entitlements have been "severed" or "chopped." The remedy given by the Constitution for takings reflects the negative masculine phallic metaphor and the second masculine strategy for dealing with castration in which exchange replaces possession. That is, the significance of the loss of any specific object is denied on the grounds that it can be cured through receipt of an equivalent object sometime in the future. And so the Fifth Amendment provides that takings are permitted so long as the government pays "just compensation"—so long as the Father(land) fulfills his promise to his sons.

It is difficult to apply this masculine imagery of takings-castration to interferences with the feminine property elements of enjoyment. Frequently when enjoyment is lost, the owner retains possession of the object of desire. The intuitively appropriate imagery is that of rape, not castration. My thing has not been taken, rather my rights have been violated. This feminine imagery similarly suggests that the Takings Clause should not apply because the remedy seems inadequate. The loss of the feminine self in violation is permanent and cannot be cured through the masculine regime of exchange.[28]

Where does this leave takings law? It is obvious that complete de-

---

28. I have suggested elsewhere that Calabresi and Melamed's property-liability-inalienability analysis of environmental nuisances is inadequate for similar reasons. It imagines all environmental nuisances in terms of the masculine imagery of castration—the taking or exchange of a thing. Property rules privilege the masculine element of possession and seek to prevent the taking (castration). Liability rules privilege the masculine element of alienation and assume that all losses (castrations) can be cured through future exchange of an equivalent thing (i.e., the payment of damages). The problem is that in the classic environmental nuisance, no "thing" is taken. Rather, one party's enjoyment of his thing interferes with another party's enjoyment of hers. As the very terminology of "pollution" suggests, the loss is not experienced as castration but as violation. Jeanne L. Schroeder, Three's a Crowd: Calabresi and Melamed's Repression of the Feminine (1997) (unpublished manuscript, on file with author).

struction of all possessory rights constitutes a "taking" because possession is the most primitive element of property. That is, one can have no
right of enjoyment or alienation unless one has at least some minimal possessory rights in the Hegelian sense. But unless we limit takings to complete, 100% deprivation of all property elements, aren't we stuck with what
Halper calls a "metonymic" approach (a taking of some part will be treated
as legally equivalent to the taking of the whole)? But doesn't this devolve
into the libertarian argument that forbids virtually all government?

To put it another way, how can I argue that property is not a random
or arbitrary collection of disparate rights (as the bundle-of-sticks metaphor
implies) but a recognizable combination of rights, yet at the same time
recognize that it is intuitively and empirically wrong to say that a property interest is always destroyed if any one of the rights that compose property is infringed? I believe that these statements are not incompatible for
the same reason that a beach is still a beach after one removes one grain
of sand; but, as anyone with shorefront property knows, as the sea keeps
removing grains of sand year after year, the beach will eventually disappear. Although property consists of identifiable elements, it is itself an
identifiable quality that cannot be reduced to a collection of elements.

D. Quality and Quantity

> *London (Reuter)—Simple laws of physics can explain one
> of life's oldest and most annoying truisms—that a dropped piece
> of toast always lands butter side down—a British physicist said
> Monday.*
>
> *"Toast falling off the breakfast table lands butter side down,
> because the universe is made that way," Robert Matthews, a
> physicist at Aston University in Birmingham, said in a
> statement.—Japan Times.*
>
> *Perhaps Professor Matthews will also discover why the rule is,
> jam tomorrow, and jam yesterday—but never jam today.*[29]

Hegel explains this phenomenon in his chapter on Specific
Quantity in *The Greater Logic*. He uses the wonderful (perhaps autobi-
ographical?) example of "the bald."[30] The hairy young man who wakes
up every morning to see a single hair on his pillow is still a hairy man—
albeit a worried one. But eventually that inevitable and tragic dawn

---

29. The New Yorker, August 21 & 28, 1995, at 114.

30. The sudden conversion into a change of quality of a change which was apparently
merely quantitative had already attracted the attention of the ancients who illustrated

breaks when he looks in the mirror and a bald man stares back.[31] Hegel's point is not that this demonstrates that the concepts "hairiness" and "baldness"—or property and no property—are irrational. In his language, these dyads are *qualitatively* different as a logical matter. It is absolutely necessary for Hegel's entire philosophical project in *The Greater Logic* to maintain a strictly logical distinction between changes in *quality* (e.g., from hairiness to baldness) and changes in *quantity* (e.g., from 1,000,000 hairs to 999,999 hairs).[32] The relation between quality and quantity is what Hegel called "measure," and the sublation of quality and quantity through measure is an essential step of the dialectical process which charts the development from pure being through to the absolute idea.[33]

Hegel argues that quantity and quality are dialectically related, identical yet different. Quantitative changes are gradual; qualitative changes are sudden. Something can have more or less of a Hegelian quantity, but it either has or does not have a Hegelian quality. The Hegelian concept of the identity of identity and difference, however, means that quantitative change reveals itself as always already becoming qualitative change.

This means that it is logically necessary, on the one hand, that quantitative changes eventually become qualitative changes, yet, on the other hand, there can be no fixed point at which the change occurs. This is because (by definition) the identification of a specific point of transition is to assign a quality to the transition point. This does not solve the logical problem, it just replicates it. We have just substituted a different question of qualitative differentiation.

---

in popular examples the contradictions arising from ignorance [of the suddenness of changes in quality]; they are familiar under the name[] of "the bald". . . . The question was asked: does the pulling out of a single hair from the head . . . produce baldness . . . ? An answer in the negative can be given without hesitation since such a removal constitutes only a quantitative difference, a difference moreover which is itself quite insignificant; thus a hair . . . is removed and this is repeated, only one of them being removed each time in accordance with the answer given. At last the qualitative change is revealed; the head . . . is bald . . . . In giving the said answer, what was forgotten was not only the repetition, but the fact that the individually insignificant quantities (like the individually insignificant disbursements from a fortune) *add up* and the total constitutes the qualitative whole, so that finally this whole has vanished; the head is bald, the purse is empty.

Hegel, The Greater Logic, *supra* note 7, at 335.

31. Those hairy readers who smile condescendingly at our metaphoric hero's plight may want, instead, to contemplate the old, gray, and wrinkled.

32. Indeed, over one-third of *The Greater Logic* is devoted to a discussion of quality, quantity, and their relationship.

33. Hegel, The Greater Logic, *supra* note 7, at 327.

An example may make this clear. We all intuitively understand that it just does not work to reword the question asked of the anxious young man standing at the mirror, "Am I bald yet?" as "Am I now at the transition point between hairy and bald?" Those of us who are confronting middle age recognize that the latter wording is not a clarification but an unacceptable attempt to avoid the issue through euphemism. Further, to name the transition point "Am I now 'semi-bald'?" just restates the problem in increasingly painful detail.

It should be sufficient for my very limited purpose simplistically to explain that "quality" to Hegel is what he calls "determinate being."[34] This is a concept derived through sublation of the logical concept of pure or *immediate* being. That is, all things that exist share the abstract concept of pure immediate being per se—they all exist. Quality refers to the specific, affirmative aspect of a thing that distinguishes it from other things that exist—that is, it is the aspect of a thing that is not shared, it is that which enables us to tell two "things" apart.

To put it another way, if being is pure and immediate, then nothing can be discerned. As a consequence, Hegel argues that pure being shares a moment of identity with pure nothing.[35] In contrast, determinative being (or quality) is the concept that *something* discernible exists. But a quality can only be defined in terms of what it is not—it is defined by its own negation in the sense of "this is not that."[36] To be bald can only be understood in terms of not being hirsute.

Determinate being, moreover, by definition, is finite (otherwise it could not be determined).[37] By this I mean that the very concept of *determining* what distinguishes one thing from another implies setting boundaries—separating one thing from another. If the thing is on this side of the boundary, it is X; if on the other side, it is not-X.

Quantity is the sublation of quality: quantity is what results when

34. I limit my discussion to the relationship of quality and quantity called "measure." This is not intended as a complete description of the complex and subtle concept of quantity. For a succinct description of this journey from pure being to essence—the beyond of deconstruction—*see* David Gray Carlson, *The Hegelian Revival in American Legal Discourse*, 45 U. Miami L. Rev. 1051, 1062–67 (1992).

35. Because immediate being in its purity has no specific content, it is identical with pure nothing. Hegel, The Greater Logic, *supra* note 7, at 82. The relationship between pure being and pure nothing is "becoming." Hegel argues that it is this relationship of becoming which sets the dialectic process in motion. It is the sublation of the pure being and pure nothing which creates determinate being (quality).

36. *Id.* at 109.

37. *See id.* at 129.

one overcomes quality's finitude. Finitude is quality's dependence on otherness—that is, the sense that a quality can only be understood in terms of what it is not, of what is fenced off. Because quantity is the expulsion of otherness, the quantity achieved by sublating any one quality is indistinguishable from and continuous with all other "ones" that similarly result from sublating all other qualities (determinate beings). In other words, qualities are plural, but quantity is unity. By definition, there must be many qualities, each separate and distinguishable from the others in the sense that the quality of baldness is different from the quality of hairiness, or for that matter, the qualities of being hot, sweet, or whatever. In contradistinction, the concept of more or less is the same regardless of whether we are talking about more of this or less of that—whether it be the number of hairs on a man's head, the temperature, or sweetness. Quantity is, therefore, indifferent to quality.

In simple English, quality is differentiation, quantity is commensuration. Quality is difference; quantity is identity. The identity of quality and quantity is the famous Hegelian doctrine of the identity of identity and difference. Qualities are the differences of self from other. Quantity, in contradistinction, is what self and other have in common. Qualitative difference is a matter of is or is not. Quantitative difference is a matter of more or less. Quality asks, "Is it X or Y?" Quantity asks, "How much Z do X and Y have?" This is why changes in quality are sudden even though changes in quantity are gradual. Nevertheless, changes in quantity eventually lead to changes in quality. This relationship between quality and quantity is called "measure."

To be free, of course, is not to have limits. As just discussed, quality (determinate being) can only be understood in terms of its finitude or limit. The very concept of any limit, however, necessarily includes within itself the concept that there is something beyond the limit. To resort to a spatial analogy, quality (determinate being) defines something by fencing it in, and this implies, in turn, that something is fenced out. True infinity consists of negating the limit of any specific quality. This is my definition of freedom—and the Feminine. Let me slow down.

If quality is the concept of identifying things in terms of that which they are not, then it is a setting of limits, a building of fences keeping some "things" on this side and some "things" on the other side. To know the true quality of a thing, we must go beyond its limit. We must climb over the fence that proscribes a quality, see what is on the other side, and then look back. In this sense, Hegel believes that logic itself requires that every time we confront a limit, we must exceed the limit.

The banal witticism "rules are made to be broken" is literally true to Hegel. The Hegelian paradox is precisely that limitation and finitude create the conditions of freedom and infinity. Freedom and necessity are, therefore, dialectically related. Freedom is the lack of limits, yet it is created by limits. Freedom is to not be bound by necessity, but limits necessitate that we seek to be free. Hegel recognizes that freedom as "the beyond of the limit" is not only a logical necessity but an ethical mandate. This is evidenced by the fact that he calls the demand to surpass all limits "the ought."[38] As we shall see, this is precisely Lacan's concept of the relationship between law and enjoyment.

Quality is "being *in*-itself." This terminology captures the idea that quality is that which makes something what it is (as opposed to what it is not). Quality is "fenced in"—enclosed within its own borders. In opposition, quantity is "being *for* itself." This captures the sense that since quantity expels otherness, it is *for itself*, not for another. Curiously, therefore, quantity (unlike quality) ends up being that aspect of being which is the opposite (or negation) of being. By this I mean: quality is the concept that there are things that really exist and that we can distinguish one from another because they are different in some meaningful way. The concept of quantity, in contradistinction, does not require the existence of anything in particular. It just posits that if something did exist and could be measured, it could be described as more or less like this or that. Quality is the assertion "This is what I am—not that"; quantity is "This is what I'm like—I have some of this and some of that." Obviously, both are necessary yet insufficient ways of understanding something.

E. The Movement of Sublation

1. NEGATION AND PRESERVATION   As I have repeatedly emphasized, a common misreading of the dialectic suppresses the preserving

---

38. *Id.* at 132. Immanuel Kant insisted that impossibility never exonerates a person from his ethical duty. Consequently, the Kantian response to the excuse "I can't" is the slogan "You can because you must!" (*See, e.g.,* Slavoj Žižek, The Metastases of Enjoyment: Six Essays on Woman and Causality 99–100 (1994) [hereinafter Žižek, The Metastases of Enjoyment], in which Žižek uses a scene from de Laclos's *Les liaisons dangereuses* to illustrate this concept.) Hegel, as always, goes a step further than Kant in recognizing that it is precisely the impossibility which changes an obligation into a duty. He writes, in effect, "You must because you can't!" *See also* Jacques Lacan, The Seminar of Jacques Lacan, Book VII, The Ethics of Psychoanalysis 1959–1960, at 315–17 (J. A. Miller ed. & D. Porter trans., 1992) [hereinafter Lacan, Seminar VII].

aspect of sublation beneath its negating aspect. It forgets that at the moment the self is negated and becomes identical with the other, it still remains differentiated and separate as the self. As property becomes nonproperty, it still always retains the notion of property. Nonproperty can only be understood in terms of property—that which it is not.

This is a crucial point to Hegel. He denies that only the positive has determinate characteristics, with the negative being a generic nonbeing.

> [T]here still lingers on the thought of this difference of [nothing] from being, namely that the determinate being of nothing does not at all pertain to nothing itself, that nothing does not possess an independent being of its own, is not being as such. Nothing, it is said, is only the absence of being, darkness thus only the *absence* of light, cold only absence of heat, and so on. And darkness only has meaning in relation to the eye, in external comparison with the positive factor, light, and similarly cold is only something in our sensation; on the other hand, light and heat, like being, are objective, active realities on their own account and are of quite another quality and dignity than this negative than nothing. One can often find it put forward as a weighty reflection and an important piece of information that darkness is *only absence* of light, cold *only absence* of heat. About this acute reflection in this field of empirical objects, it can be empirically observed that darkness does in fact show itself active in light, determining it to colour and thereby imparting visibility to it, since, as was said above, just as little is seen in pure light as in pure darkness. Visibility, however, is effected in the eye, and the supposed negative has just as much a share in this as the light which is credited with being the real, positive factor; similarly cold makes its presence known in water, in our sensations etc., and if we deny it so-called objective reality it is not a whit the worse for our doing so. But a further objection would be that here, too, as before, it is a negative with a determinate content that is spoken of, the argument isn't confined to pure nothing, to which being, regarded as an empty abstraction, is neither inferior nor superior. But cold, darkness, and similar determinate negations are to be taken directly as they are by themselves and we shall then see what we have thereby effected in respect of their universal determination which has led them to be introduced here. They are supposed to be not just nothing but the nothing of light, heat, etc., of something determinate, of a content; thus they are a determinate, a contentful, nothing if one may so speak. But as will subsequently appear, a determinateness is itself a negation, and so they are negative nothings; but a negative nothing is an affirmative something.[39]

___

39. Hegel, The Greater Logic, *supra* note 7, at 101–02. "At first, then, quantity as such appears in opposition to quality, but quantity is itself *a* quality . . . . But quantity is not only *a* quality; it is the truth of quality itself . . . . " *Id.* at 323.

The loss of property is not a mere lack of rights, it is nonproperty—a positive taking.

2. CONTRADICTION, POTENTIALITY, AND ACTUALITY In our society "contradiction" (like negativity) is considered to be a bad thing that can and must be eliminated. Consequently, it is easy to conclude that when Hegel identifies a contradiction in the abstract right of property, he is making a judgment that property is somehow incoherent or bad and in need of replacement. Nothing could be more wrong. In the Hegelian dialectic, contradiction cannot be bad and it can never be destroyed. Contradiction must be resolved, but each resolution necessarily creates a new contradiction. As a result, contradiction is not only a logically necessary aspect of the world, it is precisely that aspect of the world that creates change and dynamism.[40]

For something to be possible it must be actualized—the failure of something eventually to become actualized means that it was not, in fact, possible. As I have explained, this means that something only retroactively becomes potential once it has been fulfilled. This is why the abstract person as free will is driven to actualize its potential freedom as concrete freedom in order to reaffirm its own understanding of itself.[41] But the dialectic works the opposite way as well. The logically later concept cannot exist except for the logical necessity of the continuance of the earlier, and the earlier cannot exist except for the logical necessity of the possibility of the

---

40. Hegel is particularly hard on philosophers who try to do away with contradiction:

The *solution* . . . is transcendental, that is, it consists in the assertion of the ideality of space and time as forms of intuition—in the sense that the world is *in its own self* not self-contradictory, not self-sublating, but that it is only *consciousness* and reason that is a self-contradictory being. It shows an excessive tenderness for the word to remove contradiction from it and then to transfer the contradiction to spirit, to reason, where it is allowed to remain unresolved. In point of fact it is spirit which is so strong that it can endure contradiction, but it is spirit, too, that knows how to resolve it. But the so-called world . . . is never and nowhere without contradiction, but it is unable to endure it and is, therefore, subject to coming-to-be and ceasing-to-be.

Id. at 237–38. In his *Lesser Logic,* Hegel particularly chides these philosophers for assuming that it is intellect, and not the world, which is contradictory.

The blemish of contradiction, it seems, could not be allowed to mar the essence of the world; but there could be no objection to attach it to the thinking Reason, to the essence of the mind.

G.W.F. Hegel, Hegel's Logic 77 (William Wallace trans., 1975).

41. That is, freedom is negative and, therefore, mere possibility. Right is the actualization of freedom. G.W.F. Hegel, Elements of The Philosophy of Right 35 (H.B. Nisbet trans. & Allen W. Wood ed., 1991) [hereinafter Hegel, The Philosophy of Right].

later. The later concept is actuality, but the earlier concept is the possibility that allows it to come into being.

To resort to metaphor, the earlier moment in the dialectic is like the foundation for the subsequent edifice. A foundation is dug before the building, but in anticipation of the building. The building requires the foundation because one cannot remove the foundation after the building is built without causing the entire edifice to come crashing down. But the foundation also requires the building in the sense that unless the building is subsequently built, it is not a foundation, merely a hole in the ground. It only becomes a foundation retroactively. Similarly, the legal subject and abstract right are the foundations on which the individual citizen and the state will be built. If the dialectic is circular as claimed, the fact that when one starts with an analysis of the free person one ends up with the state means that if one instead started with an analysis of the state one would inevitably be led back to the free person. If autonomy and abstract rights are suppressed and subordinated to the state, the state will also cease to be. We would be left only with their ruins—tyranny and oppression.

3. SUBLATION AS QUANTUM LEAP Because sublation simultaneously maintains the distinction between two concepts while creating an immediate unity, the movement of sublation cannot be a gradual move. It is a change of quality, not quantity. The change from quantity to quality is, to use the language of modern physics, a quantum leap. Hegel explains how gradual quantitative change produces the quantum leap of qualitative change as follows:

> Since the quantitative determinateness of anything is thus twofold—namely, it is that to which the quality is tied and also that which can be varied without affecting the quality—it follows that the destruction of anything which has a measure takes place through the alteration of its quantum. On the one hand this destruction appears as *unexpected*, in so far as the quantum can be changed without altering the measure and the quality of the thing; but on the other hand, it is made into something quite easy to understand through the idea of *gradualness*. The reason why such ready use is made of this category to render conceivable or to *explain* the disappearance of a quality or of something, is that it seems to make it possible almost to watch the disappearing with one's eyes, because quantum is posited as the external limit which is by its nature alterable, and so *alteration* (of quantum only) requires no explanation. But in fact nothing is explained thereby; the alteration is at the same time essentially the transition of one quality into another, or the more abstract transition of an ex-

istence into a negation of the existence; this implies another determination than that of gradualness which is only a decrease or an increase and is a one-sided holding fast to quantity.[42]

Nevertheless, it is a common logical error to conclude from the fact that the qualitative change takes place through quantitative changes that the qualitative change is itself gradual. But we do this not because the former follows from the latter as a logical matter, but because it is intuitively simple.

> Since the progress from one quality [to another] is an uninterrupted continuity of the quantity, the ratios which approach a specifying point are, quantitatively considered, only distinguished by a more and a less. From this side, the alteration is *gradual*. But the gradualness concerns merely the external side of the alteration, not its qualitative aspect; the preceding quantitative relation which is infinitely near the following one is still a different qualitative existence. On the qualitative side, therefore, the gradual, merely quantitative side which is not in itself a limit, is absolutely interrupted; the new quality in its merely quantitative relationship is, relatively to the vanishing quality, an indifferent, indeterminate other, and the transition is therefore a *leap*; both as posited as completely external to each other. People fondly try to make an alteration *comprehensible* by means of the gradualness of the transition; but the truth is that gradualness is an alteration which is merely indifferent, the opposite of qualitative change.[43]

One might be tempted to argue that if, as Hegel says, changes in quality are sudden, not gradual, then one should be able to identify the exact point when the change occurs. Doesn't this suggest that the takings paradox should be easily solvable? This is, once again, a serious misunderstanding of sublation.

Žižek gives a characteristically brilliant account of why we can never identify the moment of sublation. The specific examples he uses are Hegel's descriptions of the movements from consciousness into self-consciousness, and from "in-itself" to "for-itself," but it can be generalized to all sublations.

> Hegelian "reflection," however, does not mean that consciousness is followed by self-consciousness—that at a certain point consciousness magically turns its gaze inward, toward itself, making itself its own object, and thus introduces a reflective distance, a splitting, into the former immediate unity. Hegel's point is, again, that consciousness *always-already is self-*

42. Hegel, The Greater Logic, *supra* note 7, at 334–35.
43. *Id.* at 368.

consciousness: there is no consciousness without a minimal reflective self-relating of the subject. . . .

The passage of consciousness to self-consciousness thus involves a kind of failed encounter: at the very moment when consciousness endeavors to establish itself as "full" consciousness of its object, when it endeavors to pass from the confused foreboding of its content to its clear representation, it suddenly finds itself within self-consciousness—that is to say, it finds itself compelled to perform an act of reflection, and to take note of its own activity as opposed to the object. Therein resides the paradox of the couple of "in-itself" and "for-itself": we are dealing here with the passage from "not yet" to "always-already." In "in-itself," the consciousness (of an object) is not yet fully realized, it remains a confused anticipation of itself; whereas in "for-itself" consciousness is in a way already passed over, the full comprehension of the object is again blurred by the awareness of the subject's own activity that simultaneously renders possible and prevents access to the object. In short, consciousness is like the tortoise in Lacan's reading of the paradox of Achilles and the tortoise—Achilles can easily outrun the tortoise, yet cannot catch up with her.[44]

In the passage referred to by Žižek, Lacan compares the notion of fantasy—which reflects a Hegelian sublative leap—to Zeno's famous paradoxes. In a Lacanian reading, Zeno was not merely inventing novel hypotheticals to demonstrate the teachings of Parmenides. Rather, as classicists have long since pointed out, Zeno was a brilliant satirist. He eruditely combined allusions to the tragic race to the death between Achilles and Hector in the *Iliad* with the comic race between the hare and the tortoise in Aesop's fable in order to make a profound philosophical point. Specifically, Zeno was referring to Homer's description.

As in a dream, the pursuer never succeeds in catching up with the fugitive whom he is after, and the fugitive likewise cannot ever clearly escape his pursuer; so Achilles that day did not succeed in attaining Hector, and Hector was not able to escape him definitely.[45]

As explicated by Žižek, the

point is not that Achilles could not *overtake* Hector (or the tortoise)—since he is faster than Hector, he can easily leave him behind—but rather that he cannot *attain* him: Hector is always too fast or too slow. . . . The li-

---

44. Žižek, The Metastases of Enjoyment, *supra* note 38, at 188–89.

45. Homer, The Iliad, book 22, lines 199–200, *quoted in* Slavoj Žižek, Looking Awry: An Introduction to Jacques Lacan Through Popular Culture 4 (1992) [hereinafter Žižek, Looking Awry].

bidinal economy of the case of Achilles and the tortoise is here made clear: the paradox stages the relation of the subject to the object-cause of its desire, which can never be attained. The object-cause is always missed; all we can do is encircle it. In short, the topology of this paradox of Zeno is the paradoxical topology of the object of desire that eludes our grasp no matter what we do to attain it.[46]

It is not merely empirically difficult, it is logically impossible to identify the exact moment when quantitative change becomes qualitative change—that is, when it is no longer adequate to say there is more or less of something and we must instead conclude that there has been a change of something into something else. We are always positioned either at the point where the change (i.e., in quality) has not occurred (when, in Lacanian terminology, it is the "not yet") or after it has occurred (when it is "always already"), but never at the point of the transition itself because there is no such point.

In the words of the White Queen, in sublation, it is always jam yesterday and jam tomorrow, but never jam today.[47]

Why do we insist on locating the moment of sublation, the node of takings, when it is logically impossible? Because this is the masculine moment of subjectivity and the symbolic as law. The Feminine is the dream of immediate relationship both in the sense of that which is always already lost in castration and in the sense of the not yet of the ought. She is the impossible moment of sublation which cannot be captured because it does not and cannot exist.[48] She is, therefore, simultaneously the two poles of the sublation of the change of quality—jam yesterday and jam tomorrow, yet never jam today. The Masculine is the position which claims not to be castrated, it is the element of possession—of possessing "it," of having jam today. An understanding of sublation shows that this claim is fallacious. This moment of transition within the sublation cannot be lo-

---

46. Žižek, Looking Awry, *supra* note 45, at 4.

47. In other words, is not a kind of leap from "not-yet" to "always-already" constitutive of the Hegelian dialectics: we endeavor to approach the Goal . . . when, all of a sudden, we establish that all the time we were already there. Is not the crucial shift in a dialectical process the reversal of anticipation—not into its fulfillment but—into retroaction? . . . [T]he fulfillment never occurs in the Present . . . .

Slavoj Žižek, Tarrying with the Negative: Kant, Hegel, and the Critique of Ideology 156 (1994) [hereinafter Žižek, Tarrying with the Negative].

48. Žižek comes to a similar conclusion. *See* Slavoj Žižek, The Indivisible Remainder: An Essay on Schelling and Related Matters 161 (1996) [hereinafter Žižek, The Indivisible Remainder].

cated as a logical matter. Subjectivity is split, there is a hole at its center. Subjectivity exists not because there is a there, there. Rather it is the fiction which claims existence where it doesn't exist. It is the alchemy which replaces zero with one. This process of creating subjectivity as the Masculine is the symbolic—law. Consequently, the identification of the moment of a taking, when a change in quantity becomes a change in quality, is not a matter of objective feminine logic but the act of subjective masculine judgment. This is not to imply that the Masculine as the present complements the Feminine as the past and the future. The point is that they are logically incompatible. Zeno took the masculine position that time stands still, that motion is an illusion. But if one takes the Feminine position that we are always in flux, always already gone but not yet here, then the present of jam today can never be captured.

One can see this distinction in the Old Testament concept of God. As is well known, in his Five Books Moses uses two different names for God:[49] *Elohim,* which means Rulers, and Yahweh, which means "That Which Is What Has Been And Will Be"[50] but, by implication, is not here now.[51] As my colleague Arthur Jacobson explains, Moses uses Elohim when God acts as the lawgiver, Yahweh when God is man's friend.[52] "Creation is complete, when Elohim rules. When Yahweh collaborates with [man], creation is ongoing."[53] Elohim is the God who commands us now; Yahweh is the God with whom we have interacted in the past and shall interact again in the future. From a Lacanian perspective, Elohim is the masculine image of God as the source of a static symbolic order. Yahweh is the feminine image of God who is not bound by that order but can, in the future, create something new. To be a judge, one must at one instant identify with Yahweh and collaborate with God in writing the law; but in order to do so, one must simultaneously forget Yahweh and worship God

49. Biblical historians say that this is because the Five Books are a redaction of a number of earlier manuscripts. One of the many sources is designated "E" because of its use of the name Elohim, another is called "J" for its use of the name YHWH (Yahweh, or Jehovah). Others would argue that, nevertheless, for thousands of years the Torah has been read as a single, albeit complex, work by a divinely or artistically inspired redactor-author who brilliantly used the different names and traditions of God to present the many, paradoxically inconsistent but necessarily required, aspects of the divine.

50. Arthur J. Jacobson, *Writing Law According to Moses, with Reference to Other Jurisprudences, in* Deconstruction and the Possibility of Justice 95, 96 (Drucilla Cornell, Michel Rosenfeld & David Gray Carlson eds., 1992).

51. Jeanne L. Schroeder & David Gray Carlson, *Law and Iconomics,* 47 U. Toronto L.J. 175, 181–82 (1997).

52. Jacobson, *supra* note 50, at 96–97.

53. *Id.* at 97.

as Elohim so that one can declare that one is acting justly within the dictates of a preestablished law.

F. Takings and Freedom

1. FREEDOM

> *"[W]hen [Supreme Court Justice Oliver Wendell] Holmes was a small boy his father rewarded every bright saying with a spoonful of jam."*[54]

Judges are forced to act "to-day."[55] To do so they must take on the masculine position and claim to possess "it"—to capture the moment of sublation.[56] Like the common lawyers criticized by Llewellyn, they must attempt to capture the feminine moment of sublation by collapsing a process (the symbolic) into an event (the real). This can only be done in the imaginary, in masculine fantasy. At the moment of judging we must repress the Feminine as the acceptance of castration and the concomitant knowledge that the task is impossible. Like Justice Holmes, the clever judge must speak brightly and claim his jam today.[57] As Nietzsche said, to act is to forget.

Hegel's abstract logic is impeccable, but Hegel always refuses to give the type of pragmatic advice needed by judges. How could he? He was trying to explain the nature of freedom—if he told us what to do, we wouldn't be free. On the one hand, there is a logically and intuitively recognizable qualitative distinction between property and no property. Moreover, a quantitative change in how much property one has is logically distinct from a qualitative change from having property to not having property. On the other hand, a quantitative diminution of property eventually becomes a qualitative change from property to no property.

---

54. Walton Hamilton, *On Dating Justice Holmes,* 9 U. Chi. L. Rev. 1, 22 n.30 (1941).

55. This is the problem explored by Jacques Derrida in *The Mystical Foundation of Authority,* 11 Cardozo L. Rev. 919 (1990).

56. As explained by Žižek, it precisely this impossible moment of determination, the masculine of claiming to have "it," that is Lacan's famous "quilting point" which stabilizes meaning. Žižek, The Indivisible Remainder, *supra* note 48, at 223.

57. Indeed, in defending Justice Holmes's notorious takings decision in Pennsylvania Coal v. Mahon, 260 U.S. 393 (1922), William Michael Treanor has argued that Holmes "deserves one last, posthumous, spoonful of jam." William Michael Treanor, Jam for Justice Holmes: Reassessing the Significance of Mahon (1997) (unpublished manuscript, on file with author).

This is inherent in the very logical nature of the concepts of quality and quantity. The problem in takings jurisprudence is that the declaration that a taking has occurred is precisely a judgment that the change of quantity in property has passed over into a change in quality. The relationship between possibility and actuality is traumatic.[58] And according to Hegel, there is no logical way of identifying the moment when this occurs, because it either has not yet occurred or has always already occurred. This problem is why pragmatism is always the necessary corollary to Hegelian idealism.[59]

Pragmatic decisions cannot be decided by logic but only by practical reasoning. This can only be determined by positive law (whether in the form of custom, judicial decision, legislation, or whatever). This is probably why takings cases seem so illogical and "subjective," that is, the masculine position of subjectivity created by writing law (creating the symbolic). From a Hegelian perspective, this is necessarily true.

It is also why, from a Hegelian perspective, the observation that property is both logically prior to positive law and simultaneously subject to the defining restraints of positive law is not a troublesome logical contradiction (as it is in the classical liberalism embodied in the Constitution). Most important, it suggests that, although property may be necessary for the actualization of human freedom, property may be ill suited for the role traditionally ascribed to it by liberal philosophies to "serve[] . . . in office of a wall, or as a moat defensive to a house"[60] protecting private rights from government oppression.

58. The ontological background of this leap from "not-yet" to "always-already" is a kind of "trading of places" between possibility and actuality: possibility itself, in its very opposition to actuality, possesses an actuality of its own. . . . [T]here is always something traumatic about the raw actuality of what we encounter as "actual"; actuality is always marked by an indelible brand of the (real as) "impossible." The shift from actuality to possibility, the suspension of actuality through inquiry into its possibility, is therefore ultimately an endeavor to avoid the trauma of the real.

Žižek, Tarrying with the Negative, *supra* note 47, at 157.

59. As Hegel absolutely recognized. He just thought that philosophy had nothing to add to pragmatism. When Plato recommended that nursemaids should rock babies to keep them from crying, he had left philosophy and entered prudence. Hegel, The Philosophy of Right, *supra* note 41, at 21. "A further word on the subject of *issuing instructions* on how the world ought to be: philosophy at any rate always comes too late to perform this function." *Id.* at 81. This is partly an issue of terminology. American pragmatists think of their theories as a branch of philosophy. Hegel's point is to distinguish that which can be logically demonstrated (what he calls philosophy) from that which isn't but may be adopted for good reasons. This is, of course, similar to the Popper-Kuhn distinction between science and common sense which is merely supposed to distinguish, not denigrate, the latter.

60. William Shakespeare, King Richard II, act 2, sc. 1.

2. TOTALITARIANISM   Because liberalism is based on the presumption of free, self-actuating, autonomous individuals preexisting in some hypothesized state of nature, society and the state are defined as problems. They need to be justified in light of the individual's preexisting natural rights and liberties. As we have seen, property and the Takings Clause are traditionally seen as ways of protecting the free individual *from* the state.

In contrast, as I have already explored in considerable detail, Hegel believed that the presumption of the free individual is every bit as problematic from a philosophical position as society or government. It is tempting to misinterpret Hegel as justifying the totalitarian state to which individualism, freedom, and private property are totally subordinated. This misinterpretation is based, once again, upon the usual misreading of sublation. Although the individual citizen in the developed state governed by ethical life is the last stage of development of man and society discussed in *The Philosophy of Right*, this cannot mean that the state replaces the logically earlier institution of civil society or that *Sittlichkeit* replaces the earlier relationships of morality and abstract right. To reiterate, sublation requires that the logically earlier stages always remain present and intact as the building blocks of the logically later stages. If the freedom of man as abstract person or the property rights of man as legal subject were infringed, then the ethical life of man as individual in the state (which is the eventual result of sublation of these other stages) would cease to exist.

Moreover, as I argued in chapter 3, this critique also incorrectly assumes that the organizational principle of *The Philosophy of Right* is intended to reflect the historical development of the state. Rather, it reflects the logical order of possibility, whereas history is the empirical order of actuality. The assertion that the actual is possible and the possible is actual is not a claim that possibility enfolds in any specific empirical manifestation. In this case, the logically most primitive possibility was the historically last actuality. As is so often the case, it took longer to accomplish simplicity than complexity. That is, that form of intersubjectivity necessary for a government to start to become a state which was the last to be actualized as a historical matter, was precisely the regime of abstract right—private property and freedom of contract which began to develop in the early capitalistic period.

Consequently, individuality and abstract right are not primitive in the sense of being early stages in development which the state can supplant. They are, instead, primitive in the sense of most basic. They are the immediate conditions of the state's existence as a state. It is, therefore, crucial to a state's own continued existence that it respect and preserve them.

Nevertheless, one must always remain critically aware that even if the abstract person and the developed state mutually require each other as a theoretical matter, the interests of the government and the citizen will frequently conflict as an empirical matter. Sublation preserves difference and conflict. It is painfully obvious that not all empirical governmental institutions qualify as Hegelian "states." Rather, they constitute more or less adequate manifestations of the notion of "state." Consequently, rather than subordinating the individual to a totalitarian state, the Hegelian totalizing philosophy gives the individual an external standard by which to judge the state.

The point for takings law is, once again, that society needs both individualistic property rights and some communitarian limits on property rights but there is no logical algorithm that can determine the proper balance between the two. As we have discussed, the dialectical quantum leap between property and no property is simultaneously both not yet and always already from a *logical* standpoint. Since property is not a preexisting natural right but a human creation (albeit a necessary one), its limits can only be determined by humans.

Citizens, therefore, must be in a state of constant diligence, watching the government so that it doesn't (self-defeatingly) crush human freedom. This is not merely consistent with, but required by, the Hegelian concept of actualized freedom. Freedom cannot be actualized by passively submitting to a preexisting symbolic order. It requires a constant positive affirmation of its existence through the exercise of subjectivity through the active creation of law.

Hegel leaves this actualization of law as abstract right to positive law. As I have said, this can only be promulgated in the civil society and state on the basis of morality and ethical life. We also need to consider the pragmatic decision as to who should make this pragmatic decision—the executive, the legislature, the judiciary, or the "people" (through constitutional amendment).

The specific balance of rights will, by definition, be empirical and not logical. This is because as the actualization of freedom it will have to contain a purely subjective moment. If our actions were logically predetermined, then we wouldn't be free. It will always, therefore, have an unsatisfyingly *ad hoc* or arbitrary aspect to it. There is no way around this. As Žižek said, the fundamental thesis of Hegel is that the human condition is a failed encounter *by definition*. But it is precisely this "failure" or incompleteness that leaves a space, an opening, through which humans can and must seek constantly to actualize our freedom and subjectivity by always exceeding our limits. And so, even as I emphasize the necessity of achieving the sublated feminine position of freedom as the beyond of the limit, this *first* requires the masculine moment of subjectivity which sets the limit and creates the ought.

II. THE IMPOSSIBILITY OF THE FEMININE AND THE POSSIBILITY OF FREEDOM

> Alice laughed. *"There's no use trying,"* she said: *"one can't believe impossible things."*
> *"I daresay you haven't had much practice,"* said the Queen. *"When I was your age I always did it for half-an-hour a day. Why sometimes I've believed as many as six impossible things before breakfast. . . . "*[61]

According to Lacan, ~~The~~ Woman does not exist. She cannot be captured by the symbolic or the imaginary and, thereby, exists in the real—the order that limits the other orders. From the perspective of the masculine order of the symbolic, the feminine realm of the real appears to be the impossible—the limit of possibility and the barrier to the actualization of human freedom.

A. Lacanian Freedom

> *"For instance, now,"* she went on, . . . *"there's the King's Messenger. He's in prison now, being punished; and the trial doesn't even begin till next Wednesday: and of course the crime comes last of all."*
> *"Suppose he never commits the crime?"* said Alice.
> *"That would be all the better, wouldn't it?"* the Queen said . . . .
> Alice felt there was no denying that. *"Of course it would be all the better,"* she said: *"but it wouldn't be all the better his being punished."*
> *"You're wrong there, at any rate,"* said the Queen: *"were you ever punished?"*

61. Carroll, *Through the Looking Glass, supra* note 1, at 238.

> *"Only for faults," said Alice.*
> *"And you were all the better for it, I know!" the Queen said triumphantly.*
> *"Yes, but then I had done the things I was punished for," said Alice: "that makes all the difference."*
> *"But, if you hadn't done them," the Queen said, "that would have been better still; better, and better, and better!" Her voice went higher with each "better," till it got quite to a squeak at last.*
>
> *Alice was just beginning to say "There's a mistake somewhere—. . . ."*[62]

At first blush, the Lacanian universe sounds hopelessly bleak and repressive, bound by prohibitions that make immediate human relationships impossible by definition. But a second look reveals a much different picture. By being castrated, the Lacanian split subject becomes negative (like Hegel's subject explored in *The Philosophy of Right*). But this means that subjectivity contains the capacity for freedom.[63]

This is even more true from the feminine position which is the place of that which is lost in castration. ~~The~~ Woman does not exist. But this means that she is not bound by actuality but is pure potentiality. She does not exist—yet. The law of prohibition is an alchemy that enables humans to imagine and actualize freedom. In other words, woman does not exist, she *insists*—she denies our limits.[64]

External reality is brute necessity. One cannot do certain things because they are literally impossible in the brute sense that "man cannot fly." But as conscious subjects, we do not have direct, immediate access to reality. The instant we realize we are experiencing reality, we are interpreting it—this is why *jouissance* is silent. The order of the real, therefore, is this interpreted concept of that which exists outside of our interpretation.

The psyche can only keep the realms of the real, the imaginary, and the symbolic separate through the law of prohibition—"Thou shall not merge with the real." What was impossible (merging with the world and

---

62. *Id.* at 234–35.

63. In other words, communication is rendered possible by the very feature which may seem to undermine most radically its possibility: I can communicate with the Other, I am "open" to him (or it) precisely and only insofar as I am already in myself split, branded by "repression," i.e., insofar as (to put it in a somewhat naive pathetic way) *I cannot ever truly communicate with myself*; the Other is originally the decentered Other Place of my own splitting.

Žižek, Tarrying with the Negative, *supra* note 47, at 30–31.

64. *Id.* at 188.

the others in immediate relationships) is now prohibited. One does not prohibit what cannot be. Consequently, the impossible is now reimagined as *possible but not allowed!* The real—"that which we can't speak"—now becomes "that which we mustn't say." "You cannot" becomes "Shut up!" This creates "the ought"—the desire, possibility, and necessity of going beyond a self-imposed limit.

> Thereby we have already produced the formula of the mysterious of horror into bliss: by means of it, the *impossible limit* changes into the *forbidden place.* In other words, the logic of this reversal is that of the transmutation of Real into Symbolic: the impossible-real changes into an object of symbolic prohibition. The paradox (and perhaps the very function of the prohibition as such) consists of course in the fact that, as soon as it is conceived as prohibited, the real-impossible changes into something *possible,* i.e., into something that cannot be reached, not because of its inherent impossibility but simply because access to it is hindered by the external barrier of the prohibition.[65]

The Lacanian Feminine is the negativity of subjectivity, but not in the sense of a simple negation of some masculine positivity. If she were, she would merely be the complement of Masculinity and the two sexes would together constitute a harmonious whole. The Masculine claims to have "it," but the Feminine denies that anyone still has "it," while predicting that we will obtain "it" yet. But such complementarity only exists in our fantasies, in the imaginary.[66] That is, the Feminine is the "it" which the Masculine claims to have—the paradoxical moment of sublation which is logically impossible. The Feminine is the negative of the Masculine in the sense of a denial of the hegemony of the symbolic order and its limits. She is the "not-all" (*pas tout*) in the sense of "not all things are phallic."[67] This is why she cannot be described in the symbolic or captured in the masculinist fantasies of the imaginary. The Masculine—the speaking subject—is totally captured in the phallic order of the symbolic. The Fem-

---

65. *Id.* at 116.

66. What defines the imaginary order is the appearance of a complementary relationship between thesis and antithesis, the illusion that they form a harmonious Whole, filling out each other's lack; What the thesis lacks is provided by the antithesis and vice versa (the idea that Man and Woman form a harmonious Whole, for example).

Id. at 123.

67. Slavoj Žižek, For They Know Not What They Do: Enjoyment as a Political Factor 122–25 (1991) [hereinafter Žižek, For They Know Not What They Do]; Žižek, Tarrying with the Negative, *supra* note 47, at 56.

inine is not. She is, therefore, the possibility of going beyond. The Feminine stands in the position of the negative subjectivity that is the condition of freedom.

Lacan analyzed ethics in terms of Kant's dictate "You can, because you must."[68] By this he seems to have meant that impossibility does not excuse one from one's ethical duty. But Lacan, like Hegel, went beyond Kant by recognizing that, paradoxically, impossibility creates the duty. The limit not only defines the ought, but the ought is itself the limit (i.e., the real to the symbolic).[69]

"Man cannot fly" in the real becomes "man shalt not fly" in the symbolic. Mere physical impossibility becomes in the imaginary the Icarus myth whereby man is punished for daring to fly, as well as innumerable inspirational fantasy images of angels and other winged beings that haunt the art and legends of so many cultures. Man must not fly becomes man must fly. As a result, today we have in fact gone beyond this limit and do fly—but notably not in the actually impossible (real) way of flapping our arms and flying like birds, but in a uniquely human way of using the imaginary and symbolic to invent flying machines. That is, flying is artificial—in the literal sense of "made by art"—and is, therefore, authentic to human nature.

Consequently, Lacan must rewrite the Freudian concept of the superego. The superego, as every undergraduate thinks she knows, is supposed

---

68. Lacan, Seminar VII, *supra* note 38, at 315–17. Lacan's tour de force of the Seventh Seminar is to show that the Kantian imperative is equivalent to the obscene philosophy of the Marquis de Sade, and the superego's paradoxical dictate "Enjoy!" (Lacan republished these ideas from the Seventh Seminar in an essay, *Lacan avec Sade,* which was contained in the French version of *Écrits* but was not included in the English edition.) All are radical apathological ethical dictates in the Kantian sense of being completely beyond "every element of sentiment." *Id.* at 79.

> I showed you how one can easily substitute for Kant's "Thou shalt" the Sadean fantasm of *jouissance* elevated to the level of an imperative—it is, of course, a pure and almost derisory fantasm, but it doesn't exclude the possibility of its being elevated to a universal law.

Id. at 316. *See,* Žižek, The Metastases of Enjoyment, *supra* note 38, at 67–70, 99–100.

69. "You can, because you ought"—this expression which is supposed to mean a great deal is implied in the notion of ought. For the ought implies that one is superior to the limitation; in it the limit is sublated and the in-itself of the ought is thus an identical self-relation, and hence the abstraction of "can." But conversely, it is equally correct that: "you cannot, just because you ought." For in the ought, the limitation as limitation is equally implied; the said formalism of possibility has, in the limitation, a reality, a qualitative otherness opposed to it, and the relation of each to the other is a contradiction, and thus a "cannot," or rather an impossibility.

Hegel, The Greater Logic, *supra* note 7, at 133.

to be the part of our psyche that internalizes the law of prohibition. But paradoxically, it is the superego, not the id, that constantly tells us "Enjoy!"[70] It is our guilty conscience that constantly harps on us to obey.[71] The law of the Father castrates us by forbidding our enjoyment. The symbolic—law and language—cannot exist without an order outside of the symbolic that serves as its limit. This is the real and *jouissance*. It is necessary, therefore, for the law to establish its own transgression. The only way for the superego to internalize the law is to force us to transgress the law.[72]

> We give up this enjoyment to assuage our guilt and expect to be compensated for this loss with the lesser pleasures allowed by the law—sexual maturity. But we continue to desire enjoyment which requires transgression of the law. The paradox is, of course, that it is only through the prohibition that we become subjects capable of desire, enjoyment and sin. Lacanian thought is retrospective. We conclude that the enjoyment of wholeness is forever lost because of our sin, when, in reality, it is the dream of the not yet.[73]

Hegel makes this precise point in *The Philosophy of Right* when he argues that wrong is not merely implicit in, but required by, the notion of right.[74]

70. Žižek, For They Know Not What They Do, *supra* note 67, at 237.

On this view, according to which we are simultaneously guilty and obligated to act by law, enjoyment is crime, and crime is lawful, because law is the source of enjoyment. Law is contradictory when it outlaws crime. Or, more generally, the concept of law has within it its negative. It therefore defines and is the source of crime.

Jeanne L. Schroeder & David Gray Carlson, *The Subject Is Nothing*, 5 Law & Critique 94, 100 (1993) (reviewing Žižek, For They Know Not What They Do, *supra* note 67).

71. The child creates his own guilt by retroactively writing and applying a law that is always already broken. Žižek, For They Know Not What They Do, *supra* note 67, at 105; Schroeder & Carlson, *supra* note 70, at 98–100; *and* Jeanne L. Schroeder, *Virgin Territory: Margaret Radin's Theory of Property as the Inviolate Feminine Body*, 79 Minn. L. Rev. 55, 159–60, n.395 (1994) [hereinafter Schroeder, *Virgin Territory*].

This retroactive logic is what the White Queen would have called "the effect of living backwards." Carroll, *Through the Looking Glass, supra* note 1, at 233.

72. We try to justify our castration in terms of just punishment for our violation of the law even though the law did not exist, and could not be violated, prior to castration. We, therefore, need to establish our own guilt. That is, we are not punished because we are guilty, but we are guilty because we are punished. *See* Schroeder & Carlson, *supra* note 70, at 100.

73. *Id.*

74. Hegel, The Philosophy of Right, *supra* note 41, at 115–30.

B. I've believed . . . impossible things . . .

He's dreaming now," said Tweedledee: "and what do you think he's dreaming about?"
Alice said "Nobody can guess that."
"Why, about you!" Tweedledee exclaimed, clapping his hands triumphantly. "And if he left off dreaming about you, where do you suppose you'd be?"
"Where I am now, of course," said Alice.
"Not you!" Tweedledee retorted contemptuously. "You'd be nowhere. Why, You're only a sort of thing in his dream!"[75]

In *Through the Looking Glass,* Alice finds herself trapped in a symbolic order in the form of a chess game. She is placed in the position of a pawn—woman as commodity passively moved by others. When she has the conversation with the White Queen quoted throughout this chapter, Alice, like most empirical women, is still trying to live up to a fantasy of femininity. Alice insists that she is "real," but Tweedledee is correct in insisting that she is a mere figment of the sleeping Red King's dream—a fantasy projection in the masculine imaginary.

Through the dialectic we are able to reimagine the impossible as the prohibited, and therefore as the possible. Hegelian freedom is "the ought": the ethical and logical necessity of transcending the limit. According to sublative logic, it is always already and not yet. But it is never now. Alice saw the White Queen's paradox as the impossible and she couldn't believe it. The White Queen understood that it followed from "living backwards"—the retroactive logic of the dialectic. We can bear the deprivation of jam today only because of memories of jam yesterday (the "always already") and the self-confidence that we will win jam tomorrow (the "not yet"). Of course Alice is only a child; she sees the White Queen as befuddled. But it is precisely the White Queen's understanding of, and belief in, the impossible that makes her not just free but sovereign. She is a queen—~~The~~ Woman who doesn't exist.

Why? What is the "not yet" of the failed encounter experienced in subjectivity and law? In Lacan, that which is in the real, which is beyond the limit, is feminine subjectivity. Castration is our imaginary memory of our always already of separation from the Feminine in the position of Mother-Other, and the hope of obtaining the not yet of the Feminine in the future.

From the masculine position, the Feminine and the *Phallus* look as

75. Carroll, *Through the Looking Glass, supra* note 1, at 223–24.

though they have always and already been lost in castration. But from the feminine position we see that the Feminine has only been prohibited and, therefore, is not yet. Being beyond the limit, the dream of unmediated relationships that is feminine subjectivity is the ought, not merely an aspirational goal but a logical and ethical dictate. If the Feminine is forbidden, then she must be possible. But we cannot know whether she is in fact possible until she is actualized. This means that, paradoxically, for the Masculine to exist it must both repress the Feminine and call her into being. This is what Lacan means when he says that the superego both prohibits enjoyment and commands us to enjoy.

Although the Masculine (the law) represses the Feminine as the always already lost of castration and condemns her to nonexistence, the Masculine simultaneously creates the possibility of the sublated Feminine as the not yet of freedom. As the Masculine claims to be the actuality of having the *Phallus,* it presupposes the Feminine potentiality of being and enjoying it.

The Feminine as both the always already and the not yet are terrifying as well as inspiring to the Masculine. Because the Masculine claims to have "it," the formula of masculinity is "All are subject to the symbolic order (the *Phallus*)."[76] This position is one of desperate, chronic anxiety which Freud called castration fear. The masculine position like the male organ seeks to be firm, but is fragile. This is because the simple negation of the masculine position is "There is one who escapes." It can be falsified by one counterexample.

But the Feminine is not the simple negation of the Masculine. Its formula is "Not all are subject to the symbolic order (the *Phallus*)." Although logicians might argue that this is mathematically equivalent to the sim-

---

76. Lacan sometimes, infuriatingly, represented his ideas in the form of pseudomathematical formulas or "mathemes." The formulas of sexuation are as follows:

$$\exists x. \overline{\Phi x} \qquad \overline{\exists x. \, \overline{\Phi x}}$$
$$\forall x. \, \Phi x \qquad \overline{\forall x. \, \Phi x}$$

Jacques Lacan, *A Love Letter (Une lettre d'âmour)* [hereinafter Lacan, *Love Letter*], in Jacques Lacan and the école freudienne, Feminine Sexuality 149, 150 (Juliet Mitchell & Jacqueline Rose eds. & Jacqueline Rose trans., 1982) [hereinafter Lacan, Feminine Sexuality]. The masculine formula reads "all x are submitted to the function F." The simple (masculine) negation of this is "there is at least one x which is not submitted to the function F." The feminine formula reads "not all x are submitted to the function F," which implies the simple negation "there is no x which could be exempted from the function F." Žižek, Tarrying with the Negative, *supra* note 47, at 56. The function F is, of course, castration. *Id.* at 250 n.10.

ple negation of the Masculine, psychoanalytically they are totally diverse. This is because the negation of the feminine formula is "No one ever escapes." Consequently, although the feminine position can never be verified, it can never be falsified. This is, of course, the classic problem of induction. No matter how much evidence we gather showing that every person who has ever lived has been subject to the symbolic order, there is always the logical possibility that the next example will escape. This weakness of the claims of the symbolic order is the dread of the Masculine and the hope of the Feminine. As a result, the masculine symbolic order reacts in terror and forbids the Feminine. The anxiety of the Masculine is desperate because the falsifying datum—the Feminine—is always present. As Žižek says, "the trouble with *jouissance* is not that it is unattainable, that it always eludes our grasp, but, rather, that *one can never get rid of it. . . .* "[77] Now that she is forbidden, she is not longer impossible, but possible. And as potential, she seeks to be actualized. As Lacan said, the Masculine (claims to) exist, but the Feminine insists!

Because the Masculine denies castration, it can never get beyond castration but is frozen by anxiety, trapped within the symbolic order. The feminine acceptance of castration is the realization that that which is lost is gone forever *but this means that we can mourn its passing and then can go forward and create something new.* The Feminine is the ability to say goodbye. The Feminine insists that we will never be complete *but means that there is always room to grow.* We will always desire because we will never be fulfilled. This is the criterion of freedom and creativity. The Masculine is the fantasy of present wholeness which is necessary for us to act and speak now. The Feminine, as the inevitable realization that this position is a lie, threatens to also freeze us into impotence as we mourn for a wholeness lost in the past. But the Feminine is also the position that the Masculine is a lie also in the sense that castration is a lie. The reason that we are not whole now is not that we were once whole in the past. The real seems unattainable because we experience it as though it preceded the imaginary and the real. But the truth is that the real was only created instantaneously with the imaginary and the symbolic. The three orders are mutually constituting. As a consequence, it is only the sense of loss of wholeness that we call castration which enables us even to imagine what wholeness might be. The Feminine, therefore, is the dream of a future wholeness.

As I have emphasized throughout this book, Lacan is notorious for

---

77. Žižek, The Indivisible Remainder, *supra* note 48, at 93.

insisting that the Masculine is the position of subjectivity. But Lacan is much too subtle, and subversive, to be taken at his literal word. Lacan reveals his method in one of his most influential works, his Seminar on Edgar Allan Poe's *The Purloined Letter*.[78] As is well known, in this story the blackmailing minister succeeds in hiding the eponymous letter from the police by altering its appearance and then displaying it in full sight, in the most obvious place—sticking out of a letter folder hanging from the fireplace mantle in the minister's office. By retelling this story, Lacan is also revealing that he has a secret, disguised but hidden in full sight. Indeed, he gives a further, explicit clue. According to Lacan, Poe's protagonist, Dupin, succeeds in finding the letter by imagining the room as an enormous woman, awaiting his embrace.[79]

How precisely does Lacan describe his "masculine" subject? "He" is split, "he" has a space within, a space that permits intersubjectivity, love, and creation of the new. The metaphor of the cloven, receptive, and fertile body is so obvious that we refuse to see it, so that we insist the answer does not exist. The subject *is* ~~The~~ Woman (i.e., the Feminine)—the radical negativity that is the capacity for human freedom.[80]

And so, Alice eventually gives way to her desire and goes beyond the limit to achieve a radical feminine subjectivity. At the end of *Through the Looking Glass* she achieves the impossible of both being and having the Phallic Mother. She reaches the end of the chessboard, is "queened," takes the Red Queen, and wins the chess game. At this moment, just as Lacan predicted, the fantasy comes to an end. Alice transcends the symbolic and enters the real.

C. The Necessary Loss of Virginity

Property reflects separation. But to love, we must first be separate people who can desire and cherish the feminine hope of reunion. The psychoanalytic function we call the Feminine cannot be filled by the passive, silent object of desire of which Hegel and Lacan speak. To actu-

---

78. Jacques Lacan, *Seminar on "The Purloined Letter"* (Jeffrey Mehlman trans., 1972) [hereinafter Lacan, *The Purloined Letter*], *reprinted in* The Purloined Poe: Lacan, Derrida and Psychoanalytic Reading 28 (John P. Muller & William J. Richardson eds., 1988). This essay is a substantial rewriting of Lacan's Seminar dated April 27, 1977. Jacques Lacan, The Seminar of Jacques Lacan, Book II, The Ego in Freud's Theory and in the Technique of Psychoanalysis 1954–1955, at 191–205 (J.-A. Miller ed. & S. Tomaselli trans., 1988).

79. Lacan, *The Purloined Letter, supra* note 78, at 48.

80. As Žižek has said, "Woman, not man, is the subject *par excellence*." Žižek, The Metastasis of Enjoyment, *supra* note 38, at 122.

alize human freedom, empirical woman must actualize her potential freedom and become an active mediatrix who sets the chain of desire and intersubjectivity in motion.

We must envision a feminine integrity that is not solely dependent for
its recognition on the Masculine. The Feminine insists that we are not
totally captured by the symbolic order. No doubt, submission to the
regime of market exchange is related to the commodification of women
in some deep and fundamental way. Nevertheless, the Radinian person
who chastely tries to protect the integrity of her personhood from commodification by preserving her virgin property from market intercourse
immures herself beyond the reach of community. By seeking to protect
herself from the alienation and loneliness of commodification, she instead
separates herself. Trying to avoid objectification, she so identifies herself
with her objects that she re-creates herself in the image of the traditional
masculine fantasy of woman as passive object who does not actively engage in society as a subject.

The ancient image of the Great Goddess is reduced to the Christian
image of Mary—a mediatrix to be sure, but forever Virgin, stripped of
her godhood, and dependent on the divinity of her Son. One of Mary's
most evocative titles is "Alone of All Her Sex."[81] This explicitly reflects
the fact that by virtue of her great privilege of having been immaculately
conceived she escaped the disjunction of body and soul, the pains of sexual desire, and the indignity of violation suffered by other women. But
we can now understand the double meaning which makes this title so res-
onant. Such a perfect virgin is so sadly alone.

Lacan was finally able to answer the question that so perplexed Freud:
"*Was will das Weib?* (What does woman want?)"[82] She *just wants.*[83] When
we stand in the feminine position, we experience ourselves as wanting in
both senses of the term. Moreover, in our masculine aspect we live in despair and terror of the castration we secretly know has always already occurred. Women are left wanting because it is men who are wanting the
thing we all want. Men need to insist that they have the *Phallus,* not despite their castration but just because of their castration.[84]

Hegelian theory can enrich feminist legal theory because it insists

81. Marina Warner, Alone of All Her Sex: The Myth and the Cult of the Virgin Mary
236–37 (1983).
82. Ernest Jones, The Life and Work of Sigmund Freud 421 (1955) (quoting a letter from
Freud to Marie Bonaparte).
83. Lacan, *Love Letter, supra* note 76, at 151; Juliet Mitchell, *Introduction I* to Feminine
Sexuality, *supra* note 76, at 1, 24.
84. Žižek wonderfully retells the story of *The Emperor's New Clothes* in this light. *See*

that society can never meet the minimum demands of right until every person—including women acting proudly as women and not as the reflected image of masculine fantasy—are recognized as full subjects whose recognition is worthy of desire. Lacanian theory can enrich feminist property theory by reminding us that the Feminine cannot avoid, but is dependent on, the symbolic regime of exchange that creates subjectivity. Rather than fearfully avoiding the market because it can lead to objectification that threatens the self, or grudgingly accepting limited market relations as a necessary evil, feminist theory needs to recognize that subjectivity and community—love, dignity, and justice—require the person to risk her very self in order to see herself reflected in the eyes of the Other.

Nevertheless, Hegelian theory insists that the very logic of property means that there must be some minimal objects of property that cannot rightfully be alienated in the market. Lacanian theory insists that the Feminine can never be reduced to the role imposed on her by the symbolic regime—feminine *jouissance* remains uncaptured. There must, therefore, be a place in our law for object relations, the feminine position, that are not subjected to the *Phallic* order of the market. But this does not require a disparagement of the market and traditional property, for even to analyze these object relations in terms of "property" is to subject them to the order of the market. Rather, we must consider the development of an alternate regime that would neither negate nor complement but would supplement the law of property—perhaps a jurisprudence of expanded bodily integrity. The Lacanian Feminine must, however, resist the imaginary temptations of the masculine fantasy of Aphrodite who had a lover every night but awoke a virgin every morning.[85]

The Feminine of sublation cannot be a return to the original unity of the lost Feminine. The price of marriage is the bleeding hymen. This is because the primordial Feminine never in fact preexisted its loss. Rather, she is retroactively posited as that which must have been lost in the real when the symbolic order was established. As reflected in so many traditional marriage customs, the bride's virginity is only established the

---

Žižek, For They Know Not What They Do, *supra* note 67, at 11–12, 252. What the pre-oedipal child did not realize when he blurted out the fact of the emperor's nakedness was that adults do not insist that the emperor was clothed despite the fact he was naked. Rather, we need to insist on his clothes just because he is naked. It is this fiction that is subjectivity. *See also* Schroeder & Carlson, *supra* note 70.

85. A temptation which I have been unable to resist in the past. Schroeder, *Virgin Territory, supra* note 71, at 171 (1994).

morning after by the stain of its loss on the marriage bed sheets.

Sublation is not a simple restoration. "[H]armony is restored, but this 'new harmony' has nothing whatsoever to do with the restitution of the lost original harmony—in the new harmony, the loss of the original harmony is *consummated*."[86] Once virginity is lost, it can never be restored, only mourned. But now that we have tasted the autonomy of subjectivity and glimpsed the possibility of freedom, we should not long to return to the unconscious organic unity of the lost Feminine. Rather, we seek a chosen, conscious moment of unity between free individuals.[87] And so, we must seek not restoration but transfiguration. The sublated Feminine must cast off her Vestal livery and cherish the scar of her defloration as a remainder and reminder of that which must be sacrificed for love.[88]

The Greek myth of Persephone illustrates the Lacanian Feminine. It often seems paradoxical to us moderns that she was both the goddess of spring and the queen of the dead.[89] From a Lacanian perspective, however, these two roles necessarily and inevitably go together. They are feminine enjoyment as not yet, and always already gone.

Once Persephone was called "Core," which is not a name but merely

86. Žižek, The Indivisible Remainder, *supra* note 48, at 105.

87. As Žižek contrasts the restored unity of Spirit to be achieved in the state. Spirit still will measure this new unity "by the standard of organic unity," just as the bride measures her marital unity by the standard of her lost bodily integrity and, therefore, "experience[s it] as a loss." But through a "negation of negation" Spirit returns to itself

> not by way of the restitution of the lost organic community (this immediate organic unity is lost for ever), but by the full consummation of this loss, that is, by the emergence of the new determination of society's unity: no longer the immediate organic unity but the formal legal order that sustains the civil society of free individuals. The new unity is *substantially* different from the lost immediate organic unity.

Id. at 123. That is, "Hegel's whole point is that the subject *does not survive* the ordeal of negativity: he *effectively* loses his very essence, and passes over into his Other." *Id.* at 126.

88. This imagery can be glimpsed in medieval Catholic theology of the bodily resurrection. How does one reconcile the concept that the bodies restored to us at the Last Judgment will be perfect with the necessity that the individuality of the saints be preserved and the glorious sacrifice of the martyrs forever recognized? By positing that the martyrs' wounds be healed but not in the sense of obliterated. Rather, the wounds will leave scars transfigured into dazzling ornaments to enhance the beauty of their eternal bodies. *See, e.g.,* Caroline Walker Bynum, The Resurrection of the Body 86, 128 (1995).

89. This paradox is usually explained as a simplistic metaphor for the plants which grow in spring and die in fall. This is overly simplistic, however. Unlike Persephone, the same plant does not come back to life every year. Consequently, the plant metaphor accurately describes the corn gods described by Sir James Frazer who are sacrificed every fall, but not Persephone. *See generally* Sir James George Frazer, The Golden Bough: A Study in Magic and Religion (T.H. Gaster ed., abr. ed. 1951).

the generic term for "maiden."[90] She was the virgin daughter of Demeter, the goddess of the harvest. Demeter is the Phallic Mother as ripeness or completion. Hades, the lord of the dead, abducted and raped Core so that she would rule beside him on his infernal throne. Demeter refused to allow anything to grow until her Core was returned to her. In light of this threat, Zeus was forced to intervene and ordered Hades to return Core.

This was impossible. Core had eaten of the food of the dead. She was no longer a *core*. The moment she was recalled to life in the world, she was immediately dying and leaving her mother's embrace to return to Hades. Her rapist husband tried to hold her in his icy grasp, but she was always slipping away to return to life and the warmth of her mother's arms. Like the Hegelian subject she was now both blessed and damned to divinity.

But she used this pain to buy herself an inestimable present—subjectivity. Before her violation (or what Lacan would call castration) she had her virgin integrity and was as one with the Phallic Mother in the perfect harmony of immediate relationship. But this meant that she had no separate existence and did not even have a name. Like the imaginary femininity posited by different-voice feminism, as Core, she never fully separated from her mother. Now she is Persephone, an individual speaking person. She is no longer overshadowed by her mother, nor is she passively raped by her husband. Indeed, she is a queen, but by necessity a queen of death. Her perfection is the fleeting momentary enjoyment or ripeness—union with her Phallic Mother. But the moment she merges back with Mother-ripeness, she no longer exists because she once again loses her personality. She is, therefore, even more dead when she is with the goddess of life who wishes to subsume her than she is in the land of the dead, where she is merely imprisoned and can dream of escape. Neither Demeter nor Hades succeeds in embracing her, but they now worship her simultaneously as both the goddess of spring—the future ripeness which is promised—and death—the past ripeness which is mourned.

Death seeks life, and life seeks death in the eternal, iterative sterility of the *fort-da* game. Hades, the god of death, experiences his desire for Persephone in the masculine form of *Eros*. He seeks to cure his castration in the imaginary by finding a perfect mate who will make him whole by perfectly filling his hole. Demeter, the goddess of life, experiences her desire for Persephone in the feminine form of *Thanatos* (the death wish).

90. Robert Graves, The Greek Myths 89–96 (1955).

She seeks to retreat back to a time before her violation in the real by merging with Persephone into an undifferentiated, impersonal integrity—turning Persephone back into Core. From the standpoint of Demeter and Hades, Persephone is like Eurydice, the Feminine twice lost. But from Persephone's own impossible position, she is feminine subjectivity finally found.

Epilogue:

Vesta, the Phallic Woman

The Vestal, like the shaman, was sexually ambiguous. She dressed as half bride, half wife. She was a consecrated virgin, married to the state, who ensured fertility. She was a woman with the legal status of a man. The Vestal was considered capable of mediating between the human and the divine *precisely* because she was poised in transition between all permissible social roles—she was simultaneously maiden, wife, and man, sterile and fertile, virgin and phallic.[1]

Abduction is a mediation between imagination and speech. The imaginative thinker must, therefore, be ambiguously positioned between the permissible psychic roles of masculine speaker and feminine *jouissant*. "He" becomes an imaginative thinker only if "she" is captured by imagination. The initiate became a Vestal only through *captio*. Perhaps abduction is described in the language of sexual relations because it *is* a sexual relation. Is it marriage as well as rape?

The great goddess Vesta was the epitome of the Phallic Mother: she was the most virginal and sterile of all Olympians but was addressed as

---

1. Mary Beard argues that this attempt by classicists to resolve the sexual status of the Vestals is misguided. She suggests that the symbolism of the Vestals rests in their ambiguity. They are simultaneously daughters, matrons, and men all at once, even as they are also neither daughters, matrons, nor men. That is, they combined the three possible roles of free Romans. They dressed not merely as girls or matrons but as brides—not yet women but no longer maidens. They guarded the flame, which is similarly ambiguous—both constructive and destructive, fertile and sterile, civilized and wild. Symbolically positioned on the brink of all human experience, they served as mediators between the divine and the human. Mary Beard, *The Sexual Status of Vestal Virgins,* 70 J. Roman Stud. 12, 25–27 (1980).

Mother and granted fertility. Mythographers tell us that Vesta had no myths other than her identification as the oldest Olympian entitled to priority in reverence and sacrifice over all other gods.[2] Unlike the other classical divinities, Vesta was rarely directly depicted; instead she was symbolized by her flame, the fire stick, and a ritual phallus.[3] The myths of her priestesses were limited to accounts of their miraculous impregnation by a phallus which would appear within the flame that was the manifestation of the goddess.

But was Vesta, like the Lacanian Woman, really so beyond language that she could not even be spoken of? Our knowledge of Roman religion comes entirely from Roman men — Roman women did not write and Roman men did not know Roman women's rites. What we do know is that Roman women worshiped mysterious silent goddesses who were hidden from men. The Vestals officiated at the most important religious holiday in the Roman calendar: a festival that was so mysteriously feminine that no man, male animal, or even male image could be present — a festival in honor of a deity that was so powerfully feminine that men were not even told her name but referred to her only as the "good goddess."[4] But was

2. The New Larousse Encyclopedia of Mythology 203-05 (Felix Giraud ed., Richard Aldington & Dellano Ames trans., 1968); *and* Robert Graves, The Greek Myths 74 (1955) (referring specifically to Hestia, the Greek goddess with whom Vesta was identified).

3. Leading up to Vesta's temple in the Roman Forum are a series of statues of Vestals. They are not portrayed as individuals but are idealized as types with virtually indistinguishable faces and ambiguous vestments: bridal coiffeurs and veils, matronly dress, and sacerdotal fillets. The goddess herself was rarely represented directly by a cult image but only indirectly by the flame and phallus, which may have symbolized the goddess in her de-anthropomorphized aspect. Consequently, each Vestal may have been considered a living image of the goddess. Beard, *supra* note 1, at 24. These stylized images of the Vestals — symbolic copies of symbolic copies — are indirect representations of a deity who was so ineffable that she was incapable of direct depiction.

4. That is, *Bona Dea*. Because the rites of Bona Dea were forbidden to men, they have generally been dismissed by scholars. Baldson's account is masculinist and patronizing. Because the rites were held in private homes and (like most Roman religious rites) probably included animal sacrifice, he belittles them as "crowded, smelly, and stuffy occasion[s]." J.P.V.D. Baldson, Roman Women: Their History and Habits 244 (1962). This might be a strictly accurate olfactory description but hardly a serious attempt to come to grips with Roman religion. For example, if you have ever seen the tiny size of the Curia in the Roman Forum where the Roman Senate met, and contemplated the heat of a Roman summer, "crowded, smelly, and stuffy" would also be a strictly accurate, but inadequate, description of Roman affairs of state.

There are, of course, many studies of ancient woman-centered religions. But they, too, give only passing mention to silent Vesta. *See, e.g.,* Erich Neumann, The Great Mother: The Analysis of the Archetype (Ralph Manheim trans., 1963). I believe that, although many authors of such studies identify either themselves as feminists or their research as woman-she also nameless to women? Did they know the "good goddess" as Vesta, or by some other name?[5] Was she really mythless, or did the Vestals make their *enjoyment* eloquent and sing her exploits in their seraglio?

And so let us remember that even though those of us who are positioned as women might speak in the masculine voice when we practice law, this position might also give us different access to the unconscious. Lacan wanted us to believe that this different access, *enjoyment*, is *necessarily* silent. But Lacan's point is not that the Feminine does not or cannot speak but that the legal community of fathers cannot allow themselves to listen because masculine subjectivity is created by the insistence that the Woman does not exist. Because the possibility of the Feminine is created by her prohibition, the tighter the Masculine clasps his hands over his ears, the louder the feminine voice.

Lacan insists that she was silent all along. Yet this may only mean that she has not yet spoken or that we have not yet listened.

As feminists we must strive to rewrite the Feminine—or write her for the first time. We must emphasize that the myth of castration is *imaginary*. It is a myth both in the negative sense of delusion and in the affirmative sense of a story we tell to give meaning to our lives. Unmediated relations with others cannot be a forever lost and infantile state which we can only mourn *precisely* because this state never existed. We did not even become individuals with the potential for relationship until the moment of mediation. In Hegelian terms, to return to our unmediated state is to regress to the lonely abstraction of free will. To eliminate contradiction is to eliminate movement and growth—the desire to achieve the union with the lost primeval Feminine in the real is *Thanatos*. Yet to stay at the level of simple mediated relationships identified by psychoanalytic theory is to remain at the inadequate, unsatisfactory, and "cold-hearted" level of abstract right. The Feminine as unmediated relation is, therefore, a desire, a dream, and an inspiration. The Feminine will never be *re*covered because she has not yet come into existence. She will be a creation, like the subject.

---

centered, they, in fact, adopt traditional masculine fantasies of the feminine, such as the earth mother.

5. Although the presence of the Vestals at Bona Dea's rites is suggestive, I am not proposing a simple identification of Vesta with the good goddess. Bona Dea has been associated with a number of other Roman deities but, to my knowledge, has not been identified with Vesta herself. *See* Robert Bell, Women of Classical Mythologies: A Biographical Dictionary 96, 431 (1991).

At this point perhaps all we can say is that abductions from the male position are not unique or inevitable. But will we ever be able to make our *jouissance* eloquent? Will there ever be a moment when we unbind the *virgo* and loosen her gag so that she can cease to be fasces, virgin, matron, or man, and speak as *Amata*—the Feminine beloved and violated, yet unconquered?

Index

abduction, 55–56, 101–2, 103–4, 107, 291, 335, 338

abstract personhood, 27–30, 31, 32–34, 72, 258, 262–71, 273–75, 277–80, 285–87, 291, 311, 319, 320, 337

Ackerman, Bruce, 157n. 13, 158n. 114

actuality (actualization), 3, 11, 12–13, 19, 26–27, 31, 32–34, 145–46, 182, 218, 233, 235, 256, 266, 273–75, 278, 280, 283, 291–92, 294, 295, 300, 302, 311–12, 318, 319–31, 322, 327, 328, 330

alienation: xx–xxi, 21–32, 47–51, 82–85, 91–97, 110, 111–12, 118, 130, 146, 154, 161, 169, 179, 180, 181–82, 183, 190–91, 198, 203, 204, 224–25, 226, 239–40, 241–43, 245–48, 253–54, 256–57, 260–62, 275–83, 284, 285, 287, 300–1, 305, 330, 331; abandonment, 47–48; exchange, 14, 49–51, 82–85, 105, 110, 111–12, 161, 180, 191, 198, 203, 226, 227, 231–32, 233, 234, 235, 241, 243–45, 246, 254, 255–56, 259, 260–61, 285, 287–88, 289, 291, 304, 330; gift, 48–49, 146, 260; market-alienation, 177, 179, 230, 232–34, 241–43, 245–48, 250–52, 254, 256–57, 259–62, 265, 282, 330, 331; as masculine element, xx–xxi, 82–85, 88, 89, 91–92, 96–97, 109–12, 114, 161, 162, 225–27, 230–32, 233, 241, 243–45, 287–88, 291, 304

Armstrong v. United States, 298n. 15

Augustine, Saint, 90

Avineri, Shlomo, 13n. 30–31, 14n. 32, 29n.

77, 34, 5in. 158, 256, 258n. 90, 268n. 117, 272n. 129

Aylmer, G.E., 125n. 32, 182n. 178

Baird, Douglas, 113–14, 132–44, 148, 150, 209nn. 247 and 248, 214n. 263, 227

Baldson, J.P.V.D., xinn. 2–3, xiin. 4, 6, xiiin. 10, xivn. 13, 14, 16, 18, 20, 336n. 4

Balkin, Jack, 220–21

Bankruptcy Code: 11 U.S.C. 522(f)(2), 248n. 58; 11 U.S.C. 541(a)(1), 171n. 147; 11 U.S.C. 547(e)(3), 202n. 231

Beard, Mary, xin. 1, xiin. 5, 6, 9, xiiin. 10–11, xivnn. 13, 15, 18, xvn. 20, 335n. 1, 336n. 3

Becker, Lawrence C., 224–25

Beermann, Jack M., 220n. 280

Bell, Robert, 337n. 5

Benedict v. Ratner 141–43, 146, 153–56, 200n. 225

Benevenuto, Bice, 8n. 18, 76n. 241, 77n. 242, 81n. 256, 97n. 308, 108n. 1

Benhabib, Seyla, 23, 37n. 105, 38, 42n. 126

Benson, Peter, 29, 36n. 103, 40, 46–47

Bentham, Jeremy, 29, 217n. 270

Blackstone, William, 37, 126–27n. 34, 158, 159n. 120, 162–73, 175, 179, 181

bodily integrity, 176–77, 179, 230, 234, 235–39, 243–45, 251–55, 258, 275, 277, 280–82, 297, 331

Bower, Bruce, 121n. 25

Boyle, James, 110n. 6

Božović, Miran, 49n. 147
Breitel, Judge Charles, 213–14
Brennan, Teresa, 94n. 297
Brodribb, Somer, 94n. 297
Brown, Peter, xiin. 8, 90n. 281
Brudner, Alan, 3n. 8, 15n. 35, 16–17, 18n. 49,
    20n. 54, 24n. 62, 28–29, 33nn. 90, 91,
    34nn. 96, 97, 36n. 102, 37–38, 40nn. 119,
    120, 44n. 131, 45n. 135, 47nn. 141, 142,
    51n. 157, 147n. 85
Brundage, James A., xiiin. 12
Butler, Judith, 57–58n. 177, 61n. 190, 83n.
    262, 86n. 272
Bynum, Caroline W., 238n. 20, 332n. 88

Calabresi, Guido, 45n. 133, 110n. 7, 157n.
    113, 245n. 52, 304n. 28
California Civil Code § 980(a)(1), 140n. 64
Campbell, Joseph, 6n. 13
castration: and alienation from self, 10–11,
    104, 112, 222, 227, 231–32, 245–46, 265–
    66, 322, 325–26; and anxiety, 57, 67, 218–
    19, 223, 327–28; cause of desire and sub-
    jectivity, 10–11, 55, 67–68, 81–82, 88–89,
    91, 95, 98, 105–106, 287, 290, 309, 314–
    15, 320–21, 322–25, 328–30; denial, 80,
    82–83, 93–94, 109–12, 115–16, 133, 162,
    172, 223, 225–27, 231–32, 256, 288, 291,
    292, 315, 317, 327–28, 330, 333; as loss,
    mutilation, 55, 67, 78–80, 82, 86, 88, 98,
    105, 222, 226, 243–45, 304, 315–16, 326–
    27; mediation, 87, 231, 288–89, 325–26,
    333, 337; universality, 80, 82, 86–87, 103,
    223, 288–89, 317; as violation, deflora-
    tion, 232–36, 243–45, 303–4, 328–34. See
    also law: prohibition (incest taboo)
Cardozo, Benjamin N., 110n. 6
Carlson, David Gray, 77n. 241, 78n. 243,
    87n. 274, 145n. 77, 150n. 91, 200n. 225,
    210n. 252, 221n. 282, 248n. 58, 256n. 85,
    295n. 6, 307n. 34, 316n. 51, 325nn. 70–72,
    331n. 84
Carroll, Lewis, 293, 321–22, 325n. 71, 326
Casey, Edward S., 7n. 18, 8n. 19, 9n. 22, 10
Chodorow, Nancy, 93n. 295
Clément, Catherine, 78n. 244, 91n. 290,
    94–95n. 299
Clow v. Woods, 135–36n. 50
Cohen, Felix, 159–60n. 120
commodification, 230, 233–35, 241–43,
    245–46, 251–52, 253–62, 265, 276–77,
    281–82, 288–89, 326, 330

community, 20–24, 27–29, 103, 119–23,
    184–85, 230–31, 233, 234–36, 241–43,
    253–58, 259, 260–62, 263–67, 271–74,
    283–85, 319–320 319–21, 331
complementarity, xxi, 92–94, 221–24,
    231–32, 289, 292, 316, 320–21, 323–24
conditional sales, 202–6
Corbin, Arthur, 203n. 232
Cornell, Drucilla, 58n. 173, 58nn. 178, 181,
    60n. 188, 61nn. 189–90, 62, 80n. 252, 91–
    92n. 291, 93n. 295, 94n. 298, 95nn. 300,
    302, 303, 98–99, 100nn. 320, 321, 105n.
    334, 106n. 335, 228n. 299, 290n. 170
Cramton, Roger, 5n. 12

demand, 74–75, 108, 130–31
desire, 7–8, 19–20, 30, 33, 48, 51, 53–54, 55,
    73, 75–76, 78–80, 81–82, 85, 88–89, 91, 95,
    96, 98, 105–6, 108–9, 119, 123–24, 130,
    173, 225–27, 226–27, 231–35, 258, 266–67,
    275, 282, 286, 287–88, 290–92, 323,
    328–29, 330, 333–34, 336; and eros,
    231–33, 288, 292, 333–34; and thanatos,
    224, 226, 232–33, 248–49, 288, 292,
    333–34, 336
Dolan, John, 141n. 68, 214n. 262, 215n. 266
Donahue, Charles, Jr., 164n. 130
Durham, Darrell W., 141n. 68

Eecke, Wilfried Ver, 8n. 19
enjoyment: as feminine element, xxi, 89,
    166–67, 227, 229–36, 241, 243–45, 287–
    88, 303–5; identification with objects,
    229–39, 241–49, 259, 264, 288, 330; as
    jouissance (merger with the real), xxi, 96–
    101, 105–6, 107, 232, 234–35, 241, 246,
    248–49, 287–90, 309, 315, 322, 325, 327–
    28, 331, 333, 335–36, 337–38; solipsism,
    44–45, 96–97, 231–34, 242–43, 245–46,
    253–54, 259–60, 266, 282–83; as use of
    property, xxi, 43–45, 113, 118, 146, 154,
    166–67, 181–82, 189–90, 207, 210, 224,
    226, 227, 231, 240, 242, 246–47, 254, 257,
    259, 283, 287–88, 300, 303–5, 331; virgin-
    ity (chastity), 232–34, 245–46, 254, 266,
    288
Epstein, Richard, 116n. 14, 239n. 26, 297,
    301

fantasy, 59, 61, 62, 70, 88, 93–94, 96, 103,
    105, 107–9, 223, 226–27, 235, 289, 290,
    292, 314–15, 317, 324, 326, 328–29, 330–31

Farnsworth, E. Allan et al., 186n. 190, 209nn. 247, 248

Father, 70, 71, 76–80, 81, 83–84, 86, 89, 91–92, 103, 143

Federal Trade Commission: Rule 433, 16 C.F.R. 433.2 (1994), 248n. 58; Rule 444, 16 C.F.R. 444.2 (1994), 248n. 58

Feminine, the: acceptance of castration, 115–16, 245, 288–89, 292, 317, 328, 331–32, 337; as alterity, 67–68, 69–73, 79, 95, 288–89, 291–92, 326; as the "not yet," 55, 101, 106, 113, 223, 224, 235, 289–90, 294–95, 315–17, 320, 325, 326–27, 330, 332, 337; as object(ivity), 35, 84–85, 224, 229–36, 241, 242, 244–45, 246, 251, 287–92, 316, 330; and the Phallus, xv–xvi, 14, 35, 78–80, 81, 83, 84, 85, 86, 89, 92, 95, 101, 105, 222–23, 226, 259, 285, 287, 289–92, 322–23, 325–28, 333, 335–36; as radical freedom, xxii, 12, 55, 101, 106, 223, 235, 287–92, 295, 309, 315–16, 320–26; as radical negativity (lack), xxii, 12, 55, 61, 85–86, 90–92, 94–96, 101, 104, 106, 222–23, 226, 227–28, 235, 287–92, 295, 309, 321–26, 329, 330, 332; as sexuated position, xxi, 4, 53–57, 58–61, 63, 69–70, 71–72, 77, 84–86, 89–92, 94, 96–99, 104, 106, 119, 222, 232, 235–36, 241, 244–45, 286–92, 315–16, 320–21, 322, 323–24, 325, 327–28, 330, 331, 334, 335, 337; silence, 60, 62, 97–101, 230, 234–35, 288–91, 322, 329–31, 335–37; as subject, 13, 55, 86–87, 95–96, 106, 246, 287–92, 323–24, 326–29, 331, 333–34. See also enjoyment; Other, the; Phallus, the

femininity, 61, 70–71, 93–94, 96, 103, 105, 223, 226, 235, 289–90, 292, 326, 330–31, 333

feminism: different voice (cultural), xvi, 7–8, 54, 70–72, 92–94, 103, 105, 333; postmodern, 62; radical, xvi, 92–93, 105

Fineman, Martha Albertson, 77n. 242

First English Evangelical Lutheran Church v. County of L.A., 183n. 183

Frazer, Sir James George, 3, 6n. 14, 332n. 89

freedom: as the Feminine, xxii, 12, 55, 101, 106, 222–23, 235, 287–92, 294–95, 309, 315–16, 320–26; free will (as means to one's own ends), 27–30, 36, 44–45, 48–49, 115, 117, 118, 145–46, 261, 262–63, 266, 267, 271, 272, 277–80, 283, 308, 311, 312, 317, 319–21; negativity, xxii, 12, 30,

31, 51, 55, 96, 106, 112, 145–46, 222–23, 235, 239, 267, 271–72, 287–89, 291–92, 294–95, 309, 320–26, 329, 330, 332

Freud, Sigmund, 7, 10, 54, 56–57, 67n. 206, 76, 77n. 241, 80n. 253, 84n. 262, 104, 330

Frisch, David, 164n. 128, 165n. 133, 168n. 142

Gallagher, Catherine, 249n. 60

Gallop, Jane, 69n. 215, 74n. 230, 85n. 267, 87n. 273, 95, 303n. 27

Gilligan, Carol, 70–71, 93–94

Gilmore, Grant, 140n. 66

Graves, Robert, 333n. 90, 336n. 2

Grey, Thomas C., 2n. 3, 5, 114, 116n. 14, 117–18, 124, 156–62, 163, 165n. 133, 166, 168, 170, 172, 178, 179–81, 182–85, 202, 220, 225, 227–28, 296–97n. 9, 299–300

Grosz, Elizabeth, 8n. 18, 55n. 167, 57nn. 174, 175, 58n. 181, 61n. 190, 62, 63n. 193, 65n. 199, 68n. 211, 69nn. 215, 216, 70n. 217, 72–73, 75nn. 233, 235, 236, 237, 76n. 238, 78n. 244, 79n. 245, 80n. 252, 81n. 256–58, 83nn. 260, 262, 84nn. 263, 265, 266, 87–88nn. 275–276, 93n. 295, 95n. 304, 97n. 309, 98n. 310, 100, 108n. 1, 288n. 166, 289n. 167

Halper, Louise, 303

Hamilton, Walton, 317

Hanson, Norwood R., 274–75n. 134

Hegel, G.W.F.: contradiction, 11–12, 25–27, 271–72, 289, 311–12, 337; desire, 7–8, 19–20, 33, 119n. 22, 231, 258, 275, 282, 285–86, 290; pragmatism, 147–50, 225, 275, 279–80, 283, 294–95, 315–21; presuppositions, 24–25, 27–30, 267–72, 273–75, 285–86; property, xv, 15–52, 131, 144–49, 151, 152, 153–56, 167, 173, 175, 177, 224–25, 262–85, 294, 295, 300–1, 317–21; recognition, xvi, 8, 19–20, 33–34, 40, 42, 43, 47–52, 76, 98, 119n. 22, 145–46, 147, 177, 258, 275, 278–82, 285–87, 290–91, 330–31; retroactivity, 13–14, 19n. 27, 30, 31–32, 33, 99n. 315, 264, 266, 269–71, 273–74, 291, 294–95, 311–12, 326; sexuality, 285–87; totality and negativity, 7–15, 222–23, 271–72, 289, 320–21. See also abstract personhood; actuality (actualization); alienation; enjoyment: as use of property; law: abstract right; necessity; possibility (potentiality); property; posses-

Hegel (*continued*)
   sion; quality and quantity; subjectivity;
   sublation
Hobbes, Thomas, 23, 29, 271n.124, 297
Hofstadter, Douglas R., 66n. 204
Hohfeld, Wesley Newcomb, 1–2, 4, 67, 18,
   35, 41n. 125, 45–46, 159, 161–64, 166, 169–
   70, 172–80, 184, 186–87, 190, 200–1, 208,
   220–21, 228, 230–31, 257
Holmes, Justice Oliver Wendell, 317
Homer, 185n. 189, 187, 314
Honore, A. M., 225n. 295
Hyland, Richard, 147n. 86

imaginary, the, xvi, 57, 59–60, 61–62, 63–
   65, 66–67, 69–70, 71, 72–75, 79–80, 81,
   82, 83, 85, 86, 87–89, 91, 92–94, 97,
   103–4, 105, 107–9, 112, 118–19, 120, 137,
   188, 210–11, 216, 218–19, 221, 226–27,
   231–32, 272, 279n. 144, 288, 292, 317,
   321–24, 326, 328, 331, 333, 337. *See also*
   complementarity; demand; fantasy;
   meaning
immediate relations, 33, 64, 87–89, 93–95,
   97, 106–7, 109, 111–12, 129, 131, 131–32,
   133, 137, 164, 173, 196, 215–16, 222–24,
   225–27, 230–32, 235, 241, 256, 288–90,
   307, 315–16, 322–23, 327, 333, 335, 337.
   See also enjoyment: as *jouissance*; law:
   prohibition (incest taboo); mediation;
   real, the
individualism, 7–8, 10–11, 19–24, 27–30,
   120, 144–45, 178, 184, 230–31, 234, 242,
   253–54, 256, 257–58, 260, 262–66, 267,
   268–69, 271–73, 278–79, 282–85, 319–20
individuation, 33–34, 49–50, 175–76, 239,
   242–43, 260–61, 263, 266, 274–75,
   277–83
intangible property, xviii–xix, 4, 36–37,
   113–14, 115, 118–24, 128, 129–31, 134–40,
   141–43, 146, 154–56, 159–60, 163, 165–68,
   171, 174–75, 177, 180–81, 209–10, 227–28,
   259, 297. *See also* non-custodial property
   interests; property: tangibility
Irigaray, Luce, 61n. 190, 62, 289n. 167

Jackson, Thomas, 113–14, 132–44, 148, 150,
   209nn. 247–48, 214n. 263, 227
Jacobson, Arthur J., 19n. 50, 221, 316
James, William, 5n. 12
Jones, Ernest, 330n. 82

Kant, Immanuel, 12, 20, 27–29, 262–63,
   267–68, 270–71, 276, 309n. 38, 324
Kennedy, Duncan, 17n. 42, 127n. 34, 160n.
   120, 169, 170n. 144, 172n. 150, 220–21
Kennedy, Roger, 8n. 18, 76n. 241, 77n. 242,
   81n. 256, 97n. 308, 108n. 1
Kripke, Homer, 214–15
Kristeva, Julia, 56, 100n. 320, 106
Kuhn, Thomas, xvii, 194–95

Lacan, Jacques: mirror stage, 69–73, 74–75,
   78, 83, 95; Name-of-the-Father, 76–80,
   81, 83, 86, 106; Oedipal romance, 76–80;
   presuppositions, 52–54; recognition, xvi,
   8, 53, 54, 70–73, 75–76, 77, 79, 80, 82–85,
   91–92, 96, 97–98, 285–87, 290–91, 330–
   31; retroactivity, 51, 52–53, 54, 56, 57, 62,
   63, 66–67, 68, 72–73, 76–77n. 241, 81, 83,
   85, 99n. 315, 108–9, 226, 291, 330–31, 325;
   sexuality, 55–101, 286–92, 321–24, 327–
   29; totality and negativity, 7–15, 222–23,
   289, 320–21. *See also* castration; fantasy;
   Feminine, the; imaginary, the; language;
   Masculine, the; *objet petit a*; Phallus, the;
   real, the; sexuality; subjectivity; symbolic, the
Lacoue-Labarthe, Phillipe, 8, 10n. 25
Lakatos, Imre, 194–95
Landes, Elizabeth M., 179n. 166
language, xvi, xviii, xx, 8, 10–11, 34, 53, 56,
   58–59, 60, 64–65, 67, 74, 81–82, 88–89,
   91, 96, 97–101, 107, 112–13, 120, 127, 188,
   220–22, 290, 325
Lasson, Kenneth, xiin. 6
law, xv–xvi, xvii, xviii–xx, xxii, 8, 11, 15–18,
   28–29, 49–50, 53–54, 64, 67–68, 77–78,
   79, 81–82, 88–89, 107; abstract right, 15,
   27, 29, 49–52, 83, 177, 252, 264, 266,
   267–68, 269, 270–73, 277–84, 285,
   286–87, 290, 291, 312, 319–20, 337; prohibition (incest taboo), 53–54, 63, 67–68,
   77–78, 81–82, 88–89, 98, 105–6, 232, 288,
   290, 291, 322–28, 337; mutually constituting subjectivity, xv–xvi, xviii, 8,
   23–24, 49–50, 53–54, 81–83, 107, 112–13,
   223–25, 236–38, 256, 262, 266, 267; natural law, 17–18, 20–24, 29–30, 41–42, 51,
   115, 120, 122, 145, 158, 182, 294, 296–301;
   positive law, 16–18, 41, 45, 147, 151, 153,
   225, 273, 281, 283–85, 295, 298–300, 318;
   as symbolic, xvi, 34, 64, 67, 87–88,

107–9, 111–13, 215–16, 217–18. *See also* property; symbolic, the
leases, 144, 148–50, 240–41
legal realism, 130, 185, 186–88, 190–91, 215–17
Lévi-Strauss, Claude, 8in. 259, 83–84n. 262, 85n. 269, 104
liberalism, 7–8, 15–18, 20–24, 28–29, 46, 51–52, 92–93, 115–16, 120, 121–22, 145–46, 158, 192, 184–85, 224, 239, 253–54, 257–58, 263–72, 283–84, 294–99, 301–2, 304–5, 318; libertarianism, 17–19, 20n. 54, 21–22, 41, 44–45, 51, 115–16, 120, 121–22, 182, 284–88, 296–97, 299, 301–2, 304–5; natural rights, 17–18, 20–24, 29–30, 41–42, 51, 115, 119–120, 122, 145, 158, 182, 294, 296–301; utilitarianism, 15–16, 51, 243–45, 253, 255–56, 258, 265, 266–67, 268, 297–98. *See also* abstract person-hood; individualism; public-private distinction
Lilly, John, 182
Llewellyn, Karl, 114, 137, 186–88, 190–202, 203–4, 206, 207–8, 210–11, 215–21, 227, 317
Locke, John, 17, 23, 29, 41, 115, 118, 120, 284
Loretto v. Teleprompter Manhattan CATV Corp., 183n. 181, 301
love, 19, 30, 48–49, 51, 68, 74–75, 87, 105, 108, 258, 295, 329–30, 331, 332
Lucas v. South Carolina Coastal Commission, 303

McGinnis, John O., 182
MacKinnon, Catharine, 59n. 184, 90n. 280
MacPherson, C.B., 126n. 33, 164n. 130; 182n. 177
Malamed, Douglas, 45n. 133, 110n. 7, 157n. 113, 245n. 52, 304n. 28
markets. *See* community
Marx, Karl, 26, 250n. 63, 262
Masculine, the, 54–55, 58–59, 80, 82–83, 85–87, 89, 92, 98, 99–100, 103–4, 105–6, 108–9, 111–12, 133, 166–67, 218–19, 222–24, 226–28, 230–33, 235, 241, 256, 285, 287–92, 315–18, 321, 323, 327–30, 335
Mauss, Marcel, 121–22
meaning, 57, 69, 71, 88, 223–24, 279n. 144, 303
mediation, xxi, 8, 11, 14, 19, 26, 33, 46–47,

49–50, 53, 60, 87–89, 108, 111–12, 130, 133, 162, 172–73, 215–16, 222–23, 224, 225–27, 231, 253, 256, 260–61, 265–66, 271, 275, 287–89, 330, 337
metonymy, 102–3, 221–22, 303–5. *See also* signification
Michelman, Frank, 16n. 39, 17n. 42, 183, 221, 298n. 15, 302
Miller, Jacques-Alain, 1, 9, 67n. 205
Miller v. Race, 166n. 135
misogyny, 54–55, 62, 94–95, 100–1, 223, 225–28, 230, 234–35, 246, 285–86, 291. *See also* femininity; patriarchy
Mitchell, Juliet, 52n. 160, 53nn. 162, 164, 54n. 166, 58n. 179, 59n. 184, 60n. 188, 64n. 197, 67n. 206, 72n. 220, 76n. 239, 79n. 246
Mooney Charles W., Jr., 2n. 3, 134n. 48, 135–36n. 50, 142n. 71, 148nn. 88, 89
Mother, 67–73, 74–80, 95, 96, 226–27, 292, 326
Munzer, Steven R., 41n. 124, 139–40, 160n. 120, 179n. 168, 182n. 177, 253n. 77, . 274n. 132, 283n. 154

Nancy, Jean-Luc, 8, 10n. 25
necessity, 13–14, 19n. 51, 31–32, 273, 309
Nedelsky, Jennifer, 2n. 4, 3n. 7, 17n. 45, 18n. 47, 178, 181, 296, 299–300
need, 73–74, 107–8, 118–19, 121, 123–24, 128, 129–30
Neumann, Erich, 39, 112n. 8, 336n. 4
Nisbet, H.B., 278
Nollan v. California Coastal Commission, 183n. 181, 294
non-custodial property interests, 38–42, 114, 130–36, 138, 139, 140, 141–43, 146–53, 208, 210–15. *See also* possession: physical custody (sensuous grasp)
Nozick, Robert, 17–18, 21n. 56, 117, 123, 297
Nussbaum, Martha, 239n. 24, 242

objectivity, xvi, 1–2, 8, 14, 19, 33–34, 35–37, 47, 53, 55, 88, 89, 111, 138–40, 141, 146–47, 148–56, 158, 162, 164, 166–67, 170, 173, 175–76, 184, 188, 203, 205–6, 216, 220–21, 224, 230, 231, 233, 235–36, 241, 262, 287, 290–92, 294, 295, 302, 310, 316. *See also* possession: objectification; property: intersubjectivity; property: object relations

objects, 2, 4, 35–37, 39, 43, 107–9, 111–14,
118–30, 131, 133, 134, 137–40, 157–68, 170–
79, 180, 181–82, 190–91, 196–97, 201–2,
207, 216, 218–19, 222–27, 229–30, 231–32,
234–35, 236–39, 241, 243–45, 246–52, 255,
259–60, 263–64, 275–83, 287, 296–97,
302, 331. *See also* property: object relations; subject-object distinction
objet petit a, 64, 107–9, 119, 226–27, 232,
233n. 8, 314–15
ostensible ownership, 130–39, 141–43, 144,
153, 156
Other, the, 67, 72–73, 74, 77–78, 95, 108n. 1,
109, 226, 291–92, 326. *See also* Feminine,
the

patriarchy, 55–56, 91, 103–4, 285, 291
Patterson, Dennis, 217n. 270
Paul, Jeremy, 115n. 11, 296n. 8, 300n. 18
Peirce, Charles Sanders, 26n. 67, 56, 60n.
187, 101–2, 281
Peller, Gary, 217n. 270
penis envy, 57, 80, 85
Penner, J.E., 5n. 11, 110n. 6, 160n. 120,
179n. 165, 180, 257
Pennsylvania Coal v. Mahon, 317n. 57
Penrose, Roger, 66n. 204
personality, xviii–xix, 19, 28–30, 31, 32–34,
37, 50–51, 70–71, 72, 120, 177, 252, 255,
258–59, 266, 267–68, 274–75, 277–81,
285–87
personhood, 229–39, 241–52, 253, 258,
263–65, 267, 282, 288, 302
phallic metaphor for property: as the female body, xvi, xxi, 4, 102–3, 107, 109,
112, 227, 229–62, 287–92; as the male
organ, xvi, xx–xxi, 4, 103–4, 107–228,
231–33, 243–45, 301, 304
Phallus, the: conflation with female body,
61–62, 89, 92, 102–4, 107, 109, 112, 226,
232–36, 241, 244–45; conflation with
penis, 61–62, 80, 82–86, 89–90, 92,
96–97, 102–4, 107–14, 119, 143, 218–19,
226–27, 232; as the Feminine, xv–xvi, 14,
35, 78–80, 81, 83, 84, 85, 86, 89, 92, 95,
101, 105, 222–23, 226–27, 241, 244–45,
289–90, 292, 326–27, 336; as lost object
of desire, xv–xvi, 6n. 14, 35, 61, 67, 79,
107–8, 111–12, 119, 173, 222–23, 225–28,
232, 256, 289–90, 292, 326–27; as property, xv–xvi, xx–xxi, 4, 52, 107–14, 119,
123–24, 142–43, 173, 224–25, 227–28,

231–32, 245; as signifier of subjectivity,
61, 79, 80–81, 86, 87–88, 98, 226, 289,
327–28, 330
Philco Aviation, Inc. v. Shacket, 150n. 91
Phillips, David Morris, 131n. 38, 133n. 46,
134n. 48, 135n. 49, 136n. 51
physical metaphor for possession. *See* ostensible ownership; phallic metaphor
for property; possession: physical custody (sensuous grasp); property: tangibility
Poe, Edgar Allan, 329
Pomeroy, Sarah B., xi, xiinn. 4–6, xiiin. 10,
xivnn. 18, 19
Posner, Richard, 16n. 36, 17n. 43, 27n. 74,
179, 243–44
possession, xx–xxi, 34, 35, 37, 38–46, 53–54,
73, 82–83, 96–97, 109–11, 113–14, 190–91,
230–31, 235, 239–41, 243–44, 245, 247,
254, 257, 287–88, 300–1, 304–5; of Phallus, 82–84, 226–27, 289, 315–16, 317; as
masculine element, xx–xxi, 82–86,
88–89, 96–97, 105, 109–11, 113–14, 115,
118, 130, 131, 133, 161, 162, 166–67, 218–19,
223, 227, 230–31, 232–33, 235, 243–44,
287–88, 301, 304, 315–16; objectification,
39, 137–40, 145–47, 151–56, 175–76, 203;
physical custody (sensuous grasp), xx, 3,
18, 40–41, 110, 111–12, 113–14, 115, 116,
118, 130–34, 136–40, 142–43, 146–47,
159–62, 164, 173, 175, 180, 181, 187–88,
196, 208–15, 217, 219–20, 226, 227, 301.
See also ostensible ownership; possession: tangibility
possibility (potentiality), 13, 26, 31–32, 63,
67–68, 106, 274–75, 287, 291–92, 311–12,
322–27, 328, 330, 337
prohibition: *See* law: prohibition (incest
taboo)
property: bundle of sticks (disaggregation
of property), xvii, 4–7, 16, 38, 110–12,
157, 168–70, 182–84, 186–88, 191, 202,
219–21, 225–26, 233, 305; as control of
material resources, 116–130, 174; death
or disintegration of property, 1–3, 6–7,
16–17, 111–12, 114, 116, 156–63, 170,
176–81, 185–87, 190, 202, 219–20, 231–32,
293–94, 299–302; elements of (*see* alienation, enjoyment and possession); derivation (first in time, first in right) v.
negotiation, 208–215; function, xvi,
xx–xxii, 3, 15–18, 24, 34, 40, 44, 47–51,

107, 117, 119, 129–30, 145–46, 147, 177,
178, 184–85, 224–25, 229–30, 231, 233,
236–37, 241–42, 244, 256, 259, 260,
272–73, 278, 279, 282, 283, 284, 285,
294–95, 301–2, 318; in contrast to *in personam* (contract) rights, 1–2, 144–45,
153–54, 157–61, 170–71, 173–79, 184–85,
193–200, 202–8; intersubjectivity (*see
also* objectivity), 4, 18, 33–35, 40–52,
107–8, 123–24, 139–40, 146, 151–52, 158,
161–62, 164, 166–67, 170–77, 180, 184,
226, 230–36, 242–43, 246, 254, 256–62,
264–65, 266, 272–73, 275, 282–85, 287;
limitations, 51–52, 283–85, 295, 298–300;
object relations, 2, 34, 38–50, 119–30,
157–66, 170–75, 177–78, 190–91, 201–2,
207, 208, 222–35, 236–45, 246–55, 259–
60, 265–66, 282–83, 296–97, 331; "personal" v. "fungible" property, 230–31,
232–36, 240–41, 243–52, 253, 254–55,
257–62, 264; paradigms: agricultural v.
mercantile, 194–200, 210–11; as Phallus,
xv–xvi, xx–xxi, 4, 35, 52, 107–14, 225–28,
236–39, 246–49; tangibility, xix, 4, 35–
37, 39–40, 111, 112–15, 118–34, 139–40,
157–66, 170–71, 173, 174–75, 179–80, 187–
88, 196, 208–20, 259, 301; title, 185–208,
212, 215–20, 227, 259. *See also* alienation;
enjoyment; possession; public-private
distinction
prostitution, 233–34, 243, 251–52
public-private distinction, 16–18, 21, 178,
184–85, 284, 294, 296–99, 302, 318,
319–21

quality and quantity, 200, 243–44, 276–77,
294–95, 305–9, 312–18

Radin, Margaret Jane, xxi, 16n. 39, 37n.
106, 46n. 138, 102, 179, 183–84, 229–56,
258–69, 271–72, 273–74, 275–79, 281–83,
285–86, 287 288–90, 294n. 5, 301–2
Ragland-Sullivan, Ellie, 59n. 182, 183, 68n.
207, 80n. 251, 81n. 256, 86n. 271, 87n.
275, 91, 97n. 308, 99n. 316, 109n. 3
Rawls, John, 21n. 56, 123n. 27
real, the, xvi, xxi, 8–9, 59–60, 63–64, 65–67,
68, 72–74, 75–76, 79–82, 85, 86–89, 90,
97–101, 104, 105, 106, 107–9, 111–13, 129,
173, 188, 198, 232, 241, 246, 249, 256, 272,
288–92, 317, 320–24, 325, 326–29, 331, 337;
as death, 65–66, 224, 233, 248–49, 288,

292, 334; as immediacy, 86–88, 97, 107,
109, 112, 137, 196, 198, 215–16, 224, 225–
28, 232, 241, 272, 288–92, 317, 337; as the
impossible (the limit), 65, 88, 90–91,
105–6, 290, 320–24, 325, 326–28, 331;
jouissance, 98–101, 104, 107, 232, 241,
245–46, 249, 256, 288, 292, 322–23, 325;
as object world, 65–66, 88–89, 107–9,
111, 114, 118–19, 168, 215–18, 122, 124, 137,
173, 182, 188, 192, 208, 210–11, 215–16,
217, 218–19, 226–27, 232, 241, 249, 322.
See also enjoyment: as *jouissance* (merger
with the real); need
Rehnquist, Justice William, 301
Reich, Charles, 157n. 113, 296
Richardson, William, 222n. 287
risk of loss, 207–8
Rogers, James Steven, 2n. 3
Rose, Jacqueline, 53n. 162, 56n. 171, 57n.
176, 58, 59, 64nn. 195, 197, 69nn. 212, 215,
79, 85, 91n. 288, 96, 99–100n. 317, 108n.
1, 222nn. 288, 289, 223n. 291, 226n. 296
Rosenfeld, Michel, 11n. 27, 19–20, 21n. 56,
23n. 58, 34n. 94, 269n. 119, 270–71n. 124,
297n. 12, 298n. 14
Rousseau, Jean-Jacques, 29
Rudden, Bernard, 249n. 60
Ruskin, John, 249n. 60

Salacel, Renata, 66n. 203, 68, 129–30
Sauer, Richard, 197n. 216
Sax, Joseph K., 2n. 3, 17n. 42
Scalia, Justice Antonio, 303
Schnably, Steven, 230n. 3, 247n. 56, 254n.
79
Schneiderman, N. Stuart, 8n. 18, 64n. 195,
66n. 202
securities, investment, 134–35, 151–53, 259
security interests, 131–35, 136–37, 138–39,
140, 141–43, 144–45, 146–56, 248;
attachment, 144–45; control, 151–53;
perfection, 131–32, 144–45, 147–49,
151–56; priority, 151–53, 213–15; purchase
money security interests, 148–49,
202–6
sexuality: anatomy, xvi, 53, 56n. 171, 57,
58–60, 62, 71, 76–77, 79–80, 119; artificiality, 53, 56–58; elements (*see also* alienation; enjoyment; possession), xvi, 53–
54, 73, 82–87, 96–101; language, 57, 58–
60; mutually constituting subjectivity,
53–54, 80–83, 107, 112–113; as symbolic

sexuality (*continued*)
  position, 53–54, 57–58, 71, 76–77, 285–87,
    315–17, 320–21. *See also* Feminine, the;
    Masculine, the
Shakespeare, William, 153, 229, 318
Shupack, Paul, 22n. 57
signification, 57, 71, 87–88, 96, 220–22, 223,
    226, 279n. 144. *See also* metonymy
Simpson, A.W.B., 124n. 30, 126n. 34, 167
Singer, Joseph William, 2n. 3, 16n. 37, 17n.
    42, 172n. 151, 220, 302
Slaughter, M.M., 77n. 242
Smith, John E., 26n. 67
State, the. *See* community
Sterk, Stewart E., 42n. 128
Stick, John, 123n. 27
Stillman, Peter, 270n. 124
subjectivity: artificiality, xvi, 7–8, 10–11,
    20–24, 33–34, 49–54, 107, 229–30, 253,
    256, 262, 264–65; as intersubjectivity
    mediated by objectivity, xvi, 8, 19–20,
    33–34, 45–47, 82, 88, 108, 119n. 22, 256,
    260, 270–71, 275, 280, 286, 291–92; gen-
    der of, xxi, 55, 79–98, 104–6, 223–24,
    226–27, 241, 246, 286–92, 315–17, 318,
    323–24, 326–29, 333–34, 337–38; language,
    53, 64, 81–82, 83, 120, 221, 223; mutually
    constituting law, 23–24, 49–50, 80–83,
    96, 107, 112–13, 221–22, 223–25, 256–58,
    264–65, 320–21; mutually constituting
    sexuality, 53–54, 78n. 244, 80–83, 96,
    107, 112–13; negativity, 80–81, 287, 331,
    337; split, 10–11, 55, 90, 225–27, 287, 295,
    315–16, 322, 323, 327. *See also* abstract per-
    sonhood; Feminine, the; individualism;
    Masculine, the; personhood; subject-
    object distinction; symbolic, the
subject-object distinction, 35–37, 70–71, 123–
    24, 165, 174–75, 177, 181–82, 231–32, 239,
    252, 263–64, 275–83, 288, 289–90, 292
sublation, 11–12, 25–27, 113, 235, 271–73,
    281–82, 289–92, 295, 307–8, 309–17
symbolic, the, xvi, xviii, xx, 10–11, 34, 37,
    53, 59, 60, 63–68, 71, 72, 73, 75–77, 79,
    81–82, 83–85, 87–89, 90–92, 96, 97, 98,
    99–100, 104, 105, 107–9, 111, 112–13,
    119–22, 124, 128–30, 137, 168, 173–74, 188,
    192, 198, 208, 210–11, 215, 221–27, 232,
    235, 241, 246, 256, 285, 288, 290, 292,
    315–16, 317, 321–25, 327–31. *See also* desire;
    language; law; sexuality; signification

takings, xxi–xxii, 16–18, 181–85, 293–99,
    301–5, 310–11, 317–21
*Tanbro Fabrics Corp. v. Deering Miliken,
    Inc.*, 213–15
Thurschwell, Adam, 100n. 320
Tolkien, J.R.R., 248, 249n. 59
Treanor, Michael, 317n. 57

*Uniform Certificate of Title and Anti-theft
    Act*, 150n. 92
Uniform Commercial Code (1994),
    §1–201(20), 210n. 252; §1–201(32), 186n.
    190; §1–201(33), 186n. 190; §1–201(37),
    141n. 69, 55n. 105; §2–101, 137;
    §2–105(2), §2–326(2), 211n. 254, 213n.
    260; §2–326(3), 213n. 260, 212n. 259;
    §2–326(3), 211n. 254, 212n. 259; §2–401,
    189, 189n. 194, 206; §2–401(2), 202,
    203; §2–403, 189; §2–403(1), 208n. 246,
    211; §2–403(2), 191n. 197, 211n.
    253; §2–403(3), 212n. 257; §2–501, 186n.
    190; §2–509, 189; §2–510, 189;
    §3–203(b), 208n. 246; §3–306, 209n.
    250; §3–501(b)(1), 210n. 252;
    §3–501(b)(2), 210n. 252; §7–504(1),
    208n. 246; §8–102(17), 152n. 95; §8–106,
    152n. 97; §8–106(c), 152n. 98; §8–106
    cmt.1, 152; §8–301(1), 208n. 246;
    §9–102, 155n. 105; §9–102(1), 144n. 74;
    §9–102(1)(a), 203; §9–104, 141n. 69;
    §9–106, 171n. 148; §9–114, 211n. 254;
    §9–115(5)(a), 151n. 94; §9–115(5)(e), 151n.
    93; §9–201, 147n. 84, 85, 211n. 255;
    §9–201(37), 189n. 194; §9–202, 153n. 101,
    189n. 194; §9–203, 144n. 75, 155;
    §9–203(1)(a), 144n. 74, 75;
    §9–203(1)(b), 144n. 75; §9–203(1)(c),
    202n. 231; §9–204(1), 153n. 101;
    §9–204(2), 248; §9–205, 143 n,72–73,
    155n. 104; §9–205 cmt 1., 155n. 104;
    §9–301, 145n. 76, 155; §9–301(1), 147n.
    84; §9–301(2), 149n. 90; §9–302, 155n.
    107–108; §9–306, 145n. 76; §9–306(2),
    212n. 256, 214n. 262; §9–307(1), 204n.
    237, 211n. 255, 214n. 263, 264; §9–307(2),
    212n. 256; §9–310, 145n. 76; §9–311,
    146n. 80, 204n. 237; §9–502, 146n. 82,
    202n. 231; §9–503, 146n. 81, 202n. 231;
    §9–504, 146n. 83, 202n. 231; §9–504(2),
    248n. 58; §9–505, 202n. 231; §9–505(2),
    146n. 82, 202n. 231

Uniform Commercial Code (1977),
  §8–321(2), 145n. 77
Uniform Commercial Code (1962), §2–101
  cmt., 187n. 192

Vandevelde, Kenneth J., 2n. 3, 4n. 10, 118,
  161–66, 168, 170–72, 175, 178, 179–80,
  220, 228, 296n. 8
virginity, 232–35, 245–46, 266, 288–91, 329–
  34. *See also* bodily integrity; castration;
  enjoyment

Waldron, Jeremy, 113, 115–31, 161, 167, 226,
  227, 228, 231–32
Warner, Marina, 33n. 89, 330n. 81
Weiss, Paul, 26n. 67
West, Robin, 70–71, 93n. 295, 296
Westphal, Merold, 257–58n. 90, 265n. 109,
  269nn. 119, 120, 270, 283n. 153, 284nn. 155,
  157, 285n. 158

Wilden, Anthony, 8n. 19, 9n.21, 57n. 174
Williston, Samuel, 186n. 190, 191n. 198
Wood, Allen W., 262n. 97, 266n. 114, 268n.
  118, 285n. 158
Woody, J. Melvin, 7n. 18, 8n. 19, 9n. 22, 10

Žižek, Slavoj, 9n. 19, 12, 14n. 32, 26n. 68,
  27n. 70, 53n. 161, 54n. 165, 61–62n. 191,
  64n. 195, 65n. 198, 200, 77n. 241, 79n.
  247, 81n. 255, 82n. 259, 85–86nn. 269, 270,
  87n. 274, 96n. 307, 104, 108n. 1, 109n. 3,
  217n. 270, 222nn. 288, 289, 223n. 292,
  224, 232, 235n. 13, 261, 272n. 127, 286n.
  162, 288n. 164, 289n. 168, 309n. 38,
  313–15, 317n. 56, 318n. 58, 320, 322–23nn.
  63–67, 324n. 68, 325nn. 70, 71, 327n. 76,
  328, 329n. 80, 330n. 84, 332nn. 86, 87

Designer:	Steve Renick
Compositor:	Integrated Composition Systems
Text:	10/13 Galliard
Display:	Galliard
Printer and Binder:	Thomson-Shore, Inc.